AMERICAN
VERNACULAR
INTERIOR
ARCHITECTURE
1870 ⬙ 1940

AMERICAN VERNACULAR INTERIOR ARCHITECTURE
1870  1940

JAN JENNINGS and HERBERT GOTTFRIED

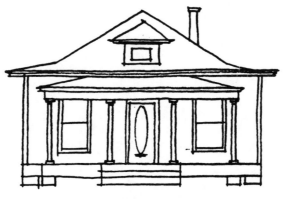

WORTH A. JENNINGS HOUSE,
CANYON, TEXAS— 1909

IOWA STATE UNIVERSITY PRESS / AMES

To our parents

Style is like a rainbow. It is a phenomenon of perception governed by the coincidence of certain physical conditions. We can see it only briefly while we pause between the sun and the rain, and it vanishes when we go to the place where we thought we saw it.

George Kubler, *The Shape of Time*

Originally published by Van Nostrand Reinhold Company Inc.
© 1988 Van Nostrand Reinhold Company Inc.

This edition © 1993 by Iowa State University Press, Ames, Iowa 50010. Text reprinted from the original without revision

⊗ Printed on acid-free paper in the United States of America

First Iowa State University Press edition, 1993

Library of Congress Cataloging-in-Publication Data

Jennings, Jan
    American vernacular interior architecture, 1870–1940 / by Jan Jennings and Herbert Gottfried. — 1st Iowa State University Press ed.
        p.   cm.
    Originally published: New York: Van Nostrand, © 1988.
    Includes bibliographical references and index.
    ISBN 0-8138-1408-1
    1. Interior architecture—United States—History—19th century. 2. Interior architecture—United States—History—20th century. 3. Vernacular architecture—United States—History—19th century. 4. Vernacular architecture—United States—History—20th century. 5. Building materials—United States. I. Gottfried, Herbert. II. Title.
NA710.J46   1993
720′973′09034—dc20   92-36000

Contents

BUILDING TYPES 269

Acknowledgments

We are grateful for the assistance we have received in putting the manuscript together and would like to acknowledge those who helped. That we were able to meet our deadline is largely due to Mary Anne Beecher and Randy Erickson. Mary Anne proved an able research assistant, and Randy developed many of the more difficult preliminary drawings.

Several archivists and librarians have been generous with their time and their collections, notably Herbert Mitchell, Avery Bibliographer, Rare Book Collection, Avery Architectural and Fine Arts Library, Columbia University; Alan Lathrop, Curator, Northwest Architectural Archives, University of Minnesota Libraries; and Lenore Swoiskin, Archivist, Sears, Roebuck and Company.

Others who helped with special services were David Roberts and Rosanne Potter for advice on the Bibliography, and Gail Stecker whose typing kept it intact. Carol Anderson, Cornell University Cooperative Extension, facilitated our access to Extension Service publications. Lloyd McGee loaned us our first millwork trade catalog; Chris and Cuth Salmon understood our logic and added to our catalog collection; staff librarians in a dozen locations were friendly and helpful; Mark Empson met all our photocopy requests with enthusiasm. We are grateful for research grants from Iowa State University's Design Research Institute and the Graduate College.

Preface

Our first study, *American Vernacular Design 1870–1940,* introduced the concept of industrial vernacular architecture. Concentrating on exterior form, this book described the materials and the elements and principles of composition in houses, commercial buildings, and churches, and it analyzed the functions that manufactured goods have in the design of vernacular buildings. This present volume describes the elements, spatial configurations, support systems, and building types of vernacular interior architecture.

The period of study remains the same, 1870 to 1940, because most building-materials machinery had been developed by 1870, and most of whatever was necessary for the development of vernacular design was produced before 1940. Similarly, patterns for the use of materials and various conceptual approaches to design systems were also intact early in the twentieth century.

Industrial vernacular architecture is unlike any other architecture. High-style work, by contrast, is architect-designed, one of a kind, intended for a specific site, very often using custom materials and finishes. This specialized kind of architecture is usually associated with concepts of style, and its vocabulary is unique to the architect or to the building itself.

Also different from industrial vernacular is folk vernacular, which is traditional building, areal in its sphere of influence, using local materials and local knowledge, constructed by an owner-builder or by workers with knowledge of local building customs. This kind of design has a unique vocabulary peculiar to a culture and a region.

Industrial vernacular, on the other hand, is a product of manufacturing. Popular in scope, it was built by many kinds of people—local builders, and owner-builders using pattern books and architects. Pattern books and trade catalogs played a large role in the diffusion of this architecture because they illustrated designs that could be replicated. This kind of vernacular is not site-specific, but some forms of it were intended to fit certain classes of building sites—houses especially suited for narrow or wide lots, for instance—and it could be adjusted to accommodate regional climates. Industrial vernacular comprises the majority of structures in the American built environment. The vocabulary for this kind of design was developed in trade catalogs, builders' periodicals, and the accumulated language of construction. It could also borrow language from high-style architecture and fit it to a vernacular context.

Vernacular architecture has become traditional. Abundant raw materials and the ability to locate manufacturing processes in almost any region, with access to regional and national transportation and distribution systems, helped diffuse vernacular design throughout the country. In this kind of architecture, design values were invested in the manufactured elements. Specific interior designs were produced by applying particular elements to arrangements of interior space, with the entire scheme tempered by a generalized aesthetic.

Many kinds of publications were used to popularize the design elements used in industrial vernacular architecture: manufacturers' trade catalogs, magazines that served the building trades, stock plan books, popular-press studies of current trends in design, manufacturers' in-house publications, and government periodicals and bulletins. The trade catalogs were particularly significant. They contained written and graphic information about materials and design concepts. Many companies included glossaries in their issues so that trade terms, which were often not traditional terms, were defined and became part of the language of vernacular design. Most catalogs suggested applications of their products, and the suggestions varied in tone. Some were prescriptive (to achieve a certain effect, one ought to do this or that), but most companies had free-market sensibilities: you could do whatever you wanted with the product as long as you bought their brand; if you were stuck for a solution to a problem, the manufacturer included a few examples for inspiration.

Magazines about construction and design were dedicated to reporting developments in new products or styles. Most articles in *Carpentry and Building* and *Keith's Magazine* were written to be informative. Their general posture was progressive: the building industry was always going forward; change was good. A new product or idea was assumed to be worthwhile. Contributors wrote about concepts and products without interpreting their significance, and a good deal of what was published was actually unsolicited material in which inventors, architects, and contractors tried to advance their businesses.

Stock plan or pattern books had a narrower focus than trade catalogs because they represented a single point of view about the requirements for effective design. They placed their architecture in the context of social values and made having a uniquely designed single-family house seem like a birthright. Plan books, which offered options in styles and costs, were published by individual architects as well as by millwork companies and ready-cut manufacturers. Interior illustrations accompanying the drawings were of living rooms with fireplaces, dining rooms with wainscots or built-in china closets, and interior vistas. Designers banked on a stock plan conveying a stock meaning. The sales pitch was direct and only occasionally subtle.

The interior design literature of 1870 to 1940 was driven by taste-makers and others who joined design to interior decoration and fashion. Book-length studies of interior trends often were organized by rooms—what to do with the living room, the library, and the like. Most of these books were directed at high-style design, and if they were aimed at all at the vernacular market they usually targeted the expensive end of it. While many authors of these books encouraged the acquisition of "taste," some campaigned for standards of design. There was also a class of hybrid book—part pattern book, part social tract, part "how-to" book—that broadcast information about techniques and materials.

Throughout the history of vernacular interiors, manufacturers of certain products published information about the use of their products and related topics. Many of these were quite valuable. For example, the Sherwin Williams Company of Cleveland produced several *Home Painting* manuals containing information about the nature and proper use of paint and varnish, color harmony, how to estimate costs, individual treatment of exteriors, the treatment of floors, walls and ceilings, and cleansers and polishes. Although the information was supposed to make painting seem easy and accessible in order to encourage paint sales, the information was also well prepared and presented in a straightforward, practical manner.

Of the different kinds of government publications having a direct bearing on the history of vernacular interiors, some of the most effective were Extension Service bulletins published by land-grant universities. The bulletins were different from every other kind of publication because they encouraged rural homemakers to learn the rudiments of design. From their inception, as Cornell University's Home Reading Course (1902), these brochures explained the need to understand organization and composition in order to create more efficient and humane environments. Topics included basic two-dimensional and three-dimensional design, room arrangements based on balance and unity of effect, the preservation of the plane of the wall, design systems and integrated design, the continuity of inside and outside space, the need for vistas through interior spaces, and the power of generally coordinated effects that could stand on their own without furnishings.

With so much available about building forms and materials, the consumer had access to a great deal of design information. Even if finances prevented some people from realizing their dreams, most of the publications of the period encouraged everyone to strive for this goal. Owning a house was a primary asset, a legitimate symbol of accumulated wealth for most American families. What people did with all this information is not clear, but if the amount of capital invested in housing and in the development of a personal aesthetic within the context of a house is any indication, the system was highly successful.

The historical development of interior materials was tied to the production of exterior work, because the mills that made cladding, gable finish, and porch rails also made hardwood flooring and wainscots. The same general cutting and planing machines, matching and sticking machines, turned out applied moldings, interior blinds, paneled doors, and architectural furniture.

But machines made more than wood products. They fashioned tile and linoleum, they stamped hardware and printed wallpaper patterns, they turned and sawed stockwork into ornament, drew metal through dies, rolled impressions onto metal and wood, made glass, and mixed paint. Every element of an interior system was machine-made by the tens of thousands.

While a vernacular interior was certainly the product of machines, it was also true that many designers, builders, consumers, and planners believed that an interior should be modulated by technology. From 1870 on, interiors accommodated successive new developments: heating and cooling devices, indoor plumbing (which necessitated kitchen and bath planning), three lighting systems (oil, gas, and electricity), and scores of conveniences. Some interior spaces became workshops or laboratories. The powerful presence of so many machine-made parts and support systems changed the nature of the vernacular buildings, giving it a new order.

The new building was unabashedly progressive. It was only partially traditional in that it might honor some time-tested vernacular convention, such as dividing houses into social spaces in the forward half and service sectors in the rear. But the new vernacular focusing on efficiency could do away with conventions, as it did when it eliminated one of the parlors of the Victorian house, or broke down the compartmentalization of interior space in favor of an open plan, or integrated the inside and the outside of a commercial building by using the same material to cover all the walls.

Approach

Industrially produced vernacular design is culturally related to folk architecture, especially in its attitudes toward building materials and the use of folk house types, and yet it is also related to the aesthetics of high style, particularly in its preoccupation with finish materials. Industrial vernacular does not have the same economic intentions as other kinds of architecture. For example, a great deal of this vernacular was built as real estate speculation in both commercial and residential buildings. The marketplace drove the development of the architecture, and most buildings were constructed in groups rather than as isolated units.

Field research is a vital part of the study of this architecture, but individual buildings cannot be explained solely by the phenomena of a particular site. The content of any industrial vernacular derives from larger frames of reference and events; this vernacular is nationally based. Any architecture underwritten by so much published material and a national inventory of manufactured elements could not be otherwise. To put this another way, it seems that this vernacular was conceived for and built in a public arena, while folk vernacular is less public. At inception industrial vernacular was rarely personal. It was by design a social art.

Moreover, we must take into account the ability of a builder to erect a vernacular building with interchangeable parts. Even without the national standardization of materials, there was enough agreement among elements to allow replication of buildings in any section of the country.

To generate a comprehensive picture of industrial vernacular, we examined several kinds of evidence associated with the building trade. From manufacturers' catalogs we gleaned an inventory of products. These represent the possibilities for design. We think of these products as design elements. Moreover, there is enough information in trade catalogs to provide a schematic conception of how elements could be used, especially in clusters. The inventory was then compared with actual structures as reported in published accounts of buildings. Finally, we examined extant vernacular buildings looking for the use of elements from the inventory and for principles of composition.

Thus, each building type has been derived from the inventory of available parts, the inventory of published buildings, and the uniqueness of particular structures. We believe the combination produced a more reliable reading of vernacular design and kept us from relying too heavily on any one resource. Assessing change is never an easy task, but we believe we have plotted the overall development of industrial vernacular architecture accurately. Vernacular interiors have always been more susceptible to change than exteriors, however, and in order to pinpoint critical modifications in long-term developments, more intensive field survey work needs to be done to identify the elements of intact interiors.

As a hedge against extrapolating too broadly, we examined architectural materials and building types sold by Sears, Roebuck from 1897 to 1940. Sears became a reality check. We assumed that despite the enthusiasm of manufacturers or the power of fashion trends operating at any one time, if Sears designed the same items that appeared in other sources, the material must have had some significance. Sears consistently produced goods for middle-income people, and its design sensibility was geared to that market. Furthermore, Sears's financial success lent another layer of credibility to its catalogs.

For instance, given the longevity of its house designs, these house types must have struck some kind of chord within consumers. Sears assessed the market demand and responded with a range of values and design systems. It did not sell just one product line or style—there was no Sears look. It sold value and designs that would endure.

One of the ways Sears did this was by democratizing its merchandise, converting the names of certain products, essentially those that represented high-style design or those that sounded expensive, to less "loaded" language. For example, Sears advertised chandeliers with opal lamps in its first catalog. By the 1920s Sears was referring to these lights as "prisms of light," not chandeliers, and soon after that they were called "fixtures," a generic name for lights of any kind.

In its strategy of democratizing the household environment, Sears also took some of the mystery out of technology. Anything Sears sold—from boilers to wallpaper—could be installed by the customer. Sears debunked the expert, the highbrow, and sold anyone the tools to do the same work at home.

Current interest in identifying Sears, Roebuck ready-cut houses is very high. We would caution that one cannot always accurately identify Sears, Roebuck's products for two reasons. In terms of design, Sears did not take much risk with its products: therefore at any given time Sears house types and interior elements were part of the general inventory of manufactured goods. Other companies made the same materials. For example, the entire contents of the Sears 1907 millwork catalog appears, item for item, in the 1909 *Stock List Catalogue* of the millwork company Roach Musser of Muscatine, Iowa. We assume Roach Musser manufactured the goods for Sears. We can find no reason why this mill would copy an entire Sears catalog that was already two years old. We also know that contracting with manufacturers for goods to carry the Sears trademark has been and still is a Sears policy.

Terminology

To arrive at definitions of terms appropriate for vernacular architecture, we searched standard language, architecture, and construction dictionaries and compared their definitions with trade catalog glossaries. We then tried to ascertain how each item was employed in practice. By standard sources, we refer to general dictionaries such as the *Oxford English Dictionary* or the *Random House Dictionary of the English Language* and to architectural sources such as Cyril M. Harris, *Dictionary of Architecture and Construction,* and R. E. Putnam and G. E. Carlson, *Architecture and Building Trades Dictionary.* We sorted variant definitions for each element and composed our own entry based on logic and frequency of use. This strategy was not always fruitful, however, because numerous terms had no definition in any source. Some terms only had a high-style or historical definition—something, for example, pertaining to historic masonry construction. These were not appropriate for the vernacular. Finally, it was clear that some terms had simply disappeared, which caused us to wonder how much vernacular language was once associated with industrially derived design and how much had been passed by word of mouth. But that is a subject for another research project.

To explain this process further let us look at one simple entry. At the turn of this century, there was a stylistic resurgence of cottage-type single-family houses. Many cottage designs included special effect windows, such as the bow window, a curved frame with curved glass. There is no definition for a bow window in any dictionary or trade catalog. There were descriptions of bow windows in millwork catalogs, but again the terminology was varied. Two catalogs published in 1900 and 1904 referred to this window as a "bow window" and a "circle-face," respectively, while two catalogs from 1911 and 1917 referred to it as a "bowed-face." Sears did not advertise a bow window.

We also reviewed the names of specific elements over time. For instance, from 1890 to the 1920s, there were several window patterns called "Queen Anne sash." From 1890 to 1915 they were known as Queen Anne, but from 1915 to the early 1920s the same patterns were referred to as *either* Queen Anne or colonial, and by the middle 1920s the same windows were given the more generic name of "divided-light window."

The so-called cottage window had a similar history. The term was not defined in any dictionary of building but it was profusely illustrated in trade catalogs. Tracking the term and the designs associated with it led us to another discovery, namely, that it is possible to bracket the incidence of individual elements chronologically. At the turn of the century, a separate catalog for moldings was developed, the *Universal Moulding Book,* and it became a standard reference. The Universal was often included as a special section in a general millwork catalog. When published this way the whole catalog was referred to as a combined book.

Eventually the concept of a "universal" broadened to include many more millwork items, which meant that more and more material could be counted on to be made from similar stock in comparable patterns, sizes, and finishes. Because of this development it became possible to establish some chronological boundaries for the emergence of specific products. A comparison of the contents of two Universal catalogs will demonstrate the bracketing method. Two of these catalogs were published in 1891 and 1898 for two different millwork companies in different locations by Rand, McNally of Chicago. To illustrate the method we will examine the development of the cottage window. No windows in the 1891 edition are identified as "cottage windows," but there are many such windows in the 1898 edition. Moreover, there are scores of catalog pages with identical materials in both catalogs; some even have the same stock numbers.

There are also pages with the same items but different stock numbers, and the contents are not arranged in the same sequence in both issues. In comparing the descriptions of cottage windows we also learned something about the emergence of the cottage window in the vernacular design system. Sometime during the eight years between catalogs the cottage window gained acceptance. We know from other sources that by the turn of the century, cottage windows appeared in catalogs all over the country. As the windows become a standard inventory item, definitions of the term *cottage window* appear in trade catalog glossaries: a window in which the meeting rails are placed above the center of the opening.

Having discovered the time period in which the cottage window emerged, we could then look for connections with other elements of the same period and for the role of the cottage window in large-scale developments. As for the latter, the most forceful aesthetic associated with cottage design in this period was the ornamental style, which would turn out to be the last gasp of earlier architectural revivals. The ornamental cottage was eventually submerged by progressive movements that stripped the excrescences from the buildings, inside and out, to create the modern cottage.

As a final point of reference we turned to Sears to see how the company had utilized the cottage window. In its initial catalog a cottage window design was referred to as an "oriel window." The example shown was a pattern associated with Queen Anne effects in that the upper light had a border of colored glass, and the lower portion a single pane of clear glass. In its 1902 issue Sears called this same window a "cottage oriel." From that we surmised that Sears had enlarged the purpose of this window. As an oriel it would have been a specialty window, usually on the second level. As a so-called cottage oriel, this window could function as a true oriel, or as the middle sash of a three-sided bay, or as a specialty window on the façade of the house. Sears offered it in either a fixed-sash or check-rail format. In any event, Sears was trying to exploit the shift to cottage design. In 1907 it called this window a "fancy front." The changes in language and usage also helped us plot the company's effort to stay abreast of its markets and create a demand for its products.

The Sears, Roebuck data on windows also facilitated our analysis of what was happening in design generally. We sorted Sears's windows by type of operation and glazing pattern from three sources: the company's general catalogs, its millwork catalogs, and its books of stock plans. We calculated the frequency of appearance for each type and added the Sears data to information from other companies. If a window pattern appeared in several catalogs for several years—in some cases, for decades—we assumed it was being manufactured and sold at high levels and was, therefore, a significant element in a design system.

As Kenneth Ames points out in his article "Meaning in Artifacts: Hall Furnishings in Victorian America" (*Common Places*, Dell Upton and John M. Vlach, eds., Athens: University of Georgia Press, 1986, p. 243), relying on trade catalogs to pinpoint the historical development of any design system is not quite accurate, in that the production of goods does not reveal all about the ways elements were used or the relative significance of one element over another. We need a statistically sound survey of elements and systems in place, and that will occur as American vernacular architecture is further inventoried and analyzed. Current evidence suggests that most production goods were installed pretty much as they came from the manufacturer; local adaptation or adjustments of trade goods occurred over time, but most initial installations remained intact for quite a while. Therefore, we feel confident that production must have had a reasonable correlation with customer interests, that it reflects the as-built condition of vernacular buildings. Lastly, we believe that styling information can be deduced from trade catalogs.

Returning to the two Universal catalogs mentioned earlier, both issues had full-size section drawings of moldings and fittings suitable for public or private buildings which could be ordered by number from local retailers and wholesalers. But a comparative study of the contents of both catalogs reveals several interesting things. Both issues have a number of identical pages grouped in clusters, for example pages 12 to 19 and 33 to 41. While the 1891 issue has no cottage window patterns, it does have other ornamental elements such as chamfered and incised trim sets. The 1898 issue has cottage windows but no chamfered and incised trim. The 1891 book illustrates a traditional five-cross-panel interior door with OG and PG moldings, but the same door in 1898 has a bead-and-cove molding. With information of this kind we can ask other kinds of questions: does the change in surface texture, suggested by the bead-and-cove, signal a shift toward more three-dimensional modeling of doors, and if that is so what is the significance of the change?

The 1891 catalog offers a molded sash door with two patterns— a circle-top single-pane light, and a segmented-head single-light. In 1898 these same doors have been redesigned so that the circle top has been divided into two identical circle-head lights, and the segment type has extended corners. The change from an item composed of one grand effect to a design with multiple effects is consistent with the shift in aesthetics and the movement toward a more ornamental design system. Reinforcing that change is the fact that the 1898 catalog has many more doors identified as cottage doors, some thirty-six choices in eleven extra pages over the earlier issue. Despite the increase in subject matter many of the stock numbers for doors were identical in both catalogs.

A third example of this development can be seen in newel posts. Each catalog has two pages of designs, but two of the turned newels in the 1891 issue have been replaced in 1898 by incised, squared models. In fact, there is less turned work in all categories of millwork in 1898.

Without going through every section of both catalogs, the pattern of changes, derived from tracking elements, should be clear. With a suitably large collection of catalogs, it is possible to bracket design elements chronologically, and bracketed elements create a data base for historical research. By bracketing certain elements in a vernacular building it is possible to estimate construction dates and to determine the significance of any one element based on its position within the sequence of things in its class.

This kind of study also establishes a data base for present use in design practice, in that a collection of elements can be construed to work as a design language, a code to be assembled from historical models. This possibility seems imminent as architects and builders continue to resurrect historical materials, patterns, forms, and ornament.

But to create an effective language more study is required. The use of milled elements has a logic and a set of values of its own. Without a comprehensive study of industrial vernacular, so that we begin to understand its ability to convey meaning, the use of vernacular materials and design language will result in applied work only, a system of historic plants on contemporary forms. There is a resonance to the vernacular environment, a sustaining tone that is based partly on perceptual experience: we recognize what we know. That is a great reassurance. There are relationships between volume and circulation, between vista and privacy that need to be explored. The historic-preservation movement has given us the opportunity to rediscover vernacular patterns, and the significance of that movement may be related to how much we allow preservation to help us redefine the concepts of house, neighborhood, and district.

The Millwork Issue

Cultural geographers have documented that American building owes much to the English system of frame construction and wood cladding. (See the works of Fred Kniffen, particularly his reflective essay "Folk Housing: Keys to Diffusion," reprinted in *Common Places*, D. Upton and J. M. Vlach, eds. Athens: University of Georgia Press, 1986, pp. 3–26). Indeed, the availability of hardwood or softwood forests in several regions of the country and the folk tradition of building log and planked buildings accelerated the development of wood-based design to a scale never before achieved by any civilization. American industrial vernacular architecture, following precedent, is overwhelmingly derived from wood elements.

Dependence on wood characterized exterior as well as interior architecture. Framed partitions and ceilings, flooring, wall finish, trim sets, doors and windows, and stairs are common features of any vernacular building. Although not part of this study, interior furnishings also relied on wood for furniture and cabinetry.

For that reason we have chosen millwork as the critical base material for interior architecture. Millwork represents the largest category of structural and finish goods, and as such it establishes a tone and a point of reference for interior systems. To our way of thinking, an accurate assessment of the role millwork plays in any historic building reveals enough information to make an interpretation of the design, including design values and cultural ideas associated with milled work. It is also our assumption that an accurate inventory of elements and an accurate interpretation will lead to a proper evaluation of the significance of individual interiors, a significance that needs to be understood in order to place the vernacular within its appropriate cultural context.

The Shape of Vernacular Time

The question of significance is not easily addressed in vernacular architecture. Arriving at any evaluation is partly a function of the methods used to study the subject. Most methods of analysis that focus on innate characteristics do not seem to satisfy. With the exception of intrinsic methods dealing with materials and technology and identifying factual information, the methods of art history are not appropriate. Extrinsic approaches describing the conditions that influence design and the social, cultural, and intellectual developments that color the work have their place, but they do not generate a methodical assessment of the elements and principles of design. The meaning of a work cannot be completed without a full understanding of the properties and qualities of the actual work.

Of the methods available for engaging a vernacular based on the industrial production of design components, we have come to believe in design of this kind as a member of a class of things, what art historian George Kubler refers to as "all material worked by human hands under the guidance of connected ideas developed in a temporal sequence" on page 9 of his book *The Shape of Time* (New Haven: Yale University Press, 1970). Kubler goes on to suggest that artifacts of any intention, whether a work of art or a tool, can be divided into formal sequences composed of prime objects and their replications. Seen this way, each article represents a solution to some problem, with the solutions linked in sequences.

Kubler's model stresses the internal coherence of events and recognizes that any sequence is composed of gradually altered replications of the same trait. The original source of any sequence of solutions to an artistic problem is a prime object, which is replicated until another invention or mutation forces solutions in a new direction. In vernacular architecture prime objects are not identifiable, because the first or best example is not known. Rather than a prime object tilting a series in a particular direction, a new product intrudes into the sequence—the way linoleum barged into floor-covering design. Therefore, any given moment in any environment consists mostly of replications and a few successful prime objects. Replications are the heart of vernacular design; in Kubler's terms, they allow sense and pattern to emerge wherever we look. Replications convey a sense of order and contribute to a sense of place.

Thought of in this way, a vernacular building is seen to be made of layers of known patterns and materials, composed in scores of sequences, with each sequence consisting of linked solutions to a design problem. Following this definition, each element of any design system is, in fact, a functional class— doors, windows, and stairs, for example. But roof plans, room shapes, and spatial configurations are classes of solutions as well.

In our approach, each vernacular building is equivalent to a historical event. Our first task in understanding this event is take a cross section, perhaps several of them, through the artifact to reveal the contents. What we see is a collection of elements each in a different stage of development. Some have just been introduced into a series, others are in their middle or late stages of development. Clustered together in this particular building, they reflect design values, most of which can be identified as belonging to a particular constellation of effects.

In vernacular architecture each sequence consists of traditional objects. Their duration is long, and change is minimal throughout their duration. For example, some window patterns have been produced throughout the entire 1870-to-1940 period, with only minor adjustments to the size of the whole window or to the window's parts—stiles, muntins, panes of glass, and molding profiles. It should also be remembered that sequences are influenced by market forces and other aspects of an economy. An example is the way the rising cost of materials and labor modifies the design of elements.

Collectively, vernacular design sequences have been open-ended, that is, solutions to specific problems were being actively derived throughout the whole period of 1870 to 1940, and in some cases they are still being derived. Not only are sequences open for new intentions or for slightly modified replications, but they are scaled. Sequences build on each other, not in a hierarchical way, but as a simple order of magnitude.

The interdependence of the sequences can be illustrated by

considering a building's design as a developmental process, beginning with a single element and going forward from there. For an interior we might start with the baseboard at the bottom of the wall, whose function is to cover the joint between the plastered wall and the flooring and to protect the wall during cleaning. In many schemes, the baseboard has accompanying moldings, a surbase and a quarter-round. Each of these things belongs to a sequence, and they are mutually dependent in order both to create an effect and to solve the baseboard "problem." Depending on the construction date, a baseboard would have its three elements in three different stages of design life. A house built in 1915 would have a quarter-round toe molding quite like other moldings of the same class, but the surbase at the top of the baseboard itself might be significantly changed or not present at all, because this element was losing favor in 1915.

Taken at the next order of magnitude, this millwork aggregate belongs to two other sequences: the organization of the entire wall, as well as the grouping of woodwork or trim sets. And these again belong to a broader conception, until ultimately we reach that state in which all the combined sequences belong to one order, a constellation in which the ultimate idea, or "mental form" in Kubler's term, is expressed as an aesthetic.

For our study we have determined four such constellations. These clusters of interlocking series of solutions are described as the *ornamental,* the *classical,* the *artistic,* and the *colonial.* How each of these is realized has never been a closed question, because there is no one solution. No one perfect order. The individuals who were responsible for assembling the elements chose items from an array of possibilities, several combinations of which could reinforce a particular constellation. Whatever the result of this integration of formal sequences, the product as a whole took a position in the duration of the constellation. A remarkable thing about this kind of architecture is that the finished work might remain as an intact event for a very long time, but it could also be altered. It is in the nature of the vernacular that the owner-builder modifies it, introduces new sequences and materials, redefines the movement of people and the use of space.

In their relative ages, the cluster of traits we call ornamental is the oldest, and that aspect of the colonial that is consciously modern is youngest. The classical and the artistic lay in between. The artistic isolated the important sequences of elements, the key series of solutions to modern design problems. The artistic elevated the design decision-making process to consider systems of design. The expression of systems became more direct within this aesthetic. While some aspects of the artistic have ceased to satisfy as they once did, the overall impact of this particular aesthetic endured throughout the period. The artistic was also associated with other issues, some social and others cultural.

All aesthetic clusters—the ornamental, classical, artistic, and colonial—serve as indicators of values and attitudes toward time, the social uses of interior space, and design.

Kubler sees the documentation of a series of prime objects and their replications, and the degree of "drift" that occurs within the life of a series, as "establishing the text," discovering the principle themes. That is precisely our goal in this book, to establish the text of one kind of architecture for one chronological period. This architecture is based on the production of unknown people, who adhered to ideas about patterns and profiles, about materials and the organization of space. We have described the vernacular sequences in time and measured the distance between versions of any one element, building type, or aesthetic constellation.

Overall we have studied what design historian John Kouwenhoven labeled the vernacular arts, "objects shaped empirically by ordinary people in unselfconscious and uninhibited response to the challenges of an unprecedented environment . . . tools, toys, buildings, books, machines, and other artifacts whose texture, shape, and so on were evolved in direct, untutored response to the materials, needs, attitudes, and preoccupations of a society being shaped by the twin forces of democracy and technology (John Kouwenhoven, *Half a Truth Is Better Than None*. Chicago: Univ. of Chicago Press, 1982, p. 23).

Assessing significance is never simple. Our first step was to identify the elements and define the terms used to construct the systems. We sorted elements by function and materials, and established patterns of assemblage. This kind of data base is in itself part of the explanation of the architecture. When an inventory of an interior architecture is complete, the discovery of the patterns is a step toward evaluation. The relative strength of the patterns, how intact they are, how well the integration of patterns was achieved, these things lead to an assessment of significance. One measure of the effectiveness of a cluster of elements is how well the design has stood the test of the marketplace. Taken altogether, this process generated our conclusions about the building types and aesthetic systems presented in the study.

Uniqueness is not an evaluative tool in this kind of architecture. The flow of designs does not trail in the wake of the one big idea or the critical invention. The pivotal objects in this vernacular are likely to be a watercolor illustration in a trade catalog or a new building in the neighborhood. This architecture is characterized by its rationality and its relationship with technology. Its value derives from these same sources, from execution and coherence among competing elements.

We would add a note on the influence of technology in vernacular interiors. The General Electric Company, among others, built demonstration houses in various regions of the country. Its advertisement in a 1935 issue of *House and Garden* asked this question: "What is the 'New American' Home? 'New American' is not a style of architecture. It is a house designed from the *inside out* to provide greater comfort, less labor and better health for the entire family." Taken from this point of view, the significance of a vernacular building would have to include a measure of the effectiveness of the original intention. And that brings us to a dimension in architectural criticism in general: the evaluation of buildings on their ability to function. Industrial vernacular is purposeful design, just as purposeful as any other product created with the expectation of delivering performance.

A final consideration of the evaluation of the vernacular concerns the plotting of each building's total effect within each constellation—as if each building's design were an event distributed across a continuum. Seen in this larger context, each building becomes an opportunity to address the demands of its period of construction. A vernacular building, because it is not fine art, always has contextual relationships. It never operates alone as a crown jewel. It gains in demeanor and value in the presence of other things like it. It is always of the world and must be judged in worldly terms.

The mass production of design elements tends to push creativity to the background so that the makers of things are anonymous. Once the building elements enter the market, the manufacturer loses control over their use. Sometimes the assemblage of elements takes on a special identity because of local customs or the presence of local workers and their concepts of good form and proper finish. But in most cases the materials are not local, and that requires some adaptation and accommodation all around.

In summary, our approach to this subject has been based on a few research conventions. As historians we sought to identify the things with which vernacular architecture was created. With that body of information, we learned how individual elements were assembled and spaces organized. We developed a chronology of elements and design concepts and tried to place these within the framework of American building. The latter task required the establishment of order among the designs by classifying the completed work. The classifications are of two magnitudes: the typology of built forms, and the sequenced clusters of aesthetic intentions. Together they comprise the historical development of the subject. There are other constellations of elements, spaces, and aesthetic intentions. Those that we identified—the ornamental, the classical, the artistic, and the colonial—were the most compelling in our first cut through vernacular interior architecture.

The Order of Things

Since the last quarter of the nineteenth century, Americans have had the opportunity to order stock parts for a new construction or remodeling. This has been a momentous cultural development, elaborated so completely that the relationship of any part of something to the whole thing is like the relationship of the element to the finished design. Put concretely, this relationship is a ratio: as a glazing bar is to the window, so the window is to the organization of wall; and the wall is to the room as the interior volume is to the form of building. No matter the level at which a reading may be taken, the result is the same. The differences among solutions to the same problem depend on the way these relationships are developed and the manner in which these ratios are expressed within the properties of the materials.

Interior architecture has been strongly affected by the presence of technology. We have labeled the various applications of technology as "support systems." These are separate, unique circuits of energy and supply, of heat and waste, and their success in altering the interior environment has been considerable. One measure of the impact of the support systems is that, well before 1940, interior space could be environmentally controlled to suit individual preferences.

A vernacular interior, no matter how minimally detailed, is not only a collection of made parts. Most designs have a conceptual framework, a referent implied by the nature of the materials used and the patterns of expression. We think of these as aesthetics, generalized constellations of values and effects. The constellations combine functional requirements and problem-solving with an aesthetic dimension. In determining the nature of a single work and its significance among like things, the elastic idea of linked solutions and sequences of traits is logical and fruitful. Change occurs within sequences, but the aggregation maintains its identity, either ornamental, classical, artistic, or colonial.

Vernacular architecture operates in an interactive mode, where modification and personal values are part of every scheme. The original models or prime objects of an aesthetic are hidden somewhere in the series of solutions. Therefore, for most people, the prime objects are irrelevant, and their interiors reflect compromise. In many interiors there is a comingling of systems and a toning of the aesthetic.

The concluding section on building types is based on our earlier work on vernacular typology. We have refined some of the definitions of these types. The names for the building types in housing, commercial buildings, and churches are based on the following: historic names as recorded in the literature of the period, names listed in the trade catalogs, and names that identify the most prominent design element.

ELEMENTS

WINDOWS Elements and Construction

For the period under study, all windows in vernacular buildings are assumed to be manufactured types, that is, each was assembled from interchangeable stiles, rails, muntins, and standardized panes of glass.

A *stile* is the vertical outer member of a sash, and a *rail* is the horizontal member. The *meeting rails* on a double-hung sash window come together when the window is closed. Plain meeting rails are the same thickness as the rest of the window. *Check rails* are thicker than the window to fill the opening between the top and the bottom sash. These usually are beveled.

Of the operable windows, the *double-hung sash window* is the most common vernacular type. A *sash* is a single wood frame to be filled with glass. A *double-hung* window has two sashes. The glass may be divided by *muntins,* or *glazing bars,* and the panes of glass are referred to as *lights.* Each window has a *trim set* made up of: the vertical and horizontal casings that cover the frame; the *stool,* a cap on the window frame; and the *apron,* a board applied to the wall directly below the stool to cover the joint made by the frame and the plaster.

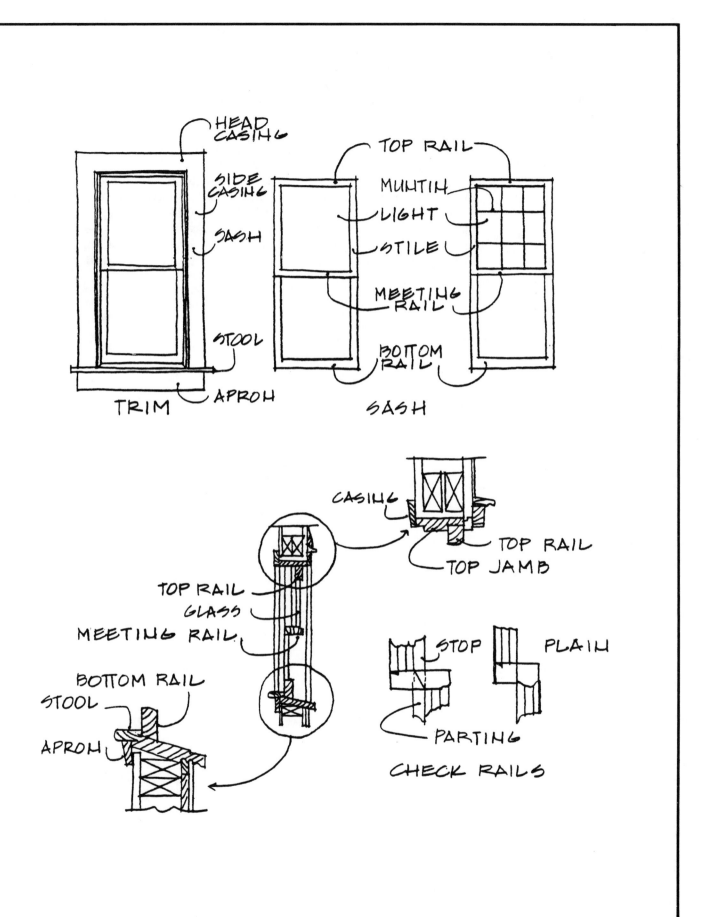

HEAD CASING

SIDE CASING

SASH

STOOL

APRON

TRIM

TOP RAIL

MUNTIN

LIGHT

STILE

MEETING RAIL

BOTTOM RAIL

SASH

CASING

TOP RAIL

TOP JAMB

TOP RAIL

GLASS

MEETING RAIL

BOTTOM RAIL

STOOL

APRON

STOP

PLAIN

PARTING

CHECK RAILS

3

Operation   Window operation includes the capacity for some part or all of a sash to slide, push, pull, or pivot in order to open. Windows that do none of these are referred to as *fixed*.

A double-hung window consists of two sashes, one that is lifted up and the other pulled down. A *single-hung* window has only one movable sash. A *casement* window has hinges on a vertical side and swings open along its entire length. *Folding sashes* are casement windows that slide in tracks when pushed or cranked.

A *fixed light* is attached directly to the framing. A *sliding* window opens by being pushed into the frame wall, and the section of wall that accepts it is called a *pocket*. *Awning* and *hopper* windows are hinged at the top and on the bottom, respectively. They are used as cellar sash and as transom lights. A *pivot* window tilts on pins at the center of the sash; usually it is an accent window or a gable sash for ventilating and lighting an attic.

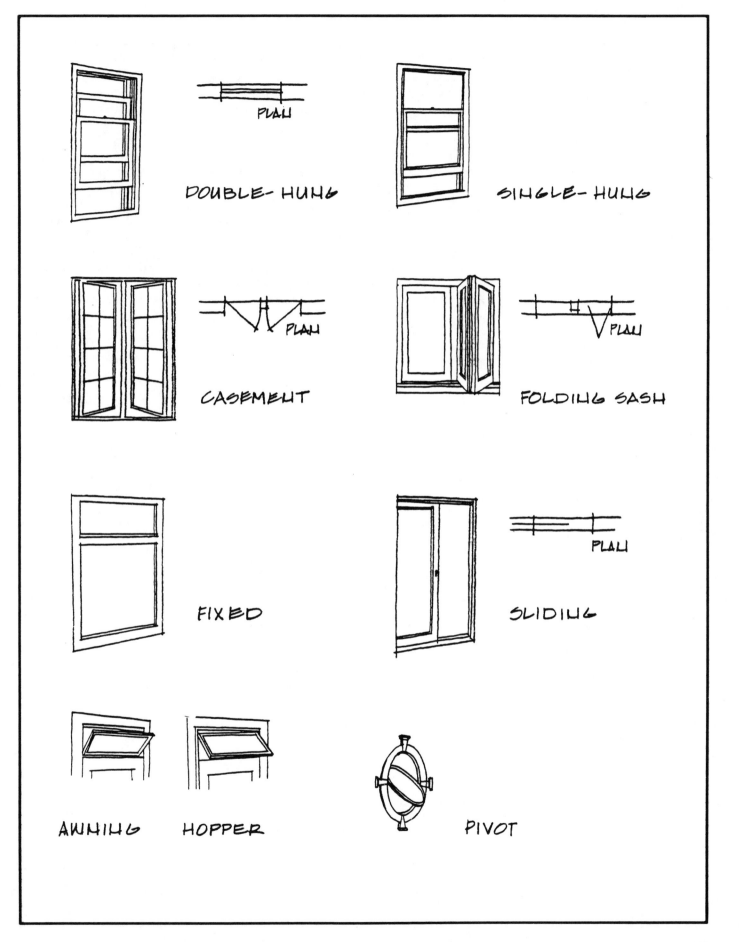

DOUBLE-HUNG

SINGLE-HUNG

PLAN

CASEMENT

PLAN

FOLDING SASH

PLAN

FIXED

SLIDING

PLAN

AWNING   HOPPER

PIVOT

A *sliphead* window slides the lower sash up through the head of the frame into the wall. This type often serves as a pantry opening into dining rooms and is sometimes called a *pocket-head* window. In a *drop* window, the sash descends completely into a pocket beneath the sill. These windows are used especially for ventilation on living and sleeping porches.

Projection Projecting windows play a significant role in interior design, because of their ability to increase light and air dramatically and to establish private spaces within rooms. These windows are of three kinds: *canted bays* forming an angle other than a right angle, *square bays* that are perpendicular to the wall, and bays with a plan in the shape of an *arc*. Of the two canted types, the *three-sided bay,* which may include a window seat, is the more popular. The *two-sided canted* bay forms a triangular space that may also hold a seat. A square bay window provides less floor space than the three-sided bay, but its double windows provide much light and air and a usable space. It is used extensively in bungalow houses.

A projecting arc is called a *bow* window; the bent glass adds considerable light to a room and may have a special effect on the space. Curved elements, like the bow window, are part of the ornamental aesthetic.

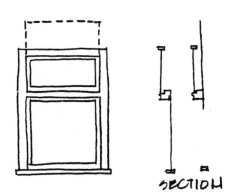

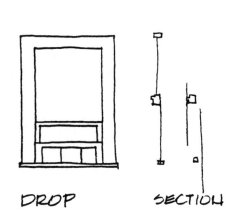

SECTION

SLIPHEAD

DROP

SECTION

PLAN

3-SIDED CANT BAY

PLAN

SQUARE BAY

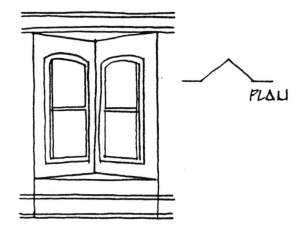

PLAN

2-SIDED CANT BAY

PLANS

BOW

Fenestration Patterns

The fenestration pattern on a vernacular building derives from a design concept that is consistent with the form of the building and is based on functional requirements. Vernacular interiors employ windows for special effects. The *single* window is the most common type. It is placed primarily to light one wall and the area immediately in front of it. Singles can be organized into a pattern of all singles, as well as being matched and clustered. Common single-window placements include hall lights, matched singles as a framework for a mantel, and stair landings. In special-use situations, the single may include art glass or an unusual glazing pattern.

Paired windows can be repeated as a type of fenestration and are also used on the façade only. The *triple* window, common in projecting bays, is a modest band of windows broad enough to light an entire room. A *band* of windows that suggests a ribbon or a narrow plane of light is part of the modern aesthetic. Some bands wrap around a corner, and other bands appear above a wainscot or a buffet in a dining room. These are especially popular in artistic treatments.

Cellar sash is usually a single, sometimes fixed, window just below the wall plate and set into the foundation wall. *Transom lights* are placed over an opening, and *stepped windows* are most commonly found as lights for stairworks. The so-called *Palladian three-part* window, consisting of side lights and a large center piece, is placed to light a stair landing or is part of a gable finish and lights the attic.

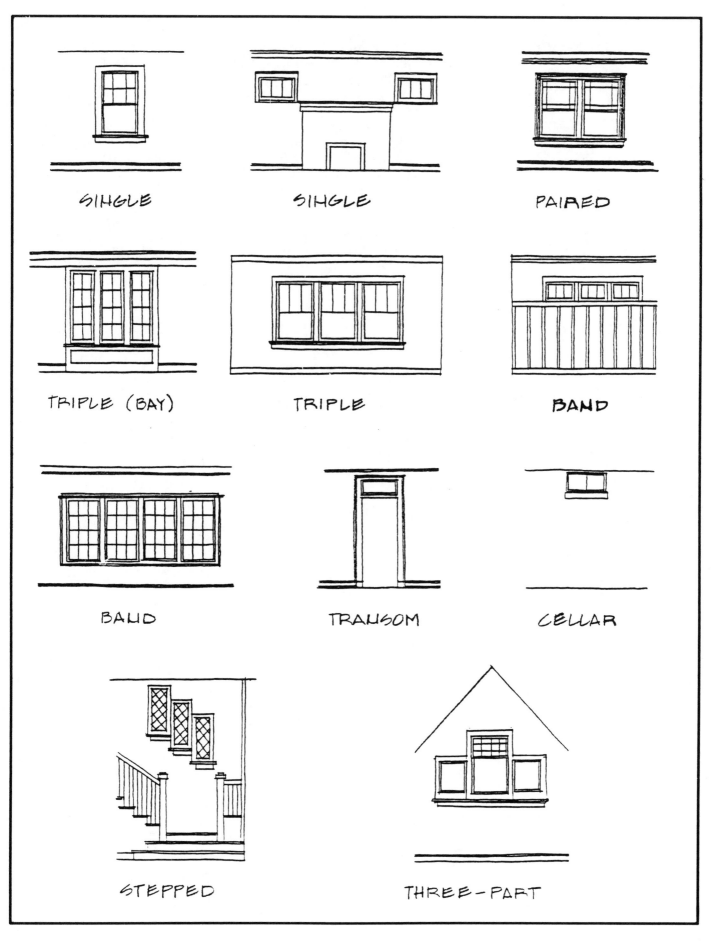

SINGLE

SINGLE

PAIRED

TRIPLE (BAY)

TRIPLE

BAND

BAND

TRANSOM

CELLAR

STEPPED

THREE-PART

Cottage Windows

The term *cottage window* seems to have been a millwork trade term. It refers to a window in which the meeting rails are placed above the horizontal midline of the opening, creating a top and bottom of different heights. Because the cottage window often is placed on the front of a house, its sash is often wider than standard units.

Many cottage windows are designed with ornamental effects in the upper sash, such as divisions of the glass into unusual patterns. The upper sash also may carry colored glass, called *art glass,* in some pattern or figure. This sash may have etched, figured, beveled, and leaded glass as well. Art glass windows were simply called "art windows" by some manufacturers, and cottage types with an elaborate pattern or figures were labeled "landscape windows," alluding no doubt to the character of the ornament in the sash and the view out the window. *Etched* glass results from treating the surface with a caustic liquid to remove glass and make a figure. All of the other patterns derive from arrangements of glazing bars.

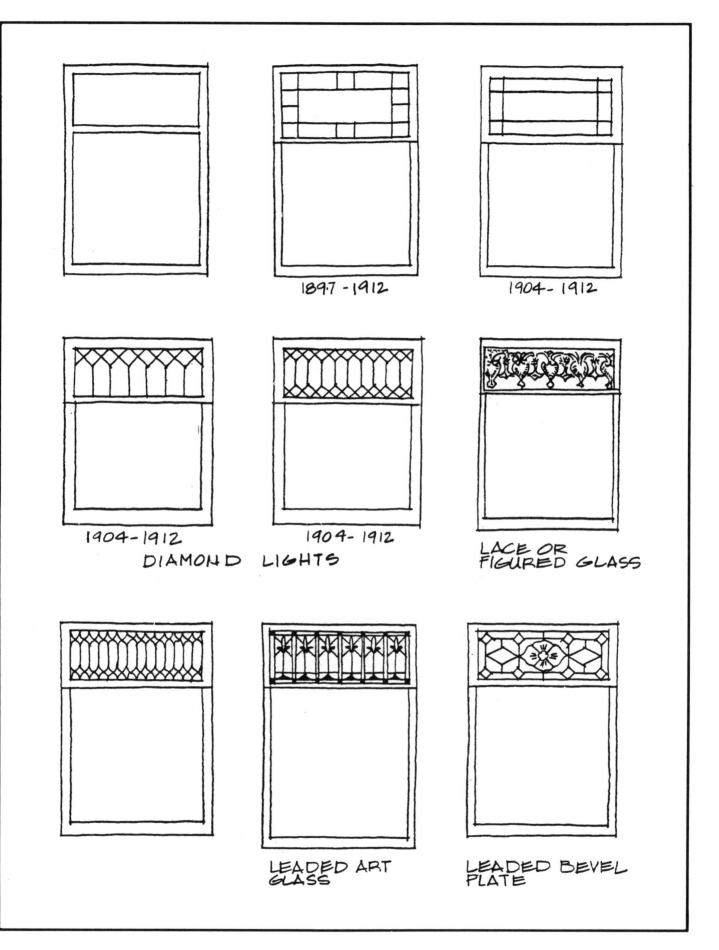

1897 - 1912

1904 - 1912

1904 - 1912

1904 - 1912

DIAMOND LIGHTS

LACE OR
FIGURED GLASS

LEADED ART
GLASS

LEADED BEVEL
PLATE

11

Divided Lights

Divided upper-sash lights were designed for use in all of the interiors of this time period. Most divided-light windows get multiple use, so that the windows illustrated are intended for use in Queen Anne–style cottages as well as in bungalows. Light division is centered on intricate patterns of muntins and panes of glass in various sizes, with polygonal shapes, such as diamonds, squares, and rectangles as primary motifs. Most light patterns reinforce the verticality of the window shape.

Queen Anne motifs emphasize color and small, square panes of glass. Color usually is limited to the primaries. These kinds of windows are seen as unique, perhaps artistic, and may be installed as one-of-a-kind windows in a house. They seem to reference themselves and nothing else.

Divided lights in bungalows seem to be more rationally conceived, even more abstract. They rely on simple rectilinear patterns. Straight lines are emblematic of the design sensibility that underlies the bungalow: it is a modern house type, and vertically divided lights reflect the modern aesthetic.

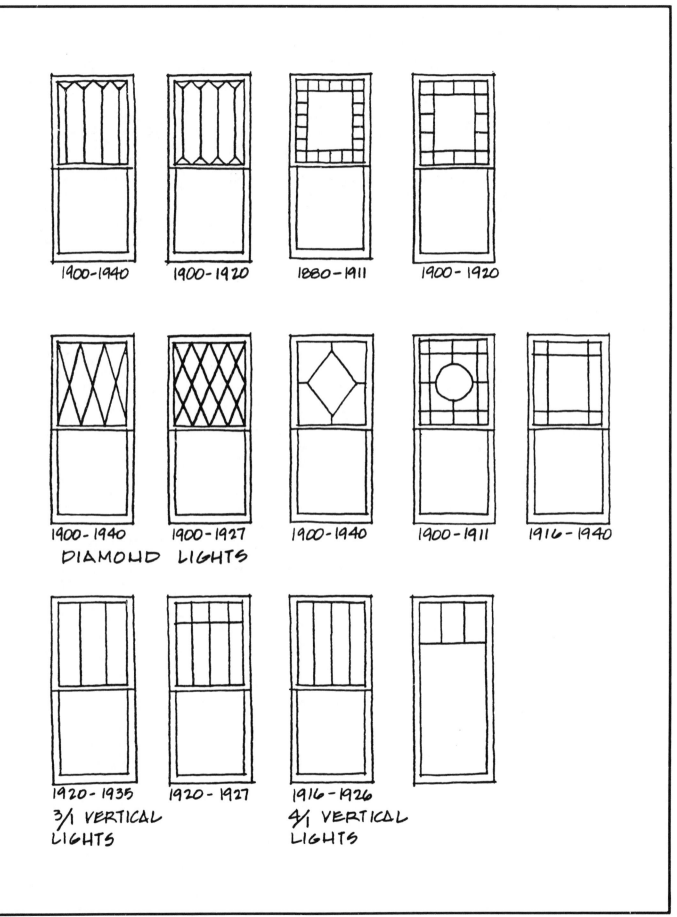

1900-1940   1900-1920   1880-1911   1900-1920

1900-1940   1900-1927   1900-1940   1900-1911   1916-1940
DIAMOND LIGHTS

1920-1935   1920-1927   1916-1926
3/1 VERTICAL   4/1 VERTICAL
LIGHTS   LIGHTS

Divided Lights

Colonial window patterns generally are based on a gridiron of lights, with multiple panes in the upper sash or in both the upper and the lower. These patterns usually are done in proportional arrangements, from 1:1 to 15:1 in upper sash treatments and from 2:2 to 12:12 when both halves are subdivided.

The array of windows illustrated represents the types most frequently produced and identified by millwork companies as being suitable for colonial cottages and bungalows. The patterns include those sold by Sears, Roebuck from 1916 to 1935. Sears sold 2/2 and 4/4 from 1908 to 1935, and most companies sold 6/6 from the beginning of the century to 1940.

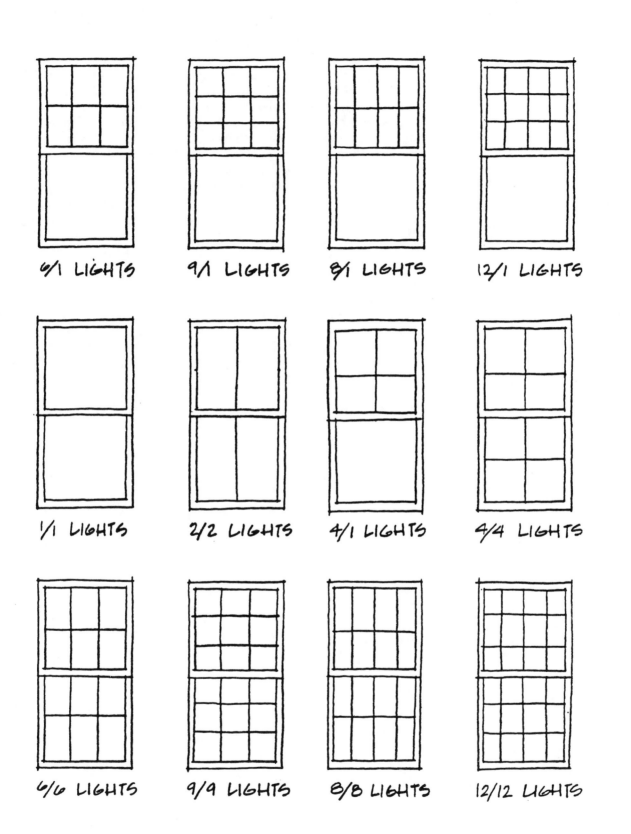

6/1 LIGHTS 9/1 LIGHTS 8/1 LIGHTS 12/1 LIGHTS

1/1 LIGHTS 2/2 LIGHTS 4/1 LIGHTS 4/4 LIGHTS

6/6 LIGHTS 9/9 LIGHTS 8/8 LIGHTS 12/12 LIGHTS

Double and Triple Windows

Double and triple windows are conceived of as individual units; manufacturers intended for them to be inserted into the wall as a set piece. The *triple front* window was derived from an historical window, the Venetian or Palladian window. The original window had a three-part organization with colonettes or pilasters for mullions, matched rectangular side lights with rounded tops, a large round-headed center window, and an entablature. In vernacular architecture the design has been abstracted into a more generic form. The outer windows are matched and may be operable or fixed. The middle sash is wider than the others and often is fixed. Some configurations of triples include a *three-part transom,* which may be glazed or otherwise ornamented in a manner dramatically different from the lower sash.

Double casement windows have hinges on the outside edge and open from the middle. These lights were especially popular with rustic cottage interiors, such as those derived from historical English motifs. The division of lights has been keyed to particular applications, with diamond shapes well suited to colonial or English houses and small squares fitting Queen Anne or artistic interiors. Casements in general often were labeled "French windows." Indeed, if the sash were extended to the floor, the double casement would be a French door.

The *landscape window* is a special first-floor façade window in which the side lights and sometimes the transom swing open for ventilation, while the large center section is fixed. These windows frame vistas of the outside world from living room or dining room. They also give framed views of interiors from the outside.

TRIPLE-FRONT
WITH TRANSOM

TRIPLE
WITH TRANSOM

DOUBLE CASEMENT
WITH TRANSOM

DOUBLE CASEMENT
DIAMOND PATTERN

DOUBLE CASEMENT

PALLADIAN

LANDSCAPE

TRIPLE WITH CASEMENTS

Church Windows   Windows associated with vernacular church interiors are of three types: the *circle-top* window, the *peak-head* window, and the *rectangular* sash. The circle-head has a half-circle or segmental top sash and usually is assembled as a double-hung sash. Circle-top windows sometimes are divided, but solid sheets seem the most frequent form.

The peak-head type has two versions: a triangular top with an abrupt point, and the Gothic arch with a curved rather than straight-line point. Peaked windows often are divided into three sections—a religious reference, no doubt. Colored glass—especially clear, deeply hued cathedral glass—is common in these windows. Here a peak-head window has provision for small squares of colored glass. Millwork companies manufactured church windows with generalized Christian imagery, such as a large field of one color with a border and a single figure—say, a cross—as the central image.

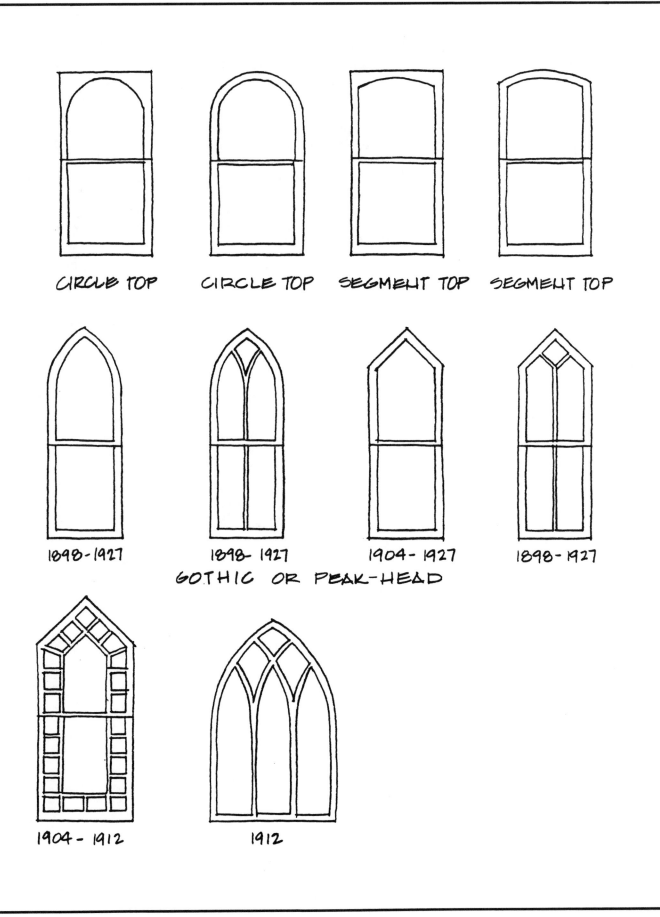

CIRCLE TOP   CIRCLE TOP   SEGMENT TOP   SEGMENT TOP

1898-1927   1898-1927   1904-1927   1898-1927

GOTHIC OR PEAK-HEAD

1904-1912   1912

Factory Windows   *Factory windows* are large sash subdivided into modular units. These windows have fire-resistant steel framing. Installed in great numbers, they provide mill or factory walls with almost continuous glazing. (Factory windows are not to be confused with windows described as "factory"; the latter are window materials of inferior quality, incorporating reasonable defects that do not weaken the sash. Much of this material was painted.)

The division of glass in factory windows ranges from 15 to 40 lights in double-hung windows. Factory windows also include casement windows, pivot types, and transoms (usually installed in series with one transom for every window on the wall), and skylights. The glazing in many of these windows is wire glass.

Skylights are used to light hallways and work spaces and are built in several shapes, including hipped and double-pitched, and a saw-tooth shape for industrial settings.

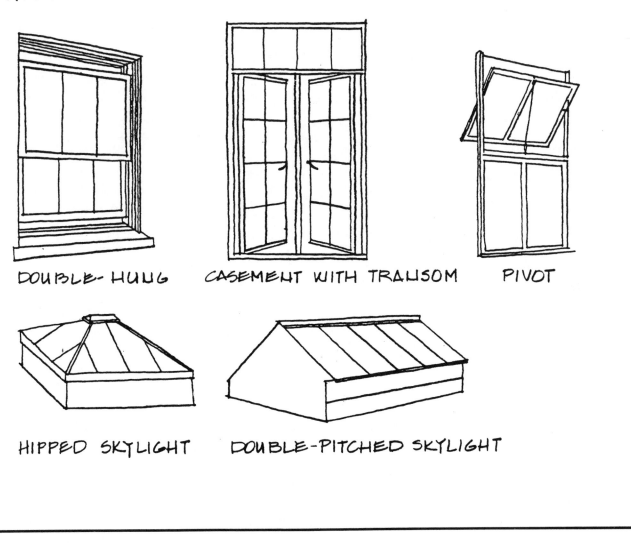

15 LIGHTS 18 LIGHTS 20 LIGHTS

24 LIGHTS

TYPES

DOUBLE-HUNG CASEMENT WITH TRANSOM PIVOT

HIPPED SKYLIGHT DOUBLE-PITCHED SKYLIGHT

Transsoms

A *transom* is a glazed opening hinged along one rail or fixed over a door or window. Transoms are minor windows that augment the primary fenestration pattern, and their glazing is likely to imitate that of the principal windows or to enhance the pattern with a special accent. Transoms are made of solid sheets or are divided, and they assume a wide range of shapes: segment, circle-top, peak-head or Gothic, quarter-circle, and so forth.

Transoms can be adapted to most any style. During the period 1870 to 1940 they were used in the ornamental, the artistic, and the colonial design systems. The *fanlight*, for example, has always been associated with the colonial style. It is a divided semicircular or semielliptical shape above a door or window. It is contained within the frame of the door or window and has radial muntins suggesting a fan.

 ONE LIGHT

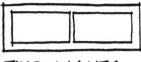 TWO LIGHTS

THREE LIGHTS

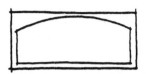 SEGMENTAL

 SEGMENT TOP

 ELLIPTIC HEAD

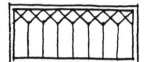 DIAMOND LIGHT

 DIAMOND LIGHT

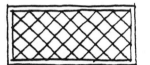 DIAMOND LIGHT

 CIRCLE TOP

 CIRCLE TOP

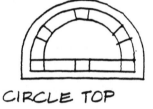 CIRCLE TOP

 BLOCK CORNER

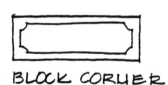 BLOCK CORNER

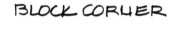 CIRCLE CORNER

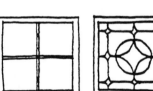 TRANSOM HEADS ABOVE CASEMENTS

 FANLIGHT

GOTHIC ONE LIGHT

GOTHIC 3 LIGHTS

GOTHIC DIAMOND

GOTHIC DIAMOND

Interior Blinds   The control of light and ventilation is a basic requirement for interior design. The use of inside *blinds* has long been part of the vernacular tradition. Blinds originally were made on the job site, but eventually they were manufactured by millwork firms.

The design of blinds for a specific building has several parameters: size of windows to be covered, the system by which blinds are to open and close, storage for open blinds, manipulation of the slats, and the amount of glazed surface to be covered with operable blinds or solid panels.

Blinds consist of rails, stiles, and slats, and are made to be either rolling (movable) or stationary. They may be furnished with segment, oval, circle-top, even Gothic heads, and some have a convex shape. They often match the woodwork in wood type and finish. The entire blind is divided into numerically ordered sections: a blind with six panels, for example, is called a six-fold type. *Folding* blinds, which are linked vertically, fold against the window jamb, the folds often fitting into a pocket. *Sliding* blinds operate like sash. There are two kinds, those with a pocket at either the bottom or the top of the blind, and those with no pocket. All blinds are furnished with hardware such as hinges, pulls, and lifts.

Venetian blinds have been a part of vernacular interiors since the 1870s. These blinds hang in the window opening and are made of movable slats held together by tape and operated by a cord. The slats were furnished in most species of wood and the tapes and cords were offered in colors and several materials.

Blinds may be thought of as gridirons of varying qualities and intensities of light. Panels of slats can be opened or closed by degrees. The relationship between solid panels and slats controls the general pattern of incoming light as well as visual access from outside. Solid panels can be ornamented with stuck or applied moldings harmonious with the woodwork system.

SECTION

SECTION

FOLDING BLINDS   SLIDING BLINDS   VENETIAN BLINDS

BLIND PATTERNS

ALL SLATS   HALF PANEL/   THREE-QUARTER   ALL
             HALF SLATS   PANEL   PANEL

Ornamental Glass

Ornamental glass is used for special effects in several cottage and bungalow house interiors. It is used in entrance doors in lieu of a panel, in windows as a headpiece, in specially located single windows, and in transoms.

To ornament common sheet glass or plate glass, the surface is subjected to various treatments, either when the glass is molten or cold. Transformation is accomplished by altering the texture of the surface, by pressing material or a pattern into the glass, or by casting the glass into unusual shapes. Methods of altering the surface include etching with a caustic, sandblasting, chipping, grinding, cutting, frosting, enameling, and rolling. Depending on the severity of the alteration, the surface is partially obscured.

Some kinds of ornamental glass are iridescent, that is, covered with opalescent glaze that aids in refraction. Others are frosted or otherwise matte-finished. In the type known in the 1870s as "roll cathedral," colored cathedral glass are assembled into conventionalized imagery and held together with strips of metal and lead; the uneven surface creates a sparkling effect. *Beveled* glass is used in doors, windows, and cupboards. It is polished plate glass cut, mitered, and leaded into geometrical patterns. As an alternative to all this, Sears sold transfer designs to make plain windows look like art glass.

SANDBLAST

LACE

ARTISTIC CHIPPED

CRYSTAL SHEET

ORNAMENTAL
PLATE GLASS

ENAMEL

BEVEL

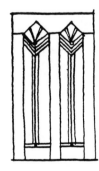

ART GLASS

Commercial Glass

Most commercial glass is plate glass, which is thicker and of better quality than regular sheet glass. *Wire* glass is fire-resistant, and has the advantage of admitting light through closed doors and windows. Wire glass may be polished and transparent, as well as ribbed, patterned, and very rough-surfaced. The last type is only semitransparent.

Figured glass is created by running soft glass under large rollers which cut a pattern into the surface. The figures break up light and obscure view. This glass is used in office partitions, transoms, halls, bathrooms, and side and rear entrance doors. It allows light to enter a room yet maintains privacy.

Prism glass is semitransparent glass about as thick as ordinary plate with either a smooth or a lenticular surface on the outside and a prismatic surface on the inside. Prism glass deflects the light from the sky into most parts of an interior. It can be cut to any size and has been used particularly as secondary lighting, as top sash in warehouses, factories, mills, schools, and as transom lights over storefronts. Usually it is glazed in metal bars and most glazing patterns are geometric: squares, diamonds, rectangles, and hexagons.

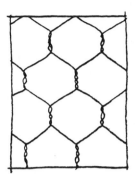

WIRE

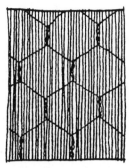

RIBBED

FIGURED GLASS

MAZE

FLORENTINE

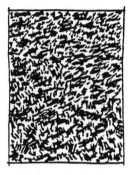

CHIP

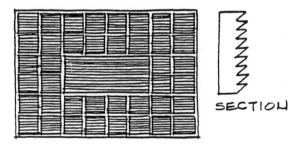

PRISM

SECTION

DOORS
Elements and
Construction

Interior doors are similar in construction to exterior doors, except that they are thinner and their paneling patterns are somewhat different. Interior doors are assembled from *stiles* (vertical members), *rails* (horizontal members), and *panels* of wood or glass. The vertical divider between the panels is called a *muntin*. Interior doors may be made of solid wood throughout or of veneer over a frame; the latter is referred to as a *compound* door. The height of interior doors ranges from 6 feet to 8 feet 6 inches.

The edges of door elements have always provided opportunity for ornamentation. Moldings, whether applied or solid stuck, have been an integral part of door design. By the 1920s builders and manufacturers had largely abandoned separate moldings applied anywhere on a door in favor of stuck molding. In this case the mold is worked out on the door element itself by putting it through a "sticker" machine to bring the edges to a desired form.

Prior to molding standardization, which is a relatively recent phenomenon, the various designations of sticking meant different things to different people. On the facing page there is an example of an *ovolo* mold. In our search through trade catalogs of the first decades of this century, we found variations on the ovolo pattern—combinations of fillets and quarter-rounds, different in each case. We did not find an ovolo, which is a classical molding, made before 1900; perhaps it was handmade during an earlier revival period. It seems not to have come back into use until colonial treatments were modernized, when its rather simple and unadorned profile made it appropriate.

Of all the stuck moldings the *OG* seems to be the most utilized. It is a combination of a cove with a quarter-round with no fillet in between—one curve flows into the other. *Cove-and-bead* mold is a combination of a cove on top and a quarter-round on bottom with a small fillet in between. A *bead-and-cove* molding is not the opposite of the previous molding, as one might assume. Instead it has three fillets, one each on the top and bottom and one between the quarter-round and cove. *PG* is a solid mold with a long bevel on the face and a small fillet on each side. The *colonial* molding shown is very similar to an OG, except that the continuous curve is interrupted by a fillet where the mold meets the panel.

A *flush* molding is an applied piece that finishes flush with or just below the surface of a panel or the surface of the stiles and rails. A *raised* molding, by contrast, is applied work that partially covers or extends above the face of a door panel or above the surface of the stiles and rails. Raised moldings were used to cover joints, such as those between the panel and the stiles and rails. Some doors, especially ornamental types, had raised panels in which the panel extended beyond the structural members.

Doors that have their stiles, rails, or panels beveled at an angle of about 45 degrees are said to be chamfered. In the style called *stop chamfer* the chamfering ends short of the length of the piece, as in the illustration.

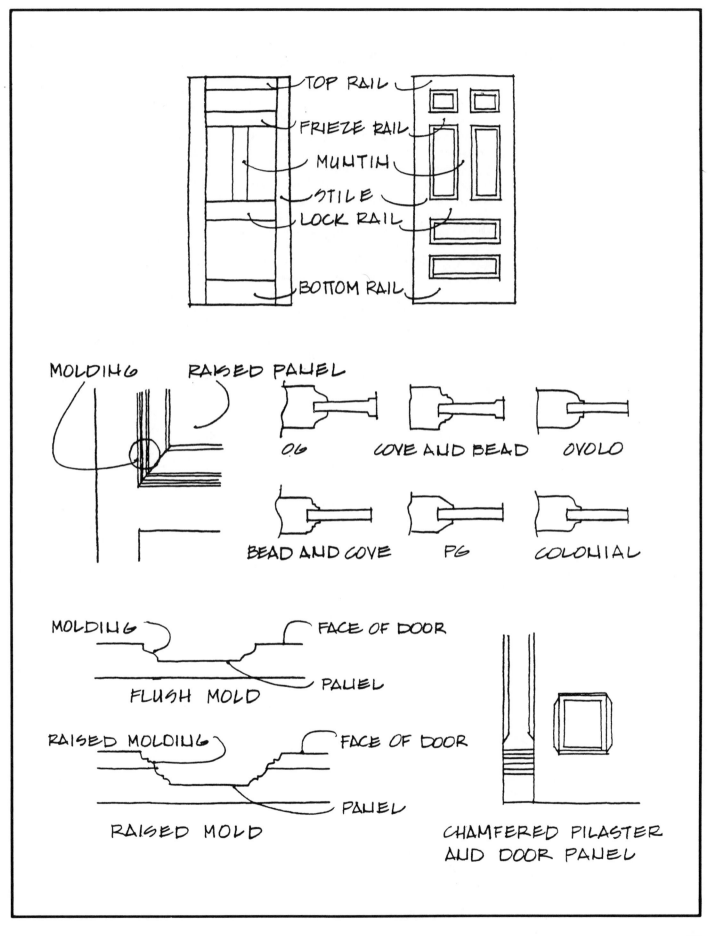

TOP RAIL

FRIEZE RAIL

MUNTIN

STILE

LOCK RAIL

BOTTOM RAIL

MOLDING   RAISED PANEL

OG   COVE AND BEAD   OVOLO

BEAD AND COVE   PG   COLONIAL

MOLDING   FACE OF DOOR

PANEL

FLUSH MOLD

RAISED MOLDING   FACE OF DOOR

PANEL

RAISED MOLD

CHAMFERED PILASTER
AND DOOR PANEL

Frames and Trim

Doors are set into wood or metal frames attached to the sides of the opening. A simple interior frame has no jamb, no lining of any kind on the frame, and no stop (a stick that stops the movement of the door). A *rabbeted* frame has a portion of its frame planed to create a stop. A *full stop* is an extra molding attached to the frame to receive the door. A *sliding-door* frame has two stops, one for each side of the door.

Casing is the framework around a window or door that covers the joint between the plaster and the frame. It may be molded or flat. A *threshold* is a piece of beveled trim under a door, used especially over a joint where two floorings meet. An *overdoor* is an ornamental pediment or hood over a doorway. It spans the opening and usually sits on a cap made of moldings. A *base block* is a rectangular block of trim at the base of a casing. It abuts the baseboard and functions as plinth for the standing pieces of the trim set.

When the edges of two doors come together they make a joint, and historically this joint has been covered with a small semicircular molding, an *astragal*. It can be an ornamental, cut with beading, or plain. In folding doors the astragal is applied to one of the pair of doors so as to form a rabbet. A *double astragal* fits sliding doors, each rabbeted on the back to receive the door and grooved on the face to make a closed joint. The *T-shaped* astragal forms a rabbet for both of a pair of folding doors, and a *cloverleaf* is simple molding that accomplishes the same thing without a rabbet.

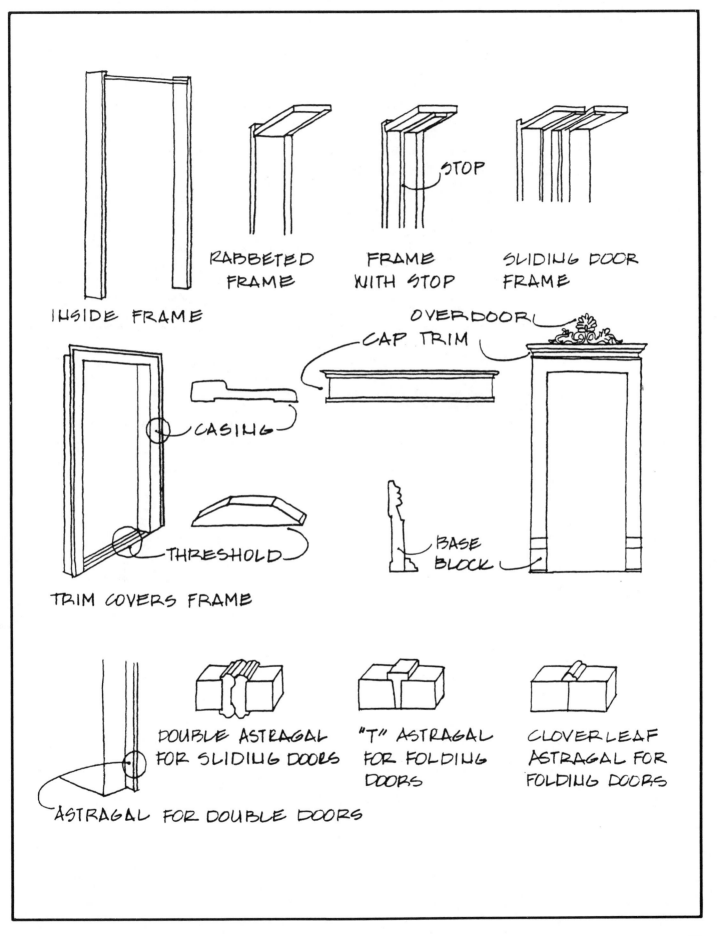

RABBETED FRAME

FRAME WITH STOP

SLIDING DOOR FRAME

STOP

INSIDE FRAME

OVERDOOR
CAP TRIM

CASING

THRESHOLD

TRIM COVERS FRAME

BASE BLOCK

ASTRAGAL FOR DOUBLE DOORS

DOUBLE ASTRAGAL FOR SLIDING DOORS

"T" ASTRAGAL FOR FOLDING DOORS

CLOVERLEAF ASTRAGAL FOR FOLDING DOORS

33

Operation   Interior doors have at least eight different kinds of operation. The *single-action,* full-sized door is the most common. *Double-action* doors, hinged to a coil spring mounted in the floor or in the door, appeared by the 1880s; a push plate on both sides of the door is standard. The so-called *Dutch* door has operation options. The top section may be swung inward while the lower section remains closed, or the entire door can be opened as a unit. A wide shelf on the lower section of this door is common in commercial settings. In the vernacular, the double action of single doors opening from the center is the feature of the *French* door.

Sliding doors are made to be singles or doubles. Both types are designed to match the pattern of other interior doors. Made of oak or pine, these doors have guides at the top and on the floor, with hangers and a trolley track. Sliding doors disappear into a pocket in the wall. A typical single sliding door has a width of 5 feet and a height of 7 feet. The Gordon-Van Tine Company noted in 1911 that "a single sliding door is very much more convenient than a pair of folding or sliding doors, as it is easier to handle."

A *rolling* door is a commercial and industrial door constructed of metal. It is framed by grooves mounted on a wall and it rolls into a coil. Rolling doors made of wood are used also in meeting rooms and church halls. An *accordion* door is a folding door with hangers and a track. The door sections usually are paneled and less than 3 feet in width. These doors typically begin with a half door and continue with full doors to the center of the opening where they meet. The accordion effect is created by folding them against the frame.

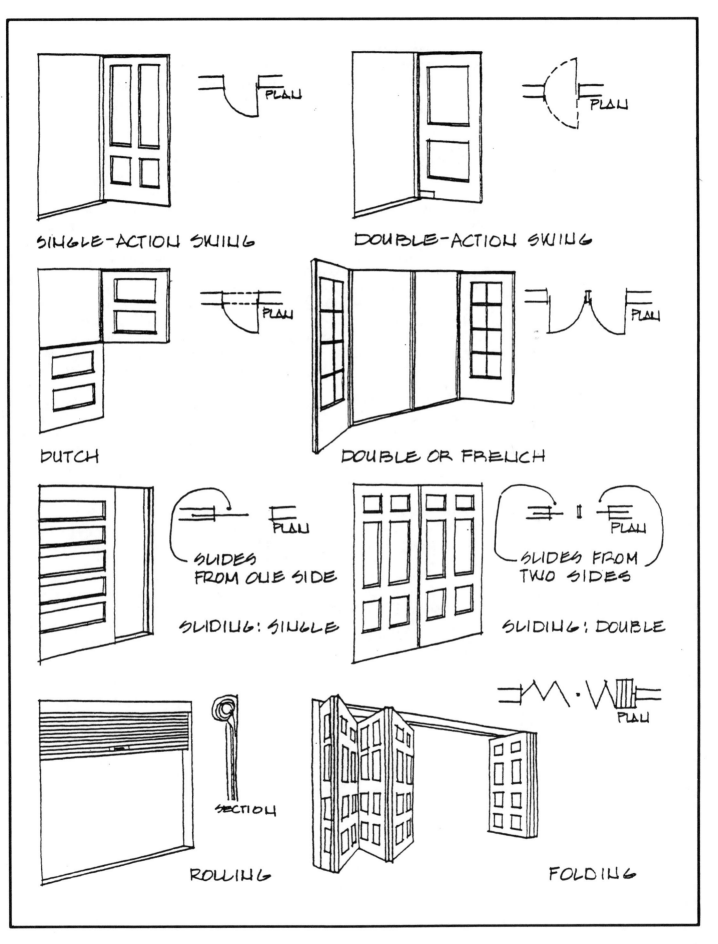

SINGLE-ACTION SWING   DOUBLE-ACTION SWING

DUTCH   DOUBLE OR FRENCH

SLIDES FROM ONE SIDE

SLIDING: SINGLE

SLIDES FROM TWO SIDES

SLIDING: DOUBLE

ROLLING   FOLDING

PLAN

SECTION

Panels   Most interior doors are paneled, with patterns ranging from a single panel up to eight panels. Panels are both horizontal, or cross, and vertical. Not all panel types were manufactured during the seventy-year period of this study.

We were able to assess the significance of the design of most doors by tracing them through Sears, Roebuck catalogs. The *one-panel* door, for example, was manufactured from 1912 to 1927, but the *two-panel* door was available from 1911 to 1935. The difference in chronology is due in part to Sears's ability to market the same door under the heading of several aesthetics. Early in its life, the two-panel was identified as a bedroom door, appropriate for a suburban cottage. In 1916 the door was seen as fitting for a "modern" home, one that could use a plain door made of oak or mahogany. In the 1920s the two-panel was seen as part of the colonial style, at home under a gambrel roof. Materials for the door had been expanded to include clear pine and fir as well as birch and red oak veneers. By 1931 the door had become the "regular two-panel design," popular wherever there was a need for simplicity and appropriate in any home.

Most panel doors have this kind of history—a range of materials and finishes and a range of applications. Sometimes the use of the door was limited to a change in one variable. The two-panel door with vertical panels, for instance, could be given a natural finish or a walnut or other dark stain. In this state it was suitable for the Mission style. If it were finished in mahogany or painted white it could fit a colonial scheme. In 1931 Sears recommended this door's proportions for *any* house, noting that its "long vertical lines add height to low rooms." The effort to extend the use of particular patterns was established early in the millwork business. For example, in 1912 the Farley and Loetscher trade catalog labeled the one-panel door "strictly sanitary" and on another page called the same door "Mission." The customer could choose health or style.

Of the remaining door patterns, the *five-panel* door with five cross panels, and the *six-panel* with six vertical panels seemed to fit into almost any design system. Some of these adaptations were facilitated by enamel paint, which tended to bind elements together.

Sears, Roebuck manufactured panel doors in every pattern category, as well as French doors, entrance doors, kitchen and rear entrance doors, storm doors, sliding doors, and mirrored doors. Its inventory, like that of all large millwork companies, addressed every door need and provided the opportunity to integrate all the doors in a building into an overall design system.

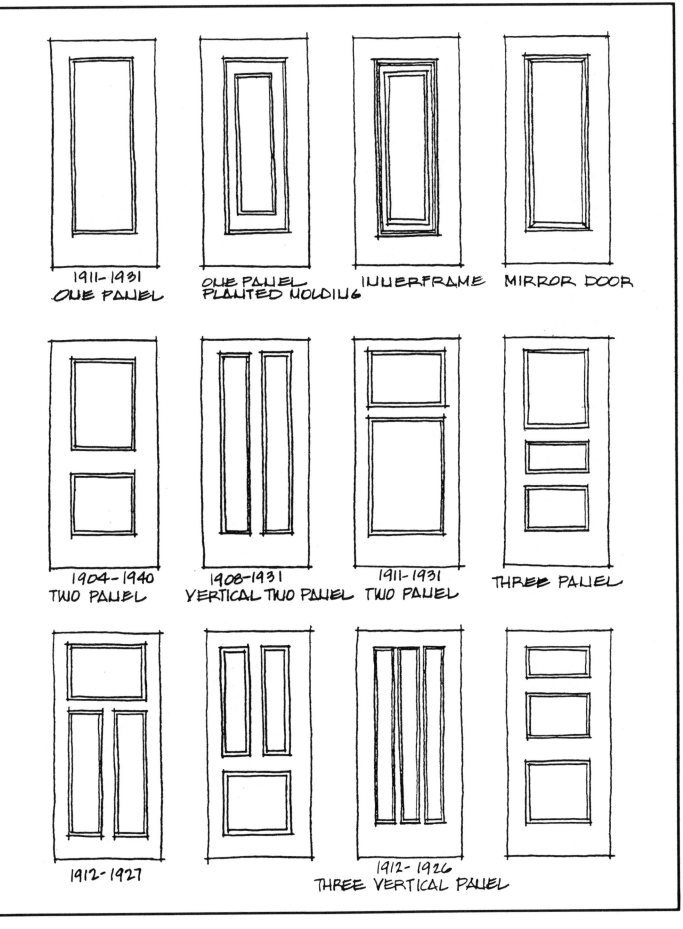

1911-1931
ONE PANEL

ONE PANEL
PLANTED MOLDING

INNERFRAME

MIRROR DOOR

1904-1940
TWO PANEL

1908-1931
VERTICAL TWO PANEL

1911-1931
TWO PANEL

THREE PANEL

1912-1927

1912-1926
THREE VERTICAL PANEL

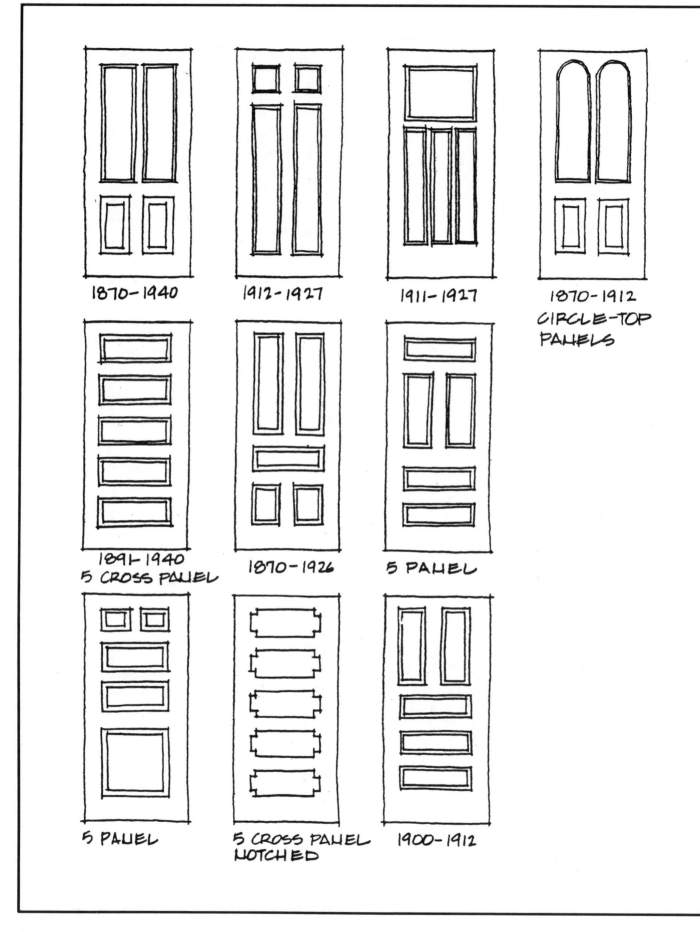

1870-1940

1912-1927

1911-1927

1870-1912
CIRCLE-TOP
PANELS

1891-1940
5 CROSS PANEL

1870-1926

5 PANEL

5 PANEL

5 CROSS PANEL
NOTCHED

1900-1912

1904-1940

6 CROSS PANEL

1880-1898
6 PANEL

1891-1898

6 PANEL

6 PANEL

1891-1898

8 PANEL

8 PANEL

1920-1930

Swinging Doors   *Swinging doors* for saloons and water closets are similar in design to interior blinds: stiles and rails enclose a series of slats and panels. Generally their length is 4 to 7 feet, their width 2 feet 4 inches to 3 feet 6 inches, and their thickness 1⅛ inch. Each door has two, three or four sections separated by rails. These doors are hung in pairs on spring-loaded hinges and are rabbeted in the same way as window blinds. The ornamental version of this door has a carved piece above the top rail and stepped or carved stile ends. Modern swinging doors are precisely rectilinear. After 1920 these doors disappeared from millwork catalogs.

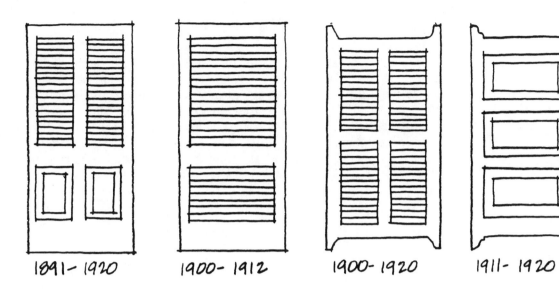

1891- 1920   1900- 1912   1900- 1920   1911- 1920

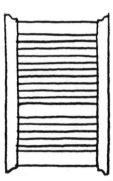

1912   1912- 1920

French Doors   *French doors* derived from French windows of the nineteenth century. Although they could be installed as single doors, they usually are found in pairs serving as passage doors from a social space—a living or dining room—to a porch or from a hallway to a living room. They are identified especially with colonial design. Typical glazing patterns include grids of 2 × 5 for ten lights and 3 × 5 for fifteen lights. Sears, Roebuck sold French doors with ten lights from 1912 to 1935, almost from the year it began making building materials. It did not introduce a fifteen light door until 1931, however. French doors, like most things vernacular, could be adapted for different aesthetics, thus there are examples of rectilinear designs with long vertical panes and very little division of the glass, which are appropriate for artistic interiors, as well as Tudor arch doors for English cottages, and elliptical- and segment-head doors for colonial interiors.

10 LIGHTS

15 LIGHTS

12 LIGHTS WITH PANEL

FOUR-FOLD

TUDOR HEAD

ARCHED OPENING

SEGMENT HEAD

Special Doors This category includes doors that had less use than other passage doors, yet there is enough evidence to suggest that their use was significant. The *slab* door, which has become very popular, appeared in the trade literature around 1911. It is a veneered door that was advertised as "completely sanitary." The severity of the slab—it is essentially a plane of wood that relies on graining for effect—made it appropriate for modern interiors and, when inlaid with a second wood such as holly or ebony, for artistic ones as well. Such inlays usually are in geometric patterns.

Reading from left to right, the first three doors of the second row are *vestibule* doors used to separate the entrance from other spaces. By the 1920s these doors were no longer part of vernacular buildings. The first vestibule door is made of beveled glass; the second is a *panel-and-glass* (or *panel-and-light*) door with a cap over the glass and a carved apron beneath it; the third door has an oval glass panel with carved corners and beaded molding around the glass.

The last door in the second row is a kitchen door (made from 1900 to 1935). Because of its placement it plays a role in the appearance of the kitchen, and it is in view in most kitchen plans. Traditionally, the kitchen door is a panel-and-glass door with much less ornamentation than is typical of an entrance door. *Lattice* doors are closet doors in which solid panels have been replaced by latticework.

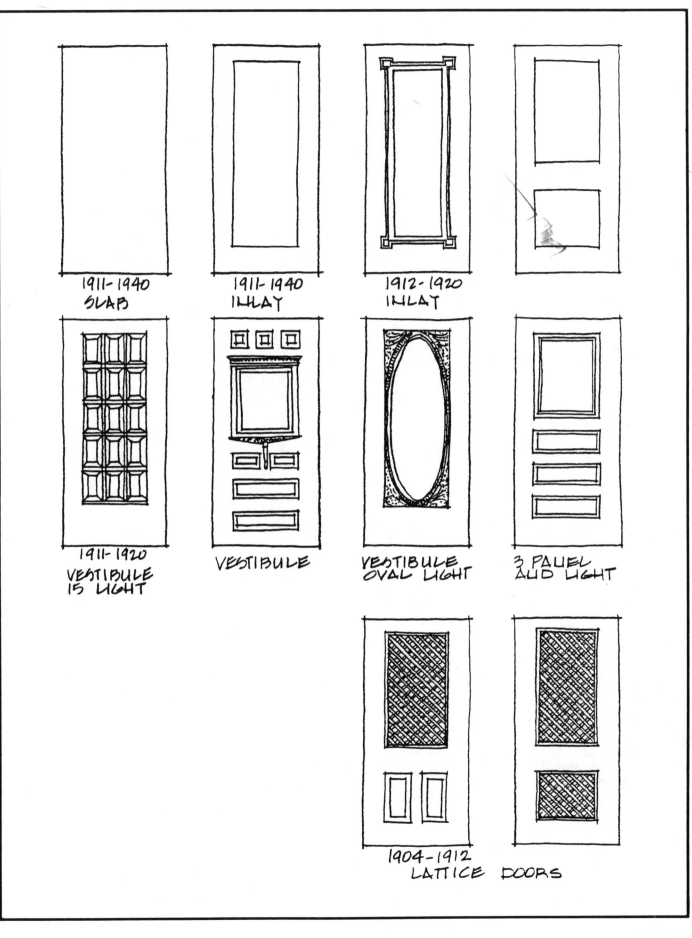

1911-1940
SLAB

1911-1940
INLAY

1912-1920
INLAY

1911-1920
VESTIBULE
15 LIGHT

VESTIBULE

VESTIBULE
OVAL LIGHT

3 PANEL
AND LIGHT

1904-1912
LATTICE DOORS

1904- 1920   1904- 1912   1911- 1920
ARCHED PANEL

PANEL AND GLASS   GRADUATED PANELS   PANEL AND GLASS

SINGLE DOORS

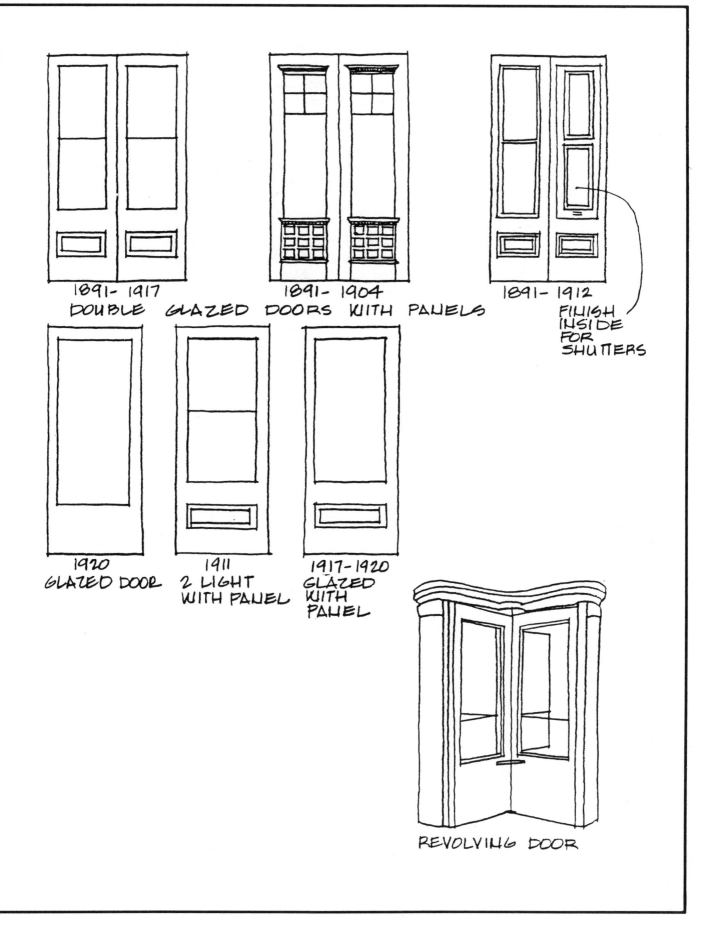

1891- 1917
DOUBLE   GLAZED   DOORS   WITH   PANELS

1891- 1904

1891- 1912
FINISH
INSIDE
FOR
SHUTTERS

1920
GLAZED DOOR

1911
2 LIGHT
WITH PANEL

1917-1920
GLAZED
WITH
PANEL

REVOLVING DOOR

Cupboard Doors

To some degree, cupboard doors are miniature doors or windows. Constructed of stiles and rails and paneled in wood or glass—the latter framed by muntins—these doors reflect most of the patterns worked up in other interior doors. At the same time, their size allows for a more delicate handling of panels, especially of divided lights.

The array of designs on the accompanying page represents patterns that appear many times in several sources. Sears, Roebuck included cupboard doors in its millwork inventory, and its products reflected both the practical and the aesthetic interests of the period. Sears cupboards built during the first two decades of this century were all wood with large raised panels. Of the three designs shown, the single-panel door and the four-panel door were manufactured for three decades. Sears made most of its cupboards from yellow pine. Sears mills identified glazed doors as "china closet sash." In this case the material could be other than pine—clear fir or oak, for instance—because china closets might be finished in natural wood rather than painted. Sears produced the one-light, the diamond-and-rhomb pattern, and the art-glass models from 1916 to the early 1930s. The popularity of these corner closets was due in part to the public's interest in colonial imagery.

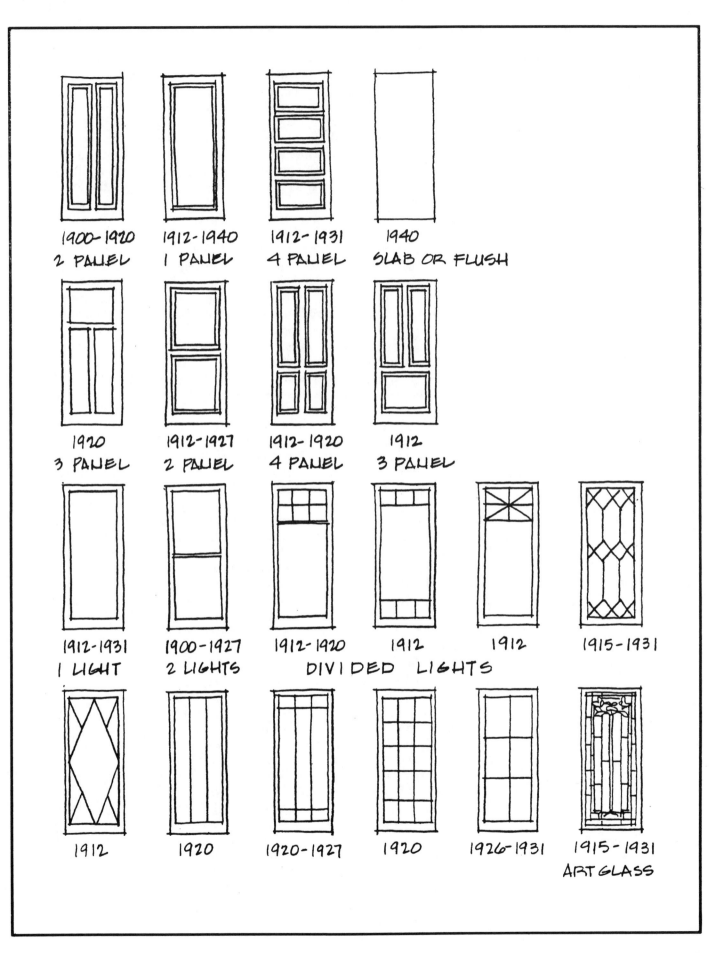

1900-1920
2 PANEL

1912-1940
1 PANEL

1912-1931
4 PANEL

1940
SLAB OR FLUSH

1920
3 PANEL

1912-1927
2 PANEL

1912-1920
4 PANEL

1912
3 PANEL

1912-1931
1 LIGHT

1900-1927
2 LIGHTS

1912-1920

1912

1912

1915-1931

DIVIDED LIGHTS

1912

1920

1920-1927

1920

1926-1931

1915-1931
ART GLASS

TRIM SETS Elements and Construction

Trim sets are part of what the trade called "standing finish"—all that is affixed to the walls—as distinct from "fittings," which includes cases, cupboards, drawers, and shelves. Interior trim sets are groupings of moldings used as casings and blocks for openings and window finish: stools, aprons, and stops. Historically, trim-set patterns were integrated, that is, each element had a design relationship to the others. Most of these linkages have to do with surface treatment.

Trim sets are made with three kinds of moldings: *applied* moldings (especially to caps), *stuck* moldings on the side and head casings, and *embossed* moldings. The latter were created by passing a stick under a large roller that pressed a pattern into the wood.

Trim sets are both practical and ornamental. *Casings* cover the space between the plastered wall and the door frame, what we refer to as the rough opening. A *window stool* caps the frame below the sill, and the *apron* is like a casing in that it masks a frame-and-wall joint under the stool. *Blocks* function as stops and integrate the intersection of casing members.

Ornamentally, trim sets add visual and physical texture to a room, and they bind the woodwork and walls together. Most of the ornamentation centers on surface design, especially linear devices—outlines, ridges or reeds, edges, and the like.

Casing design is generally of three types. One type uses corner blocks where the side and head casings meet. A second type has mitered corners instead of blocks, which creates a continuous casing. The third type relies for effect on simple trabeation—the head casing spans the opening and the width of the side casings, which butt against the head. All of these casings may be plain or ornate, but flat, molded, and rounded surfaces are the most common. There is a fourth category which uses a back-band molding applied to the outer edge.

Molded pilaster finish seems to be the most successful casing type. In this scheme thin pilasters rise from base blocks, meeting head blocks at the head of the door or window, with the entire casing being tied together by a molded head casing. Pilaster finish is symmetrical and carries common molding profiles, such as bead-and-cove, OG, and a few labeled generally as colonial. All of the pieces in the illustration are reeded; the surface design consists of a cluster of semicircular parallel ridges, just the opposite of fluting. There is also an intermediary corner block that reinforces a pattern in the wainscot. Corner blocks were preferred for casings for a time in the belief that they were reliable in keeping side casings from shrinking away from the head. This was a problem in mitered casings, and it resulted in the production of many kinds of corner fasteners.

A *round-edge* casing, once referred to as "sanitary," has no dust-catching ridges. It is a modern casing, positioned at the other end of the aesthetic continuum from an ornamental pilaster set. Round-edge casing is flat. Visually it recedes into the wall, emphasizing the plane of the wall rather than projections from it. The reference to posts and a beam has been reduced another step so that the casing becomes a geometric pattern, which contextually is a more neutral finish than molded work.

Cap trim sets are assembled from several moldings and include an architrave and cornice, both of which may be richly detailed, as the head casing. The application of sets is usually systemic: the same cap trim is used for all the doors and windows in a room or from room to room. However, there is evidence of the use of a single cap for doors with no correspondence to the head casing on the windows.

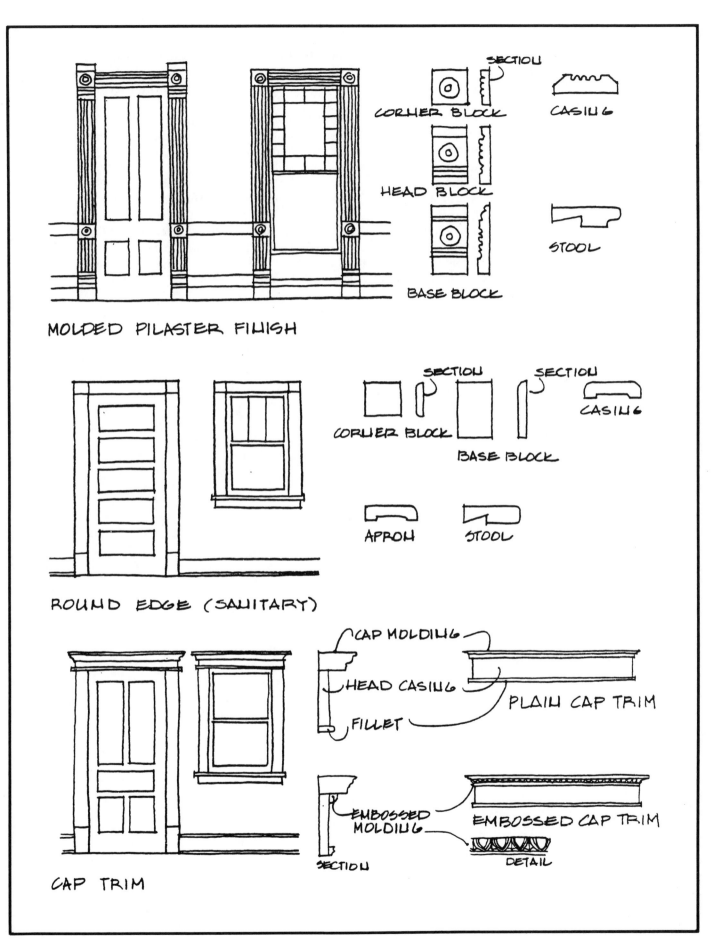

MOLDED PILASTER FINISH

CORNER BLOCK

HEAD BLOCK

BASE BLOCK

SECTION

CASING

STOOL

ROUND EDGE (SANITARY)

CORNER BLOCK

BASE BLOCK

SECTION

SECTION

CASING

APRON

STOOL

CAP TRIM

CAP MOLDING

HEAD CASING

FILLET

PLAIN CAP TRIM

EMBOSSED MOLDING

SECTION

EMBOSSED CAP TRIM

DETAIL

Elements and Construction

Back bands alter the profile of the casing by extending the outside edge. Either flat or molded, they were made to integrate with popular styles, such as Craftsman or Mission, and in a broad, unadorned style that would fit any treatment.

Much of the architectural material classified as "modern" is squared-edged in the belief that rectilinear patterns are a clear and dramatic alternative to ornamental ones. Some millwork companies made subtle distinctions between aspects of the modern. For example, Mission and Craftsman designs are sometimes distinguished by a few details. A *Mission* casing is flat and extends its head casing just beyond the side casings, giving it a lug profile. A *Craftsman* casing might have a mitered back band added to the head, which is at a right angle to the casings. A *chamfered* head casing has an angled top that gives it the appearance of a pediment, which is a traditional head-casing form. Rectilinear, flat casings are associated with the artistic aesthetic and with bungalow house types.

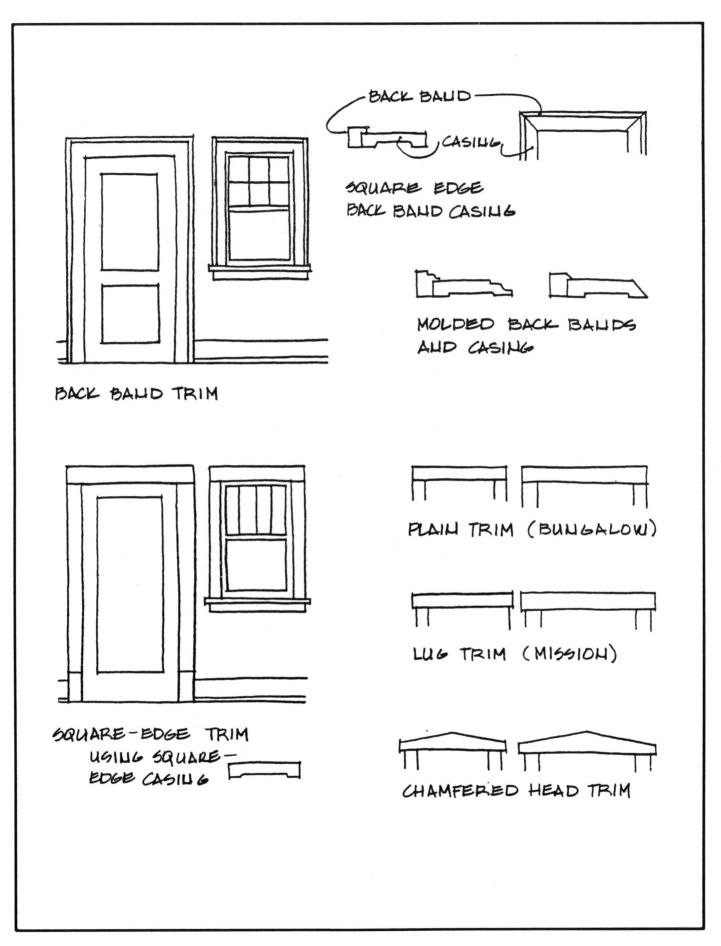

BACK BAND

CASING

SQUARE EDGE
BACK BAND CASING

MOLDED BACK BANDS
AND CASING

BACK BAND TRIM

PLAIN TRIM (BUNGALOW)

LUG TRIM (MISSION)

SQUARE-EDGE TRIM
USING SQUARE-
EDGE CASING

CHAMFERED HEAD TRIM

Blocks   *Blocks* for trim sets are of three types: *corner* blocks used where stiles and rails meet, or as a stop within a stile; *head* blocks, which terminate the casings; and *base* or *plinth* blocks, which are also stops for the baseboard and its molding. Blocks are an integral part of the ornamental design system and play a minor role in artistic approaches to interiors. They were of little significance for colonial systems, however, and disappeared from use by 1920.

The illustrations of blocks show typical patterns and shapes. Most blocks are 5½ inches wide and not very thick. Corner blocks are square and their standard thickness is 1⅛ inch. Over time they become narrower. Popular patterns include circular motifs, figures, geometrical abstractions, and conventionalized natural subjects, especially foliate forms.

Head blocks have the same thickness as corner blocks but are longer; 10 inches is typical. Head-block designs have a three-part organization. There is a molded or cut top, a molded bottom, and a field that carries the ornamentation. The pattern in the field generally is repeated in the accompanying corner blocks but not necessarily in the base blocks.

Base blocks are the thickest of the three block types, 1⅜ inch. Their width is the same as the others and the standard height is 11 inches. Base blocks have a molded top that looks like a baseboard molding, and a second mold of reeds or cove lower down. The lower half is flat and most often undecorated.

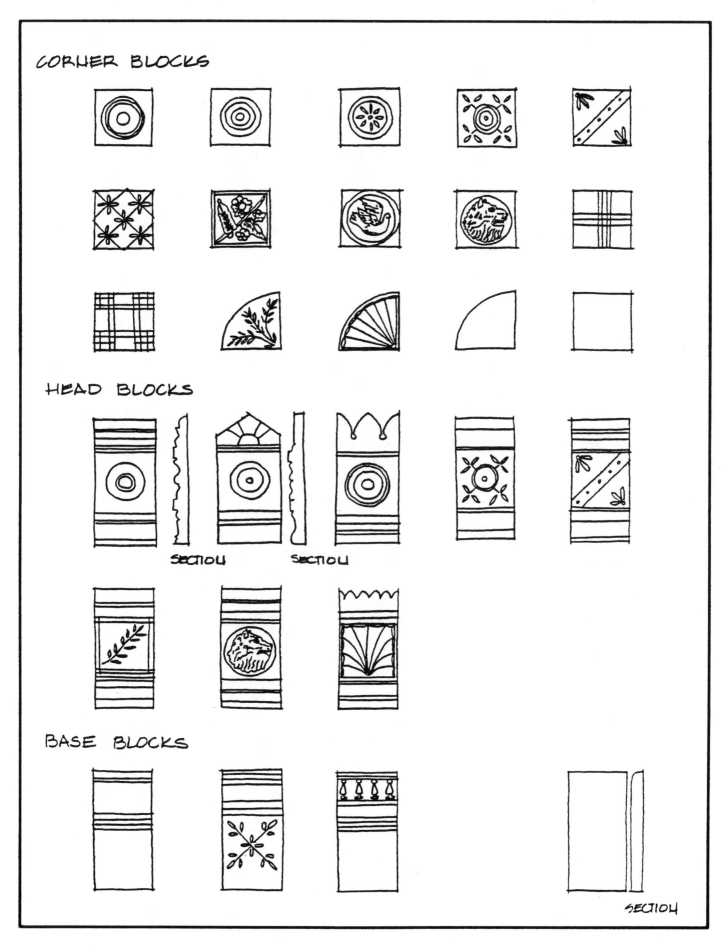

CORNER BLOCKS

HEAD BLOCKS

SECTION   SECTION

BASE BLOCKS

SECTION

55

Casings

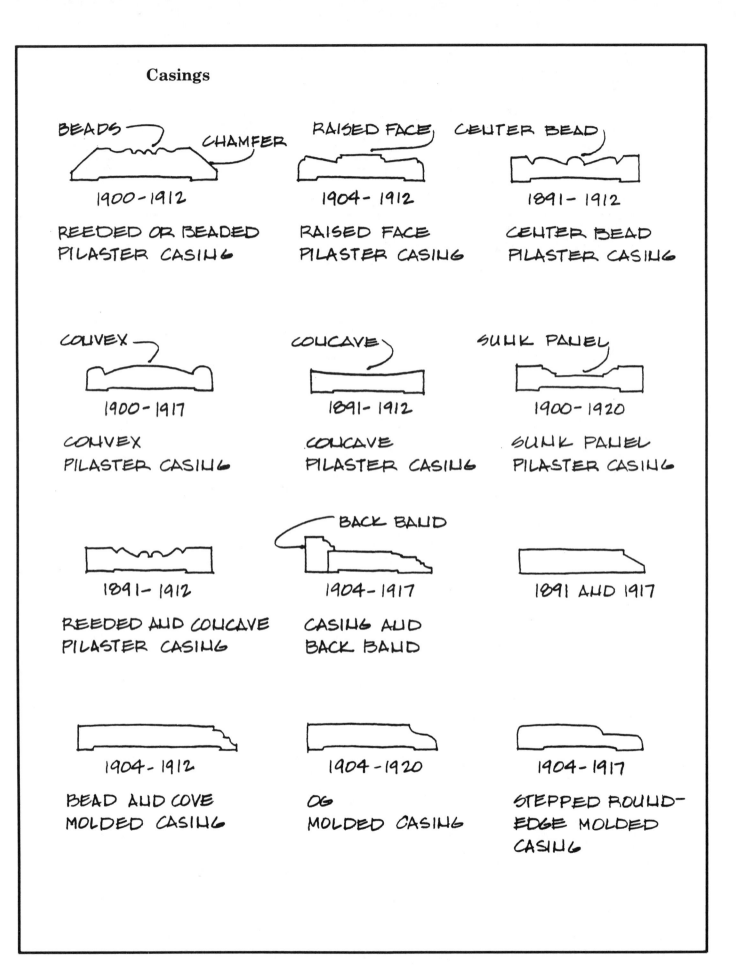

BEADS — CHAMFER
1900–1912
REEDED OR BEADED PILASTER CASING

RAISED FACE
1904–1912
RAISED FACE PILASTER CASING

CENTER BEAD
1891–1912
CENTER BEAD PILASTER CASING

CONVEX
1900–1917
CONVEX PILASTER CASING

CONCAVE
1891–1912
CONCAVE PILASTER CASING

SUNK PANEL
1900–1920
SUNK PANEL PILASTER CASING

1891–1912
REEDED AND CONCAVE PILASTER CASING

BACK BAND
1904–1917
CASING AND BACK BAND

1891 AND 1917

1904–1912
BEAD AND COVE MOLDED CASING

1904–1920
OG MOLDED CASING

1904–1917
STEPPED ROUND-EDGE MOLDED CASING

**CEILINGS
Treatments and
Materials**

This section concerns the design of ceilings in vernacular buildings, focusing on materials and conceptual approaches to the problem. We have tried to discern what materials people used to ceil, or line, the upper surfaces of rooms, and their methods of doing it. The ceiling is treated here as another plane—like the floor and the walls—whose design changed considerably over the period under study.

Most vernacular ceilings are flat. Exceptions are specialty ceilings identified with a particular room (such as a hipped ceiling in a dining room) or ceilings associated with a particular building type (such as an arched ceiling in a Spanish-style bungalow or a peaked ceiling in an English cottage.

Throughout most of the period 1870 to 1940 ceilings got special attention, distinct from that given other flat surfaces. Most treatments centered on dividing the ceiling into sections. This was carried out in almost all available ceiling materials: matched boards, metal plates, wood and plaster moldings that created ceiling panels, coffers of wood or metal, stenciling, and wallpaper. Only in a plaster ceiling was the plane left intact. Due to the differences in the nature of the materials, ceiling organization varied. Regardless of approach, the ceiling became a uniquely ornamented surface.

Most ceiling treatments were reserved for a few rooms. In vernacular houses, the kitchen, dining room, and living room got special attention. The ceiling of the 1870s and 1880s was a hard plaster affair, about 9 feet from the floor, which was at first painted white and later was tinted or papered. It was during this period that papering changed to allover patterns with borders as well as papers with multiple borders segmenting the paper into different patterns.

Beaded wood ceiling is constructed of matched tongue-and-groove boards, about 4 inches wide and ⅝-inch thick, applied in strips, with one bead at the edge and another aligned with it down the center. Made of fir, hemlock, white pine, and gum wood, beaded wood was stained or painted. This material was used to ceil porches, kitchens, and bathrooms until wood surfaces lost favor for interiors because they were thought to be unsanitary. Beaded wood was used also for wainscoting in kitchens and bathrooms of the same period.

Beamed ceilings became popular for dining and living rooms at the turn of the century. Structurally false, the beams are simple three-sided boxes arranged in parallel groupings or as a gridiron that may fill all or part of a ceiling.

Coffering is a paneling device that divides the ceiling area into shallow recessed panels, the faces of which may be ornamented. *Metal* panels will be described in detail later in this section. Essentially they derive from a modular system of multiple panels organized with a central field surrounded by a border and finished with a cornice. A similar ceiling configuration can be accomplished by wood or plaster moldings, in which the molding separates the ceiling into field and border sections.

Treatments and Materials

Plaster finish was smooth and hard until the artistic aesthetic required that flat surfaces look handcrafted, which translated into rough finish. From that point on, textured ceilings became an alternative finish. *Stenciling* is a border device that leaves the major portion of the ceiling a field. Ceiling *paper* divides the surface into sections again, with a border and a field, and the latter is often a diffused, allover pattern with much less density than wall or dado papers. *Enameled* fiberboard panels were used for ceilings in bathrooms and kitchens.

SHAPES (SECTIONS)

FLAT   HIPPED   COVED   ARCHED   PEAKED

TREATMENTS AND MATERIALS (PLANS)

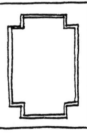

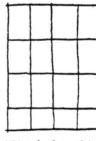

BEADED (WOOD)   BEAMED (WOOD)   COFFERED (WOOD, METAL)   PANELED (METAL)   PANELED (MOLDINGS)

PLASTERED   PAINTED   STENCILED   PAPERED   PANELED (GLASS, MIRROR, ENAMEL)

Moldings Ceiling moldings in vernacular buildings may be either simple, single pieces, as in a picture molding, or complex ensembles, as in built-up cornices or large crown-and-picture-mold combinations. A *picture molding* is an ornamental rail that provides a convex surface on its top edge to which hooks may be attached for hanging pictures against the walls. In the ornamental styles of interior design the picture molding appears with other moldings, but by the 1920s picture moldings were being used as a single molding in living and dining rooms.

Cornice, cove, and crown moldings have a similar function in that they all mediate between the wall and the ceiling, and all three are made of plaster or wood. A fully deployed *cornice* molding not only spans the angle of the intersection of the wall and ceiling, but projects and drops onto each surface. A distance of 4 to 6 inches is common in both directions. The *Cove* molding is the most modest of the three. It is narrow, yet it fills the angle, and the face has a simple concave profile. *Crown* moldings were conceived somewhat differently from the others in that they seem to cap the wall, to be the crown of the wall's organization. Historically, cove and cornice moldings are concave, while the crown is convex. As finish work became simplified, each of these pieces of molding was used by itself as the only ceiling molding in a room. Plaster moldings, in scores of profiles, were used to divide a ceiling into panels.

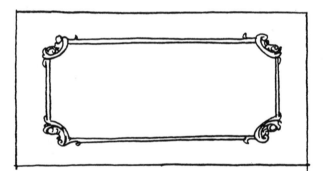

PLASTER MOLDING

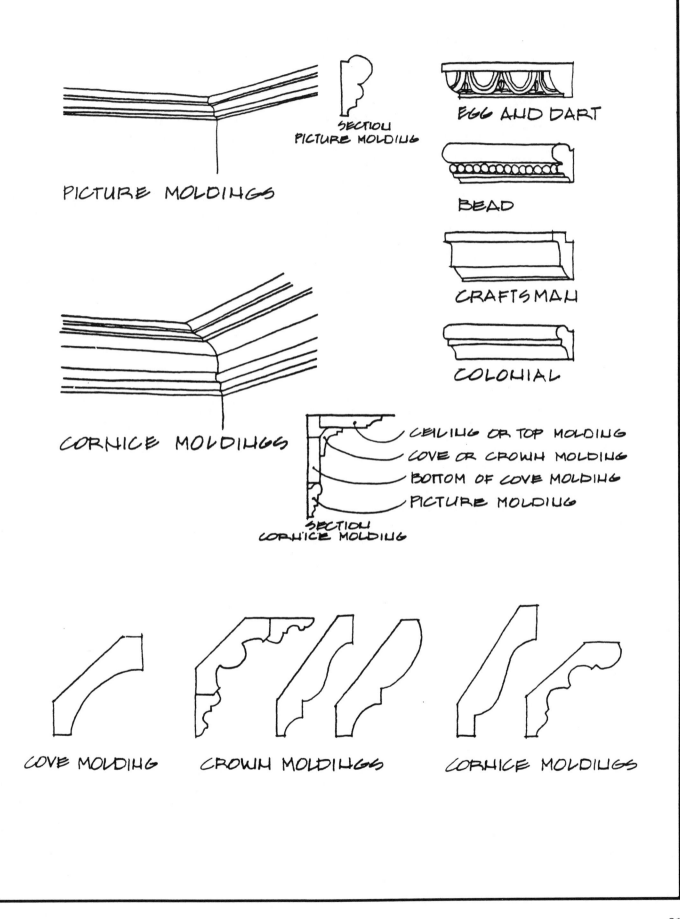

PICTURE MOLDINGS

SECTION
PICTURE MOLDING

EGG AND DART

BEAD

CRAFTSMAN

COLONIAL

CORNICE MOLDINGS

CEILING OR TOP MOLDING
COVE OR CROWN MOLDING
BOTTOM OF COVE MOLDING
PICTURE MOLDING

SECTION
CORNICE MOLDING

COVE MOLDING

CROWN MOLDINGS

CORNICE MOLDINGS

Beamed Ceilings

Beamed ceilings usually were made of oak or pine boards of generally two proportions, a narrow beam and a wide one. Which set was used depended on the size of the room: narrow beams for small rooms, under 12 feet by 12 feet, and wide beams for large rooms. Beamed ceilings were installed either as parallel beams dividing the ceiling off into long panels, or as beam and cross-beam patterns that broke the ceiling down into panels. In either case the main beam was often connected to a wall half-beam or a wall cornice. The cornice is a flat strip topped by a cove molding.

The entire system, therefore, has three parts: wall beams with an average projection of 4 inches and a drop of 2½ inches; main beams 8 inches wide with a 2½-inch drop; and cross beams 6 inches wide with the same drop. In some patterns the cross-beam drop was less than that of the main beam. Typical plans are variations on the organizational grid. Some beamed ceiling plans could be adapted to shaped ceilings, but most were installed on flat surfaces.

In metal ceiling installations, or just as beams against plaster, beamed ceilings could be made with pressed metal plates. These were approximately the same dimensions as the wood units.

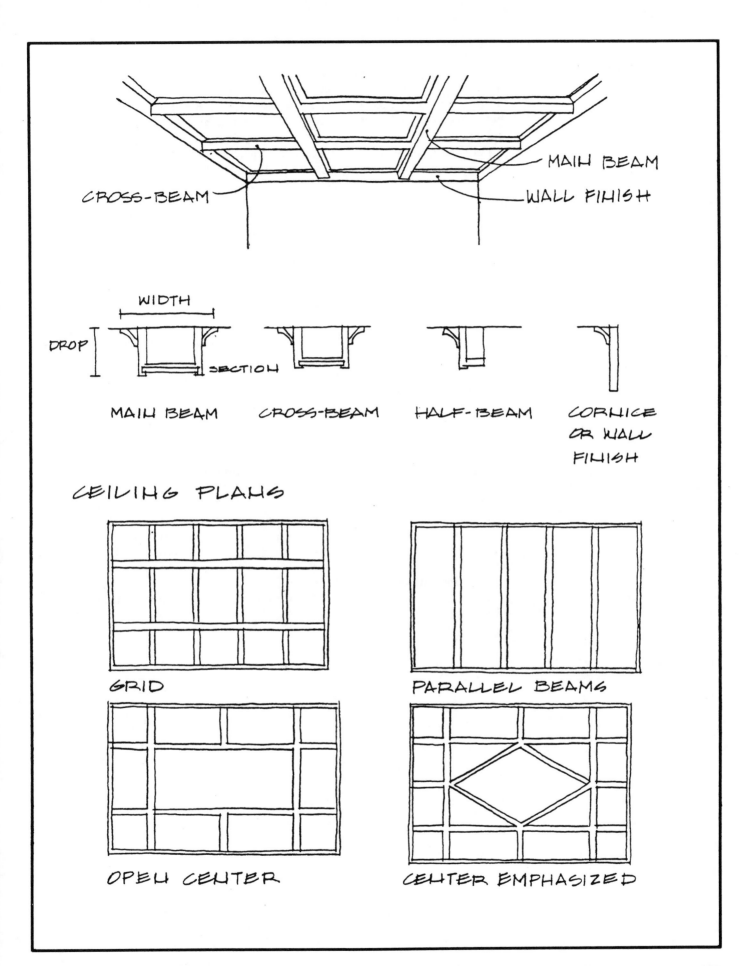

CROSS-BEAM

MAIN BEAM

WALL FINISH

WIDTH

DROP

SECTION

MAIN BEAM   CROSS-BEAM   HALF-BEAM   CORNICE OR WALL FINISH

CEILING PLANS

GRID

PARALLEL BEAMS

OPEN CENTER

CENTER EMPHASIZED

63

Metal Ceilings *Metal Ceilings* were a part of vernacular interior architecture from 1870 through the 1920s. Sears, Roebuck was still selling them in 1926. Metal ceilings were installed primarily in commercial and public buildings, but they were also part of residential design as dados in hallways and as walls and ceilings in kitchen and bathrooms.

Metal ceilings were constructed from sheets of square and rectangular pressed steel plates. The plates were stamped with historical and contemporary patterns and came in a variety of sizes. Most panels were nailed to furring strips with the joints and the nailings concealed. Plates came with a coat of oxide primer that was finished after installation.

The center of a metal ceiling, the first part to be constructed, is given to the central *field* or the body of the design. In a fully developed design, the field is surrounded by several intermediary members, including a molding and a filler, and is finished with a cove or cornice piece. The *molding* lies between the field and the filler or, when no filler is used, between the field and the cornice. The *filler* may be molded or flat. It is a strip lying between the molding and the cornice, and of sufficient width to allow the molding or the field to overlap it by 3 to 6 inches. The edge of the ceiling is the *cornice,* which extends down the wall. In a fully developed ceiling plan all of these elements are present and the size of most elements depends upon the size of the field. A second consideration in determining the plan is ceiling height, which affects the depth of the ceiling plates. Most ceiling installations enlarge the field so that it covers most of the area, finishing with a molding and a cornice.

The central field may consist of one large center piece or a series of plates. In either case, these plates are the dominant image of the design, which is supported by borders and other trimmings. *Drop-blocks* disguise joints, and because of their depth they project the ceiling into the room. A fully developed metal ceiling has projections at several levels.

The single field plate may be solid or ventilating, and it is sometimes framed by false (metal) beams. Most cornices are nailed to brackets. A complete ceiling may have secondary elements that help finish corners and intersections of moldings. These include molding ells and tees, molding crosses, border ells, inner and outer border pieces, inner and outer cornice miters, and curved corners.

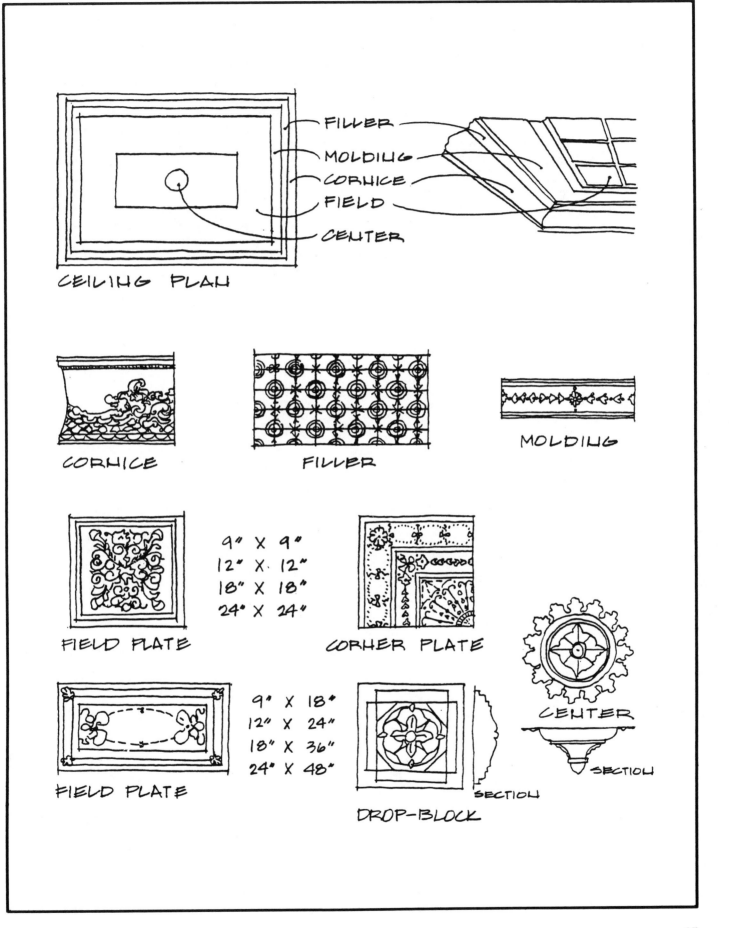

CEILING PLAN

FILLER

MOLDING

CORNICE

FIELD

CENTER

CORNICE

FILLER

MOLDING

FIELD PLATE

9" X 9"
12" X 12"
18" X 18"
24" X 24"

CORNER PLATE

CENTER

SECTION

FIELD PLATE

9" X 18"
12" X 24"
18" X 36"
24" X 48"

DROP-BLOCK

SECTION

Metal Ceilings
The drawings on the right illustrate a range of motifs available in square multiple plates and running moldings for metal ceilings. These patterns were common to most design systems. A good deal of ceiling work is modeled on plaster moldings, but the resourcefulness of the die makers and the malleability of the materials created patterns unknown to plasterers.

Twill, bead, and other sheets are alternative panels for the design of fields. All of these have raised surfaces, and all of them repeat the pattern plate to plate, creating a continuous rather than a divided effect. The depth of relief on the sheets varies; for example, a beaded plate may have full rounded beads an inch in diameter, while a crimped or corrugated sheet has shallower relief. Continuous patterns, also referred to as continuous plates, usually came in large sheets, much larger than the multiple plates.

The running moldings owe much to plaster models, both in imagery and size. In fact, there is a great deal of correspondence among vernacular moldings and other ornaments that are based on historical patterns. The bead-and-reel, for example, was used consistently in all mediums.

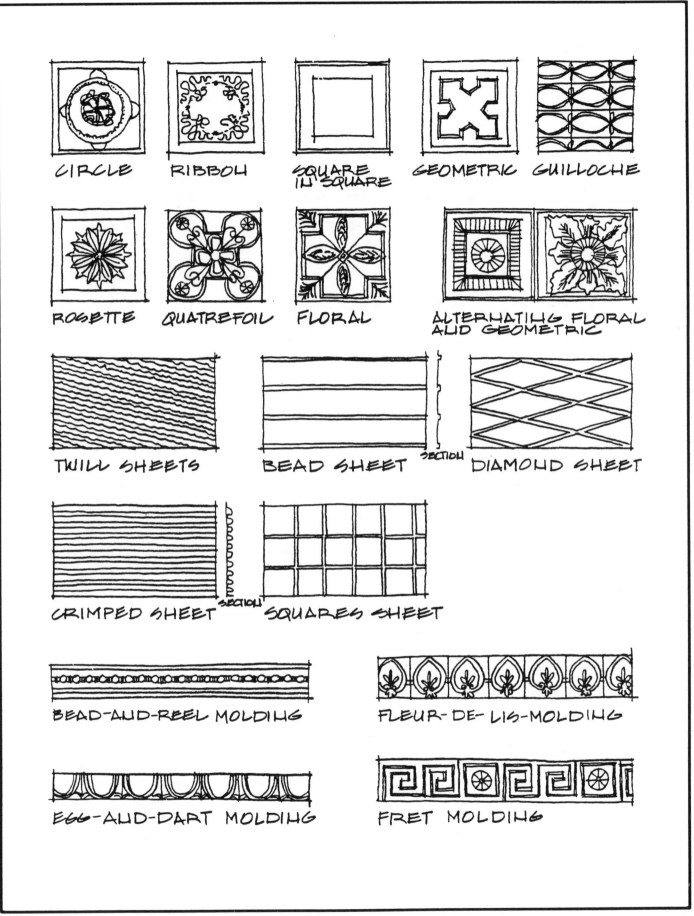

CIRCLE

RIBBON

SQUARE IN SQUARE

GEOMETRIC

GUILLOCHE

ROSETTE

QUATREFOIL

FLORAL

ALTERNATING FLORAL AND GEOMETRIC

TWILL SHEETS

BEAD SHEET   SECTION

DIAMOND SHEET

CRIMPED SHEET   SECTION

SQUARES SHEET

BEAD-AND-REEL MOLDING

FLEUR-DE-LIS-MOLDING

EGG-AND-DART MOLDING

FRET MOLDING

FLOORING
Wood Strip Flooring

Of the different kinds of flooring available for vernacular interiors, *wood strip flooring* is the most common material. Both softwood and hardwood were used for finished flooring but hardwood, especially oak and perhaps maple, was preferred. Red oak flooring installed throughout a building created a premium floor, and while this was an ideal it was expensive. There is evidence for an alternative plan in vernacular buildings: hardwood flooring on the main floor and softwood on the others. That same logic holds true for trim sets as well.

There are varieties of strip flooring but most of it is made from narrow boards, less than 8 inches wide and 2 inches thick. Strip floors are assembled primarily with tongue-and-groove or square-edged boards. Standard widths and thicknesses for this time period are illustrated on the facing page.

The quality of flooring depends upon the quality of the wood, and that was determined not only by the character of the wood but also by the sawing. *Clear* lumber was the best grade. *Select,* with minor defects, was suitable for housing. *Common* grade was used in commercial and industrial settings.

Sawing was of two kinds: *plain,* in which the boards were sliced from the tree in one plane so that the grain ran across the width of the board; and *quarter-sawn,* in which boards were sawn from the center of the tree to the outside and the grain ran at right angles to the face. Quarter-sawn flooring was preferred.

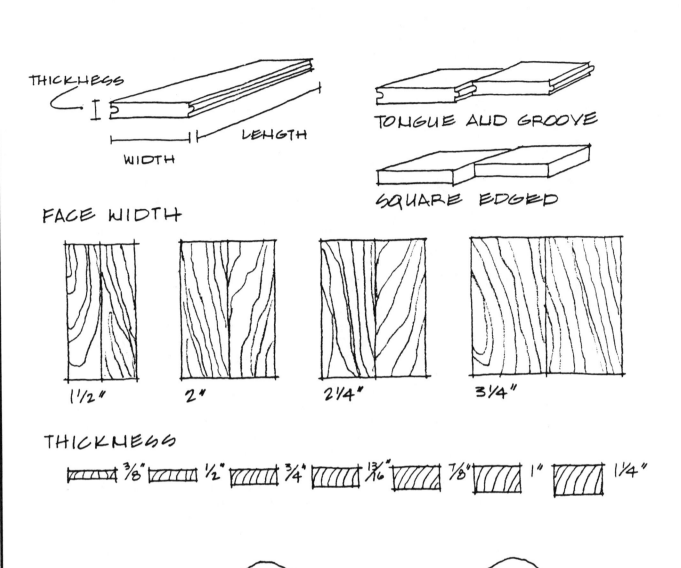

THICKNESS

WIDTH · LENGTH

TONGUE AND GROOVE

SQUARE EDGED

FACE WIDTH

1½"   2"   2¼"   3¼"

THICKNESS

⌷ ⅜" ⌷ ½" ⌷ ¾" ⌷ 13/16" ⌷ ⅞" ⌷ 1" ⌷ 1¼"

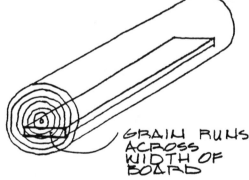

PLAIN-SAWN
(FLAT SAWN, FLAT
GRAIN, SLASH GRAIN)

GRAIN RUNS
ACROSS
WIDTH OF
BOARD

QUARTER-SAWN
(VERTICAL OR EDGE GRAIN)

GRAIN RUNS
AT RIGHT ANGLES

Wood Parquet and Carpet Flooring

Although most vernacular flooring was built from long narrow strips, a good deal of it was *parquetry*—flooring made of short strips of wood laid in a pattern. We do not know as yet how parquet flooring became part of the vernacular design: the English 19th-century designer Charles Eastlake credited the French with having invented it. The English presumably imitated it, and perhaps we, always on their heels, followed suit.

Illustrated here is a parquet flooring plan for a room with a fireplace and a three-sided bay window. The design consists of a field or center, for which there were many possible design variations, a border establishing the edge of the field, and an outside marginal section which takes the flooring to the wall.

The field, indeed the entire floor, may be laid down in single strips or in blocks of hardwood fastened together to form slabs of convenient size for laying. Both types are nailed to an underfloor. The field can vary its effect by any of these means: geometric patterning, changing the direction of the graining, and contrasting wood grain and color. The interaction between fields and borders is often dramatic, especially when the border carries deep color as well as a running pattern.

Wood carpet is made of strips of parquet-size wood glued to a heavy cotton cloth. The carpeting rolls up like an oilcloth. Roll flooring like this came in different widths—28 inches and 36 inches were common—in 5-yard lengths. The strips could be laid straight or mitered. Wood carpet could be used as a field in a parquet floor, or the entire floor could be covered with it. When the floor was installed, pieces of wood were laid between the widths to secure the strips and to hide the ends. Borders for wood carpeting also were available.

There are other kinds of wood floors that utilize slats of wood and a backing material. *Wood-block* floors were made this way by gluing blocks of slats to canvas, and laying these between flooring strips. Borders could be laid around the field of blocks. Another system laid wood blocks in mastic. These floors could be built over a wood subfloor or concrete, and the floor was thought to be fireproof.

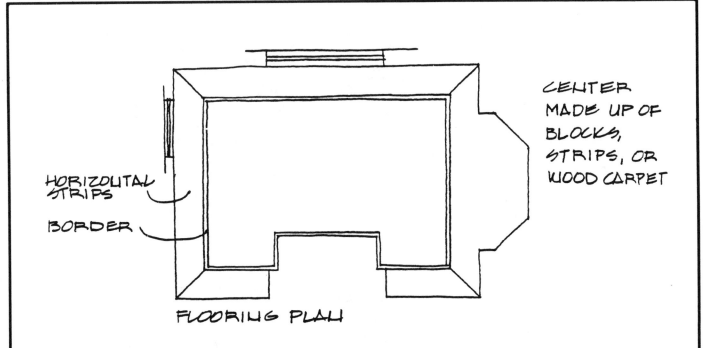

HORIZONTAL STRIPS

BORDER

CENTER MADE UP OF BLOCKS, STRIPS, OR WOOD CARPET

FLOORING PLAN

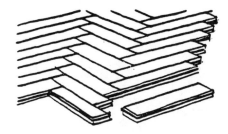

PARQUET INDIVIDUALLY LAID

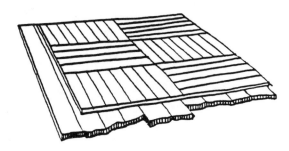

WOOD BLOCK

WOOD CARPET

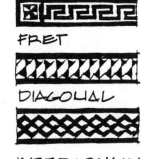

FRET

DIAGONAL

INTERLOCKING DIAMOND

BORDER DESIGNS

Parquet Designs The field designs illustrated on the facing page present some typical configurations of parquet. In the first example (above left), the angle of the blocks and the alternating pattern clearly distinguish the field from the border and the edge. In the second instance (above right), rolls of wood carpet form the major portion of the flooring. The third example (bottom left) exploits the linear properties of the parquet offset by a two-color diamond border. Border woods include mahogany, holly, walnut, cherry, maple, rosewood, and sycamore, and three-color borders are not uncommon. The last example shows an inexpensive way to lay a parquet floor by using pine for the field: this would be covered with an area rug, leaving the hardwood border and margin exposed.

PARQUET CENTER DESIGNS

BLOCKS AS CENTER

WOOD CARPET AS CENTER

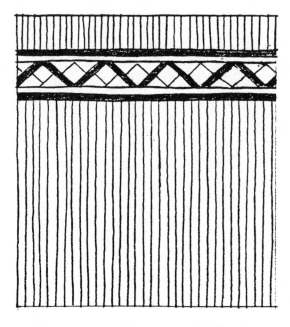

STRIPS AS CENTER

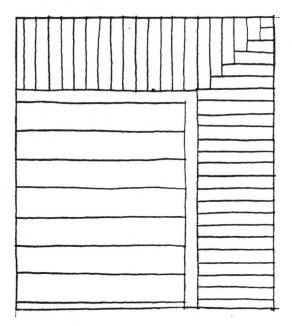

PINE FLOOR AS CENTER
(FOR RUG)
HARDWOOD BORDER

73

Ceramic Mosaic Tile

Ceramic mosaic tile is a collective term for unglazed compressed clay tiles about ¼-inch thick and less than 2 inches square, produced in a variety of shapes, sizes, and colors. These tiles were introduced into the design market in the 1870s, but they did not become significant until the turn of the century. Tiles were attached to walls, floors, or countertops with cement or other adhesives, creating durable, decorative surfaces. Ceramic mosaic tiles were marketed in sheet units.

There were other kinds of tile for flooring, such as the encaustic or glazed tiles introduced in the 1880s. For a time white was the preferred color but eventually there was greater freedom of choice. Faience tile, a glazed terra-cotta less than 6 inches square, was used as facing for fireplaces. Asphalt tile, made of fibers and binders and produced in blocks and sheets, was set in mastic. Lastly, rubber flooring composed of rubber and other materials was manufactured in standard 4-inch or 6-inch square sizes and installed with wide borders. Like asphalt tile, this tile could be laid over wood or concrete.

Besides their primary use in commercial buildings, tile floors were used also in vestibules of residential buildings. Tile patterns were tremendously varied, being assembled mostly from hexagonal, square, and round pieces. Tile was identified especially with modern design, which accounts for its presence in catalogs and periodicals in the first decade of this century.

CERAMIC MOSAICS

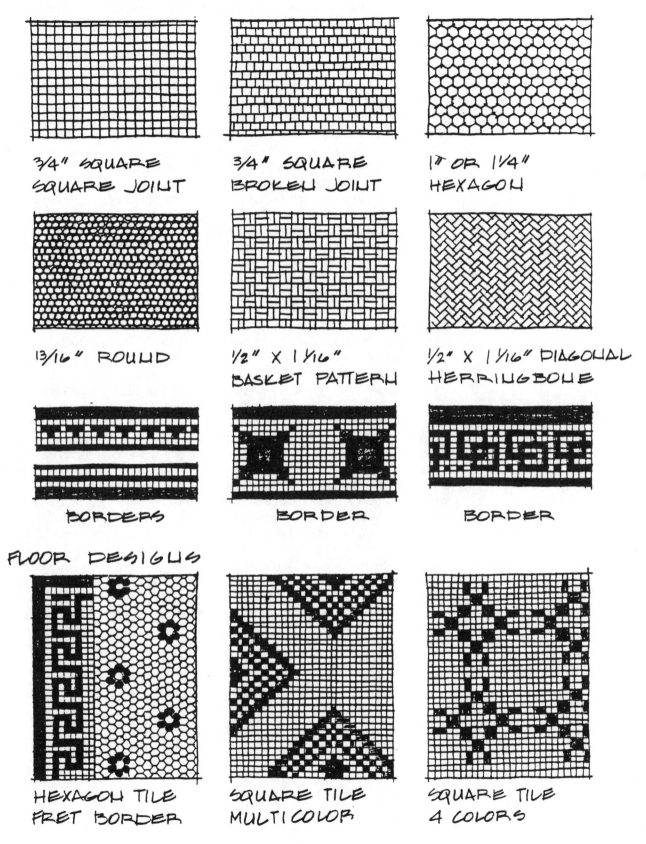

3/4" SQUARE SQUARE JOINT

3/4" SQUARE BROKEN JOINT

1" OR 1¼" HEXAGON

13/16" ROUND

½" X 1 1/16" BASKET PATTERN

½" X 1 1/16" DIAGONAL HERRINGBONE

BORDERS

BORDER

BORDER

FLOOR DESIGNS

HEXAGON TILE FRET BORDER

SQUARE TILE MULTICOLOR

SQUARE TILE 4 COLORS

Linoleum   By 1870 *linoleum* had been introduced as a flooring material. It was made on a burlap base and composed of oxidized materials—linseed oil (the primary ingredient), cork, gum, resin, coloring matter, and other ingredients. In the 1880s the process of pressing the batch material was refined by rolling the goods between the large, hot cylinders of a calendering machine. Linoleum was thought of primarily as a sanitary material, and its use was limited until after World War I, when it was marketed as suitable for all kinds of residential and commercial purposes.

Linoleum competed with fabric carpet, tile, and wood flooring, and most of its patterns imitate these materials. Some patterns became associated with specific rooms: tile effects for baths and kitchens; figured designs, rug-like treatments, and parquet patterns for dining rooms, living rooms, and bedrooms. Linoleum was produced in several formats: blocks, small sheets, and large single-piece carpets. The carpets came in standard area-rug sizes— 6 feet by 9 feet or 9 feet by 12 feet—and were available in plain, inlaid, or printed patterns in one-color, multicolor, or tapestry effects.

Linoleum was produced in different grades and thicknesses. *Plain* linoleum is solid color and when it is thin it is suitable for houses, but the heavy stock—3/16-inch and 1/4-inch thick—is flooring for commercial buildings and the decks of battleships (hence its vernacular name). *Inlaid* material has color running through the pattern to the backing. Inlaid patterns were made by rearranging cut or pulverized linoleum onto backing material and repressing it with a calendering machine. *Printed* linoleum is thinner than inlaid and of lower quality; it was made by printing oil paint onto the surface of plain stock, and over time the image would wear off.

Cork carpet is similar to plain linoleum, except that the cork and linseed mix is not so densely compacted by the rollers. Cork was used in churches and auditoriums where a soft, quiet floor was desired. *Embossed* linoleum has relief cut into the surface so that part of the pattern is raised. Tile patterns with raised faces and recessed grout lines were favorites.

Insets are designs cut from any color linoleum and cemented into a field or border. This work was custom-made, cut to order, and often personalized. *Borders* were a second linoleum laid around the principal piece. A simple border might be a strip of color or an allover pattern. Most borders were 6, 9, or 12 inches wide. The Armstrong Company made narrow Linostrips in 5/8- or 1-inch widths to be laid between the field and the border as an accent. Companies like Armstrong also offered special border effects of running patterns—wave motif, frets, laural leaf, twisted ribbon, and chevron— in 6-, 9-, and 12-inch widths. Most companies also made a passage linoleum, or hall runner, 24 inches wide with a border on each side and a field in the middle.

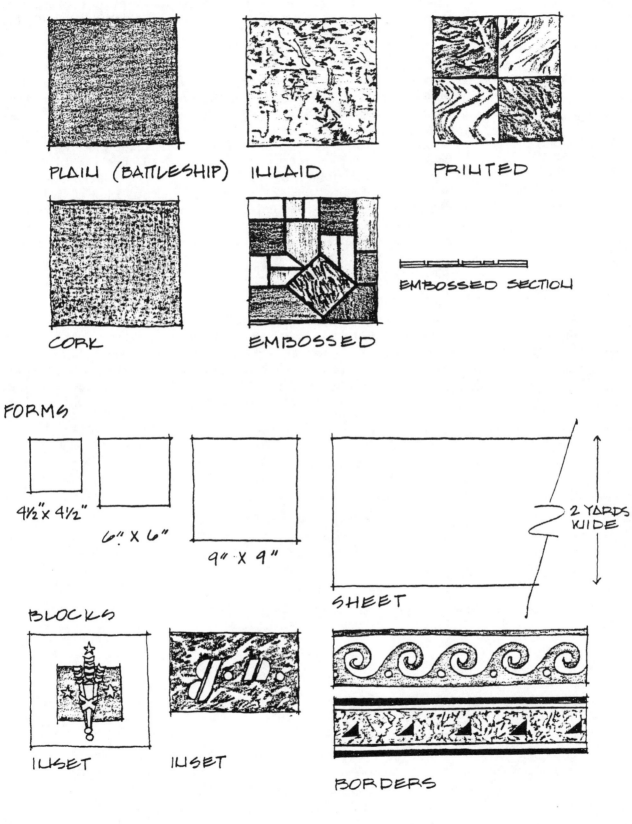

TYPES

PLAIN (BATTLESHIP)   INLAID   PRINTED

CORK   EMBOSSED   EMBOSSED SECTION

FORMS

4½"x 4½"   6" X 6"   9" X 9"   SHEET   2 YARDS WIDE

BLOCKS

INSET   INSET   BORDERS

Linoleum　　The patterns for linoleum flooring were categorized by the manufacturers. *Granite* is an inlaid pattern with a mottled face. *Marble blocks* have a single-color, allover design. *Jaspé* is related to marble; it is another inlaid type with two-toned grained or spotted colors running through the fabric. Like many inlaid types it makes a good background for rugs and furnishings.

Tile is generally an inlaid embossed design, with high contrast between the tile color and the grout lines; some patterns even have shading to create a realistic texture. Linoleum with *wood* patterns came in two designs: inlaid parquet and border pieces imitating the borders of strip or parquet flooring. *Herringbone* is a masonry paving pattern with multiple tones in an inlaid base.

Linoleum *carpet* or rug was produced as a single piece of work large enough—say, 6 by 9 feet, 9 by 12 feet, or 9 by 15 feet—to function as an independent rug on any floor, and in smaller sheets that could be arranged in patterns. Painted on felt with rich colors, this kind of linoleum had floral, tapestry, hooked rug, chintz-type, and other patterns. *Jigsaw* pattern was used for rugs; typically it had a border or double border with the puzzle portion—alternating shapes repeated every second or third element—as the field. *Plaid,* too, is a carpet pattern with three different-colored marble blocks overlaid to create the plaid.

Checkerboard is a design consisting of alternating light and dark colored blocks. The black-and-white pattern was especially popular. It and other checkerboards were used in commercial and residential settings.

Geometric patterns have been an alternative to imitations of wood or encaustic tiles. Allover geometric patterns were used in fabric carpet as well as in wallpaper. Small figures, in particular, were a reaction to the large floral designs of an earlier time. *Abstract* configurations are more contemporary, being the kind of imagery that is associated with modernity. They include implied grids and small floating squares of color as figures against a ground of generalized swirls.

GRAUITE

MARBLE

JASPE'

TILES

WOOD

HERRIUGBOUE

CARPET

JIGSAW

PLAID

CHECKERBOARD

GEOMETRIC

MODERU/ABSTRACT

WALLS
Elements and Construction

Throughout our discussion of vernacular interior systems, we have consistently made the case that millwork was an essential historical element, and that changes in aesthetics and design values could be deduced from an analysis of milled products. This method is particularly fruitful for a discussion of the organization of interior walls.

Moldings and the stickwork and panels associated with them combined with various trim sets for doors and windows—these are the framework for walls. Historically there are at least three different types of wall organization, two of which seem to have a classical heritage. The third is strictly modern.

The walls of vernacular buildings reflect the interactive relationship between manufactured materials and concepts of organization that ultimately led to manufactured elements serving as modular units. This is evident whether we cite a standard-length wall stud or a standard cabinet height. But the proportions of rooms and the divisions of the wall plane go back further than the Industrial Revolution to some fundamental ratios of parts to the whole. The walls of houses designed within the ornamental aesthetic were about 9 feet high. Finish carpenters, plasters, and painters worked with that height to create a unified appearance that could change from room to room and from building to building. Behind each scheme, however, was a bias toward a three-part division. A column breaks down into three parts—base, shaft, and capital; a pedestal and an entablature are composed of three parts each. There has been a proclivity to divide the plane of a wall into one-third for the dado, and two-thirds for the field and the frieze. The precise dimensions depend on several factors.

The divisions can be varied and a design system selected on the basis of the proportions of the room: or a system can be chosen first and that, in turn, will influence the divisions of the surfaces. These two approaches combined with the physical limitations of the room—for example, structural elements that cannot be altered or a fenestration pattern that must be accommodated—create the conditions for interior design. Overall, the tension between proportions and aesthetics—as to which will be the basis for design—has been resolved in favor of the former, because proportions are so keenly tied to manufactured materials.

Both the ornamental and the artistic systems reflect compromises between the two forces. How a room actually works, or the impression it evokes, is a question of balance.

The *ornamental design system* (a detail of which is illustrated here), has strong horizontal linear elements that are countered by the three-dimensional projections from the walls and the ornamentation on elements. The foundation of the wall is the *dado*, that space just above the floor terminating with a chair rail that protects the wall when chairs are pushed against it. The dado has three parts: a baseboard, an open space, and a cap. The *baseboard* has a two- or three-part organization that is approximately one-fourth or one-third the height of the entire dado. The central space is finished with paint, fabric, or wallpaper. When that part of the wall is lined with wood strips or panels and finished with a cap it becomes a *wainscot*. The cap on a wainscot is usually more elaborate than a chair rail, but that depends on the design of the wainscot and the general scheme in which the room is done.

The heart of the wall is the *field,* or *filling*. Its finish depends on what use the room will have, and its size is reflected in the overall dimensions of the room. In the ornamental system, the field may be divided by a picture molding, above which the field divides again into a frieze and a cornice.

Each of these elements could be carried around the entire room at the same height from the floor. Likewise, the wall organization might just as well call for only one or two continuous pieces, say, the base and the cornice, or the base, frieze, and cornice. In some treatments a frieze or some other section may be eliminated.

Over time these horizontal divisions decreased. The *artistic system,* which followed the ornamental system chronologically, eliminated some elements. The cornice and picture molding were often physically close to each other, and in the artistic mode—meaning Arts and Crafts, Mission, Craftsman— the cornice disappears and the picture molding stands alone. The height of the dado is increased significantly and often covered with a skeletal wainscot. The cap rail becomes a plate rail, a place for artifacts, not an applied or stuck molding.

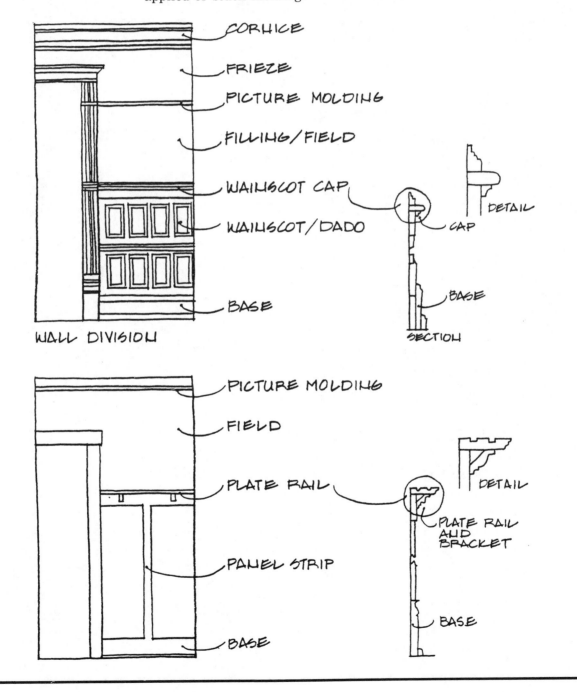

CORNICE

FRIEZE

PICTURE MOLDING

FILLING/FIELD

WAINSCOT CAP

WAINSCOT/DADO

BASE

WALL DIVISION

DETAIL

CAP

BASE

SECTION

PICTURE MOLDING

FIELD

PLATE RAIL

PANEL STRIP

BASE

DETAIL

PLATE RAIL AND BRACKET

BASE

Moldings Walls have inside and outside corners, and the outside corners are filled with corner beads. These are right-angle moldings that have turned ends in the ornamental style and straight ends otherwise. The bead protects the corner from damage and adds yet another layer of millwork ornamentation.

This section concludes with a sample of baseboard designs. Comparing the profiles reveals the different aesthetic intentions of the material. Ornamented, heavily cut surfaces give way to plain massive blocks where angles are more important than curves, and these in turn are replaced by delicately cut, plain bases for the modern colonial style. A shoe molding is required for most baseboards, and most of these are the quarter-round type.

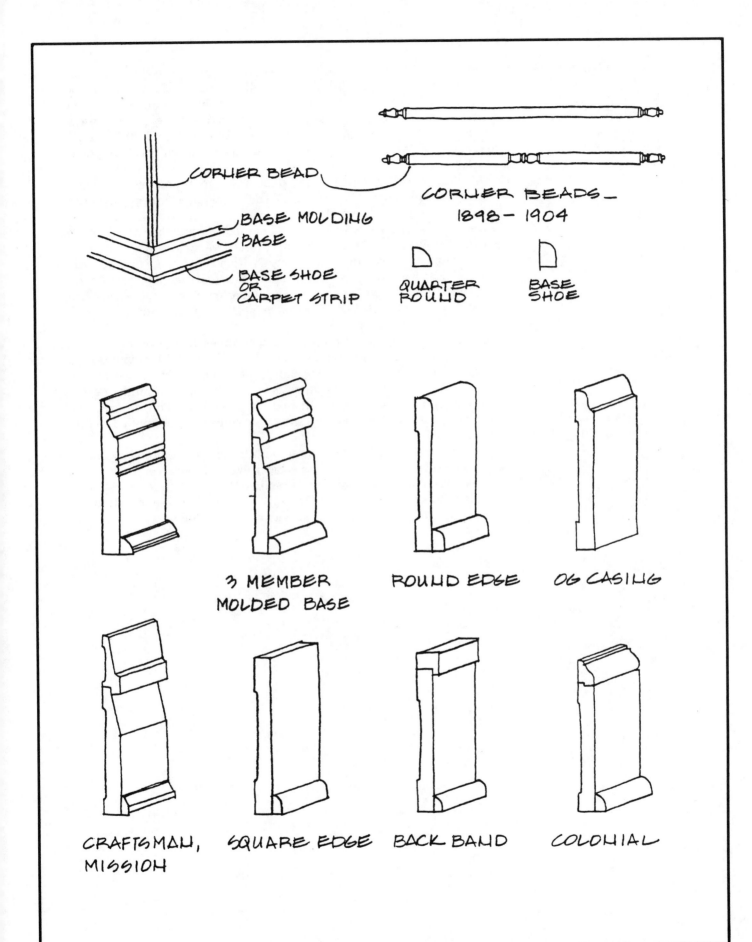

CORNER BEAD

BASE MOLDING
BASE

BASE SHOE
OR
CARPET STRIP

CORNER BEADS_
1898 - 1904

QUARTER
ROUND

BASE
SHOE

3 MEMBER
MOLDED BASE

ROUND EDGE

OG CASING

CRAFTSMAN,
MISSION

SQUARE EDGE

BACK BAND

COLONIAL

Wainscots   As defined earlier, a *wainscot* is a wooden lining on the lower portion of a wall, covering about one-third of the wall height. While important social rooms and hallways received wainscoting, for a time kitchen and bathrooms had narrow, beaded tongue-and-groove wainscots. The height of these was about 3 feet, with most wainscots ranging between 30 and 40 inches. The development of the artistic system of design raised wainscot height to 5 or 5½ feet.

Solid wood paneling with vertical panels was manufactured throughout our study period. The organization of the wainscot is three-part, with a base, a section of center panels, and a cap.

Wainscot patterns are based on a grid of modular panels marching across the wall. The design with square panels atop vertical units is a turn-of-the-century pattern that divides the area into a continuous base, on which sit vertical shafts with square capitals, and the cap serves as an entablature. The pattern to the right of this is contemporary with the vertical panel designs. The design pairs the vertical panels as twin columns, each pair supporting its own architrave.

The last two designs (bottom) are alternatives to the others. *Skeleton* wainscots, or panel strips, are assembled by laying 2-inch-wide strips of oak, 18 inches on center, with the panels between the strips covered with burlap or plaster work. In the artistic mode the plaster might be rough and tinted, and the wall above finished the same way. The cap rail in this design is a plate rail, because the skeleton wainscot was applied to dining rooms.

A wainscot made with *battens* is very similar to the skeleton type, because the battens are generally the same size, even of the same oak or birch stock as the strips. The panels are solid wood, 8 inches across in this particular design, and the battens, with a T-section and rabetted edges that overlap the panels, are placed between the panels.

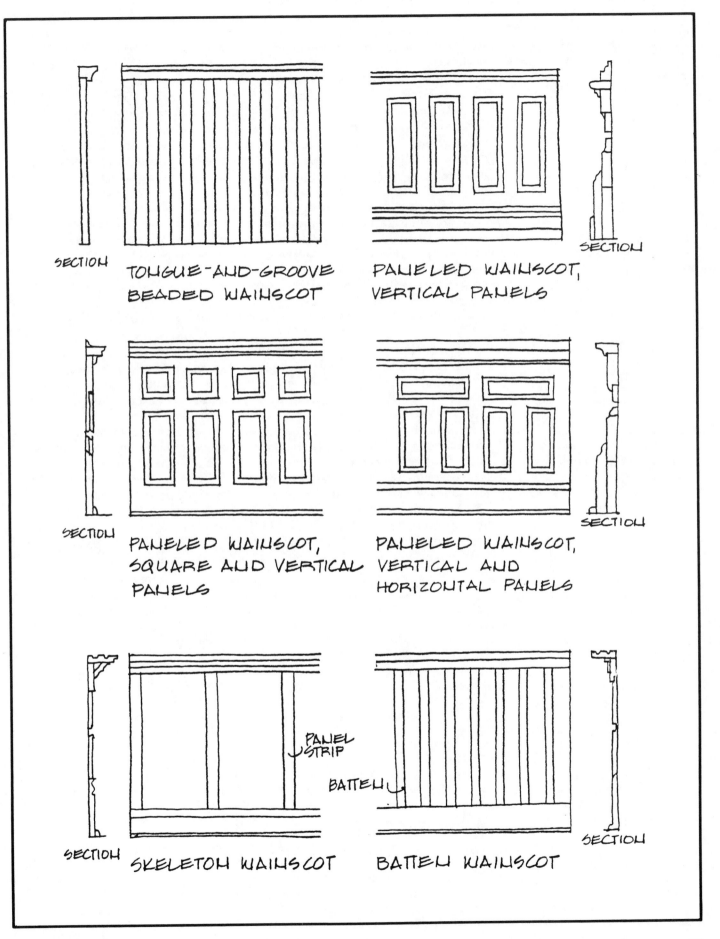

SECTION

TONGUE-AND-GROOVE
BEADED WAINSCOT

PANELED WAINSCOT,
VERTICAL PANELS

SECTION

SECTION

PANELED WAINSCOT,
SQUARE AND VERTICAL
PANELS

PANELED WAINSCOT,
VERTICAL AND
HORIZONTAL PANELS

SECTION

PANEL
STRIP

BATTEN

SECTION

SECTION

SKELETON WAINSCOT

BATTEN WAINSCOT

85

Wallpaper, 1880–1920

By the 1870s machine-printed *wallpaper* was well entrenched in interior design, but by 1940 the organization of a papered wall had changed. At first, conventional design divided the wall into three sections: a dado on the lower sector: a field, or fill, as the principal middle space; and a frieze capping the wall. Some designs included a narrow border, or trimmer, between the dado and the fill or between the fill and the frieze. A similar organization was carried through upstairs, with dados and friezes having diagonal patterns. Sears's wall plan consisted of a base, a side wall, and a border (note the change in language), and a picture molding was applied between the side wall and the border.

The illustrations concerning wallpaper have been divided into twenty-year groupings, and the first design is a Sears, Roebuck pattern from the period 1880–1900. In the ornamental design system, wallpaper is dominated by floral patterns in which sprays of leaf or blossom and scrolls saturated the wall. The amount of wall allocated to dado, fill, and frieze changes almost by the decade and can be different in particular rooms within the same building. Each room may also be assigned a tint and walls, moreover, are divided by light and dark values. The dado usually is darker than the fill, the frieze a definite contrast to the fill, and the ceiling paper very light.

Allover floral patterns were not the only kind of pattern in this period. The English Arts and Crafts Movement had an impact on American manufacturers. Catherine Frangiamore's essay in *Wallpapers in Historic Preservation* (1977), notes that subdued, grayed palettes and an interest in flat patterns and abstraction became part of everyday paper production.

Each of the designs on the facing page has a light background, cream in two cases and light green in the third. The *allover floral* is composed of sprays with terra-cotta or green scrolls and mica and bronze effects. The *rococo scroll* paper is embossed with several colors and bronze. The *tapestry* has maroon and old-gold figures. In all three designs, the border has a different palette. They are, respectively: garnet and turquoise blue; gold and bronze; and gold and silver scroll effects with dark and light green. Ceiling papers are not listed for all of them, but the tapestry paper had a Nile green background with red, gold, and silver scrolls.

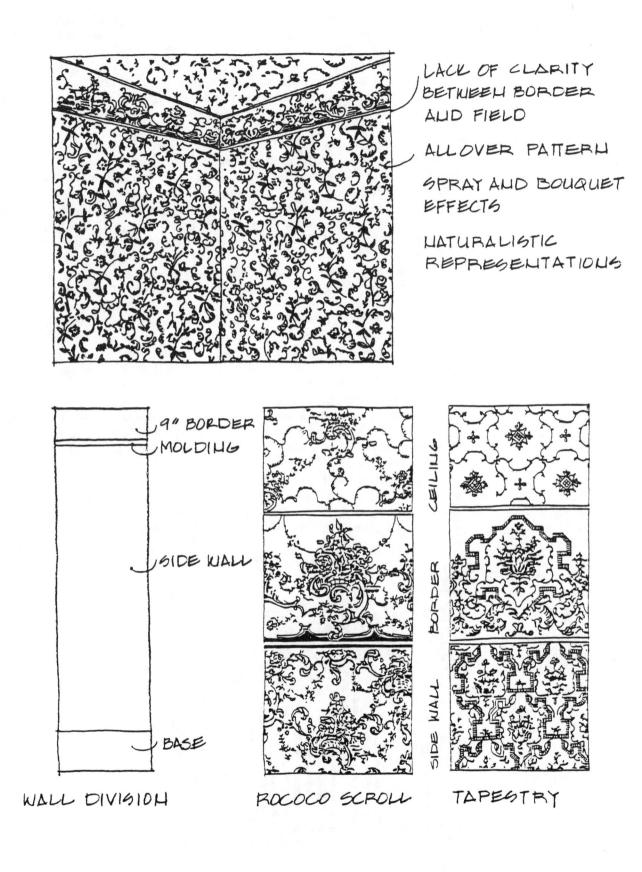

LACK OF CLARITY
BETWEEN BORDER
AND FIELD

ALLOVER PATTERN

SPRAY AND BOUQUET
EFFECTS

NATURALISTIC
REPRESENTATIONS

9" BORDER
MOLDING

SIDE WALL

BASE

CEILING

BORDER

SIDE WALL

WALL DIVISION   ROCOCO SCROLL   TAPESTRY

Wallpaper,
1900–1920

Examined from most design perspectives, the first two decades of this century were progressive, and wallpapers for vernacular design reflected the change in values. Walls were now thought of not only as something self-sufficient, but as background for pictures and furniture. In the new system, walls were to be subdued in tone, a lighter value than the floor. If the wall carried figures they were to be small, conventionalized images from nature, soft in color, and the whole paper should emphasize the flatness of the wall.

These attitudes toward wallpaper were applied to all aspects of design. The elements that constituted an ornamental design system had strong object character. Their intrinsic value was to be sacrificed for the good of the overall effect, for design as principle. No element of an interior design was allowed to dominate the treatment, to call particular attention to itself. As for wallpaper patterns, they were to be "tight to the wall," with depictions of anything expressed in two dimensions only—in length and breadth, not in thickness.

This change corresponds with the artistic aesthetic, in which the tones of wallpaper were to be an indefinite gray, rose, or blue, with barely noticeable stripes, dots, dashes, lines, or hairy flecks of color. Geometric or conventionalized flower designs also were favored in one or two of the above colors or in harmonizing colors. Scroll patterns were now considered frivolous and meaningless. When in doubt, the plain wall was always best. Even Sears, which over the years clung to traditional designs, started shifting to modern papers in the teens.

Ingrain or oatmeal paper was developed in the 1870s and stayed on the market into the 1920s. These were roughly textured papers made from cotton and wool pulp. The rags were dyed before pulping, which gave the paper an "ingrained" coloration. The finished paper was soft with no reflection, which made it good for picture display.

As for the organization of walls, in some rooms the new artistic treatment broke the wall into two sections, a border with a depth of 9, 18, or 36 inches, with the fill, or side wall, covering the rest of the wall. The change in the size of the border reveals how far the concept of border had gone.

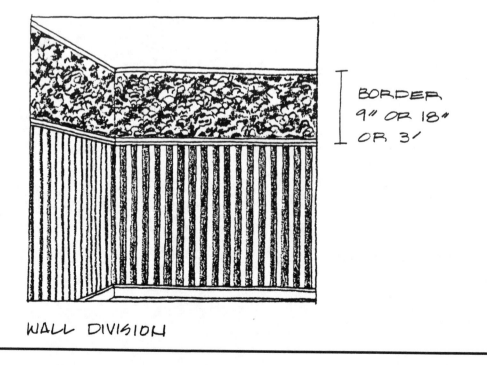

BORDER
9" OR 18"
OR 3'

WALL DIVISION

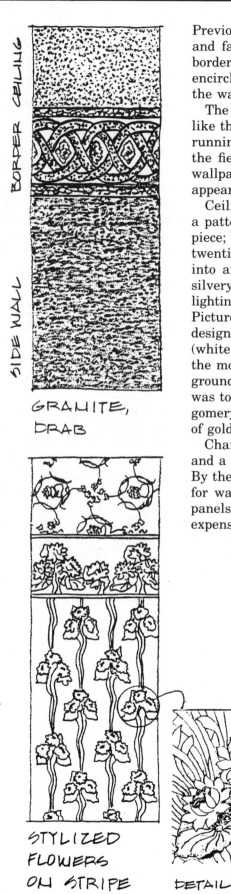

BORDER CEILING

SIDE WALL

GRANITE, DRAB

STYLIZED FLOWERS ON STRIPE

DETAIL

Previously the border was the last paper hung. It was a strip that concealed and fastened the cut ends of wallpaper, filled gaps, and hid tacks. The border was subordinate to the fill. But now there were installations that encircled a room with border, a so-called crown hanging that dominated the wall.

The patterns illustrated at the bottom of the facing page are typical, like the drab granite paper of overall granular pattern capped with a rich running border and a light gray ceiling. The stylized flower pattern and the field of vertically striped small flowers are examples of the kind of wallpaper used as a base for a crown border. They are recessive or flat in appearance, and they could function as backgrounds.

Ceiling papers generally were of three types: a border around the edges; a pattern that filled the entire area and featured a distinctive centering piece; and an overall pattern. Throughout the first four decades of the twentieth century ceiling papers declined in use, and their design evolved into an abstract, light-toned pattern of tracery or filigree, often with a silvery or frosted finish to help reflect electric indirect and semi-indirect lighting. Papered walls did not eliminate all moldings from wall organization. Picture moldings of imitation or genuine wood remained part of the wall design, but over time they became decorative. Moldings were enameled (white) and had gilt beading. This high-contrast, bright finish transformed the molding into a kind of trimmer, a bright line of green, brown, or red ground with gold relief set against the pattern. The ground of the molding was toned to complement the tone of the principal paper. The 1910 Montgomery Ward catalog advertised picture molding finished with a mixture of gold and varnish that was burnished to a high finish.

Chair rails remained part of the artistic aesthetic as did the plate rail and a cove molding as a decoration where the ceiling and side wall meet. By the 1930s Montgomery Ward was no longer advertising wood moldings for wallpaper, but it referred to them as a device with which to create panels on the side walls and recommended paper borders, which were less expensive and easier to maintain.

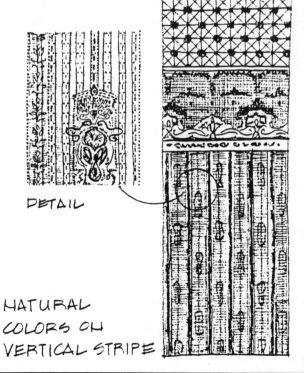

DETAIL

NATURAL COLORS ON VERTICAL STRIPE

Novelty Wall Treatments

Colored burlap and grass were wallpapers given a canvas or otherwise textile surface by pressing the material into the surface of the paper. Japanese leather paper, which was made from mulberry fiber pulp, was made similarly so that its surface texture looked like leather. Japanese grasscloths sometimes were handpainted which added an extra layer of contrasting effects to the dark paper. Both Sears and Montgomery Ward sold imitations of grasscloth and leather paper.

Several companies produced washable or sanitary wallpapers. These had glazed ground and glazed finish and were designed to look like other materials such as oak, maple, or ceramic tile. Varnished tiles were this kind of product. In 1910 Montgomery Ward sold varnished tiles for use in bathrooms, kitchens, halls, and dados. The same pattern could be used on the wall and ceiling to create the appearance of a tiled room. The colors were white and blue, and white with brown or tan. By 1925 Sears was still selling tiles with a border for wall filling, but sometime in the 1930s it dropped the tiles. It did continue to sell wall oilcloth, which it had been selling for a couple of decades. This inexpensive finish also visually imitated other materials.

The last two decades of the nineteenth century saw a great deal of experimentation with relief decoration that added a three-dimensional aspect to interior walls. The effect was achieved with embossed paper, which was made by passing the material through rollers. These papers had a fiber base on a cloth backing and a stamped finish. Other types of relief materials included papier-mâché and sheet-metal decorative plates.

The principal embossed paper was Lincrusta, developed by an English entrepreneur named Frederick Walton. Lincrusta was made from linseed oil, fibers, and resins, like linoleum, but without cork which was a key ingredient in linoleum. Lincrusta was patterned in high relief, and its first American manufacturer (started in 1883) had 150 patterns in 1885. There were motifs for any style as well as special patterns for dados, rails, fillings, and mantels. Sears had the product in its 1908 catalog. Montgomery Ward also sold it, but the starting date is unknown. Lincrusta could be colored or plain and usually was painted after installation.

Of the dozen or so products rivaling Lincrusta, most were English. A product very similar to Lincrusta was anaglypta, developed by another Englishman, Thomas Palmer, who embossed the paper while it was still in the pulp stage. It had deep relief and was lightweight, which allowed it to be used for friezes and ceilings. Anaglypta was available in three classes of relief and successfully imitated ornamental plaster.

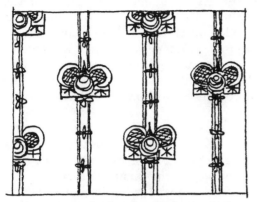

LINCRUSTA "MODERN"
MONTGOMERY WARD — 1910

LINCRUSTA FRENCH RENAISSANCE
MONTGOMERY WARD — 1910

LINCRUSTA
SEARS, ROEBUCK AND CO. — 1915

LINCRUSTA
SEARS, ROEBUCK AND CO. — 1915

BURLAP   GRASS CLOTH   VARNISHED TILES

Wallpaper, 1920–1940

Wall organization changed in the decades between 1920 and 1940. Historically, the side wall had been engaging more and more of the wall surface. Sears eliminated the dado. By 1925 Sears was selling oatmeal papers with a 7½-inch border and a 4-inch binder. The binder was actually a leftover trimming in a new role. Binders were narrow borders to be placed around panels of paper instead of moldings or used as a finish piece just above the baseboard. A binder could also replace a border in a low-ceilinged room. If a border and binder were hung on the same wall, they were to look quite similar.

The printing of wallpapers developed from *hand-block* printing, to *roller* printing in which color is applied to a moving roll of paper by an engraved metal cylinder, to *screen* printing in which color and design are deposited on paper through a silk screen, to *rotogravure* printing, a photomechanical process by which images are printed from an intaglio copper cylinder.

A good deal of traditional imagery was brought forward into the new printing processes, but the use of the imagery changed as wallpapers became iconographic, providing specific imagery for particular rooms: stripes for a low-ceilinged room, allover floral patterns for a medium or large room, plain patterns with a dainty stripe for bedrooms, and so on. This kind of categorization had been going on since the turn of the century, and by 1920 it was becoming the norm.

While wood moldings for papered walls had been reduced to a picture molding or entirely eliminated, Sears was selling linoleum moldings that could be applied to walls to frame wallpaper panels or serve as a cove. These were available in three designs and were finished in decorative colors—tan, brown, putty, white, and gold.

By 1934 every wallpaper pattern Sears offered was advertised as washable and fadeproof. Sears was also selling papers that were "independent ceilings" for use with any side wall. The relationship between side-wall and ceiling patterns had been changing throughout the last three decades. In 1910 the ceiling had a pattern related to the side wall, perhaps even to the border. They all might be linked by background tones. The 1920s continued to match ceiling and wall papers, and that idea did not die out in the 1930s, but the production of independent papers was a significant change.

The patterns of the period 1920 through 1940 exhibit a shift towards conceiving of motifs in wallpaper as small paintings. Many manufacturers advertised their lines as "art papers." In these papers a passage of the wall reads like a scene, complete with suggestions of casement windows seen vaguely in the background, with perhaps a trellis threaded through with blossoms. The pattern becomes a view out the "window," a window on the world, but also a view from the outside in. The spatiality is integrated, there is no illusion of recessional depth, only modern pictorial space, layered, reflecting some kind of continuity between the inside and the outside. These patterns owe something to French painting. Not only has the wall around the window been removed, but the whole scene has become vernacular design.

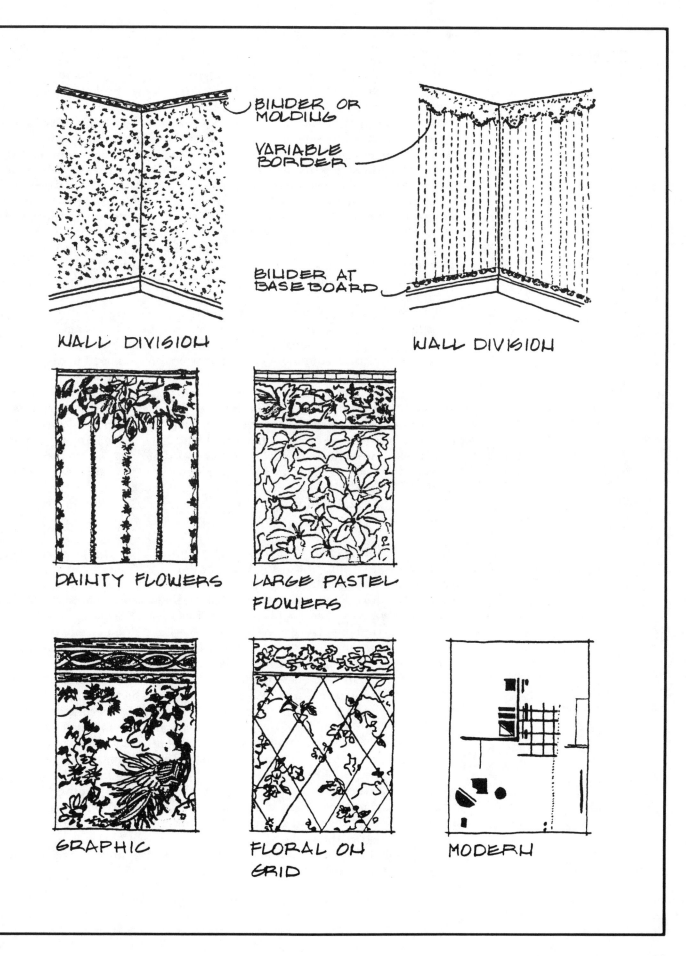

BINDER OR MOLDING

VARIABLE BORDER

BINDER AT BASEBOARD

WALL DIVISION

WALL DIVISION

DAINTY FLOWERS

LARGE PASTEL FLOWERS

GRAPHIC

FLORAL ON GRID

MODERN

Plaster, Paint, and Stenciling

From 1870 to 1940 the application of plaster to interior walls changed dramatically. At the beginning of this period plaster was made on the job site by the plasterer. Before the end of the century plaster was being manufactured and bagged for shipment to the job site. Early in the twentieth century, plaster wallboard, made of gypsum, was being manufactured in modest sizes. Besides being easy to install, wallboard aided in fire protection. By 1940 plaster boards were beginning to influence the dimensions of walls.

The application of paint to walls also changed in the period under study. In the 1870s walls were likely to be painted, calcimined, or whitewashed. Painting was thought to be best, but it was the most expensive. Calcimine was generally acceptable on account of its ease of application and durability. Whitewash, though inferior, was often the choice because of its low cost.

Calcimine is a water-based paint consisting of size (a thin solution of glue) and whiting (ground chalk). The mixture can be tinted but often it was left white: it could be decorated with flowers or figures, this treatment being called *fresco.*

Whitewash was applied to almost any kind of interior wall in any kind of building. It was a universal material that was very inexpensive to make. Depending on the intended use, whitewash was made of lime and water with sizing or other ingredients added. It was also employed in disinfecting interiors such as stables.

Whitewash could be laid on thick to effect texture, but there were other products that went on like paint yet could be used to create relief work. One of these was *plastic paint,* which was packaged as plastic powder that required only the addition of hot water and color. It was applied with a wide brush and could be worked into textures if handled while it was tacky, using a dry brush, a sponge, or a trowel. There were many of these products— notably Craftex, Morene, and Textone—and most had a range of uses. They were finished to imitate Caen stone or travertine, but they could just as easily be raked with a wire brush, flattened with a palette knife, or stippled.

Among painting effects, *glazing* is significant because it had several kinds of application in different aesthetics. For painting done in the ornamental and artistic modes, glazing means applying a layer of thin transparent wash over a ground color. This is essentially a Renaissance painting technique applied to walls to create shades and richness in the color.

A second kind of glazing entails the alteration of the glaze coat to create patterns. *Stippling* the glaze means breaking it into a dotted or pebbly surface by striking it with a dry brush. *Striating* the glaze means raking a dry brush or another instrument across the surface in parallel strokes. A third technique is *mottling,* in which the glaze is blotted with a crumpled cloth or paper. All of these treatments are visually decorative and, in addition, the unevenness of the surface creates light and shadow effects.

Several other uses of stippling are worth mentioning, for example, multicolor effects in which a foundation color is printed on by stippling with a sponge. In a related technique, several colors are laid on the wall and each color is worked out with a cheesecloth or brush, blending the colors without graying them. Scrolls can be made by using a wrinkled cloth to roughen the texture and exerting a twisting and lifting motion with the wrist. By twisting the hand without any side motion of the arm, the scroll can be made to resemble flowers, while a sweeping movement produces a more branching effect.

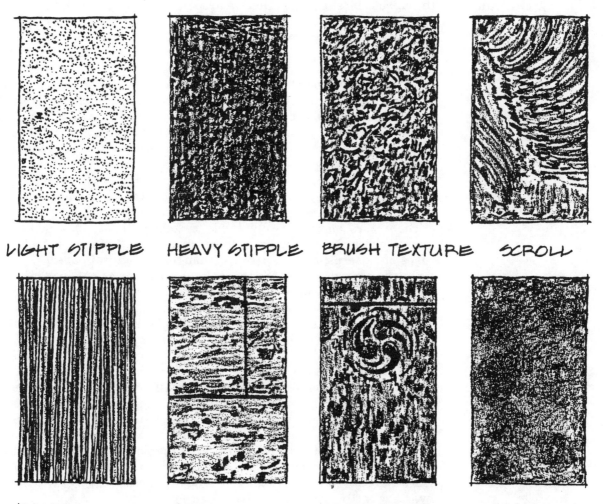

LIGHT STIPPLE　　HEAVY STIPPLE　　BRUSH TEXTURE　　SCROLL

RAKED　　SCORED　　STIPPLED AND STENCILED　　GLAZING

CONVENTIONALIZED FLOWERS　　SCROLL AND FLOWERS　　SCROLL　　STYLIZED FLOWERS

SELECTED STENCIL PATTERNS
SEARS, ROEBUCK AND CO. — 1918

Plaster, Paint, and Stenciling

Stencil painting was a significant method of decorating walls and ceilings throughout most of the period we are studying. Instructional manuals and trade publications taught people how to do it, gave examples of patterns, and described the history of the craft. Independent companies like Sears, Roebuck and Montgomery Ward sold stencil patterns and the tools to do the work.

An article by Buie Harwood in the *Journal of Interior Design Education and Research,* Spring 1986, describes stenciling as "a mechanical, decorative process characterized by the use of pattern repeats with colors conveyed in a flat, unshaded manner." The transfer of a painted design to walls was accomplished in two ways. In the simpler method the block design was complete; the whole design went on at once. In the other method, a design outline was pounded into a plate and transferred to the wall by rubbing a pencil over the perforations. The design was thus transferred as an outline, and the spaces within it were filled in by hand.

There were many different kinds of stencils, many of which produced special effects: corner stencils; band, divider, and binder stencils for the edges of patterns; allover patterns that resembled wallpaper.

On the everyday level, Sears sold stencil patterns cut into heavy oiled paper about 15 to 25 inches long. Sears recommended stenciling on calcimined, painted, and frescoed walls and on plain or ingrained wallpapers.

The patterns illustrated are typical, since floral imagery—especially conventionalized flowers, blossoms, and sprays in arabesques—and varieties of scrolls were very popular. The first two stencils are block designs, while the second two are running types. Stenciling had no stylistic limitations. It could imitate moldings and plaster work. After the initial transfer, designs could be worked over by hand to achieve highlights, extra color, and shading. Interlaced figures, garlands, swags, wreaths, patterns derived from historical, high-style sources, as well as contemporary motifs were all available.

The Sherwin-Williams paint company promoted stenciling, no doubt to compete with wallpaper. At the conclusion of a section on stenciling in its *Home Painting Manual* (1922), the company offered some rules (which were, by the way, the same rules recognized for wallpaper):

> Use borders that correspond to the proportions of the room—smaller borders for low rooms, larger for ceilings 12 to 15 feet high. Select a pattern that conforms to the character of the room. Do not use a simple border in a room that is to be decorated and furnished in a very elaborate style, and vice versa. Do not use a stencil border if the wall is of such a character that a pattern will detract from the appearance. Lastly, stronger colors are best for small borders; for large borders, colors that harmonize with the wall color are best.

Paneling   The nineteenth-century interest in colonial culture spurned the use of wood *paneling*. At first wainscots were the primary form paneling took, but the artistic design aesthetic included paneled walls that extended the height of wainscots to 5½ feet. By the 1920s full wall paneling was in vogue, carried out in three materials: hardwood panels made of stiles and rails: pine paneling of knotted wood: and veneered plywood panels set off by hardwood strips. Despite differences in the appearance of these materials, the treatments were considered colonial. Paneling was also marketed as an alternative to plaster and paint and wallpaper. Moreover, paneling could be used to cover one wall only, perhaps an end wall of bookcases and panels. A less expensive technique involved panel strips or moldings dividing a wall into baseboard-to-cornice vertical panels, with the plaster between the strips floated smooth.

From 1910 to 1935 several kinds of *wallboards* were introduced to the vernacular market as substitutes for plaster. The simplest of these were boards of layered fiber. Other products had layers of compressed fiber cemented with asphalt. The outer surface of these could even have a veneer of oak or mahogany. Some fiberboards were made of cardboard and others of wood such as white pine pulp. All of the fiberboards could be arranged as wainscot panels or as whole paneled walls by laying strips of wood over the joints between boards or by following some more elaborate pattern. Most boards averaged 8 to 12 feet in length and 32 inches in width.

Wallboards were introduced when the Mission and Craftsman styles in furniture were popular, and paneling fit those styles. Mission/Craftsman trim was heavy. When darkly stained it made a deep, bold contrast with the painted panels. In the 1920s the high-contrast technique of placing complementary colors close together to bring out the strength of each color lost ground to the more delicate strategies of harmonizing values, as well as painting everything in a room one color. Mottling and stencil work could be applied to this kind of finish, because the panels and their strips had been partially or completely painted out.

By the 1930s another material had an impact on paneled walls: fiberboard products, especially those produced by the Masonite Company. The company made insulation boards that could be used on the outside or inside of the frame. It also developed a semihard board that could be sawed, planed, sanded, nailed, cemented, painted, or lacquered for use in walls and ceilings. Another board, smooth and very hard, was made for use in walls and wainscots. It was knotless and grainless, but it could take grooving and was appropriate for residential as well as commercial buildings. It could imitate tiles for kitchen and bathroom walls, and serve as flooring material for entrance halls. The company even argued that it should be left natural, that its warm brown complemented the new interest in natural colors. Masonite tried to address modern design through the use of horizontal and vertical lines subordinated to the main effect or color. A complete Masonite wall might have beveled edges, grooved designs, and strips of metal covering the joints all on one surface.

Paneling   Ornamental plaster or composition material has been a part of interior design for a long time. Composition plaster is exceptionally versatile. In vernacular architecture plaster moldings were used to set off wall or ceiling panels and as ceiling center pieces. Composition plaster moldings were employed in ornamental and colonial systems but because of their tendency to reflect high-style design or to be freely applied, they were not part of the artistic system.

WOOD WALL PANELING

PLASTER OR WALLPAPER.

WALL PANELING WITH PANEL STRIPS OR MOLDING

PANEL STRIPS

KNOTTY WOOD OR MASONITE PANELING (FULL-HEIGHT)

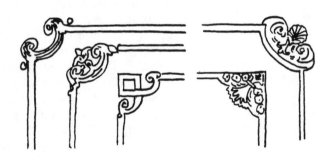

COMPOSITION OR PLASTER MOLDINGS

SECTION

V-GROOVE KNOTTY WOOD OR MASONITE

Other Wall Treatments

The last part of this section deals with remaining wall materials. The first is *oilcloth* wall covering. This inexpensive alternative to other washable, sanitary goods was hung like wallpaper. A 1915 Sears catalog entry lists three types of oilcloth: a glazed cloth for bathrooms and kitchens; a decorative dull-finish cloth for bedrooms and living rooms; and a leather or burlap type for dining rooms and paneled rooms. Sears's trade name for oilcloth was Sanitas. It came in three patterns: one that looked like tile, another that looked like wallpaper, and a border done in a fret pattern or a molding.

The social movement to sanitize interiors led designers and builders to the use of *ceramic wall tiles*. As described in a 1906 Sweet's catalog of architectural materials, glazed tiles left no corners to harbor dirt and germs, and the tiles were endorsed by doctors. The organization of glazed tile walls was simple: two parallel binders, one at the base and the other a cap on the top, with the major part of the wall a field. The base tiles were of two types: straight or cove. Glazed walls also had a set of trimmers, inside and outside angles, in half-round or rectangular shapes, and quarter stretchers. For a long time wall tile was made in white only, but that changed in the 1920s.

Metal wall plates originated in the same production system as metal ceiling plates, and they had the same extensive range of patterns. Wall plates were used for wainscoting and for covering entire walls. In the latter case, most walls terminated with a cornice that could project as much as 15 inches from the wall. A complete wall might be composed of a wainscot, a side-wall plate, a chair rail, a frieze, and a cornice. Some manufacturers referred to the side wall as a dado. Individual wall plates, 24 inches by 72 or 96 inches, were made for covering the field of a side wall. Stairway plates were furnished in sizes corresponding in width to that of the stair steps. Since the styling was generally plain, the cutting to the angle of the stairway did not mar the design. Molding strips finished the stairs with a strip along the baseboard and another in line with the handrail.

During the 1930s two new wall materials helped to redefine commercial interiors: porcelain enamel on metal, and pigmented structural glass. *Enameled metal* sheets were hung on furring strips over a stud wall, or they were veneered to a wallboard. In some uses, such as cafés and roadside businesses, a stainless-steel strip covered the sheet joints.

Pigmented glass was sold under trade names like Carrara glass, Sani Onyx, or Vitrolite. An opaque material with permanent color and a smooth, even surface, it was used wherever marble had been applied, with the exception of walls that required moldings or decorations. The glass was finished in several ways: without luster; with a soft satin finish; or polished to a bright, glossy surface. The glass was impervious to stain and did not absorb moisture or retain odors. Its reflectivity was well-suited to modern environments.

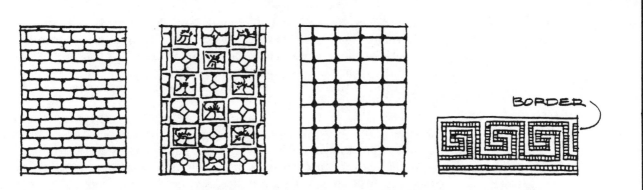

SELECTIONS FROM SEARS OILCLOTH PATTERNS — 1915

BORDER

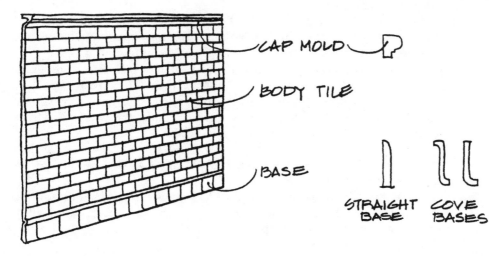

CAP MOLD

BODY TILE

BASE

STRAIGHT BASE   COVE BASES

GLAZED WALL TILE

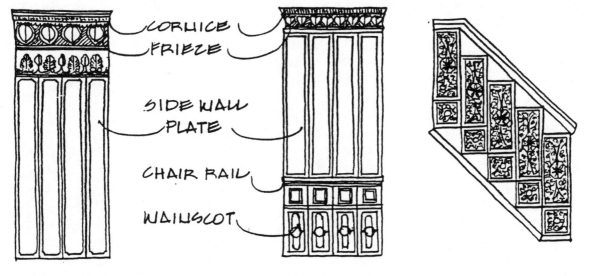

CORNICE

FRIEZE

SIDE WALL PLATE

CHAIR RAIL

WAINSCOT

METAL WALL DESIGNS

METAL STAIRWAY DESIGN

STAIRWORK
Stair Types

Stairwork was an essential element in American vernacular interior design throughout the period 1870 through 1940. Stairs were assembled from millwork products into scores of patterns suited to the aesthetics of the period. Conceptually, a stairway was derived from the plan of the stair flight and the treatment of the component parts: riser, tread, rail, baluster, stringer, and newel.

The *straight-flight* stair is the most common of all types: it extends in one direction only, with no turns, landings, or winder stairs, and with all the steps parallel to each other and at right angles to the stringers.

A *dog-legged* stair consists of two or more successive flights rising in opposite directions with a landing between them, and with no wellhole (clear vertical space) in the plan. The rail and the balusters of each flight fall in the same vertical plane, and both of the outer stringers are fixed into the same newel.

The *quarter-turn* stair turns 90 degrees as it progresses from the bottom to the top, and it has a wellhole. The turn may employ winder stairs or a landing, and the second flight is at a right angle to the first.

The *double-L* stair is a platform stair with two landings, one nearer the bottom and one nearer the top. The stair turns 90 degrees at each landing.

Helical stairs are planned in a circle with all steps converging toward the center around a central newel. The treads are winders. This stair is referred to also as a *circular* or *spiral* stair.

The *hollow* or *open newel* type is laid out so as to use two landings with a short flight between them, with newel posts at the angles. The wellhole in this plan has a rectangular shape.

Geometrical stair plans have a continuous stringer around a semicircular or elliptical well. The balustrade follows the curve without newel posts at the turns and with landings between floors. If this stair has a landing it is called a *well* stair.

Double-entry and *double-return* stair plans each have three components. A double-entry stair has two equal straight flights terminating at a landing from which a single flight, at a right angle to the first flights, rises to the second floor. The double-return plan has the reverse logic: a single flight rises from the lower floor to a landing, and two flights, one from each side, rise from there to the next floor.

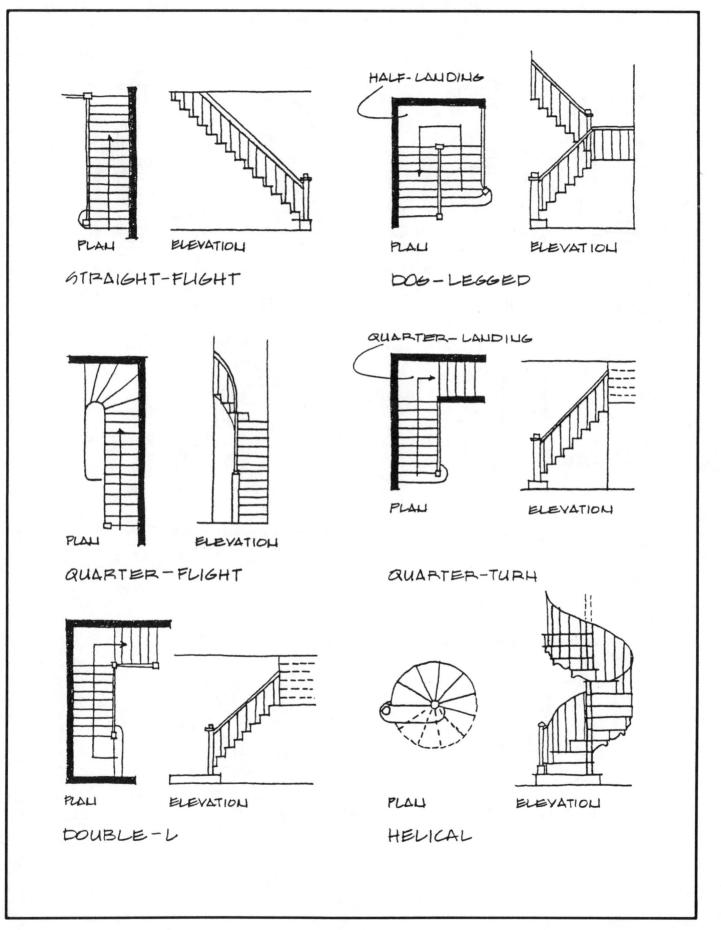

STRAIGHT-FLIGHT

DOG-LEGGED

QUARTER-FLIGHT

QUARTER-TURH

DOUBLE-L

HELICAL

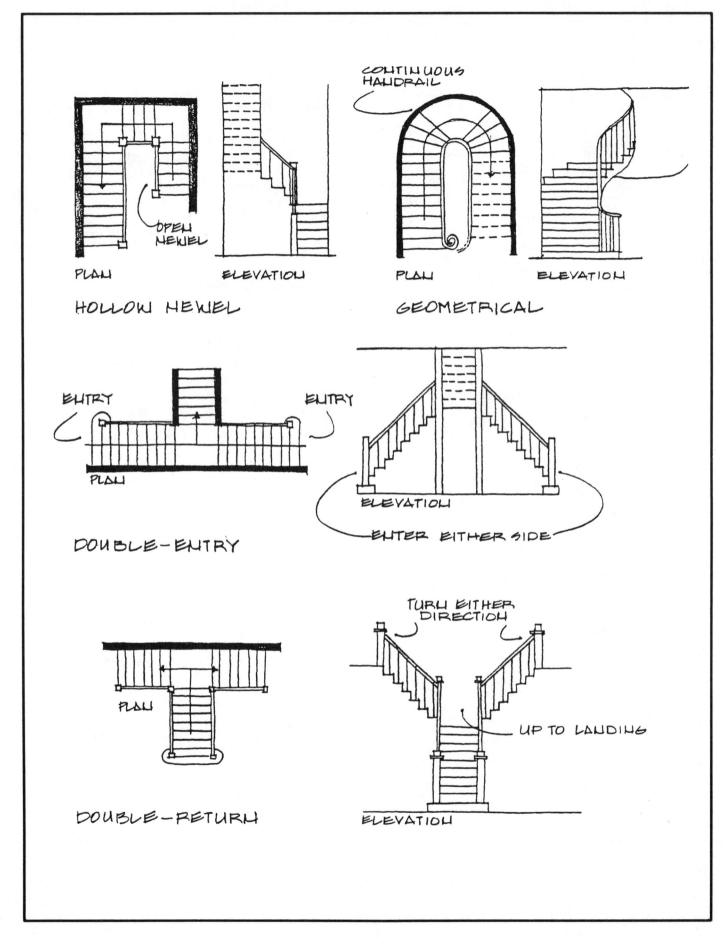

CONTINUOUS HANDRAIL

PLAN   ELEVATION

OPEN NEWEL

HOLLOW NEWEL

PLAN   ELEVATION

GEOMETRICAL

ENTRY   ENTRY

PLAN

DOUBLE-ENTRY

ELEVATION

ENTER EITHER SIDE

TURN EITHER DIRECTION

PLAN

DOUBLE-RETURN

UP TO LANDING

ELEVATION

Stairway Types There are four stairway types for vernacular interiors. *Open* stairs open on one or both sides to a room or a hall. A balustrade commonly is used on the open side and the treads are visible. A *closed* or *box* stairway is completely closed on both sides by walls and may have a door at one end. The *combination open/closed* stair occurs when stairways change as they ascend from open to closed near the top. This arrangement works with both straight or turned flights. Finally, the *disappearing* stair is a passage to an attic or loft that can be folded and swung upward into a scuttle in the ceiling when not in use.

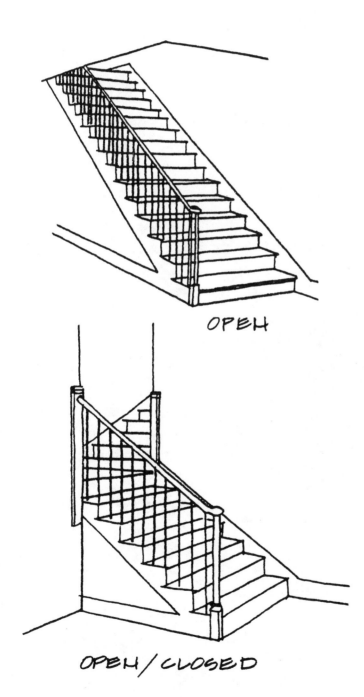

OPEN

BOX OR CLOSED

OPEN/CLOSED

DISAPPEARING

Stringers *Stringers* are the outer members of a stairway to which the risers and treads are attached. An *open* stringer (also called a *cut* stringer) has cut-in steps so that treads overhang the stringer. By contrast, a *closed* stringer has no cuts and the treads are behind it. A *wall* stringer is set next to the wall, as opposed to the outer string.

Open, outside stringers are sometimes ornamented with attached brackets, with panels, and with combinations of brackets and panels, with the pattern being repeated at each tread. Closed outer stringers may be paneled, with the repeats following the rake of the string. A closed stringer and its adjacent wall may be paneled together, and a closed stringer may be covered with a molded string board for its entire length.

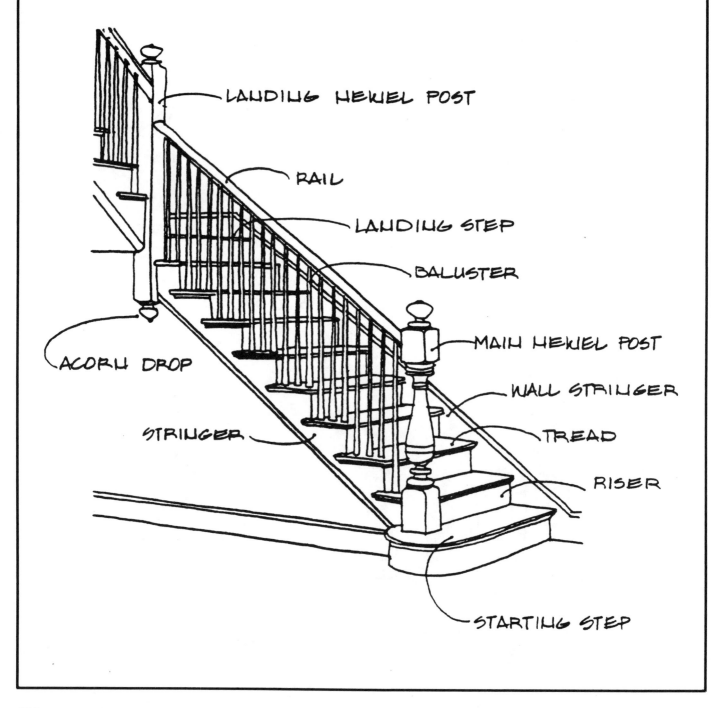

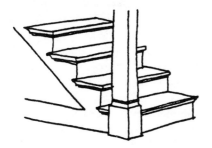

OPEN STRINGER

CLOSED STRINGER

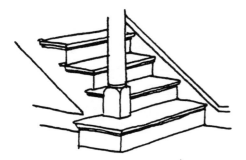

WALL STRINGER

BRACKETED STRINGER

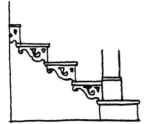

OPEN STRINGER
BRACKETS

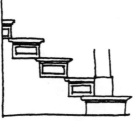

OPEN STRINGER
PANELS

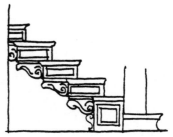

OPEN STRINGER
PANELS AND BRACKETS

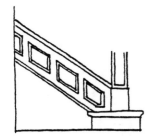

CLOSED STRINGER
PANEL STRINGBOARD

CLOSED STRINGER
VERTICAL PANEL

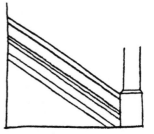

CLOSED STRINGER
MOLDED STRING-
BOARD

Step Elements and Types

The component parts of a stair are the *riser,* the vertical member that determines the height of each step, and the *tread,* the horizontal member that equals the run, or depth, of each step.

Winders are turn-steps, cut wider at one end then at the other, so they can turn an angle or go around a curve. Winders that do not radiate from a common stair are sometimes referred to as *balanced winders.*

The *starting step* establishes a design effect for the stairway. A *round-ended* starting step has an end formed into a circle. If the step extends beyond the newel post, it is called a *bull-nose* step. A *quarter-circle* starting step does not extend beyond the newel. *Square-end* steps may be built either way.

TREAD
RISER

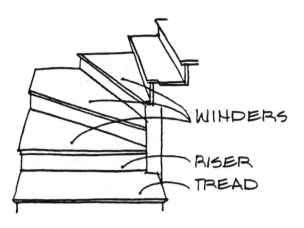

WINDERS
RISER
TREAD

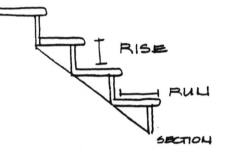

RISE
RUN
SECTION

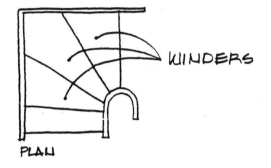

WINDERS
PLAN

STARTING STEPS

CIRCLE END   PLAN

CIRCLE END   PLAN

SQUARE   PLAN

SQUARE   PLAN

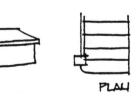

QUARTER-CIRCLE   PLAN

Rails and Crooks A *stair rail* is a bar of wood or metal used for support and as a guard. It also serves as the top member of a balustrade. Wood rails are the most common kind in vernacular design. Rails are made of solid wood or glued stock. Glued pieces have a core and four applied sides. Each stair section has two parts, a top designed for hand-holding and a bottom that accommodates balusters. Rails usually abut newel posts. The handrail sections illustrated were chosen because of their longevity as stock rails in millwork catalogs, many of them spanning all aesthetic systems.

Crooks are curvilinear rails configured with curves in either the vertical or the horizontal plane. A *gooseneck* is a curved section of a handrail used to connect a rising rail with a level rail. A *quarter-circle turn* on level rail is used around a wellhole on the second floor. An *easement* rail is curved in the vertical plane and often terminates in a newel post or a newel cap.

Platforms and landings help turn a flight of stairs at a right angle and each has an appropriate crook to facilitate the turn. A *landing* crook has a more elliptical shape and less twist than the shortened, abrupt twist of the *platform* crook.

The spiral portion of a handrail, which often supplants a newel post, is called a *volute* or *scroll*.

RAILS

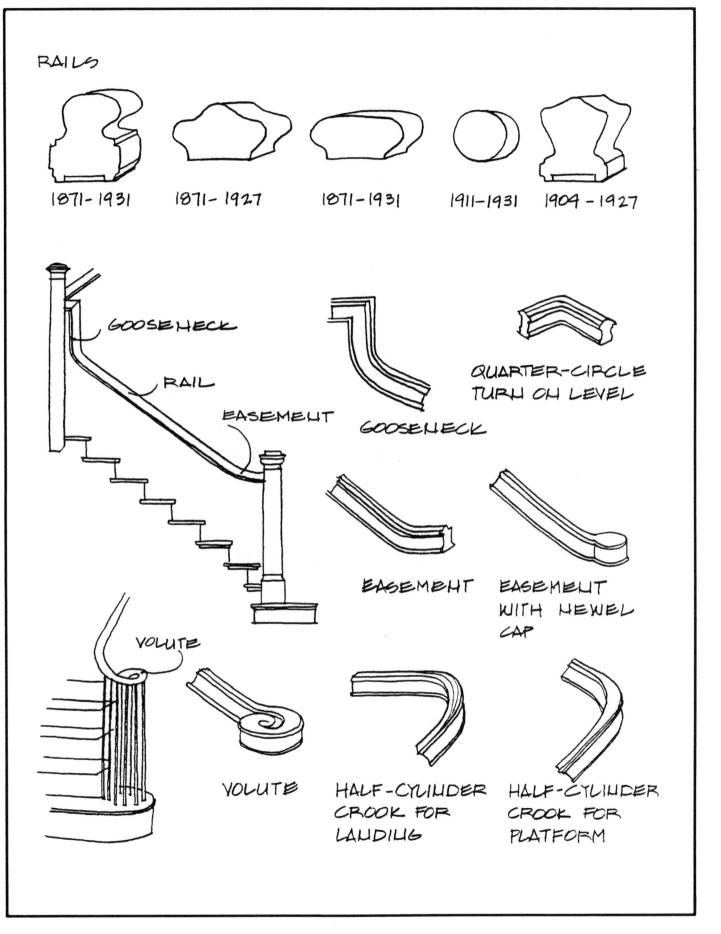

1871-1931   1871-1927   1871-1931   1911-1931   1904-1927

GOOSENECK

RAIL

EASEMENT

GOOSENECK

QUARTER-CIRCLE TURN ON LEVEL

EASEMENT

EASEMENT WITH NEWEL CAP

VOLUTE

VOLUTE

HALF-CYLINDER CROOK FOR LANDING

HALF-CYLINDER CROOK FOR PLATFORM

Newels *Newel posts* are special posts, often objects of ornamentation, that support a balustrade at the start of a stairway, at a landing, or at the end of a stairway. The newel at the foot of the stairs has always been a key element in stairway design, and historically its treatment reflects the shift in aesthetics during the period 1870 through 1940. Most newels are tapered from the bottom to the top, the base being wider than the cap or headpiece, and most newels are conceived as structures built up by varying the work done at the base, on the shaft, and at the top. Newel posts designed for ornamental treatments usually have a square base, with a surbase molding above the base, a shaft with assorted effects (turned work, panels, flat facets, carving, or chamfered edges), a neck, and a special turned piece for the head. Sometimes an electric light is attached to the top of the newel.

Fancy turned, octagon, carved, and chamfered newels were stock elements in 1890s millwork catalogs. These newels were massive; stock octagon posts were 8, 9, 10, 11, and 12 inches wide. Turn-of-the-century newels had ornamental headpieces or were square with panels and often an acorn top (Universal Millwork, 1904; Sears, 1907). The paneled newel sometimes carried an ornamental motif such as a wreath below the cap.

The modern aesthetic eliminated surface treatments so that newels had simple lines. In 1907 Sears, Roebuck produced the "anti-dust" newel that linked modern design to health. As surface work decreased, the overall geometric shape became more important. Thus, Craftsman/Mission newels became more rectilinear than their predecessors. Some modern shafts were paneled and many were plain. In 1917 the Curtis Companies introduced their tapered shaft as "utilitarian." The modern colonial remained modestly turned.

An *angle* newel, also known as a landing or platform newel, is an intermediary that supports sections of a balustrade and attaches to the rail and the stringer, and sometimes to the wall. Some angle newels have a drop at the bottom.

As for materials, historically newels were made of hardwood, but softwood, especially pine, became popular by 1920. The length of the newel for all styles was 4 feet to 4 feet 6 inches, and the width varied from 5 inches to 8 inches. Angle newels had the same width but could be as much as a foot longer.

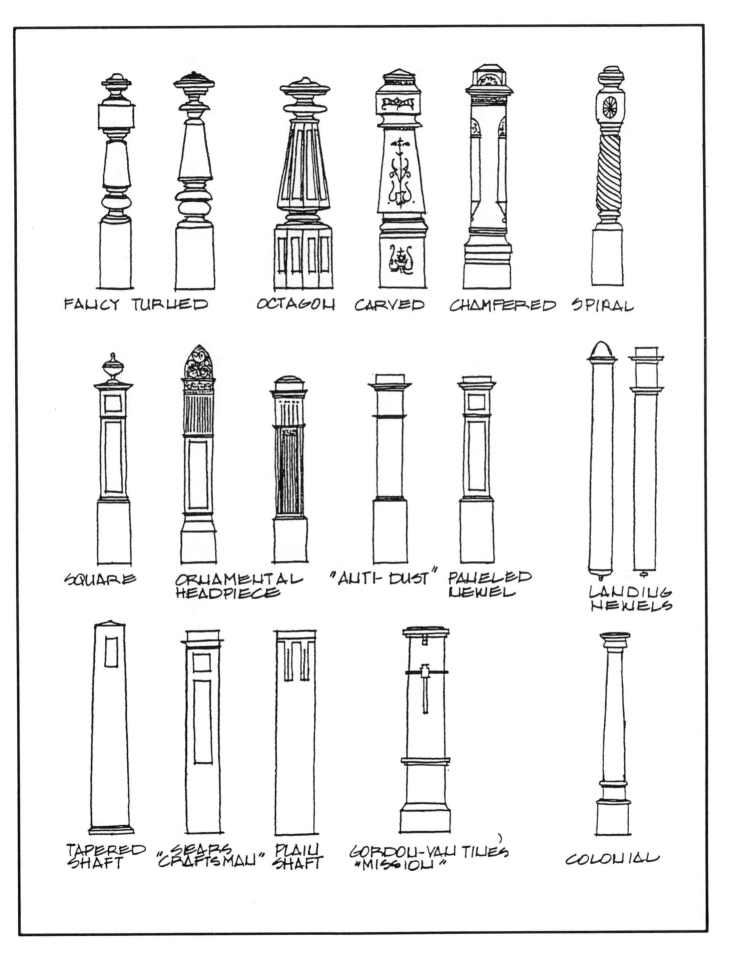

FANCY TURNED   OCTAGON   CARVED   CHAMFERED   SPIRAL

SQUARE   ORNAMENTAL HEADPIECE   "ANTI-DUST"   PANELED NEWEL   LANDING NEWELS

TAPERED SHAFT   "SEARS CRAFTSMAN"   PLAIN SHAFT   GORDON-VAN TINES "MISSION"   COLONIAL

Balusters and Balustrades

The last major element in stairway design is the *baluster* and its arrangement into a *balustrade*. The baluster is a small column or post that supports a handrail and forms an ornamental enclosure. The balustrade derives from a series or a row of balusters usually placed two or three to a step. Balusters rarely were cut less than 1 inch or more than 2 inches square, and their height was either 28 inches or 32 inches.

In the ornamental designs, balusters are characterized by turned work. Starting and ending with a square piece, a baluster is some combination of spindles, beads, spirals, reels, and plain shafts. Especially ornamented pieces were labeled by manufacturers as "fancy." A second ornamental type is the thick, heavily turned balusters. Balustrades made of sticks, no matter the pattern, function as openwork and rely on light and shadow for effect. The ornamental system also has closed balustrades made of perforated wood, units with friezes along the stringer or under the rail, and panels that fill the space between the stringer and rail. In the latter instance the balustrade is a kind of ornamented "wall."

Artistic balusters are stripped of lathe work and take round, square, or rectangular shapes. The Craftsman/Mission version of this is a wide, rectangular baluster with abstract patterns sawed into the face.

Balusters for colonial stairs are modestly turned pieces—round and straight, or round and tapered. Colonial balusters remain the most delicate, the most like furniture, and the most open of any design.

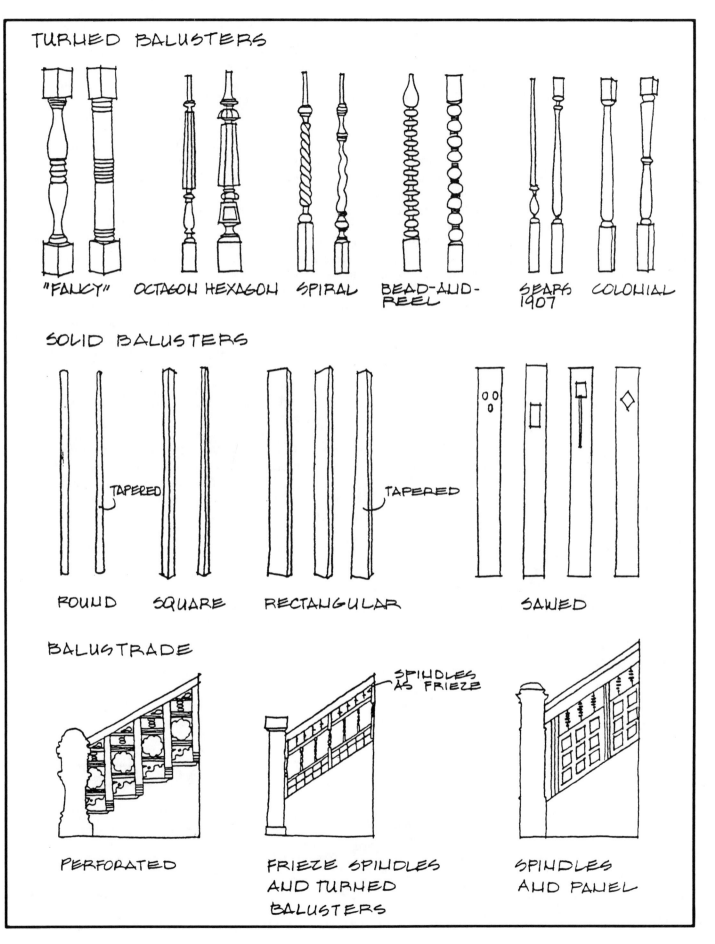

TURNED BALUSTERS

"FANCY" OCTAGON HEXAGON SPIRAL BEAD-AND-REEL SEARS 1907 COLONIAL

SOLID BALUSTERS

ROUND TAPERED SQUARE RECTANGULAR TAPERED SAWED

BALUSTRADE

PERFORATED FRIEZE SPINDLES AND TURNED BALUSTERS SPINDLES AS FRIEZE SPINDLES AND PANEL

Finishing Touches

A complete stairway has a series of small parts that finish each element and bind the elements together. The engagement of the riser with the tread becomes an opportunity to affect the design. At stake are the nature of the *nosing*—the projecting edge of the tread that extends beyond the riser—and the cove molding that covers the joint between the riser and the tread.

Most balustrades include a finished stringer, which means they add a shoe rail and its fillet to the edge of the string. The *shoe* is a molding that is usually plowed to receive the end of the baluster. The spaces between balusters are taken up with *fillets,* small pieces of wood that are generally molded on the surface.

Wood *brackets* are part of the ornamental design vocabulary. In stairwork they are applied either to the face of the outer stringer, filling the spaces between balusters, or to the underside of the handrail, filling the spaces between balusters. A scrollwork laid out in a continuous run is sometimes applied to the outer face of a closed stringer.

The final fittings for a stairway relate to the rails and include a wood *rosette*—a wall plate for the rail to strike against—and *handrail brackets* for securing the rail to the wall. The design of a bracket was tied to the hardware system installed in the building. Sometimes rails were given specially shaped endpieces, such as an acorn, which gave the rail a finished appearance.

A closed string could easily be accommodated into the adjacent wall by paneling part or all of the triangular space between the starting tread and the top. Paneling on the face of the stringer was built from planted stiles and moldings.

Iron stairways were important alternatives to millwork structures. Used mostly in commercial and industrial interiors, iron stairs rely for design effects on patterns cast in their risers. Common motifs are floral or geometric shapes, intricately detailed and cast as running pieces, with light and shade an active part of the pattern.

ELEVATION

PANEL FOR CLOSED STRING

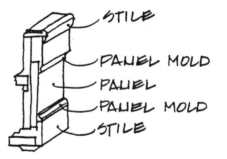

STILE
PANEL MOLD
PANEL
PANEL MOLD
STILE

IRON STEPS

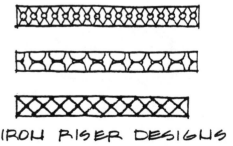

IRON RISER DESIGNS

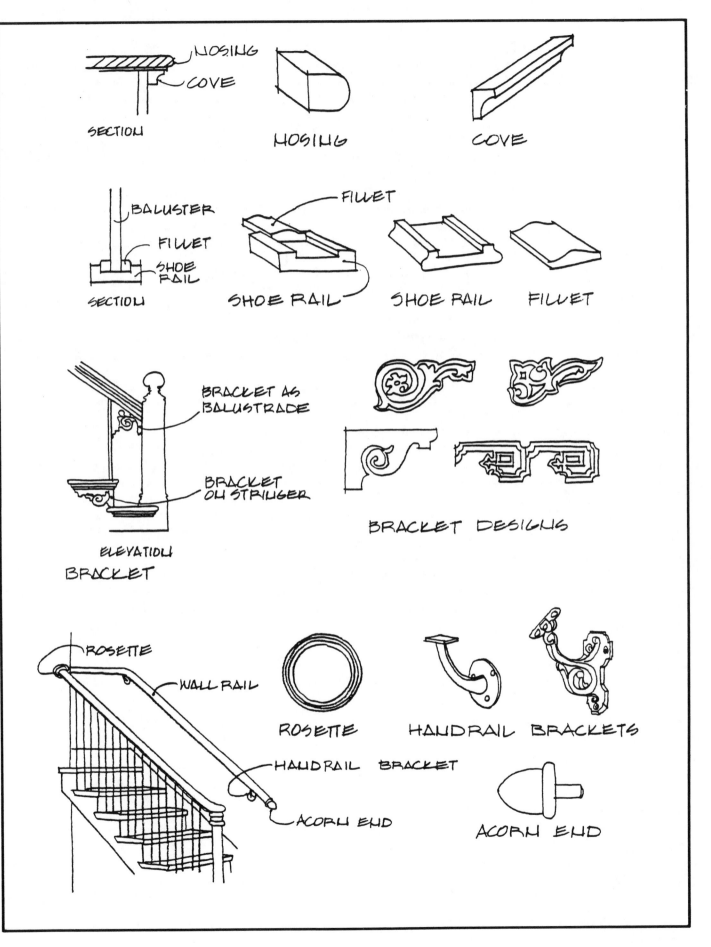

NOSING
COVE
SECTION

NOSING

COVE

BALUSTER
FILLET
SHOE RAIL
SECTION

FILLET

SHOE RAIL

SHOE RAIL

FILLET

BRACKET AS BALUSTRADE

BRACKET ON STRINGER

ELEVATION BRACKET

BRACKET DESIGNS

ROSETTE

WALL RAIL

HANDRAIL BRACKET

ACORN END

ROSETTE

HANDRAIL BRACKETS

ACORN END

117

OPENINGS
Types and Elements

Vernacular buildings have included openings in walls other than doorways. As the modern, open-plan house evolved from the compartmentalized interiors of the Victorian era, openings between rooms took on more importance. Special trim sets were applied to openings and cased openings provided opportunities for vistas, views through interior spaces to the out-of-doors. By the 1930s uncased openings also had become a part of interior systems.

An opening in a wall may be spanned or cased with a number of different kinds of grilles, with colonnades, and with trim sets, all built up from millwork component parts.

An interior *grille* is an ornamental piece of openwork that fills the upper portion of an opening. Grilles are made of wood or metal, but wood is the principal material. Historically, grilles were manufactured to suit different treatments. They were installed alone, with or without an accompanying drape (a portiere), or as part of a colonnade grille. Grilles were made first as fixed units, but later they were given loose ends so they could be cut down to fit any opening. In their most progressive form they were composed of interchangeable sections, two ends and a middle of different widths that could be doweled together.

A *colonnade* accompanying a *grille* is designed like a piece of architectural furniture. It has wood columns, usually on pedestals, and an architrave. Grilles appeared in the trade literature at the turn of the century, with columns being of secondary importance to the grille itself. The May 1901 issue of *Carpentry and Building* suggested a grille with side columns for openings "between a reception room and parlor, a reception room and staircase hall, or between two principal rooms on the main floor." Grilles were used also to span bay-window openings.

As ornamental design became less popular, the grille itself began to fade but the "side columns" emerged as larger, more significant elements in the system. The pedestals upon which the columns generally rested took on new importance as furniture. They became storage units and their design was integrated with that of other interior woodwork. As the column became more important, the colonnade was produced also in stylistic models—Mission, modern, Craftsman, and the like.

A *cased opening* is any opening furnished with jambs and trim but without doors. A partially cased opening has casing as part of the jambs or trim. Most openings like this leave the head portion uncased.

GRILLE

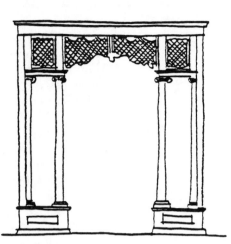

COLONNADE WITH GRILLE

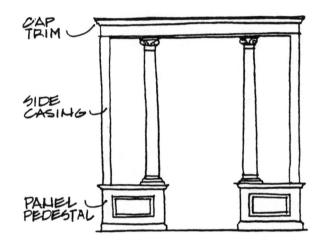

CAP TRIM

SIDE CASING

PANEL PEDESTAL

PEDESTAL COLONNADE

CASED OPENING

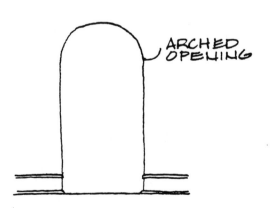

ARCHED OPENING

UNCASED OPENING

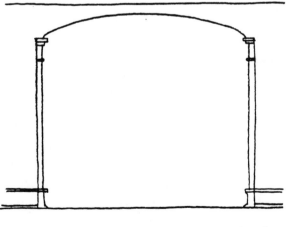

PARTIAL CASED OPENING

Grilles

Nineteenth-century millwork catalogs list grilles as "portiere work," recognizing their function of replacing a door with draperies. In practice the *portiere* was draped through the bottom member of the grille. Historically, the true portiere ceased to be part of the grille and became its own element—long drapes hung in an opening from a rod. This separation also entailed the removal of the grille from the colonnade and ultimately the loss of the grille from the interior during the 1920s.

As works of design, grilles are assemblages of turned, scrolled, sawn, and lattice work. As objects they are related to the ornamental friezes and rails on cottage porches. As stock material, grilles were manufactured to fit openings of 4 to 6 feet in width, with the drop of the grille averaging 12 to 24 inches. Grilles were thin, lacey things only ¾-inch or ⅞-inch thick. They were made from hard- and softwoods—oak was the most common—and were attached to the center of the jamb with an end shoe molding. Grilles were shipped "in the white," that is, unfinished, but on order they could be oiled or varnished in light or dark finish and matched to the grain and color of the woodwork in the building for which the grille was intended.

Some grille designs were worked in such a way that the entire panel had a flavor or an effect characteristic of a recognized architectural style, and the Art Nouveau piece here is an example of that. It features a continuous, ribbon-like scroll that clearly distinguishes it from the tighter concave-convex curves of the earlier grilles.

The commercial scroll-and spindle grille is an example of a store model: it could be set at the inner edge of a recess in a storefront to form a background for the store window. The large semicircular grille with lattice and scrollwork and a portiere in place, circa 1900, has a drop that is one-half the width, a common dimension.

Metal grilles in steel or brass were applied mostly to commercial buildings, especially low, plain grilles that served as wickets on counters in banks or stores. These designs, perhaps because of their functionality, have straightforward rectilinear schemes.

TURNED SPINDLES AND BEADS

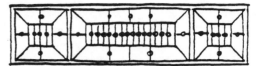

TURNED SPINDLES

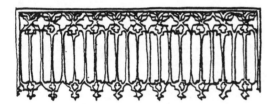

SCROLL AND SPINDLE

COMMERCIAL
SCROLL AND SPINDLE

SAWN

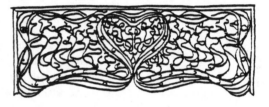

SCROLL: ART NOUVEAU

SCROLL

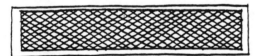

LATTICE

LATTICE AND SCROLL
WITH PORTIERE

METAL

Colonnades

The 1917 edition of the Curtis Companies millwork catalog had this to say about colonnades:

> It [the colonnade] is to serve as wall to divide the floor space into rooms, and as a doorless portal of exceptional width to give the impression of area, which one room borrows from another. . . . The colonnade is the most economical article of woodwork because it costs little more than plaster and a door for the same price. If it contains a bookcase it saves the cost of furniture. . . . It is the handsome go-between of rooms, the natural arbiter of space, a stately portal, ever open, inviting friendly intercourse and passage. If books fill its pedestals it is the storehouse of preserved wisdom, and with dainty garnitures upon its arms, a constant source of pleasure in its usefulness and beauty. . . . The desire for colonnades in his house is based on one of man's strongest instincts which leads him to plant trees along a walk. It caused him to make his early home a series of colonnaded chambers. The colonnade in our houses today permits a vista that pleases and gives a spaciousness that creates a feeling of outdoor freedom. (*Woodwork, The Permanent Furniture of Your Home*, pp. 102–3)

Despite its emotional and symbolic appeal, this advertising copy is accurate about the role colonnades played in the opening of interior walls. What was once solid, just a generation earlier, did not remain solid. Residents were now able to see through rooms, and the vistas could come at any place.

The history of colonnade composition parallels the development of the major aesthetics for the period. Early models were ornamental, the grille being more important than the column, and the columns having a base separate from the rest of the pedestal. The pedestal was treated as a wainscot with raised moldings, and the whole unit might have grille brackets on the capitals and in the corners. Grilles were often touted as having a "massive" appearance, and to reinforce this some designs included a beam between the capital and the architrave.

Structurally some columns were turned pieces, but most were assembled like porch columns: a series of partially curved, interlocking boards that looked seamless. Similarly, pedestals were paneled boxes.

When an opening was narrow, a single column with one pedestal was installed or two columns with no pedestals, because pedestals took up more floor space than columns. Columns were designed in the Tuscan and Ionic orders, with round and square columns that were plain or fluted. Capitals were made of solid wood and composition material that imitated wood. Column diameters were 5 to 6 inches, although most columns tapered toward the capital. Pedestal heights averaged 24 or 30 inches and fitted up to and around the jambs. The pedestal shelf was normally about twice the width of the jamb.

COLONNADE WITH GRILLE

PEDESTAL COLONNADE

COLONNADE WITH ARCHITRAVE

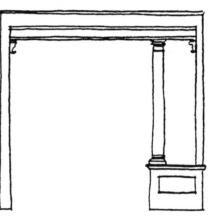

SINGLE-COLUMN COLONNADE

FULL-LENGTH COLUMNS

FULL-LENGTH COLUMNS

Colonnades   The integration of columns, architrave, pedestals, and storage compartments occurred by the second decade of this century. Shelf space in colonnades for books and china was organized into cabinets, with bookcases facing living rooms and china closets facing dining rooms. Pedestal sections were used also to create open and hidden desks, storage drawers, and bench seats. The storage function also caused the pedestal to change shape and become taller, thus reducing the height of the column. The columns were even eliminated in some designs.

Other colonnade details included ornament applied to or in place of the capitals on the columns, unusual grille patterns, and planted ornaments on the pedestal panels. The stylistic treatments of glazed pedestals were quite free, with patterns that were not necessarily imitations of window patterns. Some of the Mission units included art glass glazing on the pedestals, and others had leaded glass. The combination of special glazing and paneling turned the pedestals into cabinetry and furniture. This development also produced some experimentation, such as pairs of short thick columns.

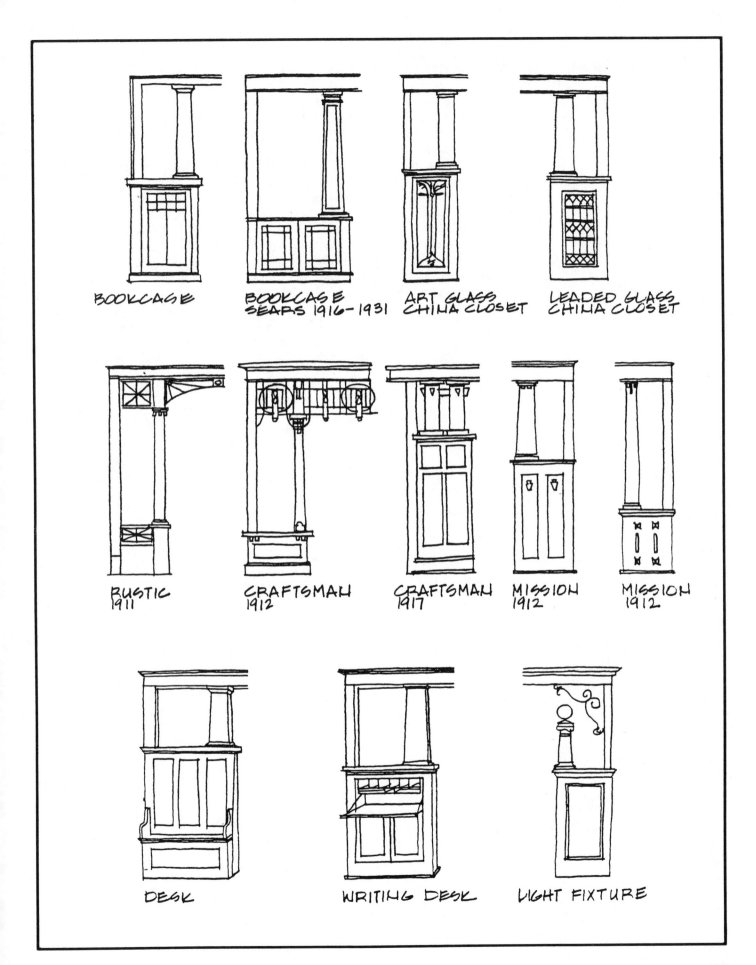

BOOKCASE

BOOKCASE
SEARS 1916-1931

ART GLASS
CHINA CLOSET

LEADED GLASS
CHINA CLOSET

RUSTIC
1911

CRAFTSMAN
1912

CRAFTSMAN
1917

MISSION
1912

MISSION
1912

DESK

WRITING DESK

LIGHT FIXTURE

Cased and Uncased Openings

The first example, a *bookcased opening,* is a Sears product derived from colonnade design. The trim for cased openings derived from the trim sets for windows and doors, so that a cased opening could be finished with a substantial cap trim. In this kind of design the trim is really an enlarged version of pilaster finish, with a plinth block at the base and a full architrave between the pilasters.

Colonial casings were composed in three ways: a pilaster casing with a cap; a flat arch with a continuous casing; and a modernized, low-profile casing that is mitered at the corners. For a while Sears, Roebuck manufactured a compromise on the cased and columned openings with a design that put narrow columns, only 7¼ inches wide, against the jambs, which were 5¼ inches, with an architrave functioning as the head casing.

Uncased *round-headed openings* were unique. A single casing of this kind of opening would not have much impact, so to extend its effect it was sometimes repeated in the house. Not only doorways, but bookcases, wall alcoves, breakfast nooks, all these might be round-headed as well in order to get a unified and effective design. Spanish- or English-style bungalows and English cottages often employed this technique. The pointed arch in church design could be accented with a partial casing of the peak.

BOOKCASED OPENING

COLUMNED OPENING

CASED OPENING, CAP TRIM

MODERN COLONIAL

CASED FLAT ARCH

UNCASED ROUND-
HEADED OPENING

PARTIAL CASED,
GOTHIC ARCH

MANTELS
Types and
Elements

All of the work that covers a fireplace or surrounds a chimney piece is referred to as the *mantel*. Like other design elements in the vernacular system, mantels were made of interchangeable parts and most were produced by millwork companies. While an entire mantel could be of cast iron or wood, most designs integrated wood with other materials: brick, tile, glass, and marble. The species of wood in mantels varied from 1870 to 1940, but generally mahogany, cherry, walnut, and quarter-sawn oak and birch were most popular. Pine began being substituted for hardwoods early in the century. Mantel finish depended on the stylistic convention used for the entire interior. For example, mantels done in the ornamental mode often were stained a dark color, regardless of wood type, whereas artistic mantels were allowed to reveal their natural color and graining under a low-luster surface. Colonial mantels usually were enameled ivory or white.

Mantel size also varied according to aesthetics. Ornamental mantels were conceived as vertically oriented so that mantel heights were 6 to 7 feet, almost twice their width. In the ornamental system, the mantel was clearly divided into two sections: the portion around the fireplace throat and hearth, and the section above that, the overmantel. Eventually the artistic system eliminated most, if not all, of the overmantel, and mantel design became horizontally oriented. Colonial designs were less horizontal than artistic and did not include an overmantel.

The nineteenth-century ornamentally designed mantel stacked design motifs on top of each other and relied on multiple elements and surfaces for effect. The shelves displayed bric-a-brac and the various layers of material projected a unique elevation into the room. The array of elements for such pieces included shelves, pilasters, columns, shelves, moldings (both solid and stuck), coves, and mirrors.

The fireplace *hearth* was integrated with the mantel. It was as wide as either the fireplace throat or the mantel. The material used to construct the hearth was sometimes carried over onto the face. Both brick and tile were popular for vernacular hearths, but by 1930 brick tile became the dominant hearth finish material, just as it had for facing.

Shelves not only supported rows of artifacts but they also helped to offset the vertical thrust of the mantel. Shelving in the ornamental style was built in several sizes, with a long shelf, about 5 feet wide, as the top of the mantel, and smaller, narrower shelves in the overmantel. The shelving system was composed of turned supports and planted moldings or worked edges. Shelves sometimes were topped by a cornice that was connected to the shelf by a broad cove.

Artistically conceived mantels were horizontally oriented and were composed to achieve a massive effect. The artistic mantel, with its thick wide shelf, sometimes set on heavy brackets, and rough-faced brick tile, had a presence quite unlike the ornamental. This kind of mantel was marketed as a key element in the organization of a wall so that bookcases or seats and windows might be combined into an entire design. Sometimes this configuration covered the narrower portion of a living room and was referred to as an end-wall piece.

Colonial shelves were single units with a thin board and lightly cut moldings connected to the pilasters and the architrave of the facing millwork.

Mirrors have played a role in both ornamental and artistic mantels. The mirrors usually were beveled, plate types, sometimes divided into panels. By the 1920s mirrors were no longer seen as an integral part of mantel design. When they were part of the overmantel, they were rectangular in shape, the horizontal side longer than the vertical.

Columns and *pilasters* also appeared in most mantel designs to frame the facing material and support the shelf. Most of these were half columns, but whole or square units also were made. Pilasters and columns were built with a plinth block at the base, and both types were made plain or fluted. Column and pilaster dimensions varied but most were 3 to 5 inches across and about 4 to 5 feet high.

The ornamental system was the only one to employ a *cove* in the mantel or overmantel. The curved face of the cove was decorated with engraving, veneered wood, paper or leather, this last being embossed.

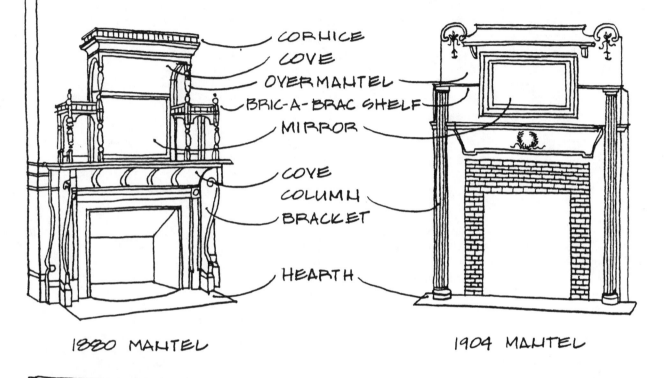

CORNICE
COVE
OVERMANTEL
BRIC-A-BRAC SHELF
MIRROR
COVE
COLUMN
BRACKET
HEARTH

1880 MANTEL

1904 MANTEL

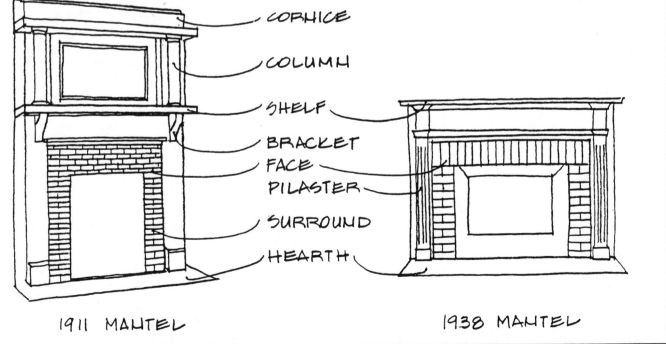

CORNICE
COLUMN
SHELF
BRACKET
FACE
PILASTER
SURROUND
HEARTH

1911 MANTEL

1938 MANTEL

Chimney Breasts The relationship between a fireplace, its mantel, and the walls of a room was often expressed by the presence of a *chimney breast*. The breast projected into the room as fireplace wall and formed the front portion of the chimney stack. The shape of the chimney breast usually was dictated by the style of the room or the style of the house, but applications were general rather than specific. Of the four types illustrated, the *sculptured,* or *stepped,* chimney breast was usually part of an artistic system or a Spanish bungalow type, and the *angled* breast, which tapered toward the top, was related to the English cottage or bungalow. The *wall-type* chimney breast extended just beyond the mantel, and the *rectangular* type was contained within the outside edges of the mantel. Regardless of shape, most chimney breasts were covered with plaster and finished like the walls.

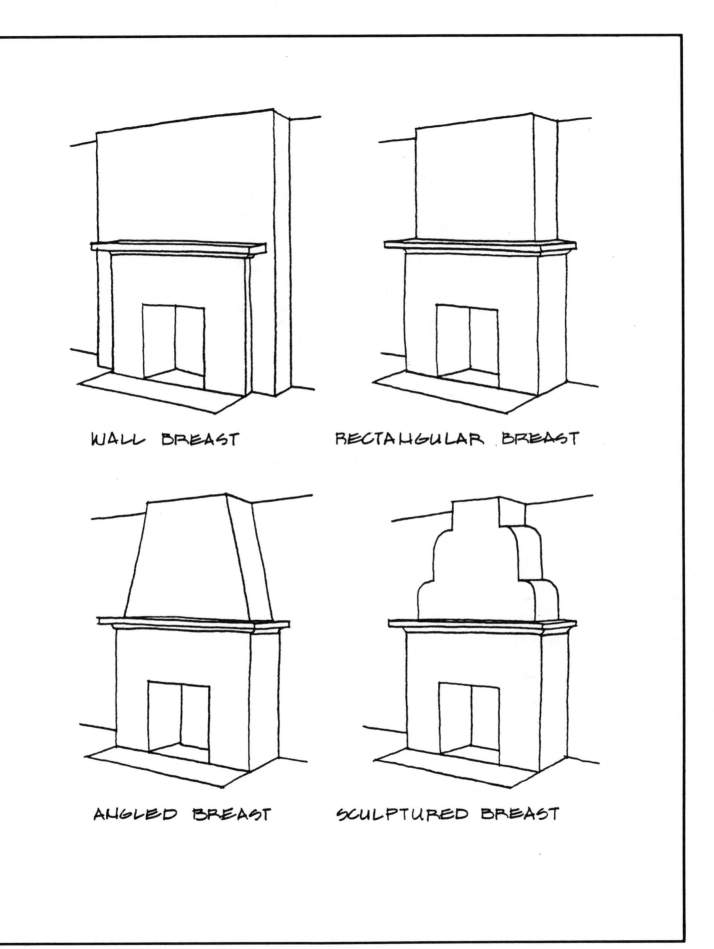

WALL BREAST

RECTANGULAR BREAST

ANGLED BREAST

SCULPTURED BREAST

Fittings   No chimneypiece design was complete without a set of *fittings,* the footnotes to the aesthetic statement of the fireplace. Fittings were part of both the closing and the enhancement of the fireplace opening. The size of the opening was determined by the size of the throat; a properly designed throat kept smoke from leaving the opening and entering the room. Each opening was lined with firebrick or cast-iron plates. When the fireplace was a key element in the heating system, it had a *grate* that held the burning fuel and contained the fire. Set or mounted grates were bolted into place, while *basket grates* were movable. Grates burned hard or soft coal and wood, and they were made of cast-iron plates, bolted together. A grate included at least one damper, perhaps an air chamber, and some method of ventilation to supply air for combustion. Because they were made of cast iron, the faces of grates were ornamental with floral or geometric patterns. When the fireplace was not in service, a *summer front,* a freestanding ornamented plate, closed off the opening. The final fitting was a metal *fender,* a railed guard that separated the hearth from the flooring and provided a footrest. If grates were unnecessary for heating, andirons, supports for logs, were integrated into the design scheme.

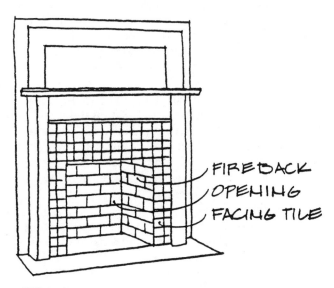

OPENING

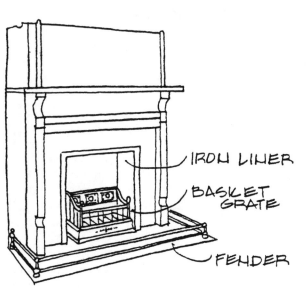

IRON LINER

BASKET GRATE

FENDER

PORTABLE BASKET GRATE

MOUNTED VENTILATING GRATE

BASKET GRATE

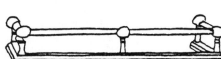

FENDER OR RAIL

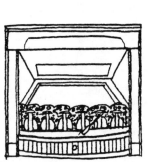

VENTILATING GRATE OPEN FOR USE

VENTILATING GRATE SUMMER FRONT

GRATE FOR ROUND-HEADED OPENING

Mantel Designs

Mantels in the ornamental tradition of the 1870s were designed in reaction to the visually and physically heavy marble, slate, and iron mantels of the revival architecture styles. The new style was referred to as *Queen Anne* (upper right) in publications like *Carpentry and Building,* and like everything else with that appellation, these mantels were elaborate compositions in wood characterized by high relief.

When an ornamental mantel is compared to a colonial type of the 1890s, the difference in aesthetics illustrates why the colonial lasted and the ornamental died out. *Colonial* designs of this period were decorative but the overall surface was much flatter than the ornamental, which helped the colonial to be perceived as something modern. And the rationale for elements and composition was clear. In the illustration here (middle row, left), the reeded pilasters terminate in a corner block yet they still relate to the architrave because of their surface pattern. The block's intrusion on the corner is minimal, the flow of the material is barely interrupted. In a modernized version of this mantel there will be no block and no shelf, just a continuous molding framing the facing brick.

Heavily ornamented work gave way to less stickwork and more surface figuration, less piling or layering and more charm. This kind of mantel (middle right) was especially suited to the last phase of the picturesque cottage designs of the last century. Mantels done in this manner were neither as high or as deep as earlier products. Indeed, a 1907 article on row houses described this type as a long oak cabinet mantel with columns and plain capitals.

The modern, artistic mantels emphasized a rugged, massive look that alluded to craftsmanship and historical designs. In fact, for quite a while they were more truly refined ornamental types, as seen in the Sears, Roebuck and Montgomery Ward pieces (lower left and right). In general there were fewer elements in each work. The columns were larger and the shelves thicker. Bold, clear, straight lines replaced curved and layered surfaces. Boldness was present in the older mantels but it was overshadowed by decoration. With less detailing, modern pieces could be integrated more easily into architectural furniture, such as inglenooks and bookcases. Furthermore, the modern mantel was thought of as one element in a design system that was, itself, part of a larger system.

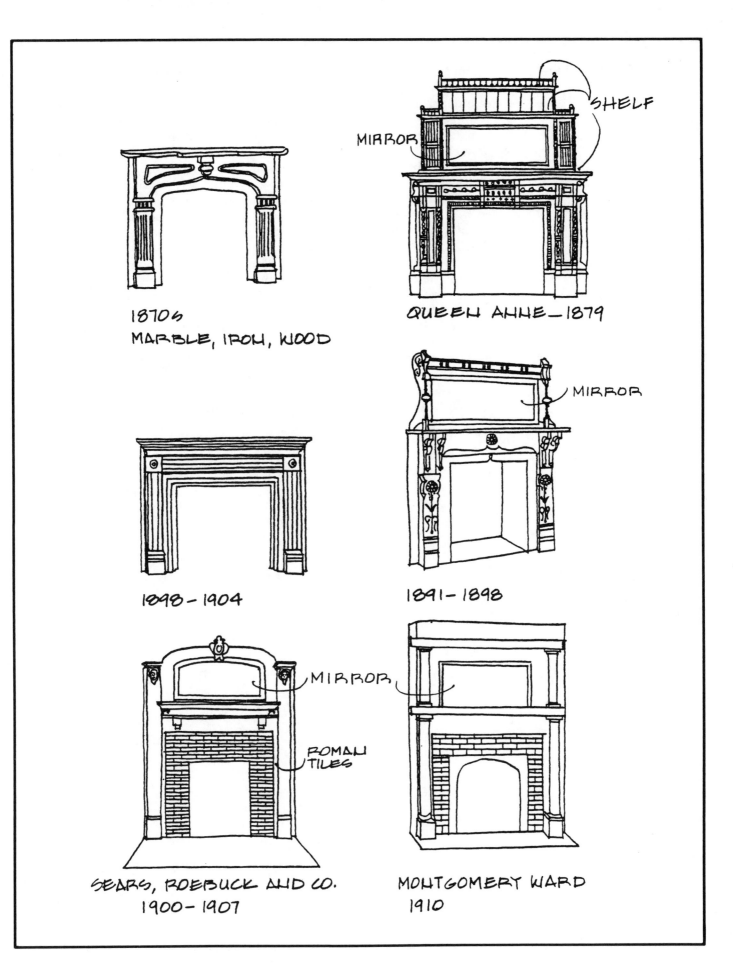

1870s
MARBLE, IRON, WOOD

QUEEN ANNE—1879

MIRROR

SHELF

1898-1904

1891-1898

MIRROR

SEARS, ROEBUCK AND CO.
1900-1907

MIRROR

ROMAN
TILES

MONTGOMERY WARD
1910

Mantel Designs

Mantels in the *Craftsman* or *Mission* style had two additional features that were important for vernacular interior design. Their horizontality related well to the opening of interior space—lowered ceilings and the feeling for vista—that was an important part of early-twentieth-century design. The second aspect was the integration of materials that made the mantels look artistic and unique: art glass, leaded glass, colored or hand-painted facing tiles, naturally finished wood. Any unusual texture, both physical and visual, could also be associated with artistic effects. For a while Sears, Roebuck addressed this concept by making an *all-brick* mantel with a decorative panel in the face. These were designed with rough or smooth faces, and used no other tile and no wood except for the mantel shelf.

Of all mantel types built from 1870 to 1940, *colonial* mantels with modest pilasters and an entablature, the cornice of which served as the mantel shelf, were the most popular. These units were painted with enamel and included brick-tile facing.

In the 1920s, the sentiment for cottage designs lingered. English Tudor cottages and English bungalows were intended to satisfy that part of the market, and they received an appropriate mantel—the *Tudor arch* type. Shaping openings had been a part of mantel design for some time, but in this period the shapes would be style-conscious. In this vein, a rough, stucco face with a brick edge would work for Spanish-inspired interiors.

BOOKCASE MANTEL — 1913-1926

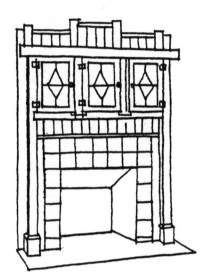

CRAFTSMAN OR MISSION
1911

SEARS ALL-BRICK
1923-1931

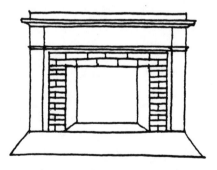

MODERN COLONIAL
1917-1940

ENGLISH
1930-1940

HARDWARE
Elements

By 1870 American hardware companies had all but eliminated their dependence on English products and were publishing their own thick catalogs of fittings and fastenings. Historically, hardware has had two classifications: *builders' hardware* and *finish hardware*. The former included a broad array of closers, latches, securing, hanging and operating devices, hinges, and lifts all treated in a few generic ways: japanned ware (with a hard, durable black finish); galvanized; or standard dull or bright finishes for bronze and brass. In contrast, the individual elements in a finish hardware set could be shaped or ornamented as a reference to an historic style. Finish work was thought of as part of the treatment of a room or a building. Over time the distinction between the two kinds of hardware blended into "builders' hardware," which encompassed everything.

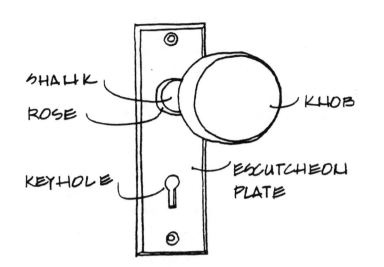

SHANK
ROSE
KEYHOLE
KHOB
ESCUTCHEON PLATE

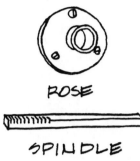

ROSE

SPINDLE

KHOB

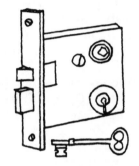

LOCKSET WITH KEY

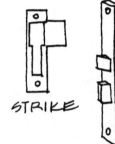

STRIKE

DETAIL OF LOCKSET

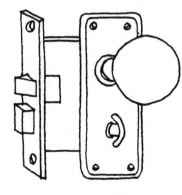

LOCKSET WITH
THUMB KHOB

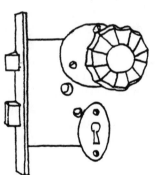

LOCKSET WITH
KEY PLATE

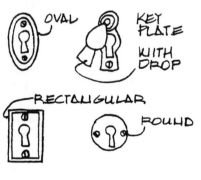

OVAL
KEY PLATE
WITH DROP
RECTANGULAR
ROUND

KEY PLATE
DESIGNS

139

Elements   Hardware finishes during the period 1870 through 1940 were diverse, but most products were made from cast or wrought metal. Wrought material was cheaper than cast and was available in brass, bronze, steel, and iron. Cast pieces were made of bronze, brass, and iron, although iron was much less significant than the others. Regardless of the base material, most hardware could receive any number of special finishes, such as:

copper plating on brass or steel
bronze or brass plating on iron or steel
nickel plating on brass
silver plating
gold plating
Bower-Barff

These finishes were not of equal value. For example, the uses of copper plating were limited because it wore off easily. Some finishes had preferred uses, say, bronze or brass finish on steel for kitchens, or plated hinges for interior doors, or, nickel plating on brass for bathrooms. The Bower-Barff process involved heating iron or steel in a special furnace until it was lustrous black.

Finish also included color. For example, brass might look its natural color, that is, with a yellowish cast either polished or dull. If it were plated brass, then the color range was extensive: verde antique (with shades of green), lemon brass, antique silver and gold surfaces, all either polished or dull. Bronze, which has a reddish cast, could be finished in different shades.

Builders' hardware went through different processing. It was rustproofed or given a base finish that could be plated. Typical finishes included dull, bright, dull with oxidized and relieved surfaces, hot galvanized, bright or matte black japanned, oil-rubbed, dull bronze, zinc, bright or dull chromium, bright or dull nickel, white bronze, and cadmium.

Hardware has always been a good indicator of design intentions, because the combinations of materials, finishes, and aesthetic inferences creates a rich design vocabulary. Hardware traditionally has been designed in sets, and a set could influence the overall design of a building in two ways: by the kind of operating principles with which the elements did their work, and by styling. Operating principles were important because certain locking or closing devices were associated with certain styles. The *thumblatch lock*, for example, was considered especially suitable for the front door of a colonial house. Similarly, there were ornamental motifs associated with certain styling concepts: the pinetree, crescent, lyre, clover, and heart-and-arrow motifs were at one time appropriate for colonial fittings. It was also true that, like most things in vernacular architecture, some elements could be associated with more than one style. A good example of this is the glass doorknob, which was sold as a colonial as well as a modern element.

Interior hardware falls into several functional categories. Most things fasten, lock, trim, hang, or pull something else. An interior door may have several kinds of functional hardware—hinges, a unit lock or spring latch, and a closing device—but in terms of aesthetics the design of the lock and its hardware is primary.

A lock system begins with a plain or ornamented *escutcheon plate* that has been adapted for attachment to the surface of a door and includes a knob socket and perhaps a keyhole. Historically, an escutcheon plate with both a keyhole and a knob socket is called a combined escutcheon plate. Knobs on either side of the door are attached to a *spindle,* a metal rod that passes through the door. By definition a *knob* is a projecting handle, usually round or spherical, for operating a lock or latch. The knob's spindle is covered by a *shank* or *collar* that connects the knob to the socket. The socket is surrounded by a *rose.* Some hardware sets employ a rose in lieu of an escutcheon plate. Most roses are circular, but square, rectangular, oblong, and hexagonal roses were produced as well.

A *lock* is a fastening of any kind operated by a key and distinguished from a latch bolt. A *lockset* consists of a lock, its trim, and a locking mechanism. Such mechanisms are of two kinds: rim locks, which are attached to the surface of the door: and locks that are mortised or built in to the door. A *strike* is the plate on the jamb that receives the bolt. A typical lock measures 3½ inches to 4½ inches, with an escutcheon 7 to 10 inches long and 2 ½ inches wide, and a knob of 2¼ inches in diameter. The size of the escutcheon is related to the size of the lock.

A lockset with a *thumb knob* has a second bolt that is extended when the knob is turned. This lock has been a popular choice for bathroom hardware. A lockset may also be designed in two parts with the keyhole mounted by itself, just below the rose. Individual *key plates* are shaped and finished according to the design system of the hardware. The 1926 Yale and Towne catalog lists twenty-four key plates, ten of them with drops that swing over the key hole.

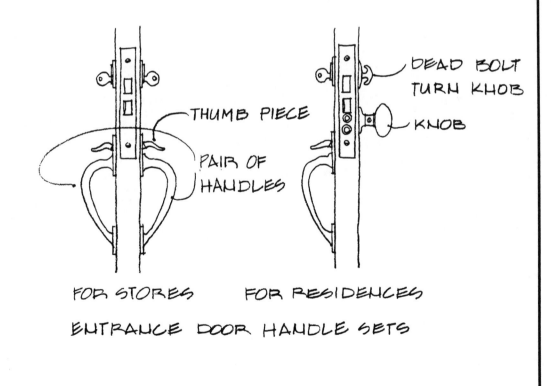

THUMB PIECE

PAIR OF HANDLES

DEAD BOLT TURN KNOB

KNOB

FOR STORES   FOR RESIDENCES

ENTRANCE DOOR HANDLE SETS

Butt and Hinge Hardware

A *butt* is a type of hinge with three parts: a leaf with holes for screws, a loose pin (it may be taken out), and a barrel or knuckle. The two leafs are brought together by the pin. These jointed plates attach one plate to the door and one to the frame, whereby the door is supported and enabled to swing. When the door is shut, the two halves of the hinge come together. A loose pin hinge also allows the door to be unhung easily. The surface of the leaf may be ornamented, especially in cast butt hinges. Interior doors usually have two butts per door, but glass doors may require three. The number of knuckles on a hinge varies too, but five is common.

Ball-bearing butt hinges use steel ball bearings between the knuckles to prevent wear and to ensure quiet operation. At one time a *mortised hinge* was referred to as an "invisible" hinge, because it was concealed from view. A *half-mortised hinge* has one plate mortised in the door and the other on the surface of the frame. *Spring* hinges are mortised to the frame and door. The barrel contains a tempered steel spring. Spring hinges are single or double action, with a tempered steel spring in the barrel, and their normal position is closed.

Swinging doors, of single or double action, are operated by *spring pivots* arranged on the vertical or the horizontal, or mortised into the floor. Some doors can be made to stand open at any angle by a foot pedal. Horizontal types are attached to the floor with a plate. A *fast joint* hinge has a pin fastened in place. Small hinges such as those for cupboards are often fast types.

A *surface hinge* is secured to the adjacent sides of a door and its frame so that the face of the hinge is visible. Consequently, surface hinges are often ornamented: the spread wing pattern is very common. Other kinds have scallops around the edges or ribs across the face.

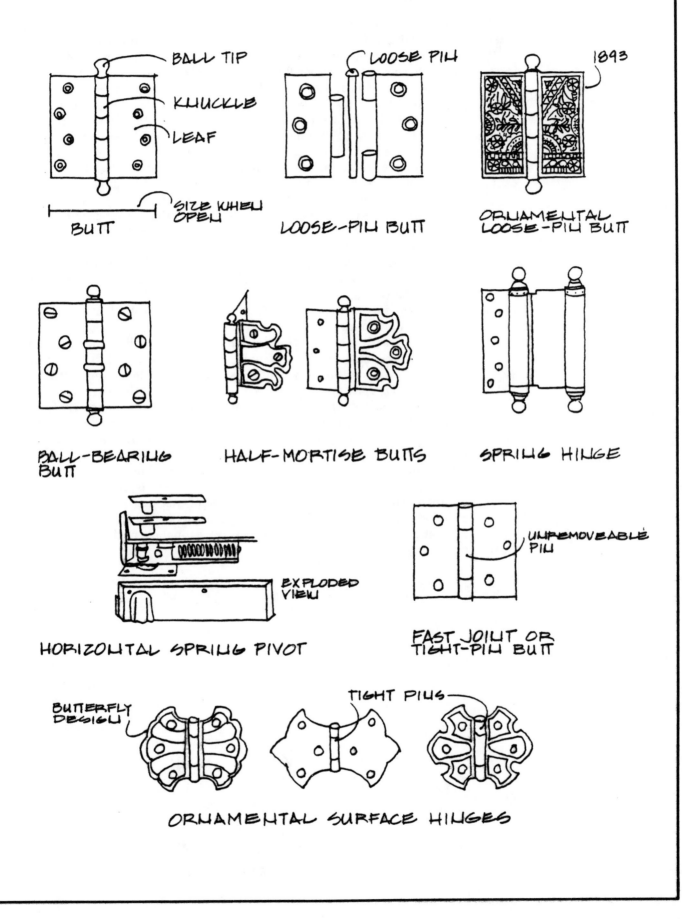

BALL TIP

KNUCKLE

LEAF

SIZE WHEN OPEN

BUTT

LOOSE PIN

LOOSE-PIN BUTT

1893

ORNAMENTAL
LOOSE-PIN BUTT

BALL-BEARING
BUTT

HALF-MORTISE BUTTS

SPRING HINGE

EXPLODED
VIEW

HORIZONTAL SPRING PIVOT

UNREMOVEABLE
PIN

FAST JOINT OR
TIGHT-PIN BUTT

BUTTERFLY
DESIGN

TIGHT PINS

ORNAMENTAL SURFACE HINGES

Window and Door Hardware

Window finish includes fasteners to keep the window tight against the stops and lifts for raising and lowering sash. Mounted on the meeting rail, a *fastener* for hung windows has two parts, one on each rail. When joined they hold the sash together. Fasteners for both hung and casement windows are latch types, with a movable bar falling into a catch. Window *lifts* are projecting bars or hooks that provide leverage for opening and closing the window. Flush lifts are cup-like fingerholds set into the sash frame with the face flush with the frame. All of these finish items were part of a design set, integrated by material, color, and pattern.

Push plates are fittings for swinging doors, designed to protect the door's finish. They are made of metal—solid brass, copper plating over steel, stamped steel, cast bronze, and glass—with beveled or slightly ornamented edges. The plates are attached with screws, and the screws themselves may have a special finish, such as nickel-plated screws in a glass plate.

A related piece of trim is the metal *kick plate* mounted over the bottom rail to protect the door's finish. These plates were designed to augment the visual properties of a design set, and usually were finished with the same color as the rest of the set.

There are several types of surface-mounted door bolts featuring a barrel or bolt and a rim strike. *Chain bolts* stay locked and are placed at the top of the door, with a chain attached for pulling the bolt against the spring that holds the bolt in place. A plain *door bolt* has a sliding bar or rod attached to a door that locks into a strike on the door jamb. Other bolts include a *foot bolt,* operated by foot and placed at the bottom of a door, and a *cremone bolt* that extends from the lock to the floor and from the lock to the ceiling, and is operated by a lever. Cremone bolts are used especially for securing French doors. A *cane bolt* is a heavy cane-shaped bolt in which the head is at a right angle to the rest. It is applied to the top or bottom of a door, and it, like the cremone, has a set of guides.

A *door stop* may be attached to a baseboard or to the bottom of a door to protect the wall. Stops have been made of cast metal, turned wood, and coiled steel, and any of them may have a rubber bumper on the end.

Sliding doors have their own trim sets consisting of a pull, a cup escutcheon, and a key.

CREMONE BOLT
FOR FRENCH DOORS

SASH FASTENER

BAR SASH LIFT

SASH FASTENER

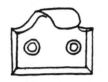

HOOK SASH LIFT

CASEMENT SASH FASTENER

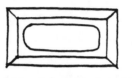

FLUSH SASH LIFT

FLUSH SASH LIFT

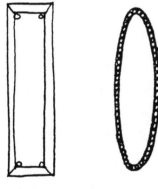

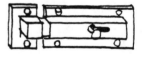

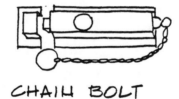

PUSH PLATES

CHAIN BOLT

DOOR BOLT

STEEL   BUMPER

WOOD

BASE KNOBS

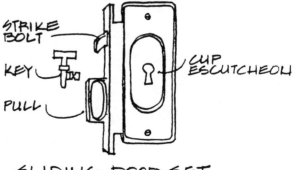

STRIKE BOLT

KEY

PULL

CUP ESCUTCHEON

SLIDING DOOR SET

Other Finish Hardware

Kitchens and pantries have trim sets consisting of hinges, catches, and pulls. The standard kitchen or pantry cupboard has a *spring catch* operated by a thumbpiece (T-handle) or a porcelain slide knob. To close a door, a *cupboard turn* requires a hand operation to change the position of the turn, but the *cupboard catch* closes by itself. Segmented, drop, and bar-shaped *drawer pulls* usually were made from wrought steel, although more expensive cast work was available.

Clothing *hooks* generally are cast pieces, but inexpensive wire hooks with screw threads were also popular. Cast hooks came in different arrangements and sizes of hooks, and models with two or more hooks were sized for different garments—small for a coat, and large for a hat.

Drawer knobs are miniature door knobs with a wood screw or a small bolt with a nut substituted for a spindle. The materials are also similar in that pressed glass, wood, and ceramic knobs were used for drawer pieces. Whatever the material, drawer knobs were selected in sets with a finish and a shape that supplemented the system's styling.

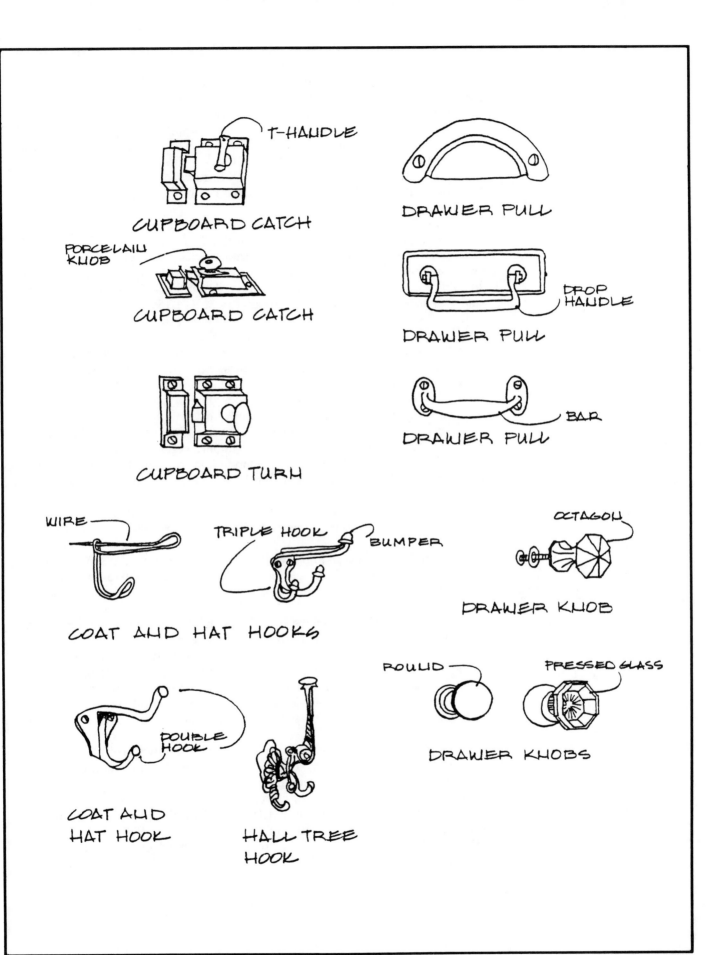

CUPBOARD CATCH

T-HANDLE

DRAWER PULL

PORCELAIN KNOB

CUPBOARD CATCH

DROP HANDLE

DRAWER PULL

CUPBOARD TURN

BAR

DRAWER PULL

WIRE

TRIPLE HOOK

BUMPER

OCTAGON

COAT AND HAT HOOKS

DRAWER KNOB

DOUBLE HOOK

ROUND

PRESSED GLASS

COAT AND HAT HOOK

HALL TREE HOOK

DRAWER KNOBS

Knobs A *knob* is a projecting handle, generally round or spherical in shape, for operating a lock. The assortment of shapes and designs on the facing page has been selected from a broad inventory. These knobs are typical of products for the entire period, and their designs are applicable to at least one of the major design systems—ornamental, colonial, classical, and artistic. The type of lock system being used on a door—whether it was a rim lock (decorated rim locks were called "French hardware") or mortise lock—and the aesthetic of the interior system indicated the kind of knob that would be appropriate.

To illustrate the range of knob design, we turn to an 1865 Russell and Erwin Company catalog. The company offered rim locks with mineral knobs with japanned mountings, porcelain knobs with hand-plated shanks and roses, silvered glass knobs, and other knobs of mineral and porcelain decorated in gold or porcelain knobs decorated in gold and flowers. Russell and Erwin had five sizes of knob, but throughout the period 1870–1940 the 2¼-inch-diameter knob became the standard size. The length of the shank generally was comparable to the diameter of the knob.

Metal knobs were the most popular, probably because they offered great variety in detailing and color, but glass, mineral, and wood knobs also were widely used. Wood and pottery knobs were less expensive than the others. Wood knobs were made of oak, mahogany, maple, gum, or birch, and were finished with varnish or stain and varnish. Pressed-glass knobs had faceted faces to make them look like cut glass. By 1930 glass knobs were available in colors—blue, green, amber, yellow, gold, and opal.

Pottery knobs were done in three colors: plain mineral (brown), jet (black), and porcelain (white). After 1915 pottery knobs were not used except for basements or attics. Knobs were made also from cast iron, the better ones covered with Bower-Barff finish. Both iron and composition knobs—the latter an aggregate material veneered with brass or bronze—were inexpensive items.

For a business or a club knobs could be personalized by applying emblems to the face of the knob. Yale and Towne Company, in 1926, offered a range of stock emblematic knobs and also provided design service to make an original pattern.

Cast bronze and brass knobs have been the quality goods of vernacular interior design. Solid knobs were the most expensive type, but they were more durable. Seamless wrought knobs, of thick material, were also good products. The seamless knob looks solid but it is really two halves of wrought steel put together and brazed. As was the case in flooring material, there is some evidence that vernacular buildings could have two sets of hardware: cast work for the main floor and hollow knobs for the other floors.

Ornamented hexagonal knobs were manufactured by Corbin; Russell and Erwin; and Malory, Wheeler and Co. in the 1870s. The hexagon illustrated was made in the 1910s by companies such as Sargent and Gordon-Van Tine as part of the artistic aesthetic.

Oval knobs with an ornamented face were produced by Corbin and by Russell and Erwin at the turn of the century. By 1900 Sears sold the "Emerald" design set which had an unornamented oval face framed by beads. Yale sold similar oval knobs as part of a colonial design set through 1926.

While round and spherical knobs were the most prevalent forms, levers and store door handles were other important types. The lever was an item of residential hardware, while the bent handle—usually mounted on a plate and provided with a lever or thumb piece for actuating a latch bolt, and applied to both the exterior and the interior—was both a residential and a commercial item.

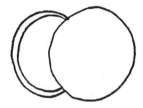

SPHEROID

PORCELAIN
JET
MINERAL
BRONZE

FLAT

ORNAMENTAL
BRONZE

CONVEX FACE
WITH A MOTIF

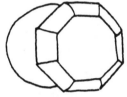

OCTAGON

PRESSED
GLASS

FACETED

PRESSED
GLASS

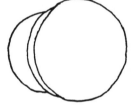

OCTAGON

CUT GLASS

CONVEX FACE

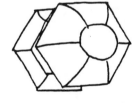

HEXAGON

SQUARE

OVAL

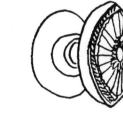

POINTED OVAL

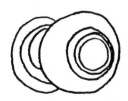

BUTTON

RING

BEVELED
RING

LEVER HANDLE

149

Hardware Sets

Hardware—like lighting, bathroom fixtures, and millwork trim—was sold in sets. A set of hardware consisted of a complete assortment of fittings for doors, drawers, windows, and hooks. Each piece was shaped and/or ornamented with the same pattern or imagery, but the application of the pattern was adapted to the shape of the piece. Each set had its own finish— polished, blackened, matte, hammered, or other. In the Sears hardware set entitled "Mayfair," the butt hinge has a plain border around each leaf, but other elements either have no border or have a different kind of border. For example, the outer edge of the cupboard catch and cupboard turn each have a different border. The sash fastener and the drawer have no border at all. By distinguishing ever so slightly among the elements, each one becomes identified with its function, so much so that the hardware installation has systems of order built into it.

The Sears 1897 catalog does not offer sets of hardware with a common pattern for all parts and a trade-name identity. But by 1900 the company was selling sets for front door locks, with "ornamented electro copper plated trimmings." There were also "genuine" bronze sets that included two knobs with escutcheons, a unit lock, and a key plate. All the other pieces had their own design. It is hard to pinpoint the year when a "hardware set" was expanded by definition. A 6-inch chain bolt with an "Ornamental Electro Plated" finish was advertised in the 1902 Sears catalog as No. 9R1303. That same chain bolt, in the same size and with the identical pattern and a "Bronze plated finish," was advertised in the 1907 catalog as Mayfair Design Chain Bolt, No. 9047408. In five years the unit price had gone up five cents. The practice of identifying products by a number and then changing to a style name or trade name was repeated by Sears for most of its products, including its mail-order houses.

FRONT DOOR
LOCKSET

INSIDE DOOR
LOCKSET

DOOR BELL

BUTT

SASH FASTENER

CUPBOARD TURN

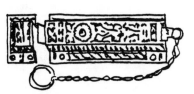

DRAWER PULL

CHAIN BOLT

PUSH PLATE

CUPBOARD CATCH

CUP ESCUTCHEON

HAT AND
COAT HOOK

Hardware Sets

From the literature of the period and from extant hardware, it seems that there were some sets whose primary design characteristic was repeated so often that it became traditional. In their imagery and textures, these sets usually refer to historical sources. In terms of placement, the distinguishing pattern is most likely to show on the face of the knob and on the escutcheon plate. Given its circular form, the knob carries its motif in a pattern that radiates from the center or circumscribes the outside edge. These hardware sets were manufactured under trade names, and we have grouped them by generic design characteristics.

The escutcheon plate has more design possibilities, given its flat surface and size. Plates commonly are composed so that the ornament is the endpiece; the motif becomes a figure against the ground of the door's stile. The figure thus is isolated against a color, usually darker than the plate, and against a grain pattern. The designs are borrowed from historical patterns, including even masonry and millwork, and the contrast between figure and ground is very distinct. Secondly, the outer edge of a plate may be ornamented with patterns comparable to raised moldings or beads. Thirdly, the escutcheon plate may have a distinctive shape, and the shape may be the equivalent of an ornamental motif. Then again, another bit of ornament may be expressed within the uniqueness of the shape.

Egg-and-dart decoration is a molding pattern applied to hardware. Historically, it is a classical pattern, sometimes identified by manufacturers of vernacular materials as of the Greek school. We found it produced from 1887 to 1926, but not always in the same manner. Plain designs are characterized by beveled escutcheon plates, curved or square corners, and no surface ornamentation. Plain sets often were made of wrought metal and included a spherical or flattened knob. Plain sets appeared in the trade literature from 1900 to 1935, categorized as both modern and colonial, and they were used extensively in bungalows.

The *oval* plate and knob motif was advertised as early as 1900. The pattern is characterized by its shape and the treatment of the edge—a bead or raised rim. There is also an understated oval with no surface work but a gently rounded edge. Sears, Sargent, and Yale had similar patterns through the 1920s.

Hexagonal motifs are identified with Craftsman styles of design. The geometrical shape of the plate, with its wide bevel, and the visually heavy design of the knob—with sharp edges between the facets—all this gives the set a massive and rustic look. We illustrate two versions of this motif, a beveled model and a stepped profile with straight rectilinear ends.

As a design motif, the *sculptured* plate has shaped ends and sides. An edge is raised continuously around the plate, moving in and out, widening along the middle section and scalloping the ends. This concave-convex elongated pattern is associated with colonial styling. Variations on it include a narrowing of the sides rather than a fattening, and an end profile that creates "ears" on the corners. The pattern seems to have been less popular than others. It appeared in trade catalogs from 1911 to 1926.

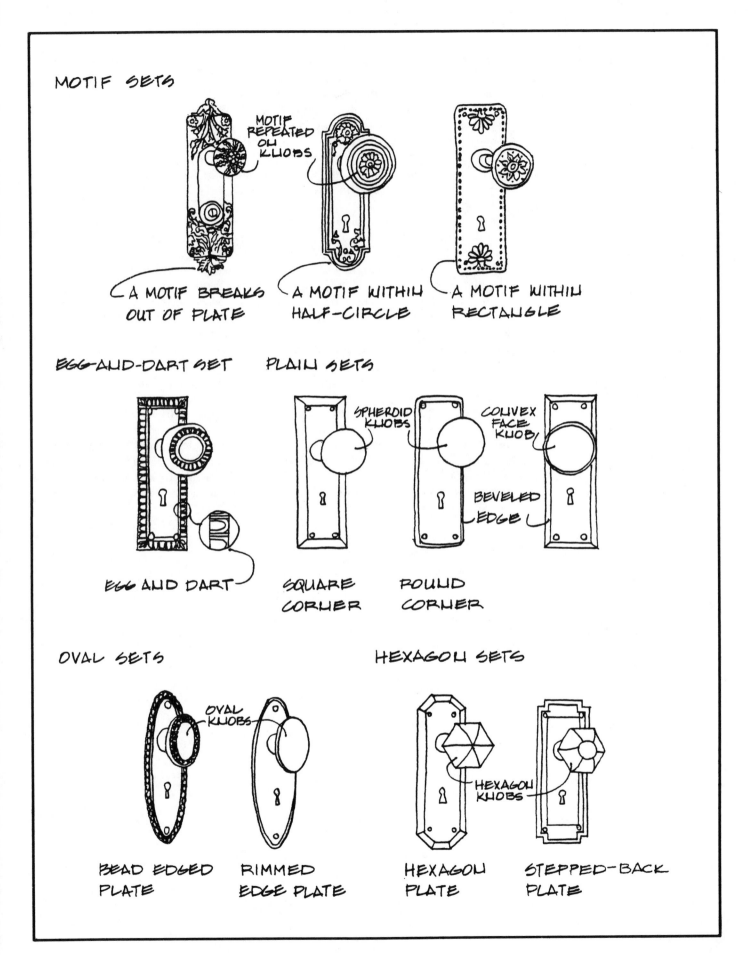

MOTIF SETS

MOTIF REPEATED ON KNOBS

A MOTIF BREAKS OUT OF PLATE

A MOTIF WITHIN HALF-CIRCLE

A MOTIF WITHIN RECTANGLE

EGG-AND-DART SET

EGG AND DART

PLAIN SETS

SPHEROID KNOBS

CONVEX FACE KNOB

BEVELED EDGE

SQUARE CORNER

ROUND CORNER

OVAL SETS

OVAL KNOBS

BEAD EDGED PLATE

RIMMED EDGE PLATE

HEXAGON SETS

HEXAGON KNOBS

HEXAGON PLATE

STEPPED-BACK PLATE

Hardware Sets

Beveled plates, on the other hand, were a constant design until the 1930s. In these the design is built upon one or more bevels. The ends might be square, gradually rounded, curved in a segment of a circle, or half-round. Knobs in this set often are designed with multiple rings. The plates are deeply modeled so that shadows are cast between the raised borders. In some designs, the space between the raised elements looks like a sunken molding, a device used to counteract the perceived severity of modern motifs. Beveled hardware has also been thought of as solid and weighty, a quality suggested by the bevel itself as it reveals the thickness of the plate.

Modern motifs have relied on shaped plates. Referred to as "modern" by manufacturers, these have at least two basic patterns: a free-form and a stepped edge. Usually the free-form owes something to the influence of the high-style Moderne design. The free-form is abstracted from these historical models, which in turn were adaptations of classical forms and patterns. This kind of plate looks carved so that the shaping becomes the motif. Some free-form designs reverse the proportional relationship between the knob and the escutcheon. Whereas in most hardware sets the diameter of the knob is the same or less than the width of the plate, such free-form pieces carry a knob larger than the plate, which tends to emphasize the plate's sculptural appearance. Knobs in these sets are made of metal or pressed glass.

The other modern pattern is a stepped-edge plate, in which the outline of the ends imitates the setbacks of high-rise buildings. This motif is also Moderne in spirit, and progressive. A Lockwood design in 1935 was manufactured with colored plastic knobs. The face of the plate is sometimes built up with pilaster strips overlapping each other from the outer edge toward the middle. The knob of both the free-form and stepped motif sets is usually a multiple concentric ring design.

SCULPTURED COLONIAL SETS

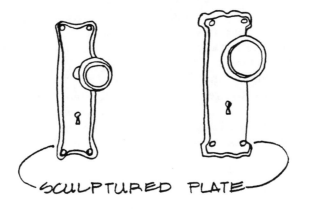

SCULPTURED PLATE

BEVELED COLONIAL SETS

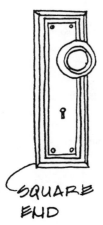 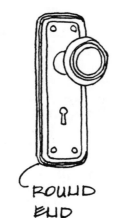 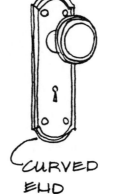 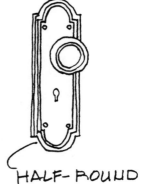

SQUARE END   ROUND END   CURVED END   HALF-ROUND END

MODERN SETS

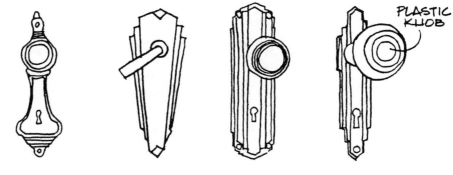

PLASTIC KNOB

FREE-FORM PLATES   STEPPED-BACK PLATES

ORNAMENTAL MOTIFS Types and Elements

Regardless of the time period or the status of certain styling ideas or the materials by which they were conveyed, interior surfaces were susceptible to ornamentation. In this section we shall look at the traditional motifs employed in decorating design elements. Many of these motifs were executed in several mediums and applied to more than one style. Most were done in wood, plaster, and glass. Millwork companies sold wood and composition ornaments in trade catalogs, and companies like Decorative Supply in Chicago made it their exclusive business. What follows, then, are illustrations of these motifs and definitions for each one.

To create an overview of the nature of ornamentation available, we have grouped the prevailing motifs with design elements to suggest the range of applications. Listed under each element are motifs that could have been used at one time period. The source is a 1904 edition of a Universal millwork catalog.

Element	Motif	Element	Motif
cottage door	festoon, scroll, panel rosette, wreath, ribbon, fleur-de-lis	mantel	panel, rosette, wreath
		overmantel	drop, wreath
stair string	oval rosette	grate outfit	figure, vase, shells, ribbon, wreath, festoon with torch, figure on pilaster
window cap trim	festoon, wreath, leaf		
pew ends	shield, quatrefoil	parquet borders	fret, rope mold
stair newel	drop, egg/dart, rosette, wreath, leaf	window glass	ellipse, scroll, circle, diamond, leaf, ribbon, festoon, shield, fleur-de-lis, rosette

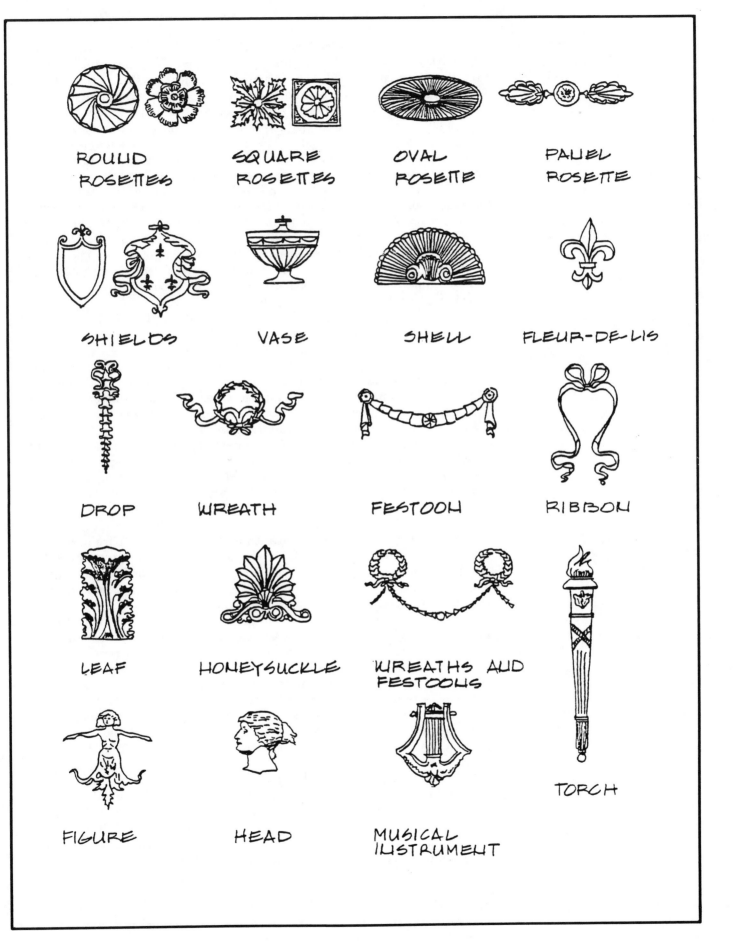

ROUND
ROSETTES

SQUARE
ROSETTES

OVAL
ROSETTE

PANEL
ROSETTE

SHIELDS

VASE

SHELL

FLEUR-DE-LIS

DROP

WREATH

FESTOON

RIBBON

LEAF

HONEYSUCKLE

WREATHS AND
FESTOONS

TORCH

FIGURE

HEAD

MUSICAL
INSTRUMENT

Types and Elements

To illustrate by example, the first element in the chart, cottage door, refers to the inside surface only, and the list following that heading suggests that this door could have been ornamented with any of these motifs— festoon, scroll, panel rosette, and so on—perhaps even with more than one motif. If a glass panel had been substituted for the upper half of the door, it is likely that yet another motif would appear there. The time period in which this catalog was issued was a transitional one, which explains the wide variety of motifs available. Many motifs were relevant to the ornamental system of interior design and a good number would fall out of favor as the new, artistic system gained ground. All of these decorative items were conventionalized images by this time, and yet the delineation of a specific motif was not standardized. Both motifs and the basic form would change over time. For instance, rosettes did not all look alike nor were all used in the same way. On a related note, some motifs would disappear from some elements. At the turn of the century, frets, wreaths, garlands, and so forth could be found as transfer designs on bathroom fixtures, but early in this century that practice stopped.

A *rosette* is a carved, molded, or turned floral motif formed by a series of leaves or petals around a central point. Rosettes were made in a range of shapes and sizes, from small circles to panels.

A *shield* is a curved scroll or tablet with elaborate borders, sometimes adorned with heraldic or other symbolic imagery. The *vase* is a rendering of classical ceramic ware, taller than it is wide. A *shell* is a conventionalized seashell, usually convex with a fluted or scalloped edge. A *fleur-de-lis* is a lily or iris simplified to stand alone or in groups.

The ornaments in the third row are linear. The *drop* is a small cylinder, a truncated cone or stem that terminates the bottom of a post or stands alone on a panel. A *wreath* is a garland in a circular form, often with ribbon streaming from the bottom. The *festoon* is another garland, this time of fruit, leaves, or flowers suspended on both ends. *Ribbonwork* is straightforward imitation of a woven strip of material.

Most solitary *leaf* forms are acanthus leaves, borrowed from classical ornamentation for their expressive character and their spiny or toothed outlines. *Honeysuckle* is also a classical motif valued for its symmetrical, shield-like design. Wreaths and festoons are key elements in *looped ornament* that usually appears as running decoration.

Figures seem to endure as ornament despite unawareness of the mythology and allegory with which they are associated. As with leaves, most sources for them are classical. *Musical instruments* are symbols of love, the *torch*, a symbol of life—without fire there is no life. Specific meanings for these symbols may differ from culture to culture, however.

Fretwork is interlaced openwork, composed in a band, as a meandering strip pattern. *Guilloche* is an ornamental strip of twisted, curvilinear bands that create circular openings between the bands. *Rope* is another twisted pattern; it is usually a molding and it gets its appearance from the strands of cord it imitates.

A *scroll* is a carved or molded spiral ornament with a continuous run of arcs or loops. A *wave* is also a stylized continuous ornament of linked scrolls or convex and concave curves. *Egg-and-dart* is another molding that consists of an ovoid shape between dart-like points; it is used in band form, as is the *ovum*, another run of engaged egg shapes. *Lamb's tongue* has a deep symmetrical profile ending in a narrow edge.

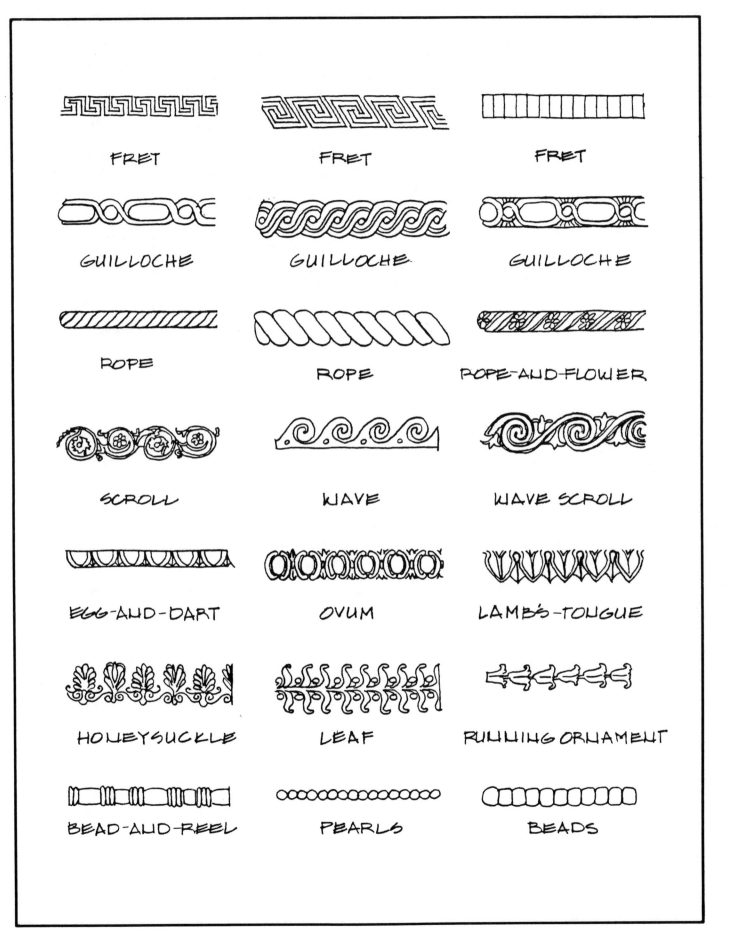

FRET FRET FRET

GUILLOCHE GUILLOCHE GUILLOCHE

ROPE ROPE ROPE-AND-FLOWER

SCROLL WAVE WAVE SCROLL

EGG-AND-DART OVUM LAMB'S-TONGUE

HONEYSUCKLE LEAF RUNNING ORNAMENT

BEAD-AND-REEL PEARLS BEADS

Types and Elements

Floral shapes, no matter how stylized, frequently serve as running ornaments, because of the delicacy of their edges or the clear outline of their forms. *Bead-and-reel* composition is a standard molding pattern with a convex profile of elongated beads alternating with disks set on edge. *Pearls* and *beads,* as strands or strings, are comparable patterns; they both imitate historical subjects and usually appear in conjunction with other shapes and moldings.

The *trefoil, quatrefoil,* and *cinquefoil* are all lobed or leaf forms divided by cusps of a circle. They have three, four, and five foils, respectively.

TREFOIL   QUATREFOIL   CINQUEFOIL

SUPPORT SYSTEMS

HEATING AND VENTILATION SYSTEMS
Types

The history of heating and ventilating in vernacular interior architecture reflects the general historic development of building technology—including new devices and new fuels—that characterizes all sectors of American architecture. During the period under study, principal heating fuels were wood, both hard and soft coal, coke, corn cobs, oil, natural gas, and electricity. Heating systems included fireplaces (some with inserted hearth or mantel furnaces), stoves, hot-air furnaces, low- and high-pressure hot water, and low- and high-pressure steam. The impact of these systems on interior design centered on the presence of grates, pipes, registers, and radiators. Many of the elements of these systems received surface ornamentation—usually a pattern—and color. The latter was applied as enamel, bronze or gold finishes, electroplating, and leaf plating. In the case of radiators, the shape and profile of the radiator as well as its placement also had an effect on interior arrangements.

Warm-Air Furnaces

The most popular space-heating systems of the 1870s were warm-air furnaces and steam. *Warm-air* systems were the cheapest. They required a centrally located heat source—usually a basement furnace, although fireplaces and room furnaces could serve the purpose. The systems relied on convection to distribute warm air and to exchange foul air for fresh. They either heated the air already present in a room or passed warmed air through the room. A typical basement warm-air furnace, as illustrated, was constructed of three parts: a fire pot, a radiator, and a casing. The radiator was located just above the fire pot and hot gases passed through the radiator, thereby heating it, on their way to the chimney. Connected with the radiator was a drum, or plenum, consisting of thin sheets of steel or cast iron, and, if required, numerous pipes leading to various rooms in the building. Some systems also included pipes that returned air from the room to the furnace. As warm air traveled upward it was often mixed with fresh air to effect air exchange.

Basement warm-air furnaces were of two types. The *set furnace* was enclosed by brick walls with a door to allow tending the furnace and a covering of some material that protected the floor joists above. The *portable furnace* was enclosed in a galvanized iron jacket and often set in a pit that was bricked around and bottomed with cement. Warm-air furnaces that relied exclusively on convection were inefficient, in that much heated air was lost to the outside grates and the distribution of heat was unequal. Moreover, they leaked combustion gases.

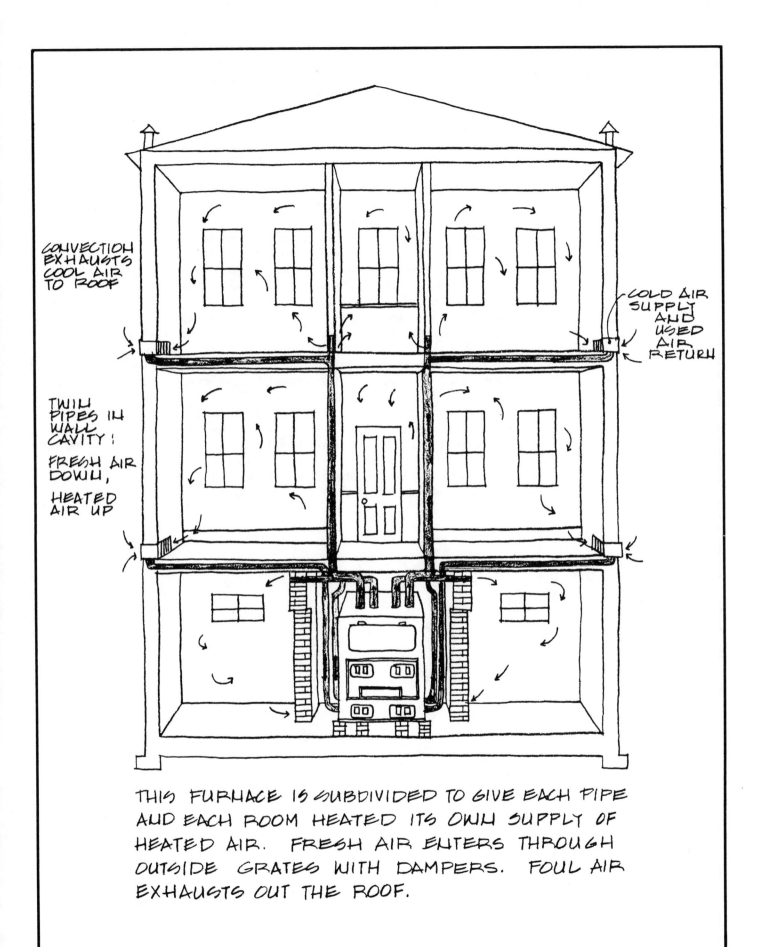

CONVECTION
EXHAUSTS
COOL AIR
TO ROOF

COLD AIR
SUPPLY
AND
USED
AIR
RETURN

TWIN
PIPES IN
WALL
CAVITY:

FRESH AIR
DOWN,

HEATED
AIR UP

THIS FURNACE IS SUBDIVIDED TO GIVE EACH PIPE
AND EACH ROOM HEATED ITS OWN SUPPLY OF
HEATED AIR.   FRESH AIR ENTERS THROUGH
OUTSIDE GRATES WITH DAMPERS.   FOUL AIR
EXHAUSTS OUT THE ROOF.

Fireplace Heating

Fireplace heating was also ineffective, but it had strong emotional appeal and has remained a part of heating to this day. The simplest fireplace system heated one room by radiation and the success of the unit depended on its drafting capability, which often was tied to the design of the fireplace throat. Most fireplaces of the last century were capable of heating more than one room, by drawing air from the room in which they were located as well as from outside and passing that air behind the firebrick to a pipe that carried the heated air to a register on the next floor. Registers were designed to stop the upward flow of air so that it would enter one room only, or to take some air and allow the rest to pass to another floor or to a second register that warmed an adjacent room.

A more sophisticated fireplace system removed the fire basket and fender and inserted a *set grate* or *mantel heater,* which produced more heat than the traditional fireplace. The design of these units was generally the same, although there were variations on how to get cold air to pass around the firepot. The pots were made of iron as were the reflective back plates. A fire clay brick lining and a series of chambers at the back and along the sides of the pot and one or two dampers, to control the fire, completed the structure. Since grates were made of cast materials, they had surface embellishments that included references to architectural ornamentation and unusual patterns for the ventilator slots. As these heaters accommodated the design values of this century, they lost ornamentation in favor of neat, plain compositions. Mantel heaters usually included a *summer front* or ornamental panel, first of iron and later of steel. These were inserted in the grate opening when the unit was not in use. Two inexpensive types of grates were the electric heater and the gas heater, complete with bulbs to simulate the red glow of burning coal or logs.

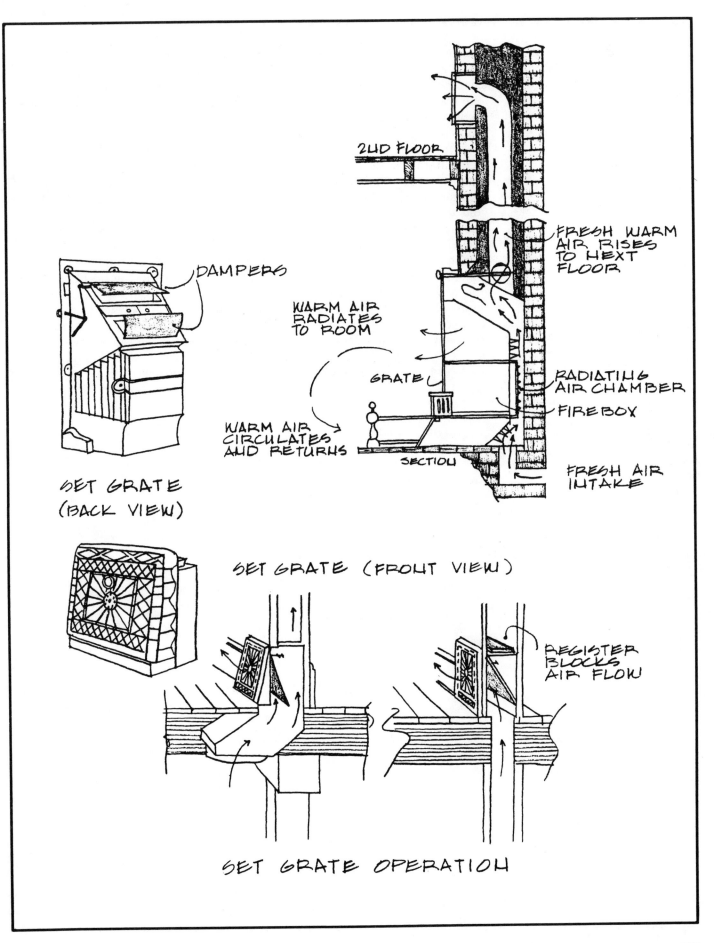

DAMPERS

SET GRATE
(BACK VIEW)

2ND FLOOR

FRESH WARM
AIR RISES
TO NEXT
FLOOR

WARM AIR
RADIATES
TO ROOM

GRATE

RADIATING
AIR CHAMBER

FIREBOX

WARM AIR
CIRCULATES
AND RETURNS

SECTION

FRESH AIR
INTAKE

SET GRATE (FRONT VIEW)

REGISTER
BLOCKS
AIR FLOW

SET GRATE OPERATION

Other Warm-Air Furnaces

Parlor furnaces were smaller versions of the portable warm-air furnace. They were sculptural in shape and took on the look of furniture. They were centrally located and used their own chimney or a fireplace chimney to exhaust gases. As simple space heaters, parlor furnaces used convection to draw cooler air off the floor into the furnace. The overall design of these units varied, but in principal they had a three-part organization. At the bottom was a raised base on legs that contained an ash drawer and the ventilators. The fire chamber, the middle and largest portion of the heater, had a cast-iron grate. The unit was completed by what was sometimes a distinctive top. The heater was wrapped in steel—sometimes polished—and trimmed with a deflector ring, side wings, drafts for the fire, and in some models an urn on the swing top. For a while, these trim pieces were nickel plated.

The basement *pipeless furnace* was safer than earlier models. It had increased capacity and drew cold air from the rooms in the building, from the basement, or from both. It burned hard or soft coal, wood, coke, and later oil. In operation, cold air passed around the fire pot, up through the furnace to a large register (made in various shapes) in the first floor, usually between the living room and the dining room in a house. Hallways and staircases helped to carry the warm air through the building, and ceiling registers allowed the warm air to pass into second-floor rooms.

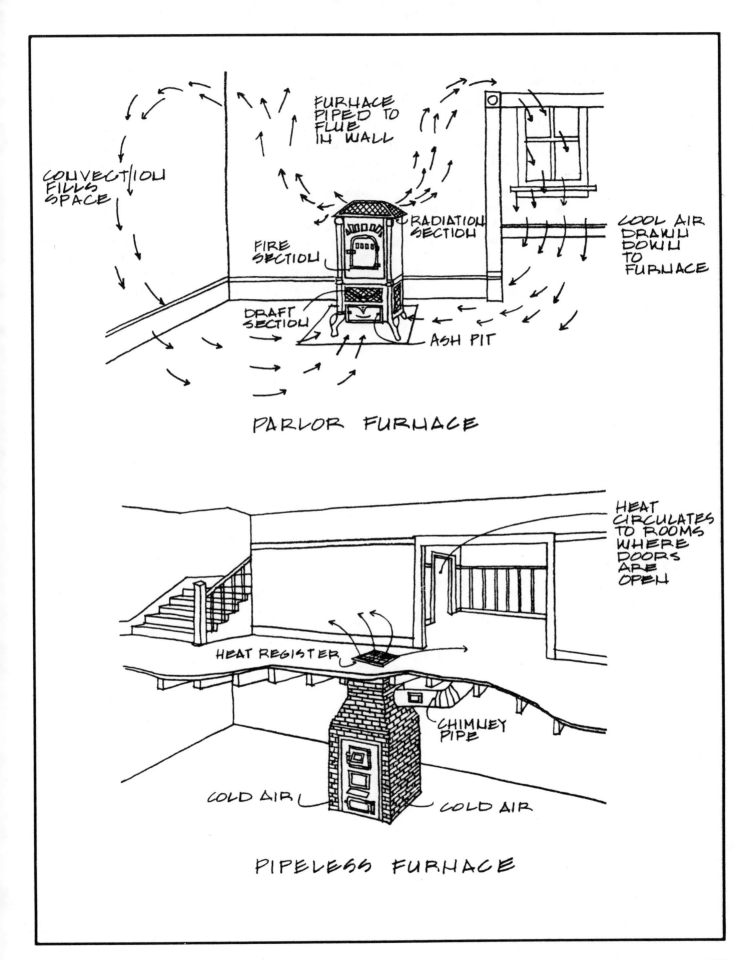

PARLOR FURNACE

CONVECTION FILLS SPACE

FURNACE PIPED TO FLUE IN WALL

RADIATION SECTION

FIRE SECTION

DRAFT SECTION

ASH PIT

COOL AIR DRAWN DOWN TO FURNACE

PIPELESS FURNACE

HEAT CIRCULATES TO ROOMS WHERE DOORS ARE OPEN

HEAT REGISTER

CHIMNEY PIPE

COLD AIR

COLD AIR

Other Warm-Air Furnaces

The development of warm-air furnaces was given a significant boost when a fan was introduced into the furnace to draw cold air, through a system of pipes, from the entire building for reheating. The fan helped to force the heated air up the round or oblong pipes. When placed within a partition these ducts were called wall stacks. Cold-air returns were located near the outside walls in order to counteract cold air currents or other infiltrations before they entered the room. Fan-assisted warm-air furnaces later were fired by oil or natural gas, which ultimately freed the basement from its fuel storage role and allowed it to assume new functions: workshop, play room for children, recreation room.

Of note in regard to heating systems is that during the time period under study, heating units—as well as kitchen ranges—often did double duty in generating hot water. In most cases, coils of one kind or another were adapted to furnaces—whether within the fire chamber or just above it— in which circulating water was heated for distribution to kitchens or baths.

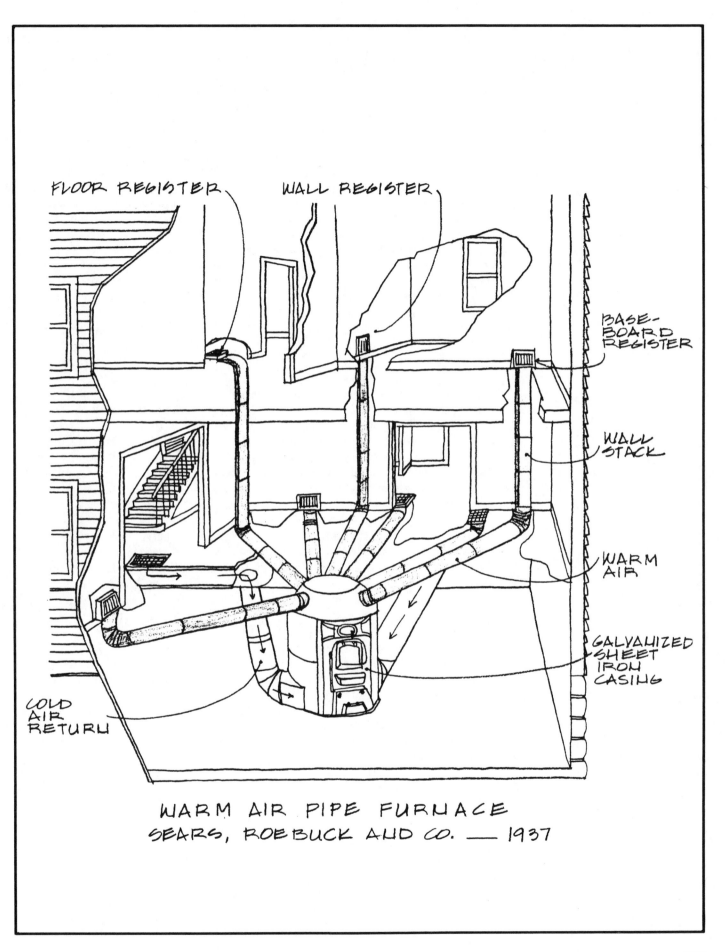

FLOOR REGISTER

WALL REGISTER

BASE-BOARD REGISTER

WALL STACK

WARM AIR

GALVANIZED SHEET IRON CASING

COLD AIR RETURN

WARM AIR PIPE FURNACE
SEARS, ROEBUCK AND CO. — 1937

Hot Water and Steam Heating Systems

The use of steam or vapor to supply heat was a direct extension of the use of steam for power. Since much of its initial use was tied to industrial developments, some time passed before steam was adapted to the level of vernacular architecture. *Steam systems* were used extensively in the nineteenth century, but hot water systems replaced them in the twentieth. The typical sophisticated steam system required a boiler, scaled down to meet the requirements of vernacular buildings (Sears, Roebuck sold easily assembled units for home use early in this century), vertical and horizontal steam supply pipes and condensation return pipes (twin pipes kept the return water from restricting the flow of the steam), and an array of radiators in appropriate locations throughout the building. Pipes often were exposed in room corners.

Radiation from the outlets was either direct, direct/indirect, or indirect. *Direct* radiation meant that the air in a space was heated by contact with the radiator in the room. Usually the radiator was fitted with both a steam valve and a return valve, which were opened and closed as the temperature required. In *direct/indirect* outfits, a fresh air supply was provided to the radiator, and the radiators often were enclosed in a screened cabinet with a register on the top. A small air duct, about 3 inches high, was taken through the outside wall at or below the window sill. Air entering through this duct was heated by convection in its passage to the top of the radiator. The *indirect* system was the most expensive of the three and usually was applied to larger buildings such as business or apartment buildings. Each living or working space had a separate radiator or metal coil suspended from the ceiling of the basement. An air duct was attached at the upper end of the radiator or coil which terminated at a register on the floor above the cellar. Higher-level floors were connected to the radiators by pipes in the walls. Many of these arrangements also had fresh-air ductwork that supplied new air to the heated air as it rose in the building.

The organization of a *steam system* sometimes utilized an overhead arrangement in which the main supply was carried directly to the attic space where horizontal runs (pipes) were carried to drops (vertical pipes) which were so located that they supplied the building's radiators on the way down to the cellar. There they converged into a main return line to the boiler. Condensation from the radiators dropped down into the pipes and flowed in the same direction as the steam, thereby preventing water barriers.

Hot-water units were organized in the same way as steam units. A boiler in the basement heated water which circulated through an assortment of radiators. The hot water forced the cold out of the system and returned it to the boiler. Some systems included a generator that accelerated the water and increased the efficiency of the system.

From the point of view of interior architecture, *radiators* were the major factor in using steam or hot water for heating. Originally, radiators were iron pipes cut off at the right length and connected at either end to make coils. Each radiator was a stack of coils screwed to a cast-iron base.

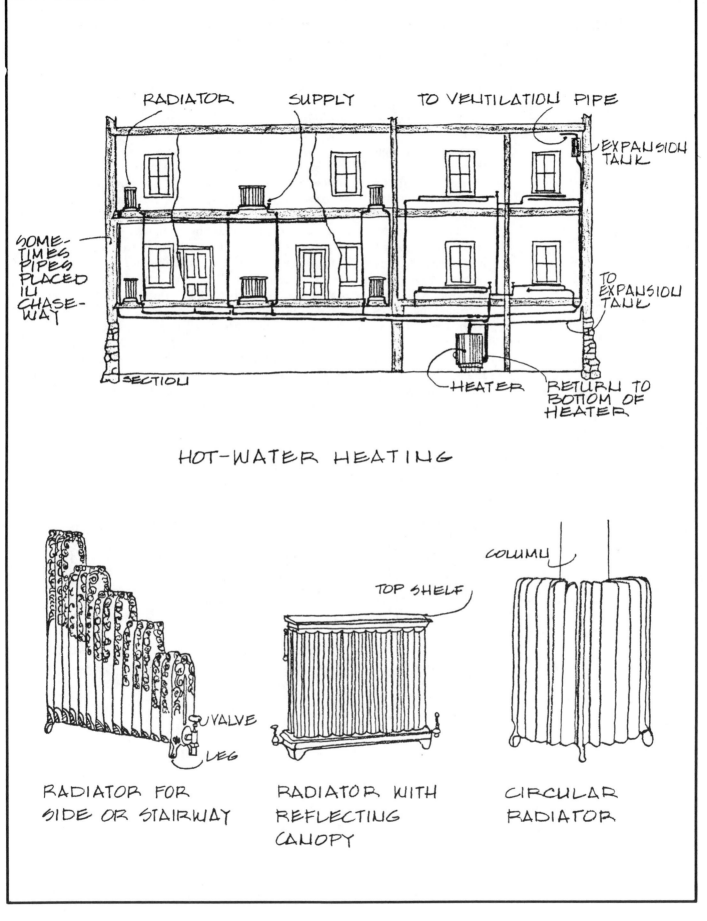

RADIATOR   SUPPLY   TO VENTILATION PIPE

EXPANSION TANK

SOME-TIMES PIPES PLACED IN CHASE-WAY

TO EXPANSION TANK

SECTION

HEATER   RETURN TO BOTTOM OF HEATER

HOT-WATER HEATING

VALVE

LEG

RADIATOR FOR
SIDE OR STAIRWAY

TOP SHELF

RADIATOR WITH
REFLECTING
CANOPY

COLUMN

CIRCULAR
RADIATOR

Hot Water and Steam Heating Systems

The first advance in radiator design was the development of completely cast units, which not only produced better radiator sections but allowed for the application of ornamental motifs on the surfaces of the coils and for the production of new profiles for the coils and new special-location shapes for the radiators. Cast-iron units were replaced by pressed-steel ones which were smaller and weighed less, thereby lightening floor loads. Most radiators were thin-edged, 8 to 9 inches wide and 20 to 45 inches high. In this century radiators were made less obtrusive by the use of lightweight copper and brass heating surfaces, and even when exposed, their new tubular designs made the units more attractive.

Most radiators were placed close to sources of cold air, such as just under windows. A front-entrance radiator was placed in a wall and covered with a grille or in the floor by the door for indirect radiation. Some ground floor halls got a single unit by the stairs, and if the hall was especially large, there might be another radiator on the stair landing. In larger building installations, *stepped radiators* were aligned with the run of the stairs. In houses with pantries or in restaurants there were small plate-warming radiators with sections of pipe laid on the horizontal. Bathroom configurations included low types with a seat on top and indirect radiators under the floor with a register on top. Generally, radiators were adapted to suit spaces, such as window sizes and shapes and the dimensions and locations of available walls. Some design considerations were practical in another way in that bedroom units often got high legs for ease in cleaning under them, and radiators far from the riser pipes got high legs to allow for a proper pitch which was necessary for the gravity flow of the return pipes.

REFLECTING HOOD

PARTIAL RECESS

WOOD CABINET AND GRILLE

PLUMBING SYSTEMS AND BATHROOMS

Bathroom design from 1870 to 1940 centered on the development of the modern bath and parallels much of the creation of the modern kitchen. The bathroom (first written as two words) became recognized as a key ingredient for the modern building. It was, in many respects, an extension of the plumbing system. The bathroom was a special-use room in which water was made to serve the purposes of cleanliness and sanitation.

For our purposes, modern plumbing consists of two series of pipes and branches. One series is for *drainage*—for taking sewage away from a building—and includes a line of air pipes open to the atmosphere. The second series is for *supply*—bringing hot and cold water to various fixtures. Early plumbing systems had several possible sources of pumping power: windmills, gravity flow, hand pumps, and pressure within public water lines.

In this section, we are concerned with the overall design of bathrooms, with inventorying the elements of bath design, and with describing the interaction between systems and elements that produced interior design.

For most vernacular buildings, running water was available even before bathrooms, and both were available before 1870 in the East. The immediate impact of plumbing on interiors was the installation of a tub, which could receive cold water directly from its supply source and hot water from a range coil or tank in the kitchen. However, it was not long in modern bath development before the freestanding hot-water heater was connected directly to the bathroom tub.

Water heaters are a key element in this history. Typical of the early types was the instantaneous model that produced hot water on demand at the rate of about two to three gallons per minute. Some of these were gas fired and mounted on the wall between the tub and the lavatory, with a pipe to vent combustion gases rising through the bathroom ceiling to the roof. There were other kinds of gas heaters. One was attached to a water tank—much like the coal or wood range and waterback in the kitchen—with a copper coil running from the bottom to the top of the boiler and gas burners heating the coil. A second type had a burner and coil in the bottom of a hot-water tank surrounded by an insulated covering. A flue took gases to the chimney and the unit could be controlled by a thermostat. These models also had pilot lights and relief valves and were located in the basement or the kitchen.

Gas and electric emerged as the preferred methods of heating water by the 1930s, but there were other heating practices still functioning at that time. One was a pipe coil in the furnace that absorbed heat from the fire chamber. Another was a system whereby furnace-heated water circulating in a small tank heated another coil that led to a pipe for the bath and kitchen fixtures. Another system placed a coil in the chimney flue or smokestack, and the water in it took up the heat from the gases going up the stack. There were electric heaters that relied on household current and a strainer-like attachment to a faucet; as soon as the faucet handle was turned, current flowed through a resistance coil which heated the water flowing over it. Electric heat evolved into a freestanding, steel-jacketed tank in which water was heated by resistance coils. Finally, there were kerosene or range oil automatic water heaters designed like other jacketed insulated models, except for having an attached burner.

The acceptance of household bathing tubs and the availability of hot water were not the only factors in the creation of the modern bathroom. Installing water closets was a complicated matter and often required overcoming the fear of sewer gases. As traps and vent pipes became recognized solutions to the gas problem, the toilet completed its migration from the back yard, to the porch, to a room of its own, even to a room within a room. The plumbing stack was the key to sewer gas control. The pipe was usually 4 inches in diameter and led from the basement or crawl space to the roof. From the foot of the stack, a sloping pipe extended along a basement wall or under the floor, through the foundation wall, where it connected with a tile pipe extending to a sewer, septic tank, cesspool, or nearby body of water. At the top of the stack a pipe passed up through the roof, where it was open to the air. Fresh air circulated through the stack, and fixture waste pipes were connected to it. Traps, which prevented sewer gas from entering rooms, were inserted between each fixture and soil pipe. These traps were loops of pipe partially filled with water. When a fixture discharged, waste water flowed through the loop into the soil pipe and some water remained as a barrier.

The water closet—in England the term *closet* stood for toilet for a long time—was developed well before 1870, but adequate cleaning systems for the bowl were not developed until the 1890s. By design most water closets could hold water, but to be successful the bowl-and-tank combination needed to cleanse the bowl properly every time and remain an effective trap for sewer gas. There were three principal types of design: washout, washdown, and syphon. The washout was the least sanitary; successfully emptying the closet depended upon the force of the water injected into the bowl. The water in the bowl usually was too shallow to complement the injected water effectively. The washdown unit was better because it contained a large body of water in the bowl, and its rim injection of water was an improvement, but its discharge was very noisy. In the syphon, also called the syphon jet, incoming water was divided, part entering the rim and part entering at the bottom of the bowl as a pressure jet. When the closet flushed, the entrance of a stream of water in the bottom of the bowl started the closet emptying by syphonic action (suction). The bowl's sides were washed by the rim flow and the bowl was filled by afterwash.

Water closet design, especially bowl design, reflected the ways manufacturers tried to build syphoning and washing functions into the bowl shape. In profile and sectional views most bowls had an organic look, especially after bowls became molded and fired vitreous china. The bowls often revealed the tubular arrangements of the trap as well as the containment features of the bowl. Lastly, the top of the bowl and the base had different shapes. The overall design of the water closet also was tied to the type and placement of the water tank. At first, tanks were placed high on the wall above the bowl. Low-down models, called combinations, emerged early in this century, but the unification of the bowl and tank does not seem to have occurred until the 1930s. Turn-of-the-century toilets had a decorative dimension in that transfer prints and hand-painting decorated the sides of the bowl, and the tank sometimes had a decorative motif on the front. Ultimately toilet design aesthetics centered on the integration of materials, on bowl and tank treatments, on the choice of seat design, and on the style and finish of trimmings.

Water closet materials followed the same pattern as tubs and sinks, in that wood, metal, enameled iron, and ceramic goods were used in both bowl and tank design, with ceramic becoming the preferred material. Whether made of enameled iron or china, fixtures were white until the 1920s, when colored fixtures were introduced. A short article in the *American Builder* (April 1927) announced the introduction of colored fixtures but did not mention the company producing them.

As the use of water closets increased, special units were developed, including chemical toilets and the hopper closet for cold climates. The hopper usually had the trap and supply valve deep in the ground with the valve activated by a pull chain or by the seat.

Two final features of water closet design were closet location and ventilation. Unlike English and European systems, the American water closet typically was not located in a separate room or compartment. Tenement houses and commercial and industrial buildings might have such a space, but most vernacular buildings placed the toilet in the same room with other sanitary fixtures. A minor accommodation along these lines was the inclusion of a water closet alcove in the bathroom. Ventilation most often was related to the positioning of the toilet beneath or near an outside window. Some closet design included a local ventilator connected to a flue or a register at the back of the closet which would circulate air. Sometime during the 1930s the ceiling exhaust fan began to take over this function.

Tubs often were installed before lavatories and water closets, because their use had been well established before indoor plumbing was an option. Tubs were made of wood, sheet metal, cast iron, and ceramic materials. Historically the tub was a portable item, and late-nineteenth-century tubs reflected that heritage. They had legs and special hoses that siphoned the water out; Sears and others sold a folding tub. As the tub gained acceptance, it abandoned portability and became recessed or fitted to a corner.

Showers were thought of first as a type of bath, and they were not popular alternatives to the tub bath. For people who were willing to engage in showering modestly, in 1902 Sears sold a shower-bath yoke, which was a hose the bather placed around his neck out of which water streamed down his body. Shower baths originally were designed like a piece of furniture—freestanding, pipe-framed, curtained, with a shallow basin for a base. The shower became integrated with the tub as well as built into its own alcove by the 1920s.

Lavatory design encompassed all of the following: the material from which the lavatory was made, the shape of the entire fixture and the shape of the basin (as seen in plan view), the thickness and shape of the slab, the profile of the back piece, the method of support, the location of the lavatory in the bathroom, the color of the fixture, and the pattern and finish of the hardware and supply and waste pipes. With design parameters that wide-ranging, the selection of products was extensive. Moreover, the subtleties of lavatory design could be worked among the elements. For example, the method of support for a lavatory could make a contribution to the design scheme. Historically, supports were attached iron brackets, legs, pedestals, and "invisible" wall hangers on which the lavatory was hooked. For three of these supports, the design and finish of the support could establish a tone for the bathroom system.

ITALIAU MARBLE SLAB LAVATORY, NICKEL-PLATED BRACKETS
SEARS, ROEBUCK AND CO. 1902

ROLL RIM ENAMELED LAVATORIES, ORNAMENTAL EXTERIOR, SEARS, ROEBUCK AND CO. — 1902

In summarizing overall bathroom design, there were several conceptual approaches to the arrangement of fixtures and the use of space. In the late nineteenth and early twentieth centuries the bathroom was a large room containing loosely arranged fixtures, with little relationship among the diverse parts. The reform movement in housing design had an effect on baths that resulted in a smaller bathroom and the development of the room as a workshop for personal health. The third version of the modern bathroom took the workshop a step further and created a gleaming white laboratory for personal health and grooming. The final treatment reduced the bath space even more and relied on integrated compact units, with all the practical concerns, such as sanitation, taken for granted. In this stage aesthetics entered the bathroom scene as a primary consideration.

Design parameters for relationships among fixtures include: height, width, and depth dimensions: the logic of placement as it related to room use (the lavatory near the door, the tub away from it), and the relationship among materials. China and enameled cast-iron fixtures might be found in the same room, or a mixture of china and metal trimmings, or there might be a unified material look in which everything was either ceramic or painted enamel. Also of interest were the types of supports for fixtures—bases, pedestals, legs, brackets, hangers—and the configuration of each fixture: referential types such as a fish-shaped water closet, purely functional forms, or designed or "artistic" shapes. Likewise, the edges of fixtures and their surfaces might be treated similarly; edges were cut, rounded, or rectilinear, and surfaces were recessed and featured cups, rims, and other raised elements. Lastly, there were trimmings to be integrated.

To give some idea of the design options that underlay the final appearance of a bathroom, consider the following categories of water closet elements and how they might be fused into a scheme.

Element	Types	Element	Types
materials	china, enameled iron (plain, porcelain)	flush lever	push button, flip lever, pull chain or rod
bowl action	washout, washdown, syphon jet	seat design	round, saddle, horseshoe, extended lip, assorted colors and finishes
bowl shape	oval, round, reflecting trap design, extended lip, raised lip	trimmings	hinges (bar, XS, S bar, horseshoe bar), bolt cap, connector, escutcheon
tank type	high on wall, low, integrated		
tank material	wood, cast iron, ceramic		

As alluded to earlier, there was also the issue of ornamentation. Even though transfer-printed designs, most leg types, elaborate bases, and textured pedestals were dropped from the design vocabulary, other aspects of design—lines, patterns, bevels, and color, including at first accent color—were still important.

Lavatories, tubs, and shower baths had similar options. To create unified effects, plumbing manufacturers sold bathrooms as complete installations priced according to the quality of the materials, finishes, and methods of operation of the components. In this strategy, the manufacturers followed the unit approach that millwork manufacturers used in selling kitchen design. Once this unit, or "outfit," idea caught on, it presented a new design opportunity: coordinated design effects. For example, the 45-degree-angle cut at the corners of the lavatory back could be repeated on the inside corners of the basin and on the corners of the apron. The beveled corner could also be applied to the base of the toilet and the edge of the tank cover and the edge of the tub.

Similarly, the hardware of all the fixtures could be made of the same material and have the same style and finish. Generally, the detailing of the system was carried out in all the trimmings: toilet paper and soap holders (whether the projecting or recessed type), tumbler and toothbrush holder, towel bars, and shelf brackets. Although plumbing companies did not manufacture bathroom lights, the range of choices among lighting products made it possible to complement bath fixtures well enough to give the 1930s bathroom the ambience of total design.

Tank and Bowl Assemblies

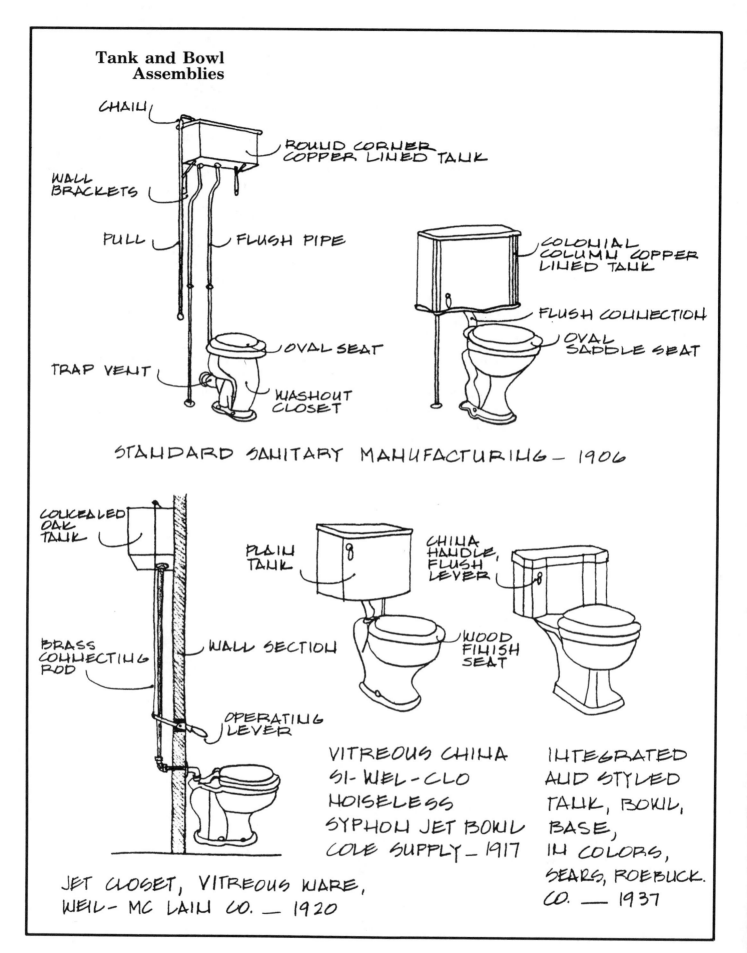

CHAIN

WALL BRACKETS

PULL

FLUSH PIPE

ROUND CORNER COPPER LINED TANK

TRAP VENT

OVAL SEAT

WASHOUT CLOSET

COLONIAL COLUMN COPPER LINED TANK

FLUSH CONNECTION

OVAL SADDLE SEAT

STANDARD SANITARY MANUFACTURING — 1906

CONCEALED OAK TANK

PLAIN TANK

CHINA HANDLE, FLUSH LEVER

BRASS CONNECTING ROD

WALL SECTION

WOOD FINISH SEAT

OPERATING LEVER

JET CLOSET, VITREOUS WARE, WEIL—MC LAIN CO. — 1920

VITREOUS CHINA
SI- WEL - CLO
NOISELESS
SYPHON JET BOWL
COLE SUPPLY — 1917

INTEGRATED
AND STYLED
TANK, BOWL,
BASE,
IN COLORS,
SEARS, ROEBUCK.
CO. — 1937

Toilet Seats and Bowls

REVERSE TRAP SYPHON BOWL

SYPHON WASHDOWN FOR HIGH OR LOW TANK

1¼" ROUND SEAT AND COVER

SYPHON WASHDOWN BOWL WITH EXTENDED BACK OUTLET

FLOOR OUTLET WASHDOWN, NO. 3 PLAIN OVAL

1½" HORSESHOE SEAT AND COVER

PLAIN OVAL SYPHON JET BOWL FOR HIGH OR LOW TANKS

JUVENILE SYPHON JET, CONCEALED JET PIPE

1½" EXTENDED LIP, FULL SADDLE SEAT

SYPHON JET BOWL, EXTENDED LIP

SYPHON JET BOWL, RAISED FRONT LIP, CENTER OUTLET

SADDLE SEAT AND COVER

Water Closet Parts

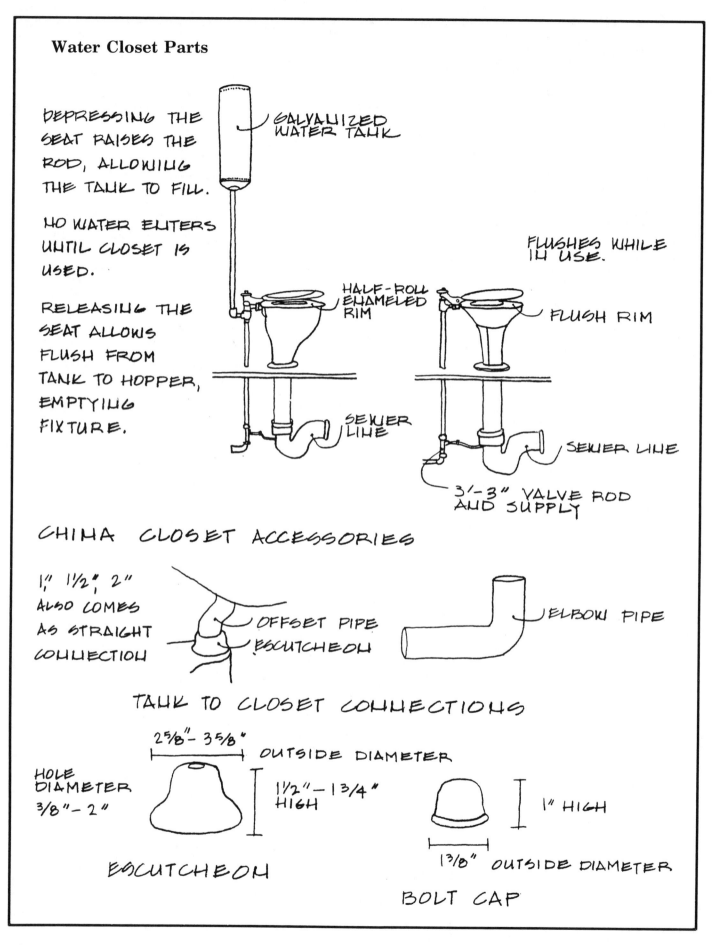

DEPRESSING THE SEAT RAISES THE ROD, ALLOWING THE TANK TO FILL.

NO WATER ENTERS UNTIL CLOSET IS USED.

RELEASING THE SEAT ALLOWS FLUSH FROM TANK TO HOPPER, EMPTYING FIXTURE.

GALVANIZED WATER TANK

FLUSHES WHILE IN USE.

HALF-ROLL ENAMELED RIM

FLUSH RIM

SEWER LINE

SEWER LINE

3'-3" VALVE ROD AND SUPPLY

CHINA CLOSET ACCESSORIES

1", 1½", 2" ALSO COMES AS STRAIGHT CONNECTION

OFFSET PIPE ESCUTCHEON

ELBOW PIPE

TANK TO CLOSET CONNECTIONS

2⅝"- 3⅝"

OUTSIDE DIAMETER

HOLE DIAMETER 3/8"- 2"

1½"- 1¾" HIGH

1" HIGH

ESCUTCHEON

1⅜" OUTSIDE DIAMETER

BOLT CAP

Tub Designs

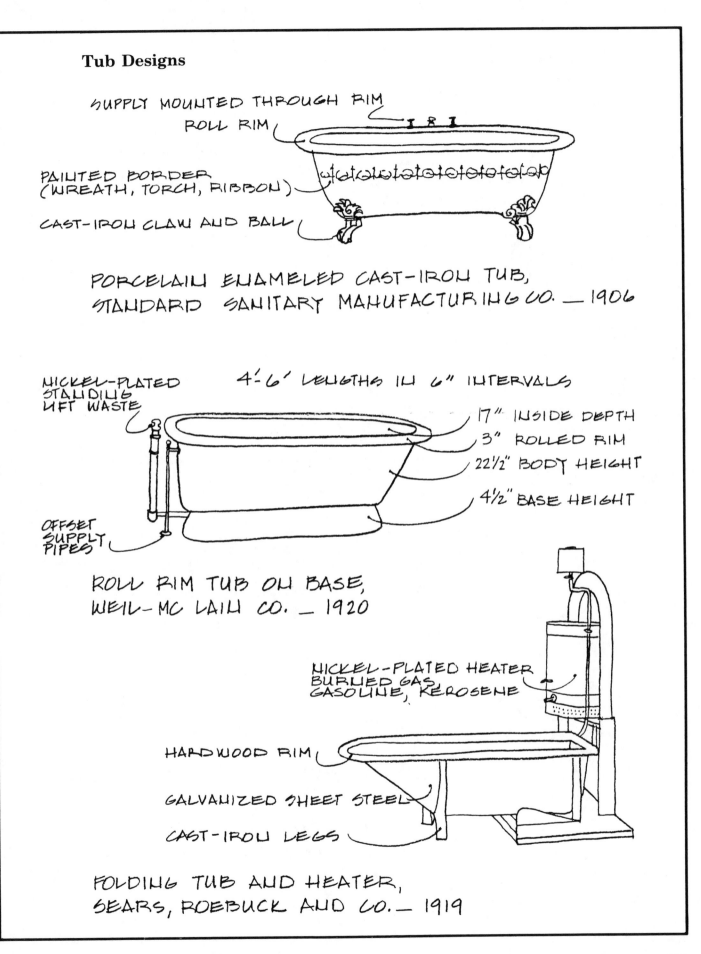

SUPPLY MOUNTED THROUGH RIM

ROLL RIM

PAINTED BORDER
(WREATH, TORCH, RIBBON)

CAST-IRON CLAW AND BALL

PORCELAIN ENAMELED CAST-IRON TUB,
STANDARD SANITARY MANUFACTURING CO. — 1906

NICKEL-PLATED
STANDING
LIFT WASTE

4'-6' LENGTHS IN 6" INTERVALS

17" INSIDE DEPTH

3" ROLLED RIM

22½" BODY HEIGHT

4½" BASE HEIGHT

OFFSET
SUPPLY
PIPES

ROLL RIM TUB ON BASE,
WEIL-MC LAIN CO. — 1920

NICKEL-PLATED HEATER
BURNED GAS
GASOLINE, KEROSENE

HARDWOOD RIM

GALVANIZED SHEET STEEL

CAST-IRON LEGS

FOLDING TUB AND HEATER,
SEARS, ROEBUCK AND CO. — 1919

Tub Designs

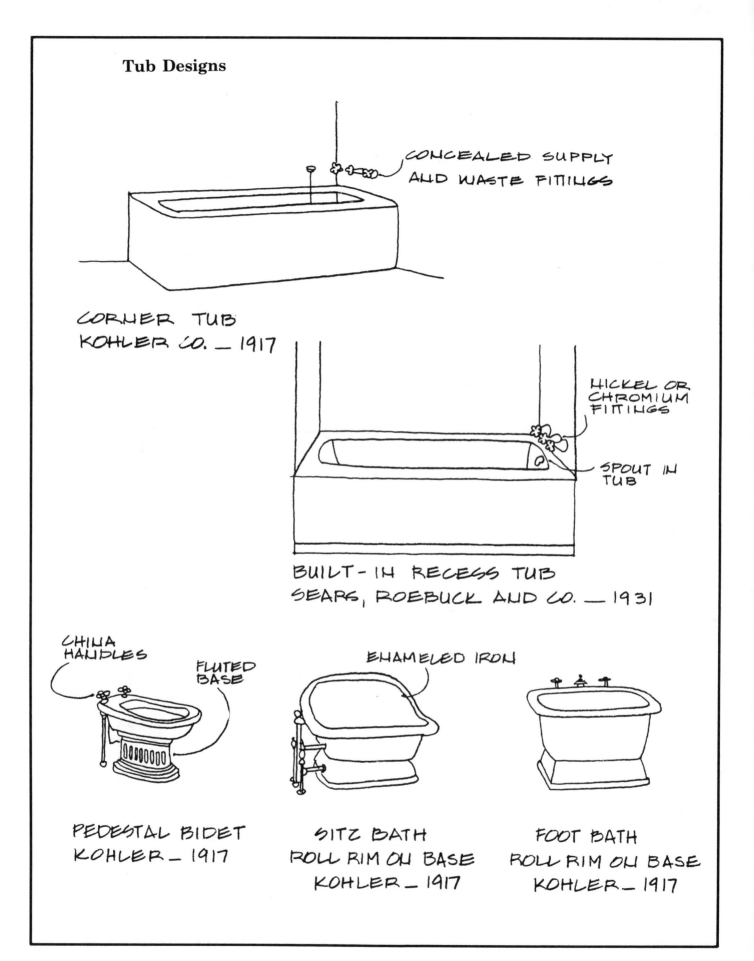

CONCEALED SUPPLY AND WASTE FITTINGS

CORNER TUB
KOHLER CO. — 1917

NICKEL OR CHROMIUM FITTINGS

SPOUT IN TUB

BUILT-IN RECESS TUB
SEARS, ROEBUCK AND CO. — 1931

CHINA HANDLES

FLUTED BASE

PEDESTAL BIDET
KOHLER — 1917

ENAMELED IRON

SITZ BATH
ROLL RIM ON BASE
KOHLER — 1917

FOOT BATH
ROLL RIM ON BASE
KOHLER — 1917

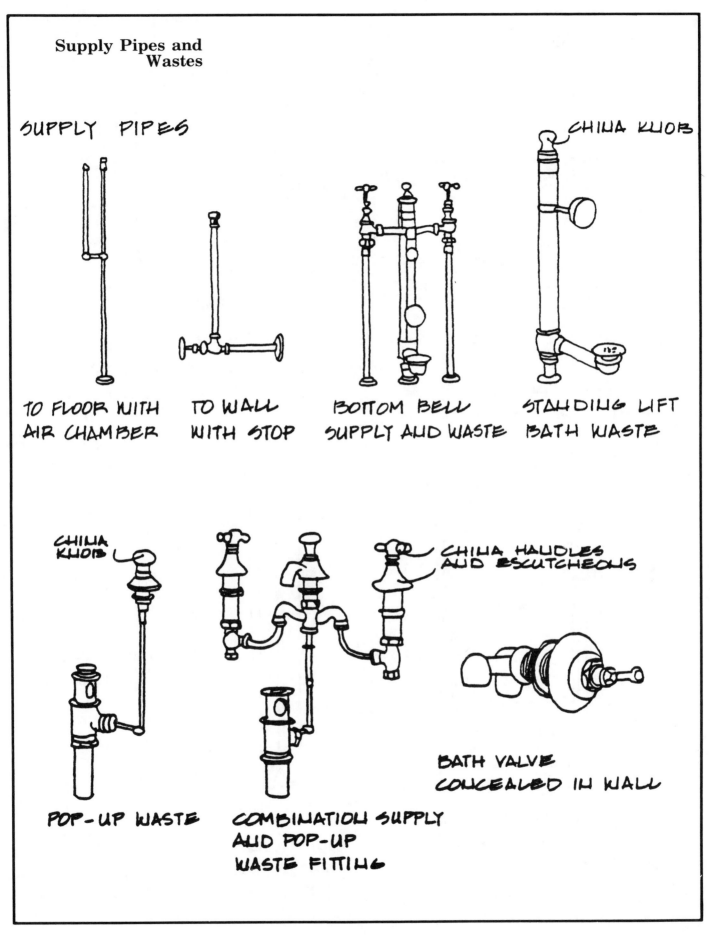

SUPPLY PIPES

CHINA KNOB

TO FLOOR WITH AIR CHAMBER

TO WALL WITH STOP

BOTTOM BELL SUPPLY AND WASTE

STANDING LIFT BATH WASTE

CHINA KNOB

CHINA HANDLES AND ESCUTCHEONS

POP-UP WASTE

COMBINATION SUPPLY AND POP-UP WASTE FITTING

BATH VALVE CONCEALED IN WALL

Showers

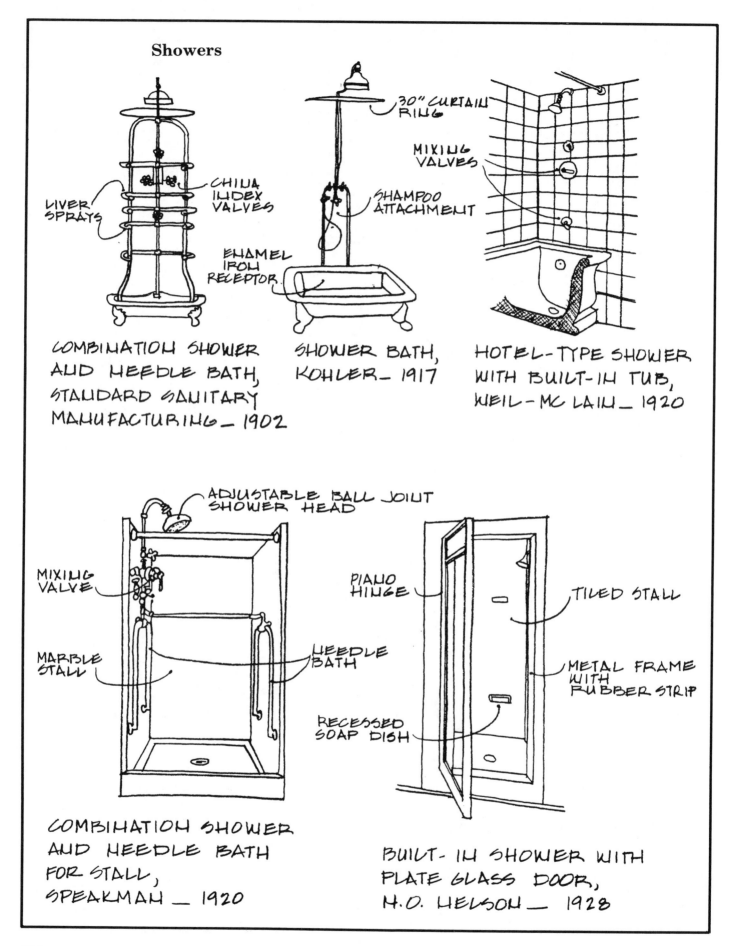

COMBINATION SHOWER
AND NEEDLE BATH,
STANDARD SANITARY
MANUFACTURING — 1902

LINER SPRAYS

CHINA INDEX VALVES

ENAMEL IRON RECEPTOR

SHOWER BATH,
KOHLER — 1917

30" CURTAIN RING

MIXING VALVES

SHAMPOO ATTACHMENT

HOTEL-TYPE SHOWER
WITH BUILT-IN TUB,
WEIL — MC LAIN — 1920

ADJUSTABLE BALL JOINT
SHOWER HEAD

MIXING VALVE

MARBLE STALL

NEEDLE BATH

COMBINATION SHOWER
AND NEEDLE BATH
FOR STALL,
SPEAKMAN — 1920

PIANO HINGE

RECESSED SOAP DISH

TILED STALL

METAL FRAME WITH RUBBER STRIP

BUILT-IN SHOWER WITH
PLATE GLASS DOOR,
H. O. NELSON — 1928

Lavatory Elements

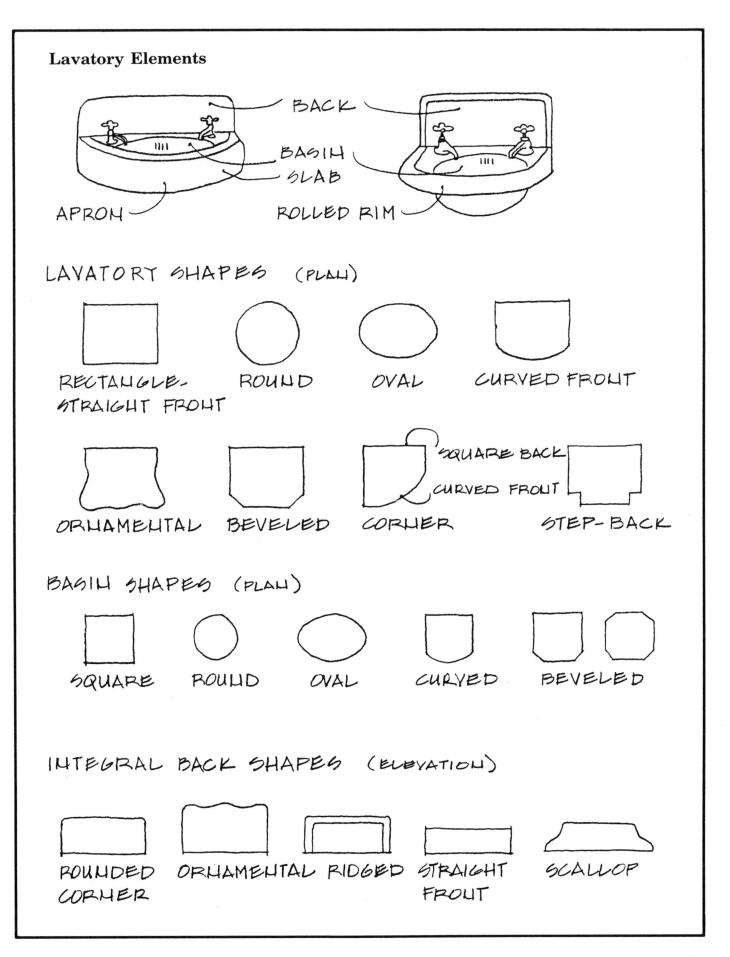

BACK

BASIN

SLAB

APRON

ROLLED RIM

LAVATORY SHAPES (PLAN)

RECTANGLE-STRAIGHT FRONT   ROUND   OVAL   CURVED FRONT

ORNAMENTAL   BEVELED   CORNER   STEP-BACK

SQUARE BACK

CURVED FRONT

BASIN SHAPES (PLAN)

SQUARE   ROUND   OVAL   CURVED   BEVELED

INTEGRAL BACK SHAPES (ELEVATION)

ROUNDED CORNER   ORNAMENTAL   RIDGED   STRAIGHT FRONT   SCALLOP

Lavatory Design,
1917

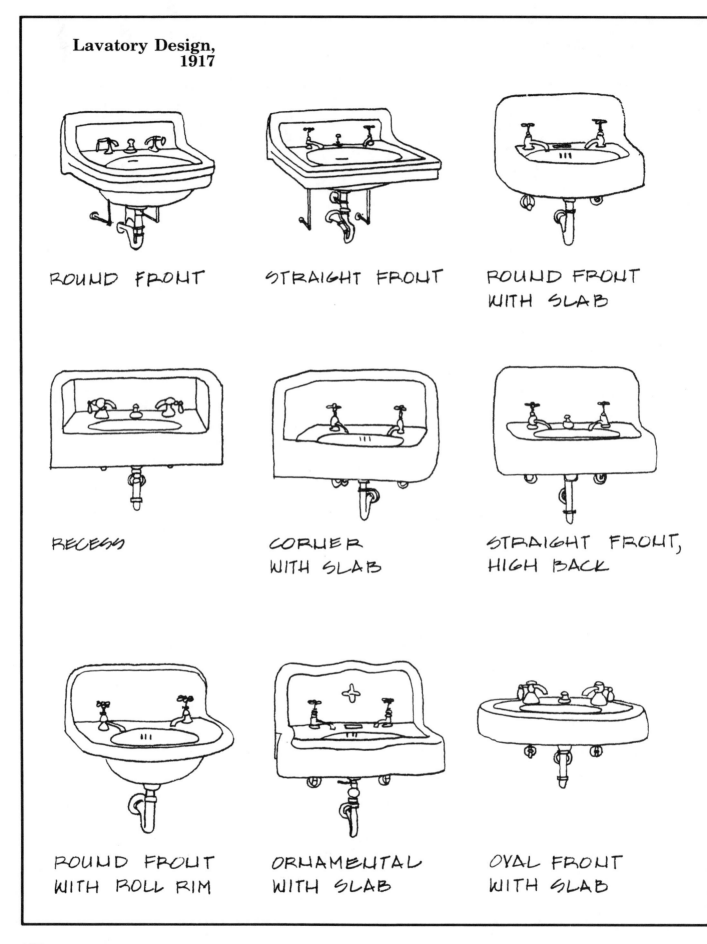

ROUND FRONT

STRAIGHT FRONT

ROUND FRONT
WITH SLAB

RECESS

CORNER
WITH SLAB

STRAIGHT FRONT,
HIGH BACK

ROUND FRONT
WITH ROLL RIM

ORNAMENTAL
WITH SLAB

OVAL FRONT
WITH SLAB

ROUND BASE

URN-SHAPE PEDESTAL,
ELLIPSE SLAB
KOHLER — CIRCA 1890

FLUTED PEDESTAL,
OVAL SLAB
STANDARD SANITARY
MANUFACTURING — 1906

ROUND PEDESTAL,
OVAL SLAB
KOHLER — 1917

SQUARE-BASE PEDESTAL
STRAIGHT-FRONT LAV,
SQUARE BASIN
COLE SUPPLY — 1928

Lavatory Pedestals and Bases

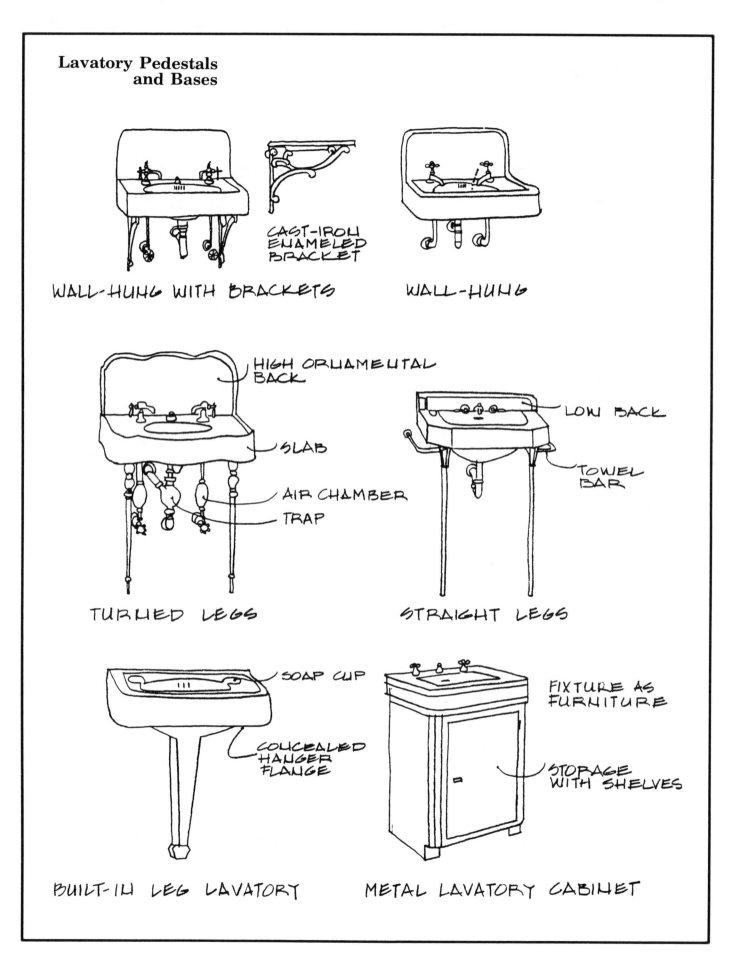

WALL-HUNG WITH BRACKETS

CAST-IRON ENAMELED BRACKET

WALL-HUNG

HIGH ORNAMENTAL BACK

SLAB

AIR CHAMBER

TRAP

TURNED LEGS

LOW BACK

TOWEL BAR

STRAIGHT LEGS

SOAP CUP

CONCEALED HANGER FLANGE

BUILT-IN LEG LAVATORY

FIXTURE AS FURNITURE

STORAGE WITH SHELVES

METAL LAVATORY CABINET

Lavatory Fittings

BASIN COCK / FAUCET TYPES

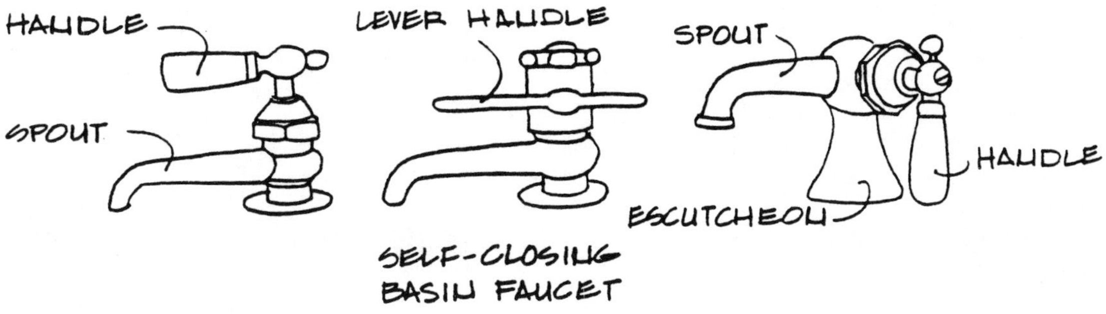
HANDLE
SPOUT
LEVER HANDLE
SELF-CLOSING
BASIN FAUCET
SPOUT
HANDLE
ESCUTCHEON

HANDLES

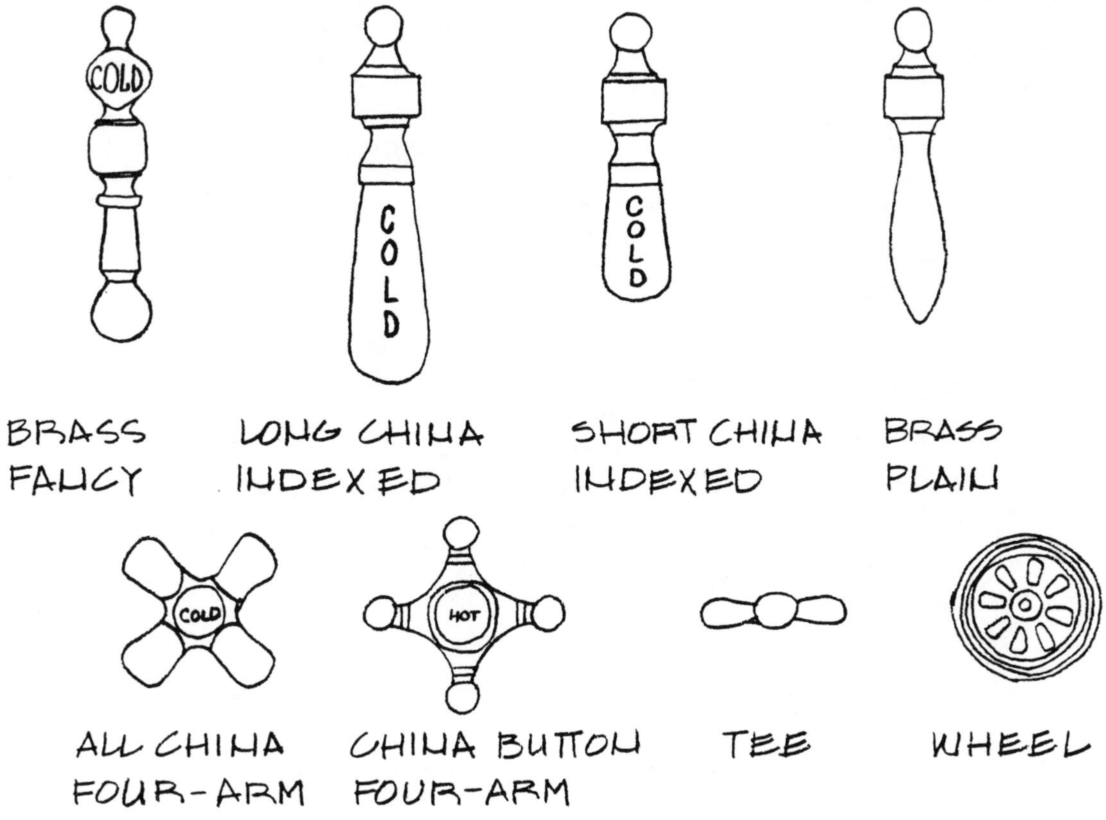
COLD
COLD
COLD
BRASS
FANCY
LONG CHINA
INDEXED
SHORT CHINA
INDEXED
BRASS
PLAIN
COLD
HOT
ALL CHINA
FOUR-ARM
CHINA BUTTON
FOUR-ARM
TEE
WHEEL

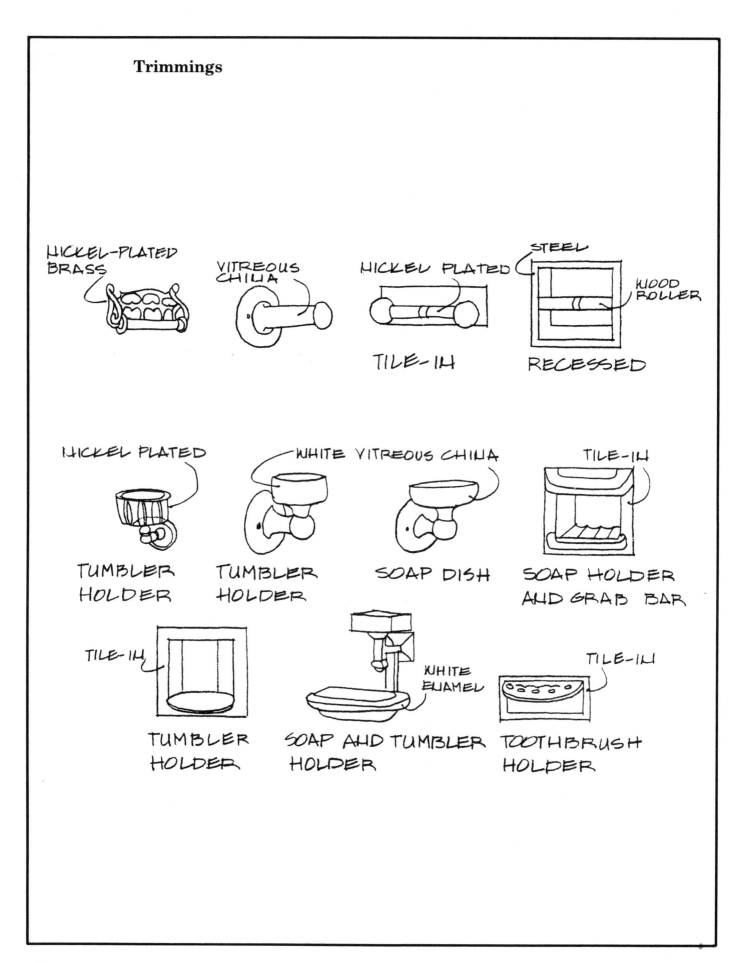

NICKEL-PLATED BRASS

VITREOUS CHINA

NICKEL PLATED

STEEL
WOOD ROLLER

TILE-IN

RECESSED

NICKEL PLATED

WHITE VITREOUS CHINA

TILE-IN

TUMBLER HOLDER

TUMBLER HOLDER

SOAP DISH

SOAP HOLDER AND GRAB BAR

TILE-IN

TUMBLER HOLDER

WHITE ENAMEL

SOAP AND TUMBLER HOLDER

TILE-IN

TOOTHBRUSH HOLDER

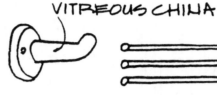

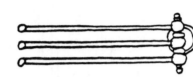
VITREOUS CHINA

TOWEL HOOKS   ROBE HOOKS   TOWEL ARMS

TOWEL BAR

SQUARE TOWEL BAR

WHITE ENAMEL

TOWEL BAR AND
GRAB RAIL

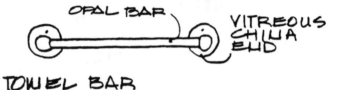
OPAL BAR   VITREOUS
                           CHINA
                           END

TOWEL BAR

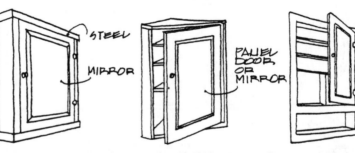
STEEL

MIRROR

PANEL
DOOR
OR
MIRROR

MEDICINE CHEST   CORNER CHEST   RECESSED CHEST

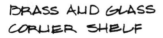

BRASS AND GLASS   PROJECTING TILE-IN
CORNER SHELF   OPAL GLASS SHELF

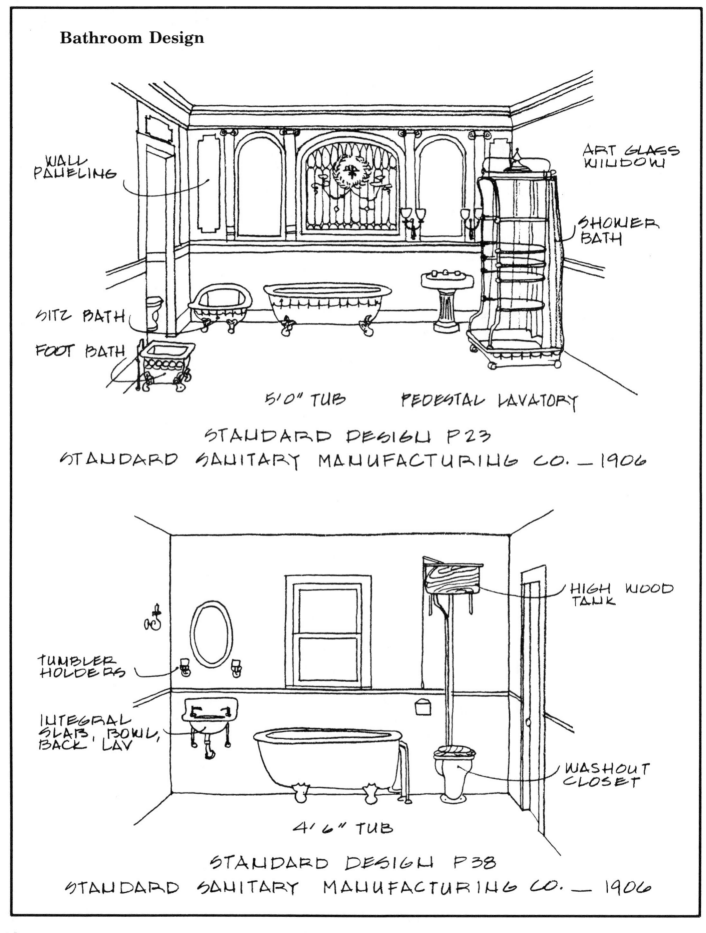

WALL PANELING

ART GLASS WINDOW

SHOWER BATH

SITZ BATH

FOOT BATH

5'0" TUB   PEDESTAL LAVATORY

STANDARD DESIGN P23
STANDARD SANITARY MANUFACTURING CO. — 1906

TUMBLER HOLDERS

INTEGRAL SLAB, BOWL, BACK LAV

HIGH WOOD TANK

WASHOUT CLOSET

4'6" TUB

STANDARD DESIGN P38
STANDARD SANITARY MANUFACTURING CO. — 1906

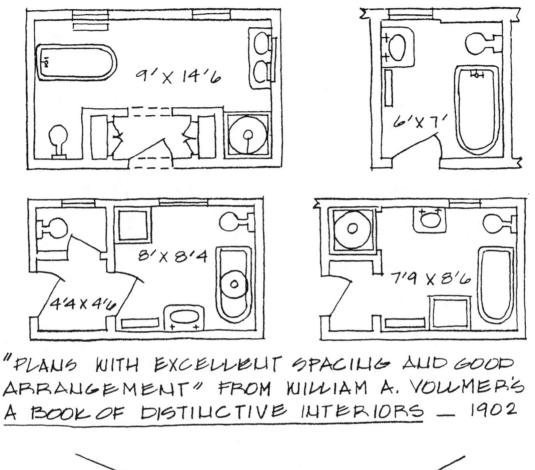

"PLANS WITH EXCELLENT SPACING AND GOOD ARRANGEMENT" FROM WILLIAM A. VOLLMER'S A BOOK OF DISTINCTIVE INTERIORS — 1902

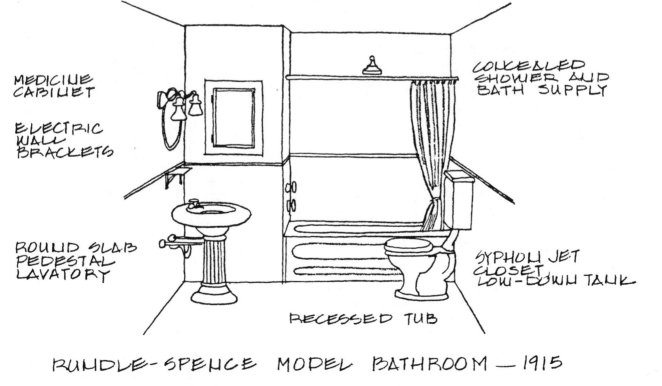

RUNDLE-SPENCE MODEL BATHROOM — 1915

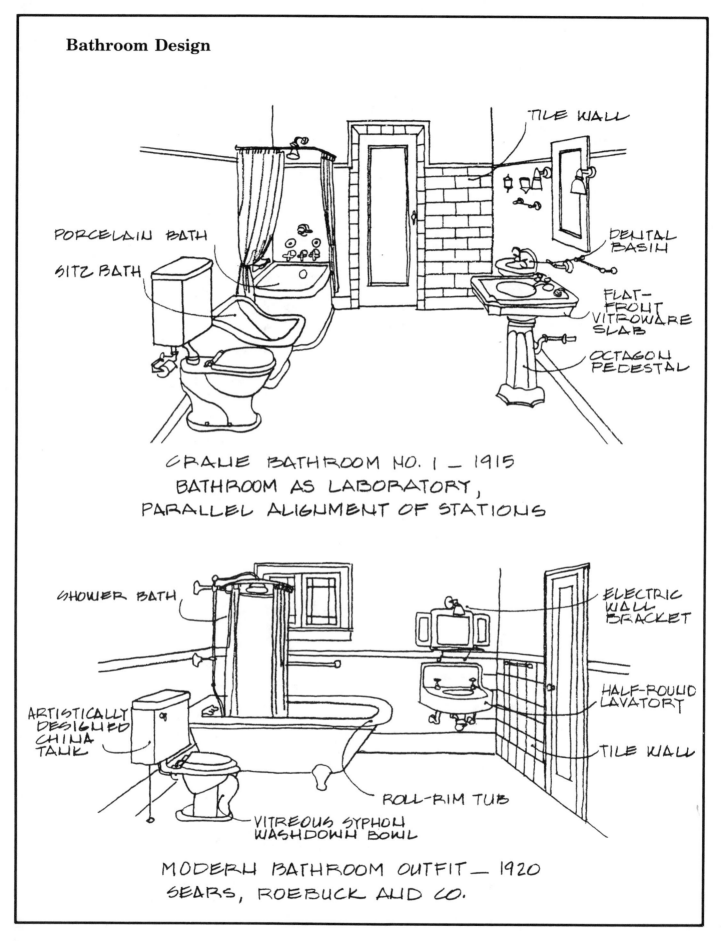

PORCELAIN BATH

SITZ BATH

TILE WALL

DENTAL BASIN

FLAT-FRONT VITROWARE SLAB

OCTAGON PEDESTAL

CRANE BATHROOM NO. 1 — 1915
BATHROOM AS LABORATORY,
PARALLEL ALIGNMENT OF STATIONS

SHOWER BATH

ARTISTICALLY DESIGNED CHINA TANK

ELECTRIC WALL BRACKET

HALF-ROUND LAVATORY

TILE WALL

ROLL-RIM TUB

VITREOUS SYPHON WASHDOWN BOWL

MODERN BATHROOM OUTFIT — 1920
SEARS, ROEBUCK AND CO.

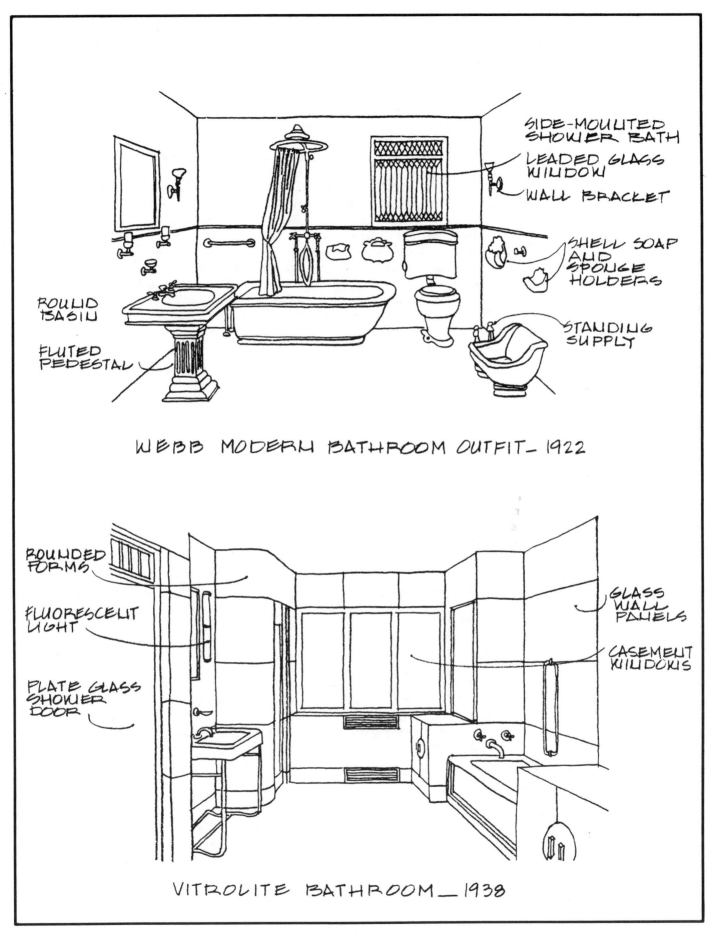

SIDE-MOUNTED SHOWER BATH

LEADED GLASS WINDOW

WALL BRACKET

SHELL SOAP AND SPONGE HOLDERS

ROUND BASIN

FLUTED PEDESTAL

STANDING SUPPLY

WEBB MODERN BATHROOM OUTFIT _ 1922

ROUNDED FORMS

FLUORESCENT LIGHT

PLATE GLASS SHOWER DOOR

GLASS WALL PANELS

CASEMENT WINDOWS

VITROLITE BATHROOM _ 1938

195

KITCHENS The history of the kitchen focuses on the elevation of a back room into a special place, with clearly established functions and special equipment. The evolution took place in the single-family home. Kitchens in buildings other than residential were adaptations of the residential model.

Prior to the development of the modern kitchen, which begins in the last quarter of the nineteenth century, the kitchen was a place to store provisions, prepare food, wash cooking utensils, wash and iron clothes, change clothes, take care of personal grooming (shaving, washing hair), eat, and pass through on the way to other rooms. Moving beyond this eclectic space to the kitchen of the 1920s and 1930s meant concentrating activities related to the use of food in the kitchen proper and relegating all other functions to other spaces. The parallel developments of the bathroom and the laundry room greatly relieved congestion. Moreover, pantry spaces—for storing dinnerware and table service, for storing provisions, and for serving food—were another early solution to redefining kitchen space. In response to these and other changes, and to the need to reorganize the kitchen to relieve the drudgery of house work, the kitchen was allocated less square footage and given new purpose.

By 1870 the kitchen had equipment and finish materials that would remain, in some form, part of its design for a long time. There was a refrigerator—an insulated wooden box with a space for food and another to hold blocks of ice; a range or stove that could bake, roast, and heat water; a storage unit or two, at least one shelf, a sink, a work table and chair, a washable floor, and a clock. The organization of this kitchen was loose, with wide spaces between equipment or work stations. In one sense, the history of kitchen design is the story of how these units became physically connected to make the work area more efficient and labor-saving.

Water service was available for the nineteenth-century kitchen. In cities water was pumped under pressure through lead and galvanized iron pipes to residences and businesses. In rural areas water was brought into houses by gravity flow from springs and cisterns, by wind power, or by hand-operated force pumps connected to wells. Early water systems had exposed pipes with supply and return pipes running across ceilings and along walls. Some sections of pipe might run under a floor or through a partition, and some ran in modest chaseways with wood cappings. The exposure of the pipes was looked upon as practical because repairs and adjustments to flow could be made easily. Each line could have stop cocks, traps, and bleeders. The presence of the pipes had another effect, the symbolic reinforcement of the idea that house development, especially in rooms like the kitchen, was tied to technological advancement. The pipes' presence made the room look progressive. Most plumbing systems had access to some hot water, through either the range heater or a separate unit. The hot-water storage tank also was placed in the kitchen. Sometimes hot-water lines ran to the attic and returned from there, and air lines that prevented hammering and air bounding were also taken off the attic lines.

This kitchen was serviceable, but it took its toll on the women who worked in it. Despite improvements, the kitchen needed a new conceptual approach, and that was taken up by reformers who saw in kitchen design issues that stood for the role of women in family life and for the significance of their labor. Kitchen studies in academic domestic-science programs established standardization. Kitchen size, for example, was not to exceed 150 square feet.

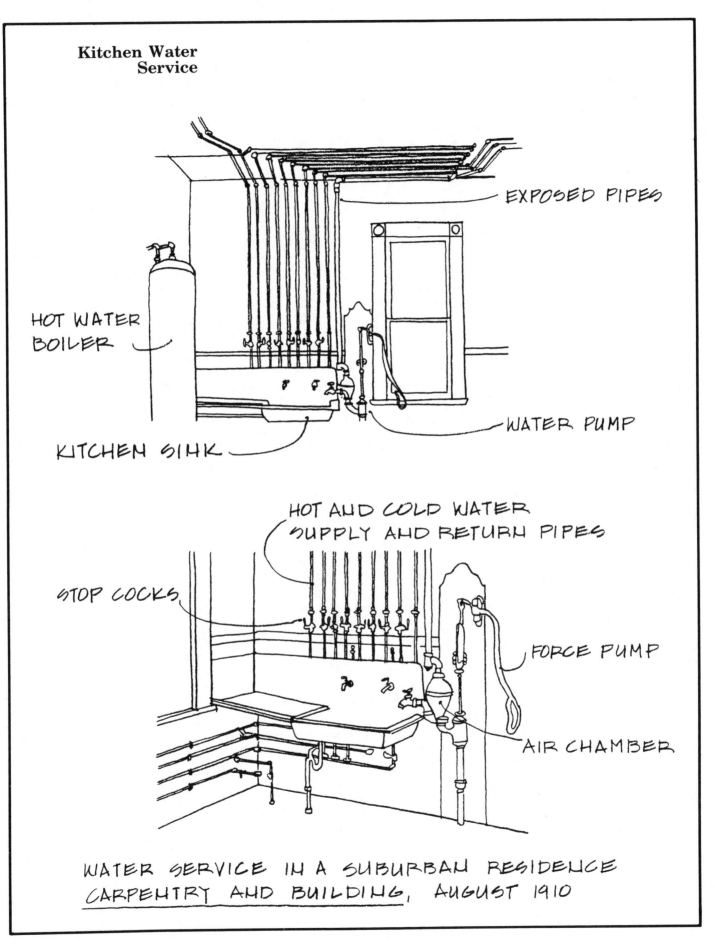

EXPOSED PIPES

HOT WATER
BOILER

WATER PUMP

KITCHEN SINK

HOT AND COLD WATER
SUPPLY AND RETURN PIPES

STOP COCKS

FORCE PUMP

AIR CHAMBER

WATER SERVICE IN A SUBURBAN RESIDENCE
CARPENTRY AND BUILDING, AUGUST 1910

Among the reformers, there was divided opinion as to the shape of the kitchen—oblong, L-shape, or the more popular square—but there was agreement about the need for windows on two sides and for light and ventilation. They agreed about the need to restrict the use of the kitchen as a passageway by reducing the number of doors opening in to it. Four doors was the maximum: an outside door, a pantry door, a cellar door, and one to the dining room. Reduction to two or three doors was even better, and their placement should be on adjacent walls, to avoid lines of travel through the work area and to leave two sides of uninterrupted wall space. Windows were to be placed 3 feet 6 inches from the floor to allow for table space beneath the sill. Counter and table heights were examined to establish appropriate working levels to reduce strain. The reorganization of the kitchen was tied to redefining the service functions in general.

Kitchen design—even before the kitchen was thought of as the workshop of the home—was tied to the development of a few key work stations, such as the sink and the range/stove. Sink design was the same as that for bathroom tubs and lavatories. Early wooden sinks gave way to carved soapstone, and later to models mass-produced in porcelain, enameled iron, and graniteware. Water was supplied from spigots, either in the wall or built into the sink, or from attached hand pumps. Sinks had rolled or flat rims, low or high backs of either wood or cast iron, and aprons. They might fit into corners or stand alone, with single or double basins. The sink was also a work station and its dish drainboards, whether attached or integral, served as food preparation areas. The boards were made of wood (oak), then metal, and finally enameled or porcelained cast iron. Sink support came from integral or attached legs, brackets, wall hangers, and, finally, cabinetry.

Storage

Storage function and storage capacity changed several times from 1870 to 1940. The 1870s kitchen had very little capacity. Foodstuffs were kept in small amounts and fresh goods were bought more frequently. Garden produce was home-processed and stored in root or fruit cellars and pantries. Immediate kitchen storage for utensils and service items was often relegated to a "dresser," a movable piece of furniture, and to the implements shelf by the sink and the range. In the 1870s, reformers already were calling for the use of storage cases and closets to help in the reorganization of the kitchen.

Like almost everything in vernacular design, early casework was done on the job site by the finish carpenter. Gradually, ready-made elements, at first drawers and cupboard doors, were introduced. These were augmented by casework that was fabricated completely at the mill. The rapid increase in the production of cases and competition among shops led to experimentation in case organization so that variations in shelf and drawer size, adjustable units, special-use bins, and specially shaped closets all developed quickly.

The trend toward packaged foods led to increased storage capacity, and that led to the accumulation of more household goods. When these accumulations were tied to the desire to alleviate kitchen congestion, that prompted the design of pantries as separate spaces. Basically a pantry was a cabinet located near the kitchen or between the kitchen and the dining room. In the latter situation, the pantry was used for serving food; it might have a variety of cabinets, a sink with hot and cold water, a pass-through door with a floor hinge for opening both ways, or a small pass-through opening in the wall for serving food and collecting dishes. Casework in both kitchens and pantries often featured glass doors over the upper sections, with beveled, leaded, or art glass glazing.

Sinks

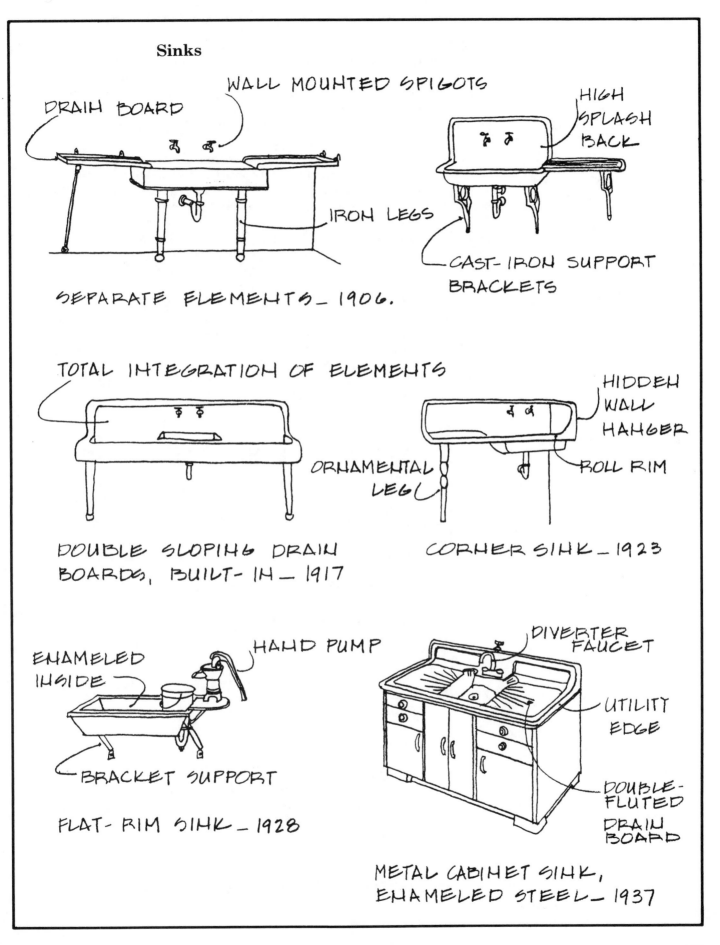

DRAIN BOARD

WALL MOUNTED SPIGOTS

HIGH SPLASH BACK

IRON LEGS

CAST-IRON SUPPORT BRACKETS

SEPARATE ELEMENTS _ 1906.

TOTAL INTEGRATION OF ELEMENTS

HIDDEN WALL HANGER

ORNAMENTAL LEG

ROLL RIM

DOUBLE SLOPING DRAIN BOARDS, BUILT-IN _ 1917

CORNER SINK _ 1923

ENAMELED INSIDE

HAND PUMP

DIVERTER FAUCET

UTILITY EDGE

BRACKET SUPPORT

DOUBLE-FLUTED DRAIN BOARD

FLAT-RIM SINK _ 1928

METAL CABINET SINK, ENAMELED STEEL _ 1937

Once manufactured cabinetry had taken hold in the marketplace, the development of kitchen storage was based on the linking of storage units, at first into specific work centers and later into continuous cabinets. The ultimate success of this system all but eliminated the serving pantry from American housing. With floor-to-ceiling cabinets, organized on a gridiron principle for efficiency and ease of manufacture, the pantry's square footage could be captured for another purpose.

One final aspect of storage needs to be mentioned; built-in storage or work units. These appear in manufacturer's trade catalogs during the 1910s as set pieces that supplemented casework or served as work stations. Ironing boards that folded down from a wall-mounted cabinet, dumb waiters for food and goods delivery, package receivers built into outside walls, folding tables for temporary tasks, desks for planning and relaxation (the "quiet corner"), and breakfast nooks that informalized family meals were all aspects of this development from the 1870s through the 1920s.

Walls, Ceilings, Floors

Historical materials for kitchen walls and ceilings reflected sentiments about sanitation and efficiency. A chronological inventory of materials reads as follows: wood wainscots, 1- or 2-inch tongue-and-groove boards with a cap rail; the same boards, sometimes referred to as "kitchen board," for ceilings; hard plaster covered with oil-base enamel paint; oilcloth that could be washed regularly or torn off and replaced; washable wallpapers such as varnished wall tiles; glazed ceramic tile for walls, usually at wainscot

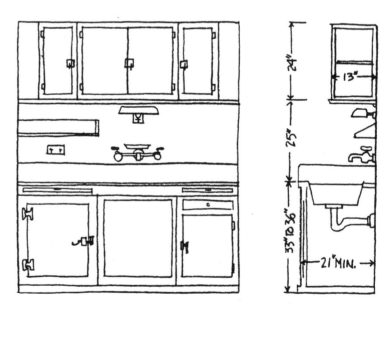

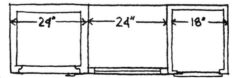

STANDARDS FOR WORK CENTER

height; and metal side wall coverings in sheets or in square or oblong blocks nailed to furring strips.

The kitchen floor consisted of a subfloor covered with a hardwood such as maple. Sometimes the floor was enameled for ease of maintenance. Oilcloth, ceramic tiles, including quarry tile, linoleum (patented in the 1860s), rubber mats, and cement also were used. Over the entire period it was linoleum-type products, in a wide range of colors and patterns, that carried the day.

Lighting

Kitchen lighting followed the historical patterns of the period, but the kitchen was seen particularly as a place where natural lighting would alleviate eye strain and enhance the general ambience. Artificial light sources from 1870 to 1940 included oil lamps set on metal wall brackets to light the sink and stove, gas fixtures as wall brackets and pendants hung from the center of the ceiling, and electric fixtures—as single bulbs, as clusters of bulbs in direct and indirect modes, and as bracket lights for work centers.

Beyond the concern for converting the loosely organized kitchen into a tightly grouped workshop, the kitchen was one of the primary theaters (the bathroom was the other) for the household campaign against unsanitary conditions. The desire to control disease by inhibiting the proliferation of germs had ramifications for kitchen design. The period 1900 through 1920 included a push for plain, smooth surfaces for moldings and cabinets, a rebuff to the ornamented surfaces of the last century. Ornamented edges and concave/convex surfaces collected dust, and dust was the medium for germs and bacteria. Smooth materials, especially those impervious to water, were easier to clean, and when combined with lots of sunlight and fresh air they produced a healthful and protective environment. The design concept that produced this enthusiasm for cleanliness was the *kitchen as laboratory*, a gleaming white room where the results of time-and-motion and nutrition studies could be implemented. A related minor development, generated by the technological character of the modern kitchen, was the presence of a house incinerator with a chute in the kitchen. After garbage collection became common, this feature disappeared.

Once the idea of the modern kitchen was fully inculcated into house design, it was inevitable that kitchen design would return to aesthetic issues as a basis for modernity. The route to aesthetics was through a negative reaction to the harsh white interior and a positive campaign for the application of color to the room. At first color accents were confined to stencil work or accent tiles, but soon there were campaigns to tint the walls—cream, light tan, green, or gray. By the 1930s floor coverings were more dramatically colored and kitchen equipment and utensils were manufactured tinted so that a kitchen might have one solitary tint or a two-tone effect. The increased use of color seems to have had a correlative increase in window lighting. Some kitchen critics even called for a formula deriving glass area from the room's square footage, with an area equal to at least one-fifth of the floor area to be devoted to glass (30 square feet of window for a kitchen of 150 square feet).

The call for color and other design accents was partly an appeal to the housekeeper to establish her own individuality in this work space. Now, as the manager of a standardized kitchen system—complete with measured counter heights, interchangeable cabinets, work centers arranged for the fewest steps between units, environmental controls such as heating, cooling, lighting, cooking, exhaust, and health control—she should introduce her personal aesthetic to unify the entire system.

Kitchenettes Once the integrated kitchen was successfully manufactured and marketed, it could be adapted to any kind of kitchen space. One especially significant effort in this vein was the miniaturization of the entire kitchen into the *kitchenette,* a scaled-down, tight grouping of cabinets, sink, refrigerator, and stove. The same logic transformed the pantry into the *pantryette.* The illustration accompanying this section was part of a 1921 advertisement by the Aladdin Company of Bay City, Michigan, makers of manufactured housing. Aladdin was selling the idea of the "Aladdinette," an apartment "that separated itself from other apartments and became a house." With proper proportioning and the adaptation of all accessories—the kind used in "expensive apartments, private railroad cars, and the like"—the single-family could live in an apartment-size house. The Aladdin kitchenette was designed to keep everything in reach, and included a refrigerator, sink, four-burner cookstove, a work table, and cabinets. The Aladdinette had 912 square feet of area that featured multiple-use rooms: living room/bedroom; dressing room/bath; dining room/bedroom; kitchen; and sun room/bedroom. The sleeping rooms had Murphy wall beds and eating was assigned to a dining alcove. The Aladdin products were made of wood, but steel kitchenettes could be had at this time from other manufacturers.

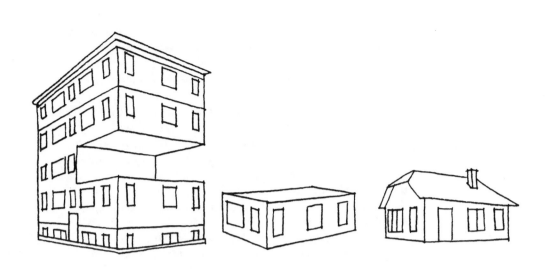

EVOLUTION OF ALADDINETTE HOME — 1921

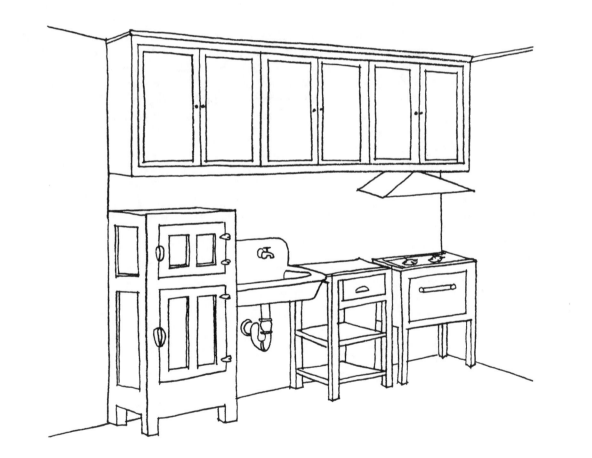

ALADDIN KITCHENETTE FOR ALADDINETTE HOME

Breakfast Nooks	Another kitchen design specialty was the development of the *breakfast space,* sometimes referred to as a "Dutch breakfast room" but eventually called a breakfast nook. These rooms began appearing in the trade literature around 1915. As for design, 8 feet by 10 feet was considered adequate, and it was recommended they have lots of windows (casements were popular) and be oriented to a porch or within a projecting bay. The furnishings for breakfast rooms were informal, with easily modified arrangements of chairs and a small table. Since the breakfast room was a very expensive addition, its function was served in most houses by an alcove or a nook in the pantry or kitchen. The nook was intended to save work for housekeepers and save wear on the dining room furniture. It was to be naturally ventilated and lighted with natural and artificial light. The atmosphere was to be cozy and charming, with color accents and an eastern exposure to get the morning sun. Nook size was generally square, about 5 feet 6 inches to 7 feet along one side. Design options for nooks were an arched or cased opening and movable or folding seats and table; folding types were called Pullman nooks. Seat and table designs were generally of two kinds, open-ended or solid, with the latter often having storage compartments under the seats. Most tables were the trestle type with straight, turned, or wide solid endpieces. Ornamentation consisted of scroll saw cuts in the table or bench supports and painted decoration.

Breakfast nooks were classified in trade catalogs as another kind of built-in furniture, and even featured electric convenience outlets on the wall or built into the table to put percolators and toasters within reach. The nooks were especially popular during the 1920s. While they sold for practical reasons, their success probably was related to the social transformation of the workshop-laboratory-kitchen into a family room, because family activity was associated with the nook. The table could be used for food preparation, dressmaking, ironing, childrens' play, letter writing, meal planning, and school work.

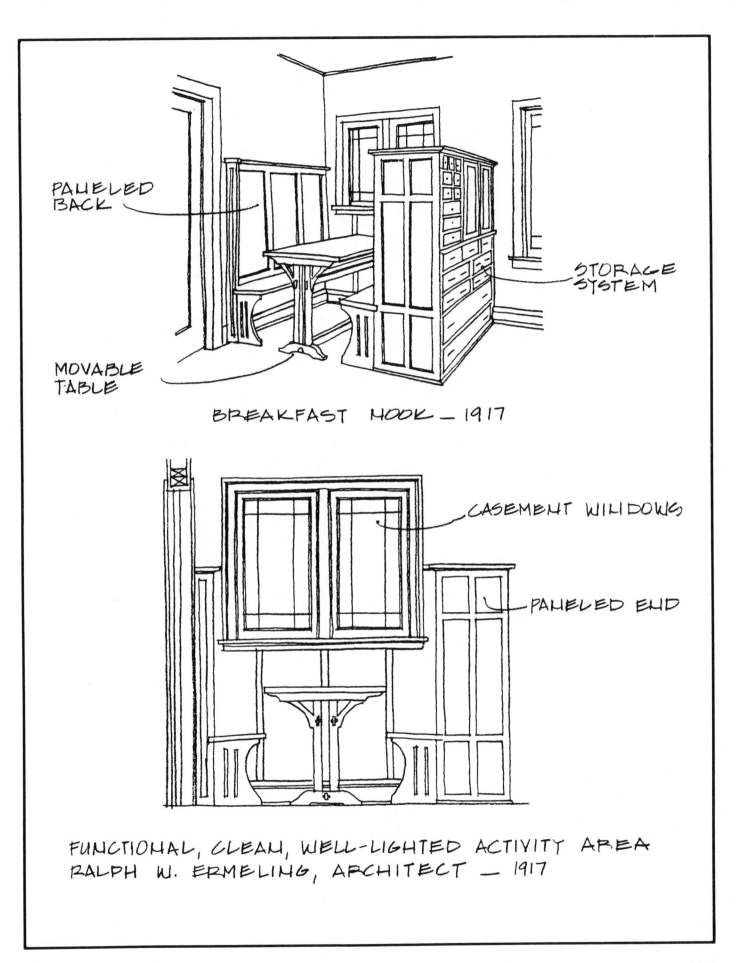

PANELED
BACK

STORAGE
SYSTEM

MOVABLE
TABLE

BREAKFAST NOOK — 1917

CASEMENT WINDOWS

PANELED END

FUNCTIONAL, CLEAN, WELL-LIGHTED ACTIVITY AREA
RALPH W. ERMELING, ARCHITECT — 1917

205

Modular Units   There was an interest in the *standardization* of kitchen elements early in the twentieth century. Home economists' bulletins and home-study reading courses, such as those published by Cornell University (as early as 1902), recommended that cupboards or dressers be 2 feet 8 inches high and from 20 to 24 inches wide, with a 12- to 15-inch open space between lower and upper cupboards. The demand for standards had its roots in a rational, scientific approach to kitchen planning. Essentially, this approach examined kitchen uses and functions and planned space accordingly. But the scientific approach also meant measured spaces, double uses, and standardized work patterns. Georgia B. Child, in *The Efficient Kitchen* (1925), put it this way:

> The problem that confronts us in the building and equipping of our kitchens is the developing of a standard type that will be adapted to the universal needs of the present day, and that can be modified to meet special needs without vital changes in the essential principles of construction.

The standardization issue was also part of the reform effort to improve the lot of housekeepers, whose work was made harder because of poorly planned and arranged equipment. The manufacturing system had been capable of responding all along, but the production of integrated cabinets in modular sizes wasn't well established until the 1930s. Kitchen design, by that time, utilized combinations of ready-made units, their widths based on 6-inch intervals (from 6 to 30 inches or more), and on heights of 24, 28, and 35 inches.

Moreover, by the 1930s cabinet design was so specialized that kitchen planners had choices of *special-use cabinets* to suit individual needs. With standardized units, which easily accommodated sinks, stoves, refrigerators, and dishwashers, the solution to a successful kitchen design lay in configurations that suited the house plan, the square footage available, and the housekeeper's aesthetics. It was the latter appeal that carried the kitchen into the era of conspicuous consumption, that pushed historically based design principles aside in favor of other values.

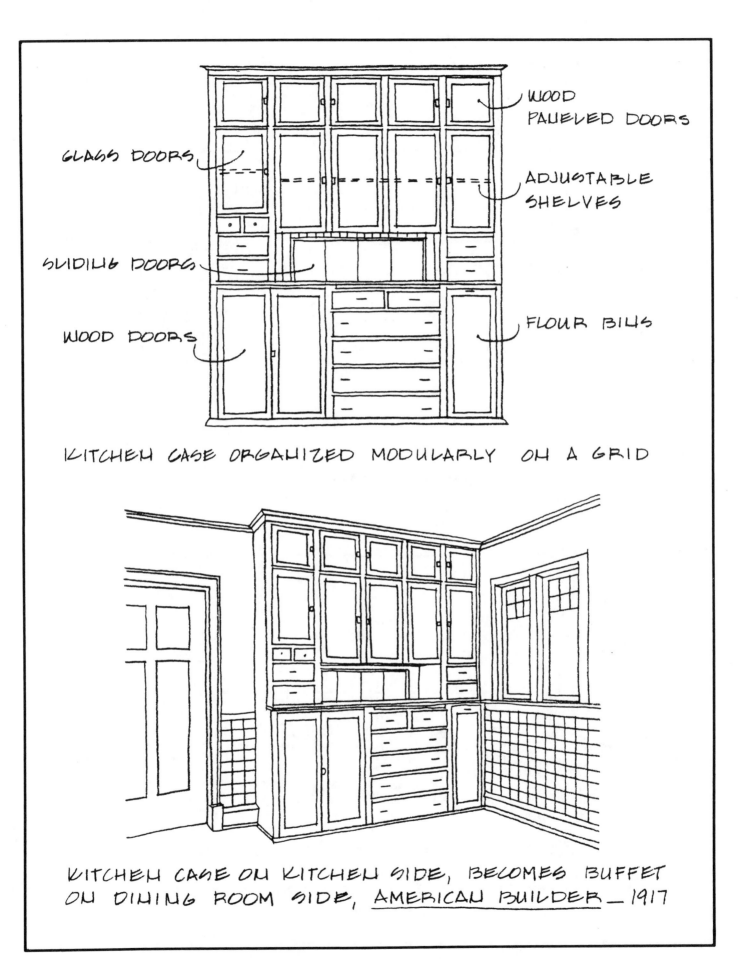

GLASS DOORS

WOOD PANELED DOORS

ADJUSTABLE SHELVES

SLIDING DOORS

WOOD DOORS

FLOUR BINS

KITCHEN CASE ORGANIZED MODULARLY ON A GRID

KITCHEN CASE ON KITCHEN SIDE, BECOMES BUFFET ON DINING ROOM SIDE, AMERICAN BUILDER — 1917

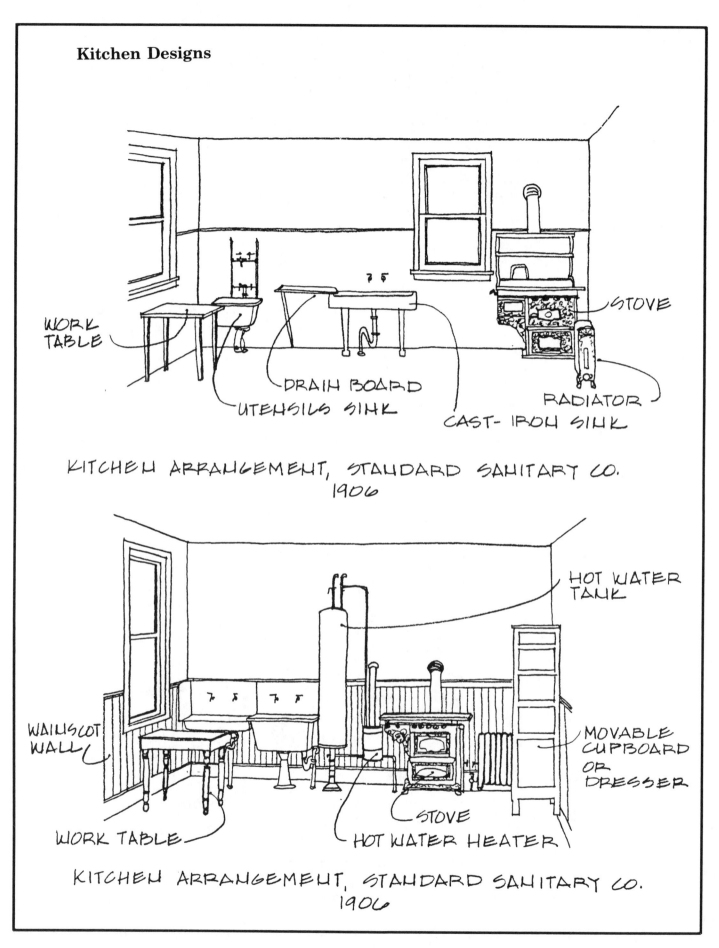

WORK TABLE

STOVE

DRAIN BOARD

UTENSILS SINK

CAST-IRON SINK

RADIATOR

KITCHEN ARRANGEMENT, STANDARD SANITARY CO.
1906

HOT WATER TANK

WAINSCOT WALL

MOVABLE CUPBOARD OR DRESSER

WORK TABLE

STOVE

HOT WATER HEATER

KITCHEN ARRANGEMENT, STANDARD SANITARY CO.
1906

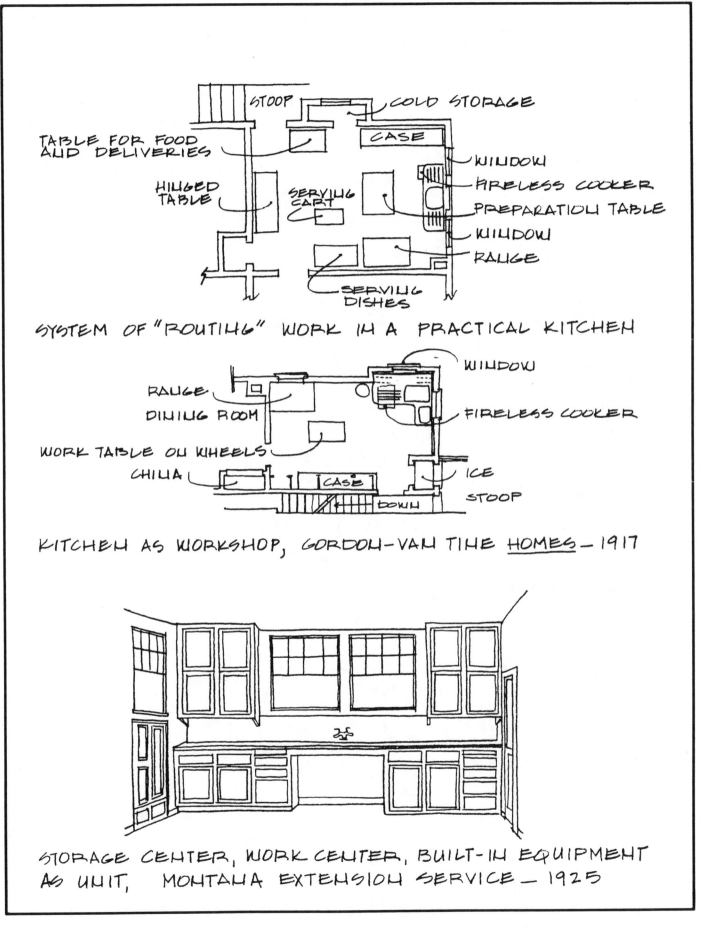

SYSTEM OF "ROUTING" WORK IN A PRACTICAL KITCHEN

Labels: STOOP, COLD STORAGE, TABLE FOR FOOD AND DELIVERIES, CASE, WINDOW, FIRELESS COOKER, HINGED TABLE, SERVING CART, PREPARATION TABLE, WINDOW, RANGE, SERVING DISHES

KITCHEN AS WORKSHOP, GORDON-VAN TINE HOMES — 1917

Labels: RANGE, DINING ROOM, WORK TABLE ON WHEELS, CHINA, CASE, DOWN, WINDOW, FIRELESS COOKER, ICE, STOOP

STORAGE CENTER, WORK CENTER, BUILT-IN EQUIPMENT AS UNIT, MONTANA EXTENSION SERVICE — 1925

Kitchen Designs

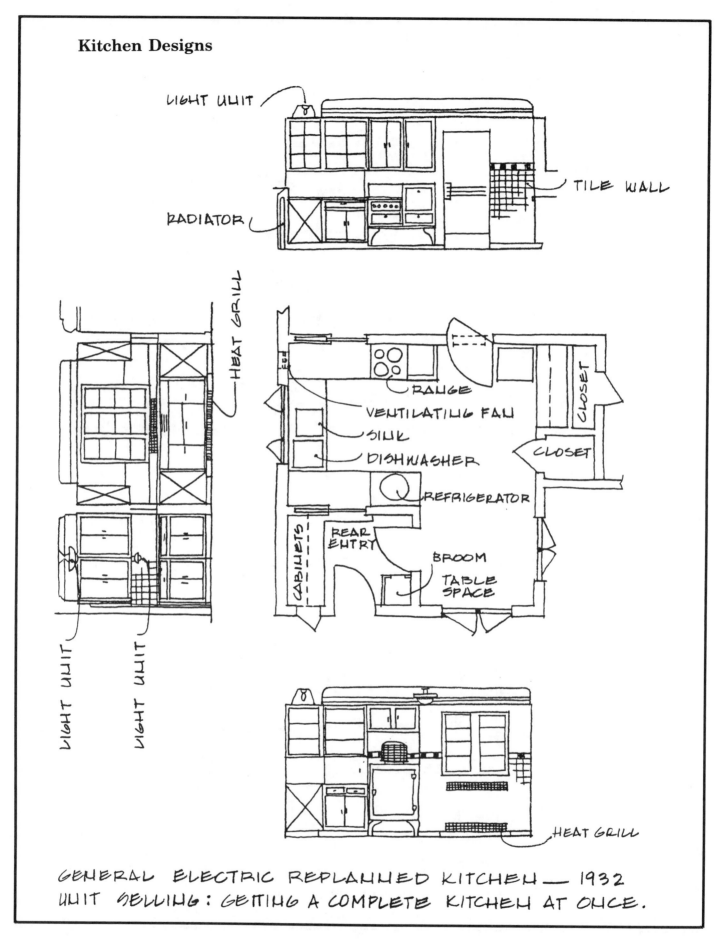

LIGHT UNIT

TILE WALL

RADIATOR

HEAT GRILL

LIGHT UNIT

LIGHT UNIT

RANGE

VENTILATING FAN

SINK

DISHWASHER

REFRIGERATOR

CLOSET

CLOSET

CABINETS

REAR ENTRY

BROOM

TABLE SPACE

HEAT GRILL

GENERAL ELECTRIC REPLANNED KITCHEN — 1932
UNIT SELLING: GETTING A COMPLETE KITCHEN AT ONCE.

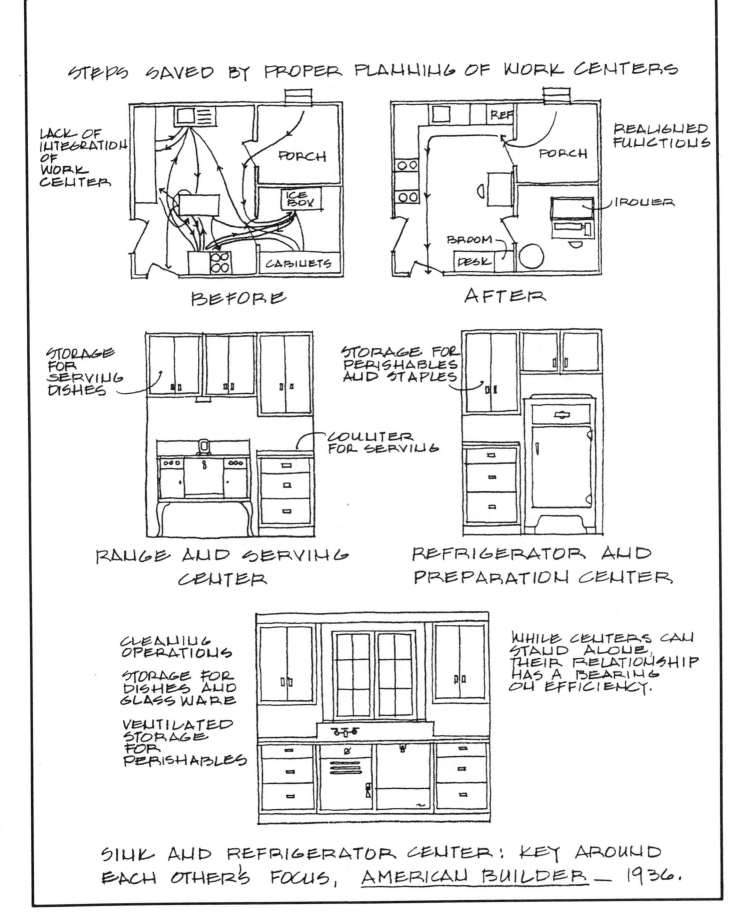

STEPS SAVED BY PROPER PLANNING OF WORK CENTERS

BEFORE

AFTER

LACK OF INTEGRATION OF WORK CENTER

PORCH

ICE BOX

CABINETS

REALIGNED FUNCTIONS

REF

PORCH

IRONER

BROOM

DESK

STORAGE FOR SERVING DISHES

COUNTER FOR SERVING

RANGE AND SERVING CENTER

STORAGE FOR PERISHABLES AND STAPLES

REFRIGERATOR AND PREPARATION CENTER

CLEANING OPERATIONS

STORAGE FOR DISHES AND GLASSWARE

VENTILATED STORAGE FOR PERISHABLES

WHILE CENTERS CAN STAND ALONE, THEIR RELATIONSHIP HAS A BEARING ON EFFICIENCY.

SINK AND REFRIGERATOR CENTER: KEY AROUND EACH OTHER'S FOCUS, AMERICAN BUILDER — 1936.

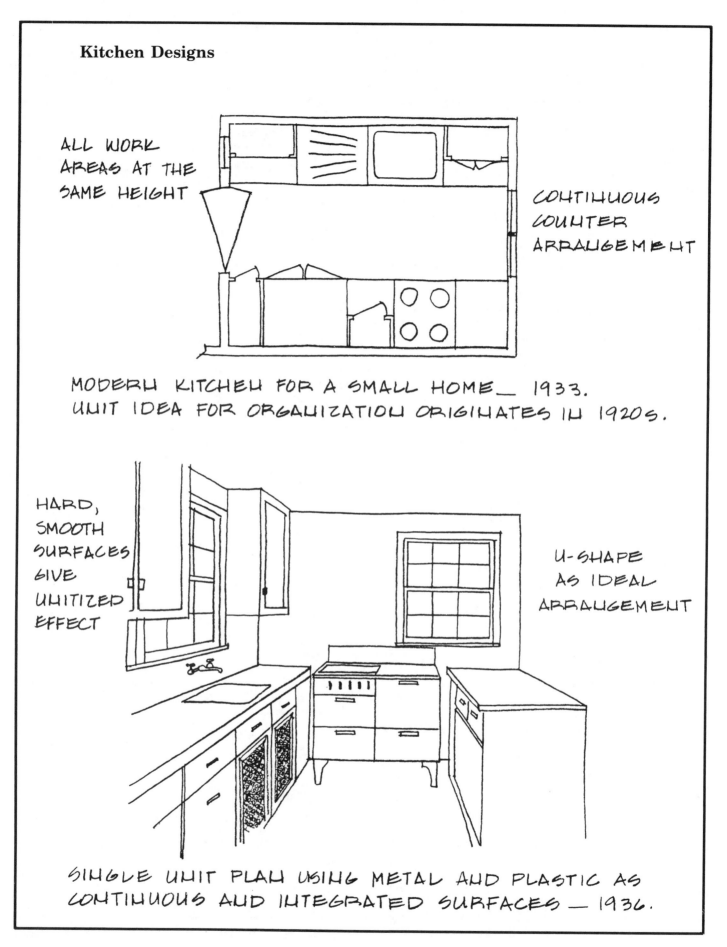

ALL WORK AREAS AT THE SAME HEIGHT

CONTINUOUS COUNTER ARRANGEMENT

MODERN KITCHEN FOR A SMALL HOME _ 1933.
UNIT IDEA FOR ORGANIZATION ORIGINATES IN 1920s.

HARD, SMOOTH SURFACES GIVE UNITIZED EFFECT

U-SHAPE AS IDEAL ARRANGEMENT

SINGLE UNIT PLAN USING METAL AND PLASTIC AS
CONTINUOUS AND INTEGRATED SURFACES _ 1936.

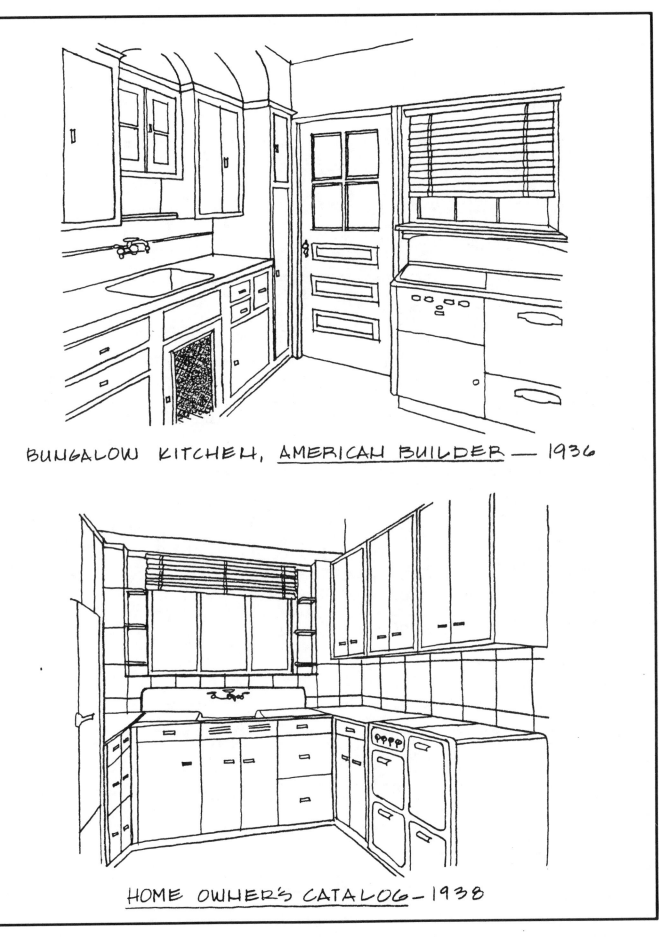

BUNGALOW KITCHEN, <u>AMERICAN BUILDER</u> — 1936

<u>HOME OWNER'S CATALOG</u> — 1938

**Stock Cabinets for
Any Kitchen**

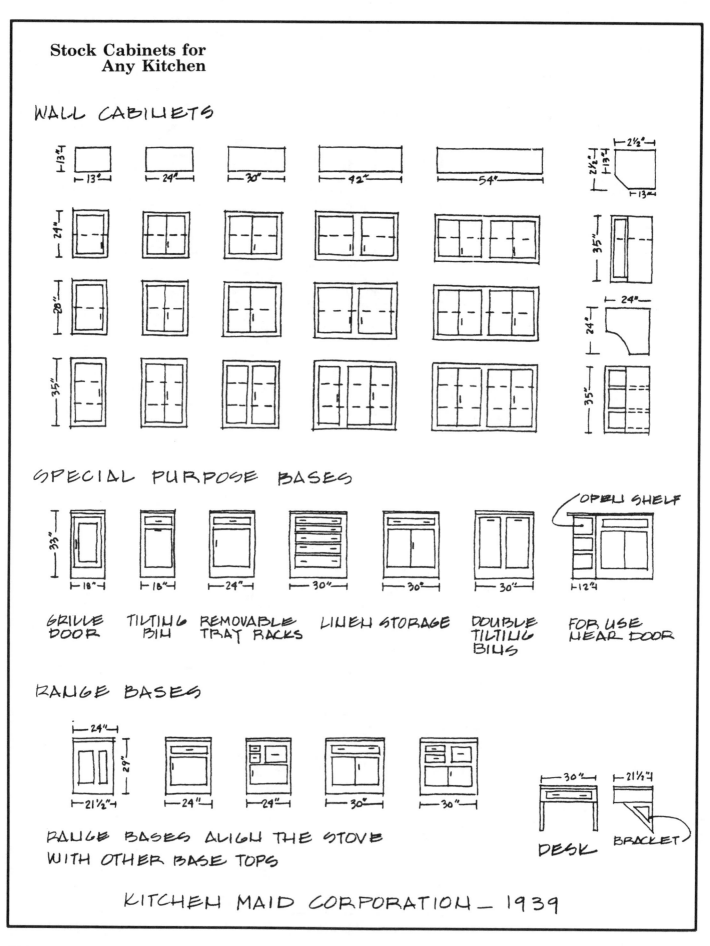

WALL CABINETS

SPECIAL PURPOSE BASES

OPEN SHELF

GRILLE DOOR TILTING BIN REMOVABLE TRAY RACKS LINEN STORAGE DOUBLE TILTING BINS FOR USE NEAR DOOR

RANGE BASES

RANGE BASES ALIGN THE STOVE
WITH OTHER BASE TOPS

DESK   BRACKET

KITCHEN MAID CORPORATION — 1939

LIGHTING Lighting design in vernacular interiors depended, in the first place, on the type of lighting power available. Power systems from private or municipal suppliers date from approximately the last decade of the nineteenth century. The first broadly based system of illumination was street lighting by natural gas supplied by private companies or municipal authorities; this system soon branched into lighting for residential, public, commercial, and industrial buildings. Small gas plants were also available for lighting individual vernacular buildings. One type, the acetylene plant, had a gas generator and gas holder and used carbide crystals for fuel; it could be automatically fired by a clockwork motor. Another type, the gasoline unit, generated gas in a carburetor placed underground at some distance from the building it served; air under pressure from a compressor or pump impregnated gasoline, making gas which passed to a governor in the basement of the building. Lastly, there was the bottled (blau) gas unit, using gas bottled under high pressure in steel containers.

Electric power systems were well in place by the 1920s. Offering multiple uses and improved lighting, electric systems replaced gas very quickly. Turn-of-the-century systems were not reliable, but that was overcome with better engineering and manufacturing. Besides area-wide systems, there were also low-wattage house electric plants for power and lighting which consisted of a storage battery, a small engine, a dynamo, and a switchboard. The plant was placed in the cellar or in a garage and required ventilation for safe operation. Three types of engines were used for driving the dynamo—gasoline, kerosene, and hot-air engines. Public and free-enterprise utilities companies made individual plants obsolete in urban areas by the 1930s.

By the 1920s standards for wiring and for outlet, switch, and fixture locations had been established, and there was not much deviation from them over the next two decades. One circuit was required for every 500 square feet of floor space, and all rooms were served by at least two circuits to prevent interruption. In general, three essentials were recognized for electric systems: 1) a sufficient number of outlets to suit taste, but at least one convenience outlet (for appliances) and one lighting outlet for every 50 square feet of floor space; 2) convenient control, a switch accessible to every doorway; 3) permanent installation, because wiring was strung within plaster and lath walls.

Outlets were the key to expanding electrical use in vernacular buildings. In 1931 General Electric estimated that from 1920 to 1927 the average number of outlets in a six-room house had increased from 21 to 53. Convenience outlets, as they were called, were the single or duplex type, with one or two plugs. The duplex units often were placed on the horizontal. Baseboard and wall locations for outlets typically were 18 to 24 inches above the floor. Some installations included waist-high outlets in hallways for vacuum cleaners and other cleaning equipment. In the bathroom and kitchen twin outlets were installed 36 to 48 inches from the floor. This height was also appropriate for basement outlets. Point-of-use became a significant criterion in planning systems, and over time additional standards crept into practice, such as placing a convenience outlet for every 10 feet of unbroken wall space in living rooms and bedrooms. Common to most vernacular design is the development of options or specializations within a class of elements. By the 1930s there were specialty outlets: floor, radio, telephone, pilot light and switch control, heavy-duty polarity outlets, all in flush or weatherproof designs.

By 1870 vernacular buildings were lighted by oil, especially coal oil (kerosene), and natural gas. Oil lamps faded from use around this time, because of the low quality of the light and the need to keep the fixtures clean and filled. But the systematic placement of oil lamps and the general design of oil-lamp fixtures established patterns that were followed in the eras of gas and electricity. Hanging lights for general use, 26 to 30 inches in height, hall pendants (some adjustable) of 41 to 45 inches, and side lamps with reflectors for special effects or for task lighting laid a groundwork for fixture design. There were also chandeliers with a center support post and two to four fixtures branching from the post, each comprising a font, globe, and chimney. In general, gas and electric lighting fixtures were variations of these types—with the addition of a few new forms, such as the candle light—until the stylization of fixtures and the exponential growth of electrical usage took lighting to a new dimension. This growth was accompanied by the development of specialty lights and the use of new materials for fixtures.

The majority of all light fixtures have been suspended from or attached directly to ceilings, with the remainder being attached to walls. Fixtures were suspended on metal hangers, solitary or branched stems, and chains or chords. To ensure equal radiation, lighting fixtures, regardless of the light source, were symmetrical in design. In hangers and pendants the fixture was placed on the center line of the support: in chandeliers branches with fixtures radiated from the center. Most suspended fixtures were located in the center of the room they serviced or were placed on center axis in a hallway.

Gas lights inherited the functional elements and forms of oil lamps: similar pendant frames, iron supports, tubular pieces, glass globes, chains for adjusting lights, and globe clasps or set screws. Oil fixtures usually were single units, one to a branch, all in the same plane. Gas lighting expanded on this and layered the lights—large globes on the bottom and smaller ones on the top, arranged in concentric rings. In another change, the side lamp evolved into the bracket light without reflector. Since gas lights were brighter, shade design was changed to diffuse and mask the new light, and wall mounting was modified. The gas light could be extended on its supply pipe 6 to 12 inches from the wall. Jointed arms, a feature of oil side lamps, were incorporated in the design vocabulary of gas brackets.

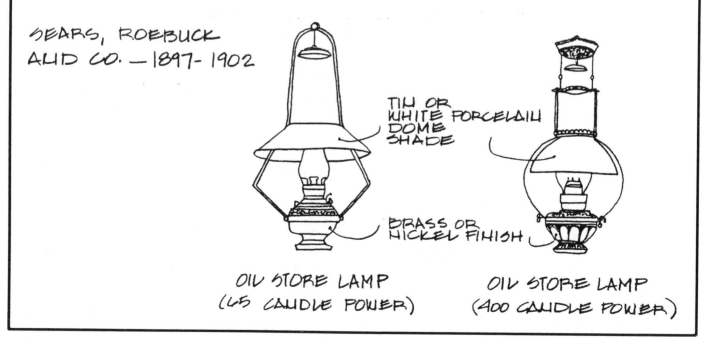

SEARS, ROEBUCK AND CO. — 1897- 1902

TIN OR WHITE PORCELAIN DOME SHADE

BRASS OR NICKEL FINISH

OIL STORE LAMP (65 CANDLE POWER)

OIL STORE LAMP (400 CANDLE POWER)

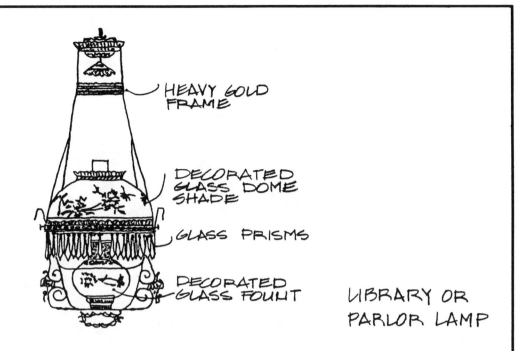

HEAVY GOLD FRAME

DECORATED GLASS DOME SHADE

GLASS PRISMS

DECORATED GLASS FOUNT

LIBRARY OR PARLOR LAMP

As alluded to above, natural-gas lighting had advantages over oil-lamp lighting. Not only was the light quality better, but the piping of gas lines through the walls increased the number of available light sources and added permanent light location as an element in interior design. Gas lighting also encouraged fixture experimentation, including linking lights to design systems and examining the role of reflectivity in quality lighting. Gas lighting established a precedent for the development of electrical fixtures, providing light anywhere it was needed with variations in functional and atmospheric effects.

Historically, gas-light fixtures were confined to being set upright with a font at the bottom, a carryover from oil lamps, and a burner above. In the 1880s an inverted gas burner was developed but it was not introduced until the turn of the century. The inverted burner made the gas fixture more effective for direct illumination: more light was thrown downward and shadows were eliminated. Mantles were made shorter and double woven, and an air mixer was added to burn less gas. Other changes in fixture design included a shift away from heavy iron supports toward tubular supports with brass or bronze finishes, a modification of the fixture shade from a small-necked to a wide type, and shades that were cut, frosted, etched, ribbed, and painted. Overall, fixtures became visually and materially lighter.

AIR MIXER

GAS COCK

GLOBE

INVERTED GAS FIXTURE

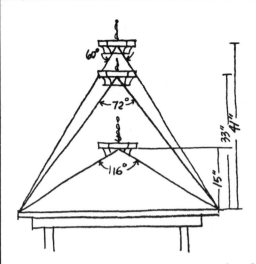

HANGING HEIGHT DETERMINED BY THE DIAMETER OF OPENING THROUGH WHICH LIGHT IS EMITTED AND DISTANCE OF LAMP FILAMENT ABOVE OPENING.

As electricity gained popularity, combination gas and electric fixtures were created for pendant, chandelier, and bracket lights. Trying to compete with ranges in lamp wattage, gas units featured chains for adjusting the gas flow and the light intensity. Fixture designs that integrated the two light sources had the same shade shape, finish, and support pieces. The supports were made mostly of brass or bronze with an assortment of finishes: gilt, polished brass, old brass, nickel, green bronze, copper, ormolu, and silver. Many of the design elements were cut from sheet metal, which gave the fixtures a lighter and more linear design quality.

Electric lighting systems were assembled in much the same way as gas systems. There was a supply line diverted into circuits, with a switchboard delivering lines to rooms in the building. The turn-of-the-century system had open or knob-and-tube wiring. Insulated copper wires needed for each circuit were stretched from point to point, supported by white porcelain knob or cleat insulators. Knobs held one wire, cleats two. Where the wires passed through framing, such as wall studs, porcelain tubes were used as insulating sleeves. Fuses for circuits were installed in porcelain blocks and mounted on the basement ceiling or the attic floor joists. Some systems had fuse cabinets in a pantry or the kitchen.

Since electric lighting was a technology-based development, and given the reform atmosphere of the time in which it was being introduced to the public, it is not surprising that the use of electric lighting was subjected to "scientific" study. Most of these studies had to do with the application of electric lighting to residences. The nature of illumination was of interest, and a number of publications, such as *American Carpenter and Builder* and *Keith's Magazine,* ran articles explaining the types of illumination necessary for a complete lighting system. Writers argued that electric units could provide more diversified lighting effects, and that generalized light qualities could be redefined to suit specific sites and tasks. To do that properly meant integrating the three kinds of illumination: direct, indirect, and semi-indirect.

Direct illumination, the oldest type, was limited at first by the kind of lamps that were available. Thomas Edison's carbon lamps were inefficient, and the discovery that tungsten could be utilized for light filaments improved lighting considerably. But the first filaments of this kind were pressed tungsten, which was brittle and fragile. In 1911 William Cooledge's process for making tungsten ductile so that it could be drawn into fine wire solved the problems of efficiency and fragility. Tungsten filament lamps made it possible to develop indirect and semi-indirect illumination.

Direct illumination fixtures sent light directly to where it was needed. Shades controlled the spread of the light. The *pendant* was a typical direct-illumination light. Aided by a dome-shaped shade, the pendant provided controlled light. To enhance its appearance, parchment, textiles, or art glass were used in the dome. To improve its diffusing properties, frosted lamps and quality glass were required. There was experimentation with the size of apertures, and most were reduced to just a few inches, especially for domes over dining room tables.

Indirect illumination achieved the opposite effect, in that all the light was directed toward the ceiling which in turn acted as a large reflector and distributed the light throughout the room. Indirect illumination provided subtle effects in light, color, distribution, and intensity. In some instances it corresponded to the lighting effect of the sky. The typical indirect light was a bowl, with a silvered glass reflector concealed in an ornamented housing. Indirect lights often were concealed in some kind of architectural detail.

The third condition, *semi-indirect illumination,* reflected most of the light toward the ceiling but allowed some light to be transmitted down toward the floor or laterally through the fixture bowl. The amount of direct illumination was controlled by the density of the glass beneath the aperture of the opaque reflector. Glass of light density allowed a lot of light to pass through, while a very dense glass made the bottom of the fixture barely luminous. The luminous bowl combined direct and indirect effects, with the indirect effect coming from silvered reflectors; in the center a second lamp illuminated the parchment, silk, or glass and an aperture. Other semi-indirect combination lights included direct units with candle lights, shower lights with a bowl, and bowl-and-candle combinations.

Different kinds of illumination became identified with specific rooms or groups of rooms. Direct illumination was suggested for the living room, dining room, and library: indirect for the music room, den, reception room,

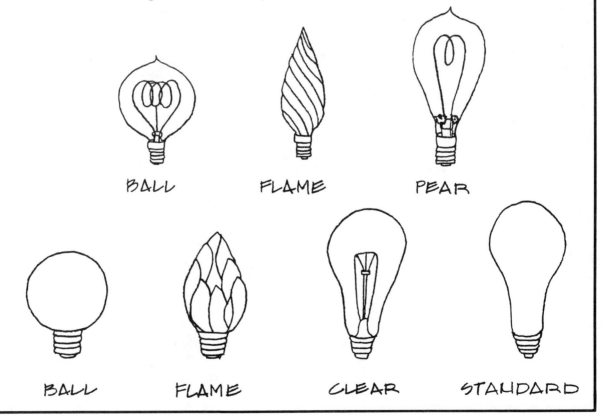

BALL   FLAME   PEAR

BALL   FLAME   CLEAR   STANDARD

kitchen/pantry, and sewing room; and semi-indirect for sleeping and dressing rooms, billiard and card rooms, halls, and bathrooms. Most of the lighting for these spaces was complemented by wall brackets and portable lamps.

Besides illumination strategies, electric lighting was subject to studies of fixture heights and aperture openings as related to the cones of light coming through them. M. Luckiesh, *Lighting Fixtures and Lighting Effects* (1925), diagramed the relationship between the diameter of a fixture's opening and the distance of the lamp filament above the opening as determinants for fixture height above the table. By this formula it was possible to light the dining table with pleasant and adequate light without direct light entering the eyes of the diners.

Luckiesh also offered recommendations for control switches and convenience outlets. A summary of the "rules" follows:

1. Have a wall switch on the knob side of a door through which you enter frequently
2. Locate baseboard outlets to accommodate furniture placement
3. Place two duplex outlets on different sides of important rooms
4. Actuate a light in the closet by an automatic door switch in the jamb
5. Provide hall lights with a three-way switch, allowing for off/on operation from either direction
6. To avoid casting shadows, place no light opposite a window shade
7. Have side wall lights in bedrooms
8. Have a central light in the attic
9. Have more than one center ceiling light in a house
10. Install a switch with a red "reminder" for the cellar light.

New light fixtures were designed to exploit the possibilities of electrical illumination. One that enjoyed great success was the *shower light*. It was a direct-illumination light composed of a cluster of small lamps hung by chains, with the lights attached to a plate in order to spread the light. Shower lights had two to five lamps, at first covered with bell-shaped shades: they ranged in drop length from 30 to 36 inches and in spread from 12 to 20 inches. The shower light and the indirect light in a bowl or urn replaced many pendants. The bowls and urns simply held more lamps and thus provided opportunities for different effects. Efficient indirect lighting and special-effect lighting required a reflective room finish. In the 1920s, cream-color paint laid on smooth plaster was the preferred scheme. On the issue of efficiency, not all lighting requirements were reduced to satisfying percentages. Any loss of light by the indirect method was considered offset by improved quality of illumination and better conditions for seeing.

By the 1920s specific kinds of lighting effects were linked to certain illuminations and fixtures. If the house were, in the language of the period, "the theater of life," then lighting could play a key role in the activities, moods, and social affairs of that theater. Lighting became decorative. The *living room* got one or two indirect or direct luminous bowls supplemented by wall brackets and portable lamps. Integrating the units required balancing general and local light with expressive effects. The latter often were carried off with concealed lamps in indirect fixtures. Urns, vases, corbels, capitals, cornices, moldings, plaques, decorative panels, wall boxes, window boxes, window sills, rosettes, domes, friezes, artificial windows, niches, skylights, and finials all were used in this way.

Dining room lighting centered on illuminating the table. There were several placements that succeeded in bringing a cone of soft white light to the table. One required 24 inches between the top of the table and the bottom of the fixture's dome. A second dimension for a dome was 54 inches from the floor to the bottom of the dome. If a shower light was used, then 36 inches was recommended. Candle light fixtures could be even higher— 45 inches from the table to the bottom of the shade. Cylindrical or bud-shaped shades were better at confining the light of shower lamps than were the traditional bell-shaped shades. Glass shades had been colored from the beginning of electric lighting, but more attention began to be paid to providing tinted bulbs and glass that would create special effects in the dining room. The so-called artistic styles of design modified the color of the transmitted light and used shades that harmonized with the room finish. Wall brackets with colored bulbs and shades also were used in dining rooms; they were mounted 6 feet from the floor and used low-wattage lamps.

Bedroom and *bath* spaces often received a central fixture. In bedrooms, wall brackets placed about 6 feet above the floor were sometimes the primary lighting. Small portable lamps on a dresser or dressing table provided local lighting. In the bathroom, twin bracket lights were placed at a height of 5 feet above the floor, one on either side of the mirror over the lavatory.

Kitchen lighting required a centrally placed *luminaire* close to the ceiling with a glass reflector to distribute the light around the room. Bracket lights, notable for their smooth, easily cleaned surfaces and dense opal-glass shade, were placed above the sink, about 5 feet off the floor. In large kitchens, local lighting was recommended also for the range. Breakfast nooks were to have a semi-indirect light that illuminated the eating area and the storage around it.

The *entrance hall*, which could be either a type of reception room, or merely the intermediate space between the front door and the rest of the building, usually was lighted. Generally a low-wattage lamp, close to the ceiling, sufficed for the informal hall. Reception halls called for more elaborate fixtures: urn-shaped enclosing globes with indirect lighting, candle- and torch-type wall brackets, and multiple-light drop fixtures on chains.

Special-use rooms such as laundries and utility rooms were to have high-level illumination. Dome reflectors, plain porcelain sockets, ceiling lights with an all-enclosing globe, or kitchen lights if the laundry was finished were acceptable fixtures. The den or sewing room also needed high-intensity illumination, divided between a central fixture of moderate intensity and a portable lamp for close work. Closet illumination was carried out by a ceiling light or bulb socket with a pull chain within the closet or by a wall bracket placed to direct light into the closet.

One final dimension to the standards for electric lighting was the attempt to establish wattage levels for lamps in specific rooms. In the early 1930s such recommendations were as follows: living room and dining room ceiling lights should be 40-watt, with wall brackets of 25-watt frosted or 40-watt colored or tinted lamps; kitchen ceiling wattage should be 100 for a frosted lamp and 150 for a daylight lamp, with 75-watt units over the sink and stove; bedroom central lights should be 40-watts whether frosted or tinted; wall brackets should have the same wattage as those in the living and dining rooms.

Throughout the first decades of this century there were continuous developments in lamps, in their efficiency and the quality of their light. Some lamps, such as the Lumiline series, stretched a filament for 18 inches and with the help of a long reflector created linear light effects. These tubular lights prefigured the fluorescent units that were to make a strong impact on vernacular commercial and residential buildings.

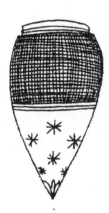

CUT GLASS
STALACTITE
HOLOPHANE

HOLOPHANE
REFLECTOR

221

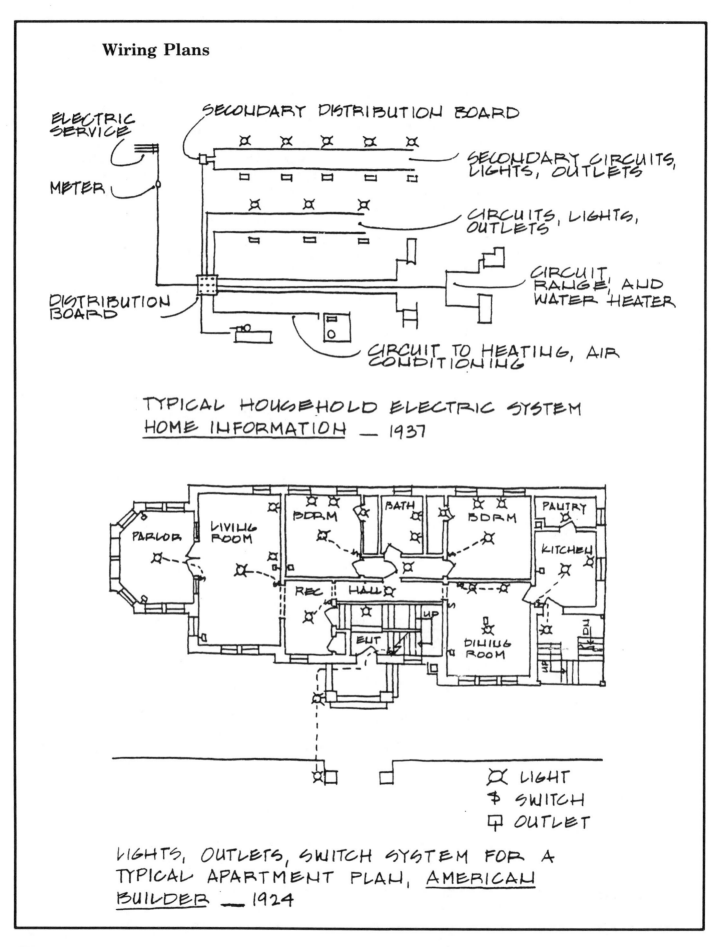

ELECTRIC SERVICE

SECONDARY DISTRIBUTION BOARD

SECONDARY CIRCUITS, LIGHTS, OUTLETS

METER

CIRCUITS, LIGHTS, OUTLETS

CIRCUIT RANGE, AND WATER HEATER

DISTRIBUTION BOARD

CIRCUIT TO HEATING, AIR CONDITIONING

TYPICAL HOUSEHOLD ELECTRIC SYSTEM HOME INFORMATION — 1937

PARLOR

LIVING ROOM

BDRM

BATH

BDRM

PANTRY

KITCHEN

REC

HALL

UP

EUT

DINING ROOM

UP

LIGHT
SWITCH
OUTLET

LIGHTS, OUTLETS, SWITCH SYSTEM FOR A TYPICAL APARTMENT PLAN, AMERICAN BUILDER — 1924

Outlets and Switches

OUTLETS

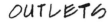
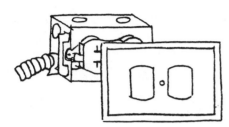
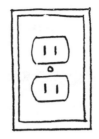

CONVENIENCE
OUTLET

TWIN
CONVENIENCE
OUTLET

SINGLE
CONVENIENCE
OUTLET

SWITCHES

KNIFE
SWITCH

STANDARD
DIAL SWITCH

PUSH BUTTON
SWITCH

ROTARY
FLUSH SWITCH

PLATES   COMBINATION PLATES

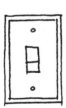

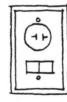

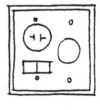

FLUSH
SWITCH

TWO-GANG
FLUSH
SWITCH

TUMBLER
SWITCH,
PILOT
LIGHT

TUMBLER
SWITCH,
OUTLET

TUMBLER
SWITCH,
CONVENIENCE
OUTLET,
PILOT LIGHT

**Types of
Illumination**

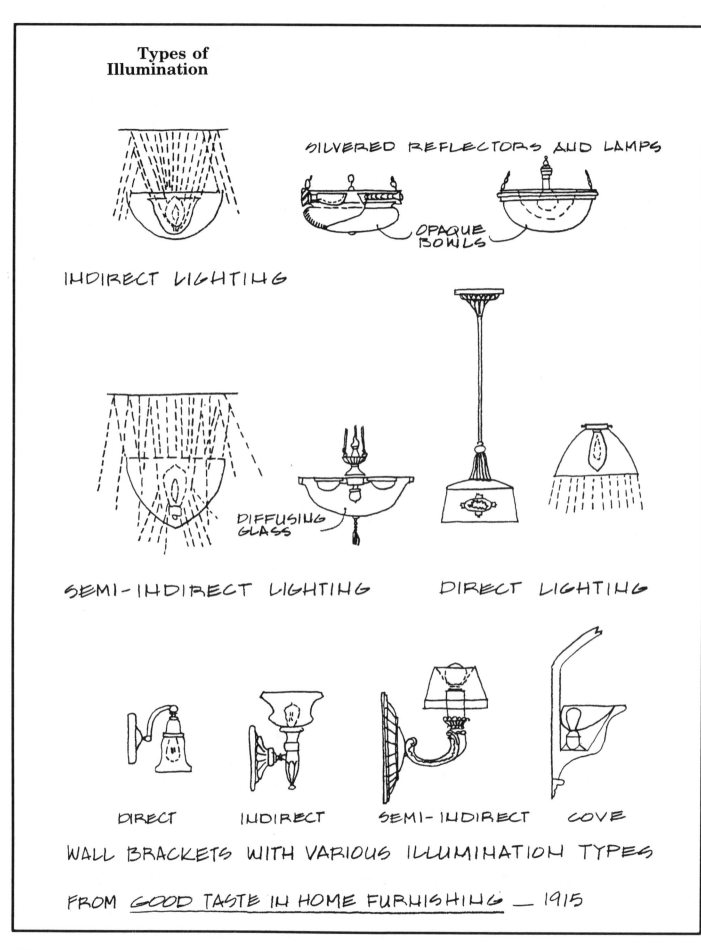

INDIRECT LIGHTING

SILVERED REFLECTORS AND LAMPS

OPAQUE BOWLS

DIFFUSING GLASS

SEMI-INDIRECT LIGHTING

DIRECT LIGHTING

DIRECT

INDIRECT

SEMI-INDIRECT

COVE

WALL BRACKETS WITH VARIOUS ILLUMINATION TYPES

FROM _GOOD TASTE IN HOME FURNISHING_ — 1915

Fixture Elements

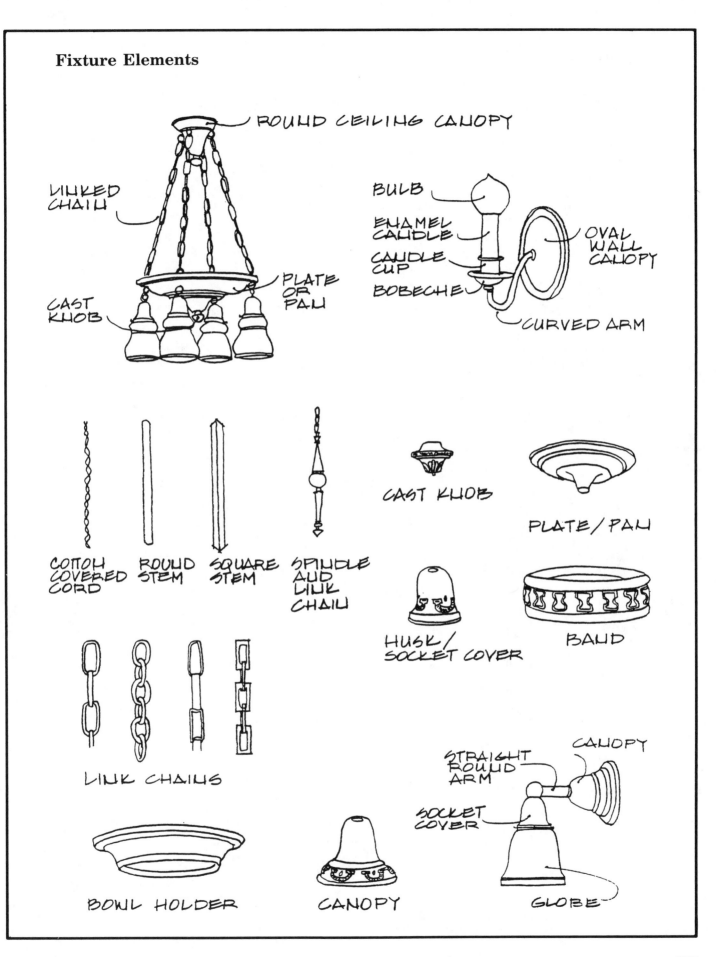

ROUND CEILING CANOPY

LINKED CHAIN

CAST KNOB

PLATE OR PAN

BULB

ENAMEL CANDLE

CANDLE CUP

BOBECHE

OVAL WALL CANOPY

CURVED ARM

COTTON COVERED CORD

ROUND STEM

SQUARE STEM

SPINDLE AND LINK CHAIN

CAST KNOB

PLATE/PAN

HUSK/ SOCKET COVER

BAND

LINK CHAINS

STRAIGHT ROUND ARM

CANOPY

SOCKET COVER

BOWL HOLDER

CANOPY

GLOBE

Fixture Elements

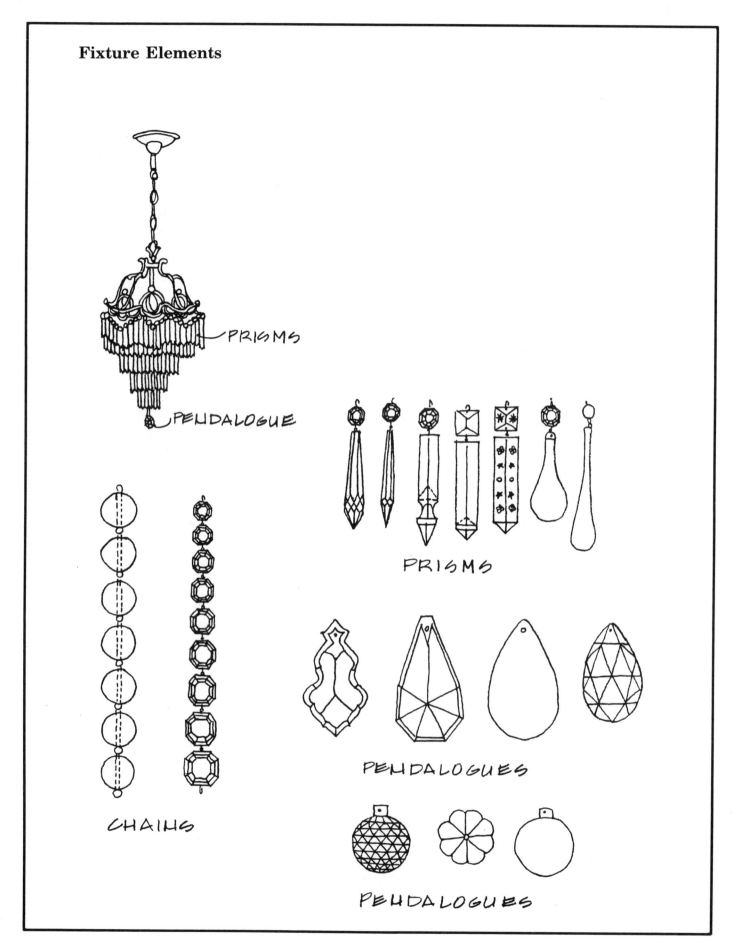

PRISMS

PENDALOGUE

PRISMS

CHAINS

PENDALOGUES

PENDALOGUES

Shades

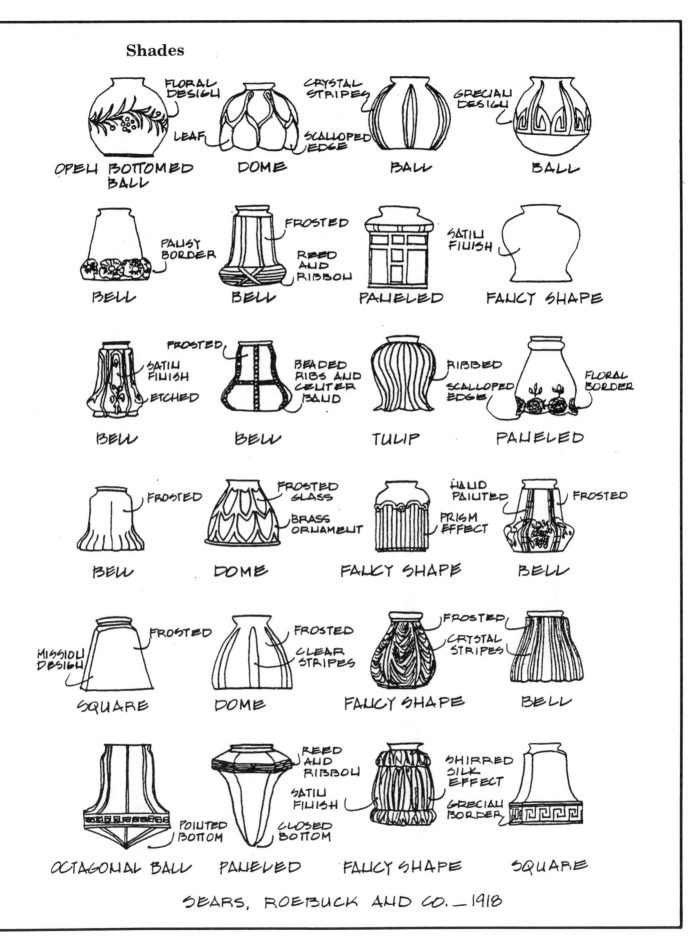

OPEN BOTTOMED BALL — FLORAL DESIGN, LEAF

DOME — CRYSTAL STRIPES, SCALLOPED EDGE

BALL

BALL — GRECIAN DESIGN

BELL — PANSY BORDER

BELL — FROSTED, REED AND RIBBON

PANELED — SATIN FINISH

FANCY SHAPE

BELL — FROSTED, SATIN FINISH, ETCHED

BELL — BEADED RIBS AND CENTER BAND

TULIP — RIBBED, SCALLOPED EDGE

PANELED — FLORAL BORDER

BELL — FROSTED

DOME — FROSTED GLASS, BRASS ORNAMENT

FANCY SHAPE — HAND PAINTED, PRISM EFFECT

BELL — FROSTED

SQUARE — MISSION DESIGN, FROSTED

DOME — FROSTED, CLEAR STRIPES

FANCY SHAPE — FROSTED, CRYSTAL STRIPES

BELL

OCTAGONAL BALL — POINTED BOTTOM

PANELED — REED AND RIBBON, SATIN FINISH, CLOSED BOTTOM

FANCY SHAPE — SHIRRED SILK EFFECT, GRECIAN BORDER

SQUARE

SEARS, ROEBUCK AND CO. — 1918

227

Pendants

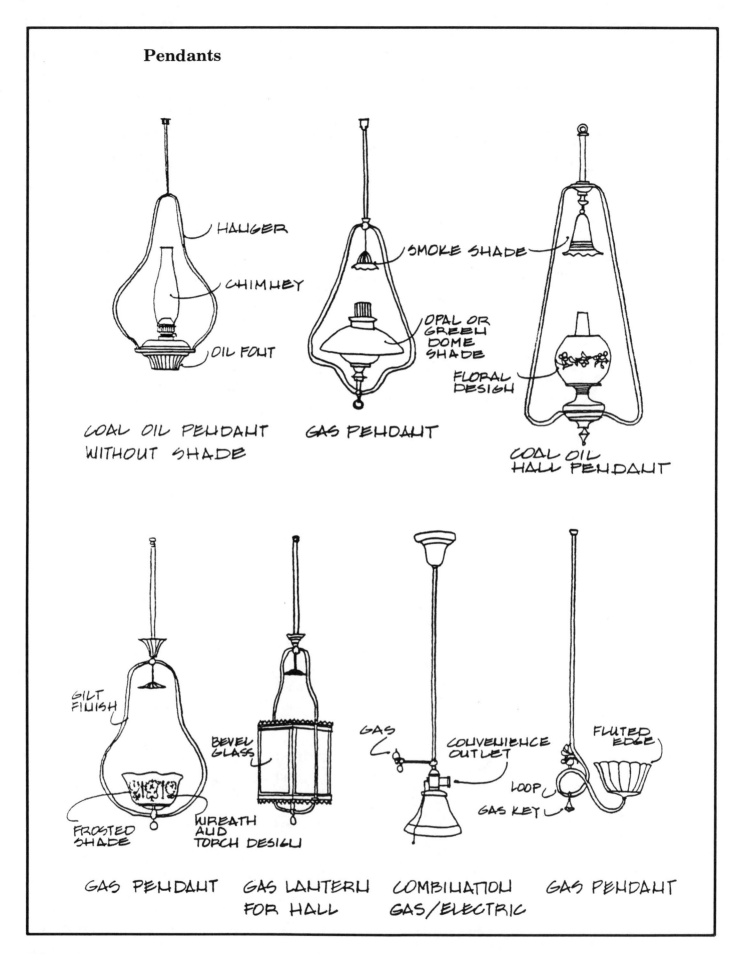

HANGER

CHIMNEY

OIL FONT

COAL OIL PENDANT
WITHOUT SHADE

SMOKE SHADE

OPAL OR
GREEN
DOME
SHADE

FLORAL
DESIGN

GAS PENDANT

COAL OIL
HALL PENDANT

GILT
FINISH

FROSTED
SHADE

BEVEL
GLASS

WREATH
AND
TORCH DESIGN

GAS

CONVENIENCE
OUTLET

LOOP

GAS KEY

FLUTED
EDGE

GAS PENDANT

GAS LANTERN
FOR HALL

COMBINATION
GAS/ELECTRIC

GAS PENDANT

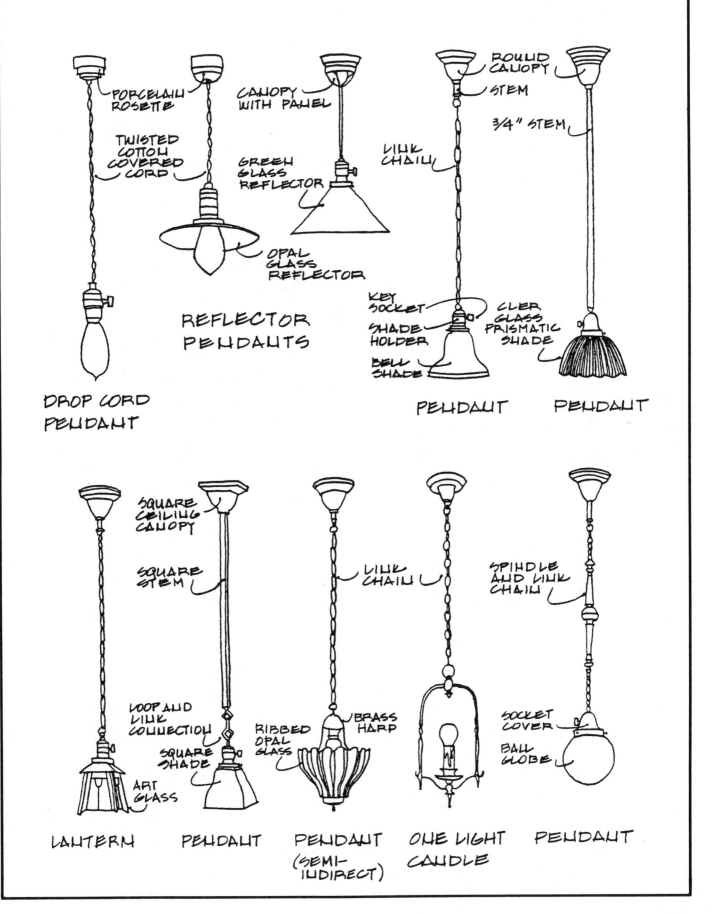

PORCELAIN
ROSETTE

CANOPY
WITH PANEL

ROUND
CANOPY

STEM

3/4" STEM

TWISTED
COTTON
COVERED
CORD

GREEN
GLASS
REFLECTOR

LINK
CHAIN

REFLECTOR
PENDANTS

OPAL
GLASS
REFLECTOR

KEY
SOCKET

CLER
GLASS
PRISMATIC
SHADE

SHADE
HOLDER

BELL
SHADE

DROP CORD
PENDANT

PENDANT

PENDANT

SQUARE
CEILING
CANOPY

SQUARE
STEM

LINK
CHAIN

SPINDLE
AND LINK
CHAIN

LOOP AND
LINK
CONNECTION

RIBBED
OPAL
GLASS

BRASS
HARP

SOCKET
COVER

SQUARE
SHADE

BALL
GLOBE

ART
GLASS

LANTERN

PENDANT

PENDANT
(SEMI-
INDIRECT)

ONE LIGHT
CANDLE

PENDANT

229

Branched Fixtures

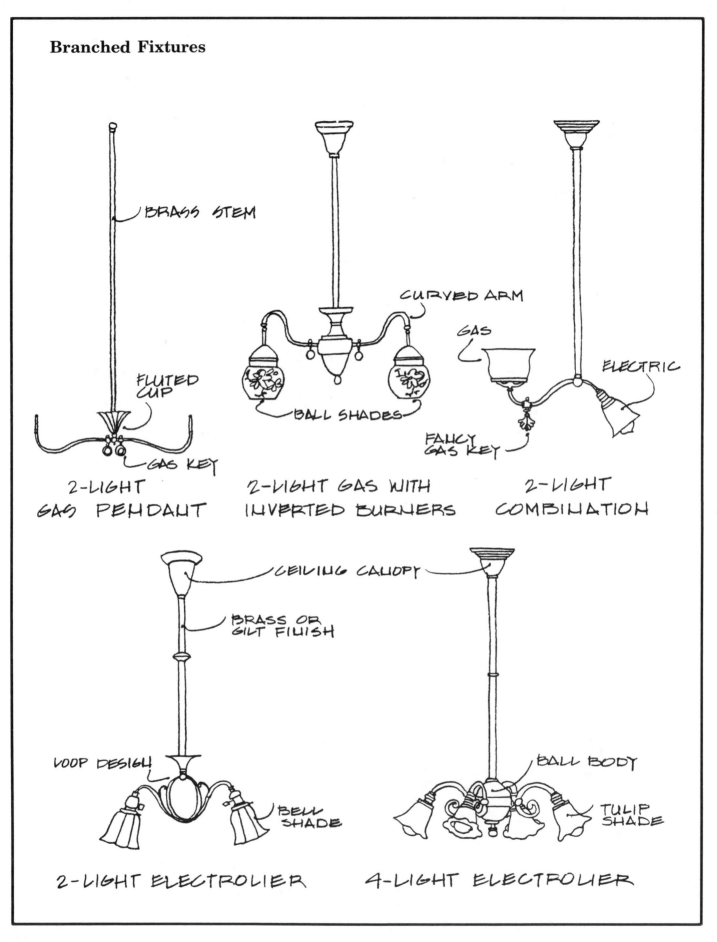

BRASS STEM

FLUTED CUP

GAS KEY

2-LIGHT GAS PENDANT

CURVED ARM

BALL SHADES

2-LIGHT GAS WITH INVERTED BURNERS

GAS

ELECTRIC

FANCY GAS KEY

2-LIGHT COMBINATION

CEILING CANOPY

BRASS OR GILT FINISH

LOOP DESIGN

BELL SHADE

2-LIGHT ELECTROLIER

BALL BODY

TULIP SHADE

4-LIGHT ELECTROLIER

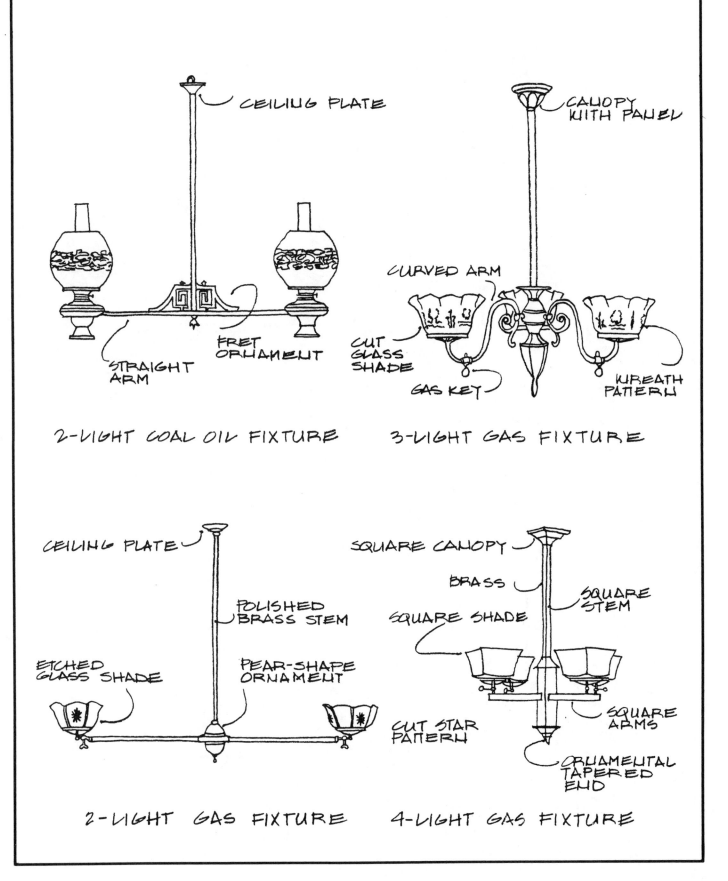

CEILING PLATE

STRAIGHT ARM

FRET ORNAMENT

2-LIGHT COAL OIL FIXTURE

CANOPY WITH PANEL

CURVED ARM

CUT GLASS SHADE

GAS KEY

WREATH PATTERN

3-LIGHT GAS FIXTURE

CEILING PLATE

POLISHED BRASS STEM

ETCHED GLASS SHADE

PEAR-SHAPE ORNAMENT

2-LIGHT GAS FIXTURE

SQUARE CANOPY

BRASS

SQUARE STEM

SQUARE SHADE

CUT STAR PATTERN

SQUARE ARMS

ORNAMENTAL TAPERED END

4-LIGHT GAS FIXTURE

Branched Fixtures

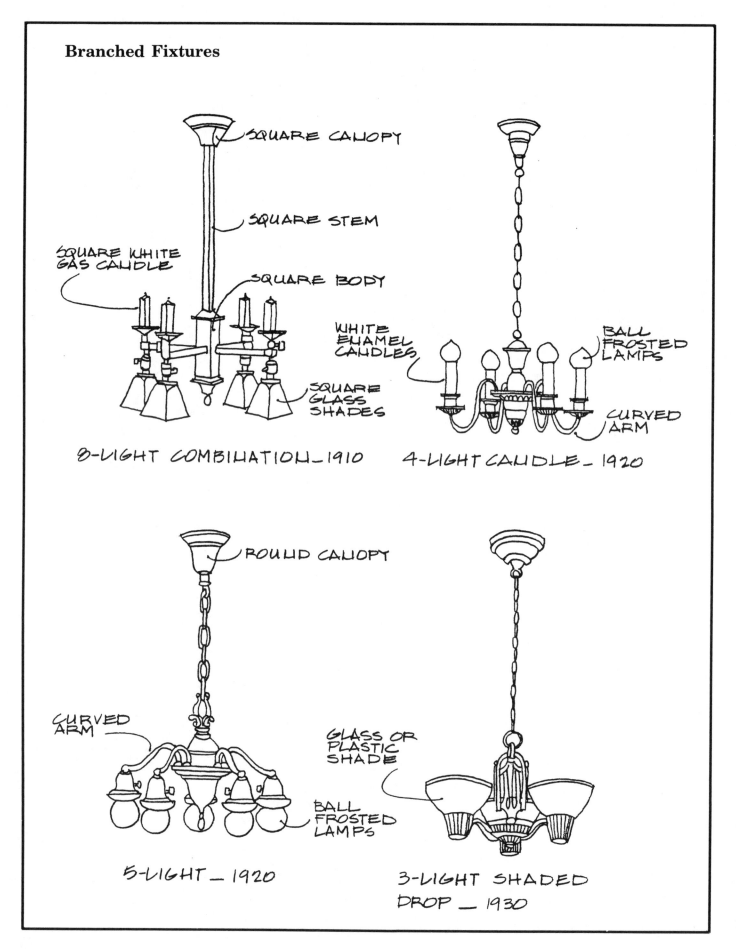

SQUARE CANOPY

SQUARE STEM

SQUARE WHITE
GAS CANDLE

SQUARE BODY

WHITE
ENAMEL
CANDLES

SQUARE
GLASS
SHADES

BALL
FROSTED
LAMPS

CURVED
ARM

6-LIGHT COMBINATION — 1910

4-LIGHT CANDLE — 1920

ROUND CANOPY

CURVED
ARM

GLASS OR
PLASTIC
SHADE

BALL
FROSTED
LAMPS

5-LIGHT — 1920

3-LIGHT SHADED
DROP — 1930

Domes

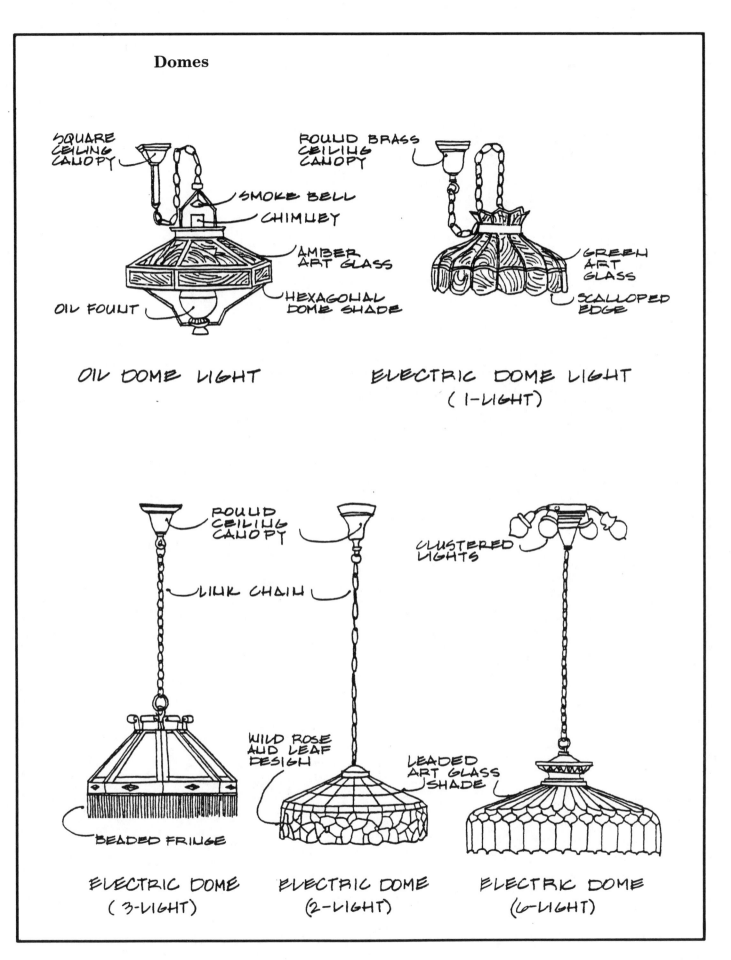

SQUARE CEILING CANOPY

ROUND BRASS CEILING CANOPY

SMOKE BELL

CHIMNEY

AMBER ART GLASS

GREEN ART GLASS

HEXAGONAL DOME SHADE

OIL FOUNT

SCALLOPED EDGE

OIL DOME LIGHT

ELECTRIC DOME LIGHT
(1-LIGHT)

ROUND CEILING CANOPY

LINK CHAIN

CLUSTERED LIGHTS

WILD ROSE AND LEAF DESIGN

LEADED ART GLASS SHADE

BEADED FRINGE

ELECTRIC DOME
(3-LIGHT)

ELECTRIC DOME
(2-LIGHT)

ELECTRIC DOME
(6-LIGHT)

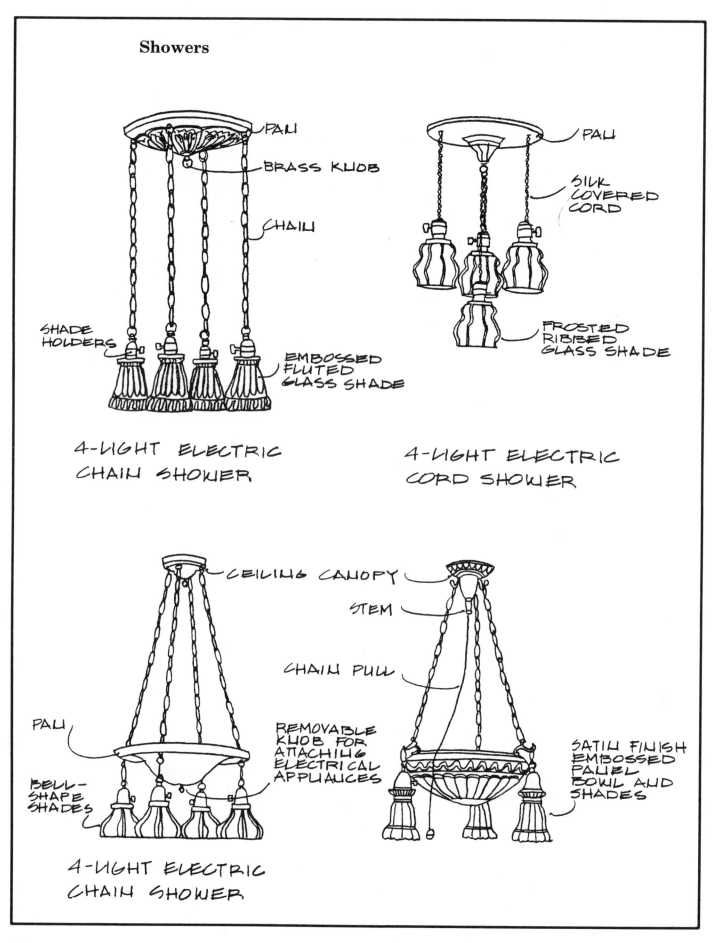

PAN

BRASS KNOB

CHAIN

SHADE HOLDERS

EMBOSSED FLUTED GLASS SHADE

PAN

SILK COVERED CORD

FROSTED RIBBED GLASS SHADE

4-LIGHT ELECTRIC CHAIN SHOWER

4-LIGHT ELECTRIC CORD SHOWER

CEILING CANOPY

STEM

CHAIN PULL

PAN

REMOVABLE KNOB FOR ATTACHING ELECTRICAL APPLIANCES

BELL-SHAPE SHADES

SATIN FINISH EMBOSSED PANEL BOWL AND SHADES

4-LIGHT ELECTRIC CHAIN SHOWER

Semi-indirect Bowls

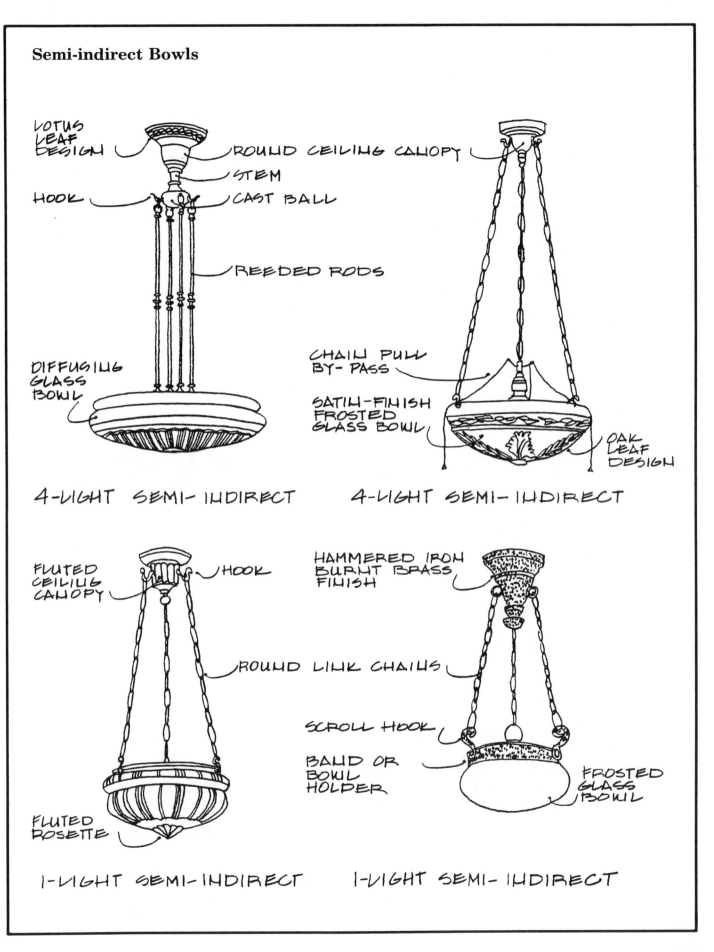

LOTUS LEAF DESIGN

ROUND CEILING CANOPY

STEM

HOOK

CAST BALL

REEDED RODS

DIFFUSING GLASS BOWL

4-LIGHT SEMI-INDIRECT

CHAIN PULL BY-PASS

SATIN-FINISH FROSTED GLASS BOWL

OAK LEAF DESIGN

4-LIGHT SEMI-INDIRECT

FLUTED CEILING CANOPY

HOOK

ROUND LINK CHAINS

FLUTED ROSETTE

1-LIGHT SEMI-INDIRECT

HAMMERED IRON BURNT BRASS FINISH

ROUND LINK CHAINS

SCROLL HOOK

BAND OR BOWL HOLDER

FROSTED GLASS BOWL

1-LIGHT SEMI-INDIRECT

Wall Brackets

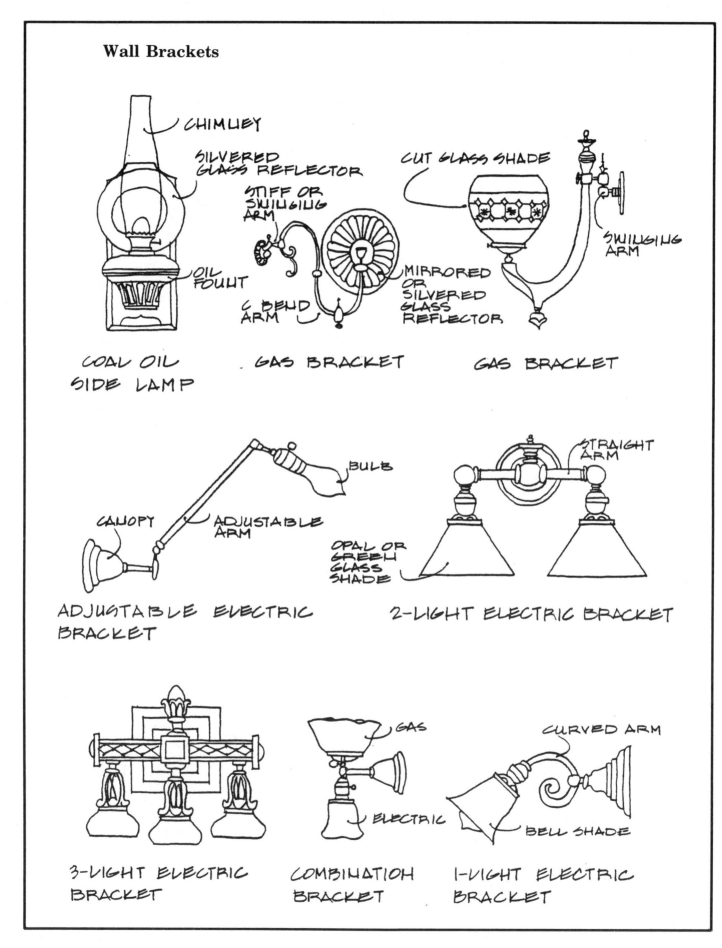

CHIMNEY

SILVERED GLASS REFLECTOR

STIFF OR SWINGING ARM

OIL FOUNT

C BEND ARM

CUT GLASS SHADE

MIRRORED OR SILVERED GLASS REFLECTOR

SWINGING ARM

COAL OIL SIDE LAMP

GAS BRACKET

GAS BRACKET

BULB

CANOPY

ADJUSTABLE ARM

OPAL OR GREEN GLASS SHADE

STRAIGHT ARM

ADJUSTABLE ELECTRIC BRACKET

2-LIGHT ELECTRIC BRACKET

GAS

ELECTRIC

CURVED ARM

BELL SHADE

3-LIGHT ELECTRIC BRACKET

COMBINATION BRACKET

1-LIGHT ELECTRIC BRACKET

FOR 2 LIGHTS

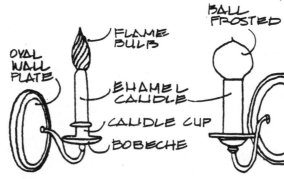

OVAL WALL PLATE

FLAME BULB

ENAMEL CANDLE

CANDLE CUP

BOBECHE

BALL FROSTED

WALL BRACKET OR ANGLE SOCKET

1-LIGHT CANDLE BRACKET

2-LIGHT CANDLE BRACKET

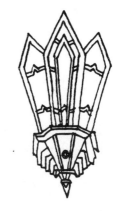

WHITE OPAL GLASS SHADE

1-LIGHT LANTERN BRACKET

BATH OR KITCHEN BRACKET

1-LIGHT POCKET BRACKET

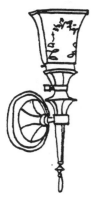

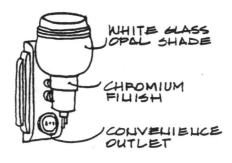

WHITE GLASS OPAL SHADE

CHROMIUM FINISH

CONVENIENCE OUTLET

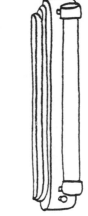

1-LIGHT TORCH BRACKET

1-LIGHT SHADED TYPE BRACKET

LUMILINE WALL BRACKET

Ceiling Lights

CEILING PLATE

1-LIGHT CEILING FIXTURE

MULTI-LIGHT CEILING FIXTURE

MIRRORED OR SILVERED GLASS REFLECTOR

DOUBLE-CONE REFLECTOR

OVAL PLATE

EMBOSSED CAST METAL

BALL BULB

2-LIGHT CEILING FIXTURE

CAST METAL PLATE

5-LIGHT CEILING FIXTURE

BOWL HOLDER

FROSTED GLASS BOWL

BOWL CEILING LIGHT

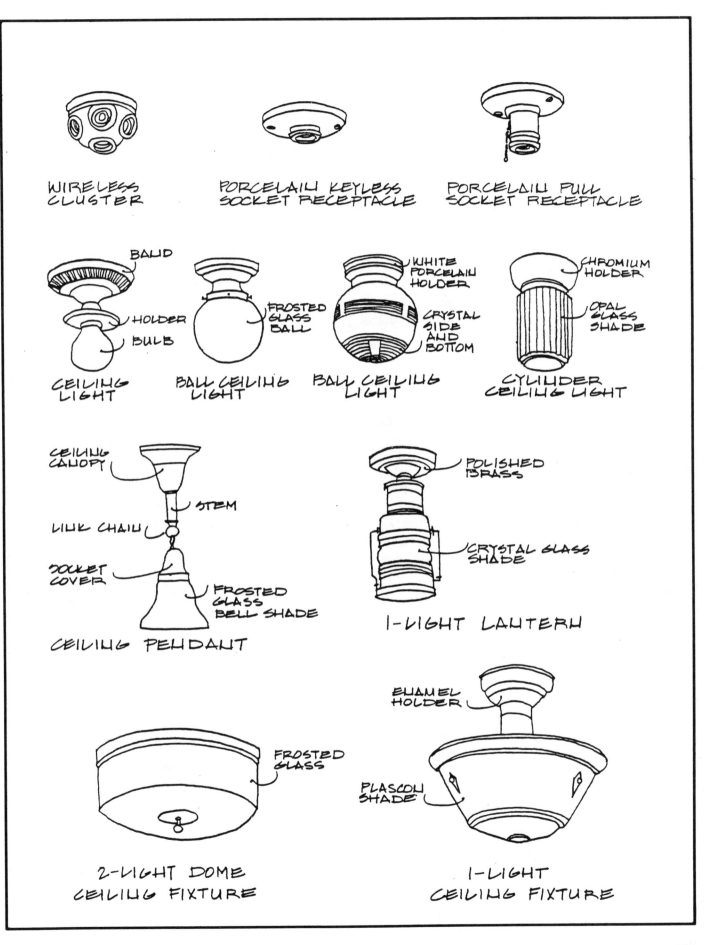

WIRELESS CLUSTER

PORCELAIN KEYLESS SOCKET RECEPTACLE

PORCELAIN PULL SOCKET RECEPTACLE

BAND

HOLDER

BULB

CEILING LIGHT

FROSTED GLASS BALL

BALL CEILING LIGHT

WHITE PORCELAIN HOLDER

CRYSTAL SIDE AND BOTTOM

BALL CEILING LIGHT

CHROMIUM HOLDER

OPAL GLASS SHADE

CYLINDER CEILING LIGHT

CEILING CANOPY

STEM

LINK CHAIN

SOCKET COVER

FROSTED GLASS BELL SHADE

CEILING PENDANT

POLISHED BRASS

CRYSTAL GLASS SHADE

1-LIGHT LANTERN

FROSTED GLASS

2-LIGHT DOME CEILING FIXTURE

ENAMEL HOLDER

PLASCON SHADE

1-LIGHT CEILING FIXTURE

239

Commercial Fixtures

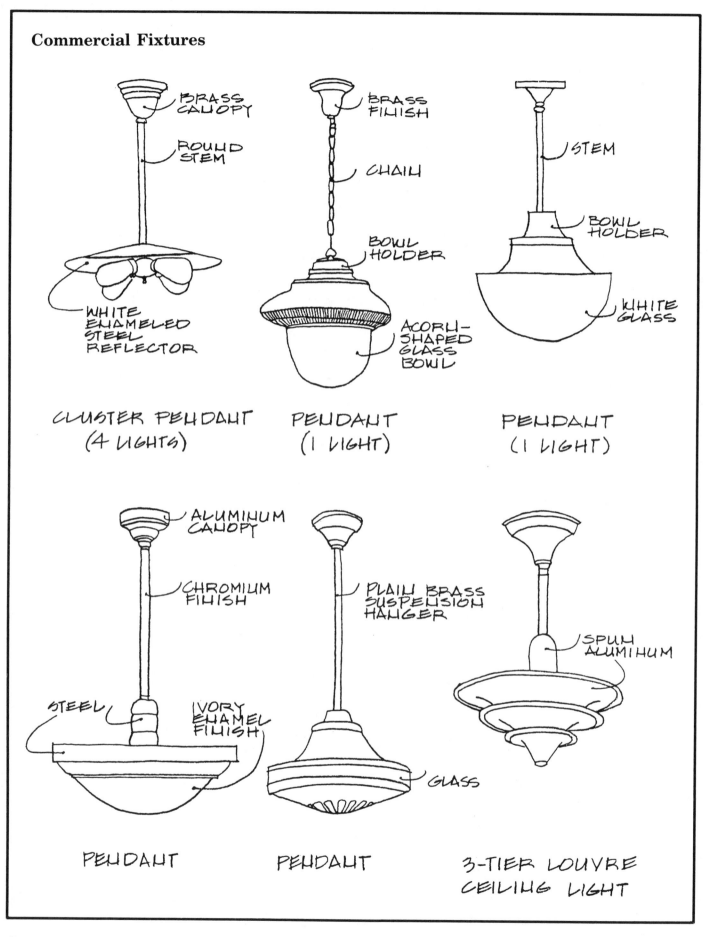

BRASS CANOPY

ROUND STEM

WHITE ENAMELED STEEL REFLECTOR

CLUSTER PENDANT (4 LIGHTS)

BRASS FINISH

CHAIN

BOWL HOLDER

ACORN-SHAPED GLASS BOWL

PENDANT (1 LIGHT)

STEM

BOWL HOLDER

WHITE GLASS

PENDANT (1 LIGHT)

ALUMINUM CANOPY

CHROMIUM FINISH

STEEL

IVORY ENAMEL FINISH

PENDANT

PLAIN BRASS SUSPENSION HANGER

GLASS

PENDANT

SPUN ALUMINUM

3-TIER LOUVRE CEILING LIGHT

Bungalow Set

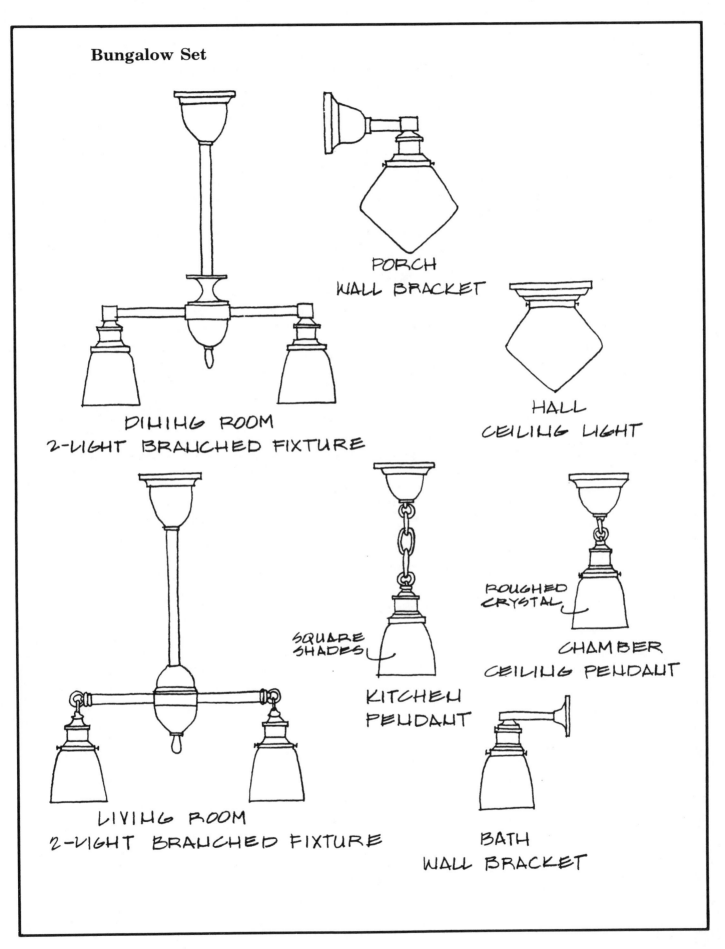

PORCH
WALL BRACKET

DINING ROOM
2-LIGHT BRANCHED FIXTURE

HALL
CEILING LIGHT

SQUARE
SHADES

ROUGHED
CRYSTAL

CHAMBER
CEILING PENDANT

KITCHEN
PENDANT

LIVING ROOM
2-LIGHT BRANCHED FIXTURE

BATH
WALL BRACKET

CONVENIENCES

The technological aspect of vernacular architecture generated several things we might label interior conveniences, some of which are still functioning. They can be grouped categorically under three headings: chutes, traps, and receivers.

Coal chutes and *laundry chutes* had an impact on basements. Coal chutes were referred to by their location, which was either on grade level or in the wall as a window chute. Laundry chutes were built into wall cavities from upper floors to the basement.

Among trap devices, two were fairly standard: *ash traps* built under fireplaces at the base of the chimney, and galvanized *garbage receivers* located outside near the kitchen door or on the back porch. Before centralized garbage collection was provided, much waste material was taken care of on the site. For example, some houses were equipped with basement incinerators with access chutes in the kitchen or hallway. Otherwise, people burned their trash in outdoor units.

As for *receiving units,* the package receiver set into a kitchen wall was handy for deliveries of milk, groceries, and other goods. The boxes were metal-lined, often with steel, and had two doors, one outside and one inside. A package receiver could also be built into the entrance door of individual apartments in a multifamily building.

There were communication devices, including annunciators of one kind or another, and door chimes and buzzers. Mailboxes with internal chutes or plain slots were part of this category. So were telephone cabinets or niches, which were built into a partition wall with a shelf for the phone and space for the wires and bell box. Dumbwaiters helped transfer material from one level to another. In vernacular design, these were small, hand-operated, and set into their own framework rather than in a pocket in the walls.

There were a few more helpful built-ins—other than the furniture we have discussed already—such as ironing boards built into the wall or attached to a door, and built-in beds. Lastly, there were window, wall, and ceiling fans for dispelling odors and moisture in kitchens and bathrooms, and exhaust fans in attics or in windows for cooling.

DESIGN SYSTEMS

INTRODUCTION   It appears, from both archival and field research, that from 1870 to 1940 there were no formulas for designing interiors and no overarching styles that dictated the use of elements and materials. Although there were different aesthetics operating in the period as part of design systems, there were no strict rules of application. An assessment of millwork in a given environment will indicate the presence of a specific aesthetic. Changes in millwork composition reflected shifts in design values, taste, fashion, and no doubt profit margins. What follows then is a discussion of the four dominant aesthetics for the period: the *ornamental,* the *classical,* the *artistic,* and the *colonial.*

THE ORNAMENTAL AESTHETIC   The *ornamental aesthetic* for vernacular interiors derived from the various revival styles of nineteenth-century architecture. The revivals gave the vernacular a predilection for decorative motifs applied in various sizes and in several mediums, for layered surfaces, and for three-dimensional modeling. The ornamental was popular during the last three decades of the last century, but it gradually gave way to the "artistic" and the "colonial."

In this system decorative motifs were applied to almost any surface. Theoretically, there seems to have been no limit to the amount of decoration— at least no easily recognized limit. In millwork, images were carved into the surface or applied to the surface as whole finished work. The imagery included natural and geometric figures, and was usually part of something else: for example, an image would be part of a panel of a newel post rather than standing alone as an isolated figure. This kind of ornamentation had something in common with the design of furniture in the same period. Both were likely to have surface areas covered with something, and illusion was an integral part of the work. What you saw was not all there was to the design. Indeed, what you saw may not be what you thought it was. There was a degree of sham—papier-mâché, veneered work, composition work, and the like—built into the system.

The ornamental system of design produced a layered interior in which the effect of the design was cumulative. In millwork, moldings and panels were built upon each other, which altered the surface character of each element. Layering also took place on the horizontal. A typical wall organization in the ornamental consisted of a high baseboard composed of two or three pieces of wood, a dado or wainscot (the latter with a cap rail), a large section of wall that would most likely be papered, and a wallpaper frieze. If wallpaper covered the entire wall—dado to frieze—the motifs in each layer would be different, and the ceiling finish, whether paper or plaster, would add a fourth motif. The transition from one section of wall to another often was accomplished by adding wood or plaster moldings— as a picture molding, a cornice, or one or more ceiling moldings.

A secondary kind of layering involved the color and natural pattern of materials. For instance, the ornamental living room and dining room would have pieces of built-in furniture, with each piece made from a different species of wood: cherry, walnut, oak. The wood was left its natural color or stained to look like something else. (The same thing happened in furniture.) Furthermore, the ornamental style permitted a lot of painted graining as a surface treatment, regardless of the grain pattern of the original wood. The variegated patterns of a marble mantel face and shelf were yet another layer of imagery to relate to the wood patterns and the color treatment.

The third dimension of the ornamental system was its propensity to project multiple surfaces. The sectional and plan views of moldings and panels, rails and doors, reveal an internal logic only; the elements are self-referential, deriving their development only in terms of themselves. A curve or an edge in one section of work must be answered by another curve or edge, usually one going in another direction or having a different shape. There appears to be no hierarchy, no movement toward some cumulative effect with the final element—say, the top of the newel post—being the most important.

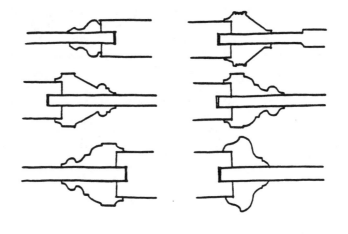

DOOR STICKINGS

This condition of Victorian design was no doubt related to the associational values that revival styles sought in elements and forms. It is not clear what ideas or values were being linked to vernacular elements in the ornamental style system. Despite its vague classicism (classical moldings and applied orders), it seems that the ornamental was related to present time. Its decoration and forms turned inward. The turnings and squares of a baluster, for example, related to each other only on that stick and on the others immediately by it. Those turnings related to nothing else in the room. Symbolically, this kind of design suggested a complicated world, a world of parts for which the logic of assembly was not readily available.

Also characteristic of the ornamental was the way specific elements were clustered. Passage doors had raised moldings and raised panels with chamfered stiles, rails, and casings. Folding or pocket doors had similar stickwork and added an astragal to the leading edge. Architraves of ornamental patterns or special work over the door were also common. The trim sets for doors and windows included pilaster casings with base, corner, and head blocks and elaborate apron panels under the windows. The windows themselves often had panes or whole sections of art glass, which added another layer of imagery and color.

Ornamental flooring included the use of different species of wood for graining and color, and numerous patterns of parquet flooring. Parquet was laid in blocks or short strips with a border and a center, each with different design.

As for wall organization, we have referred previously to the division of walls by wallpaper. Wainscots provided a similar division, the wainscot built up from the baseboard to cover about one-third of the wall with paneled sections of wood, plaster, or textile. The wainscot was finished with a cap. In walls that had no wainscot or casing, a bead was placed on the outside corners.

Ornamental plaster for walls and ceilings, done in molding patterns, was a significant element in this style. The plaster work was done in varying widths and thicknesses, and placement was most typically as a center piece—a block or a rosette in the living room or over the dining room table. Plaster molding was used also to divide a ceiling and walls into panels, a motif present also in wallpaper.

Openings in walls most often were finished with pilaster casings on the face of the wall: grilles with scrollwork, beads, or spindles spanned the opening. Individual colonnades also were placed in openings and could be linked by grilles. A piece of drapery, a portiere, often completed the arrangement. Folding doors and sliding doors were popular devices for controlling the use of space in this design system. The visual effect of these elements was to add a temporary wall of wood panels to what was more than likely a paneled interior.

The final, permanent element of the ornamental system was the fireplace

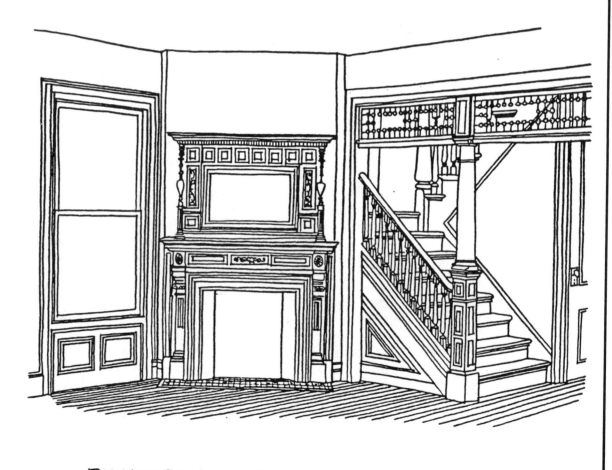

RECEPTION HALL AND MANTEL

mantel. This element has been a focal point in all design systems for vernacular interiors. In the nineteenth century the mantel was a primary source of space heating as well as an opportunity to celebrate the aesthetic. Ornamental mantels had two parts: a lower section with hearth, fireplace opening, and shelf: and an upper portion, the overmantel, which could have additional shelving, a wide, ornamented cove, and a mirror. The shelf and the face of the mantel often were made of marble, but the face and openings could be made of wood or cast iron. The grate and lining were iron. Mantel faces most often were executed in a classical mode, with pilasters, half columns, or brackets carrying an entablature.

The ornamental design system was not carried out in the same manner throughout its period any more than the other systems were. There was no strict rule about elements and their application, and, since industrially based vernacular was characterized by change, modifications were common. Changes might be made to encourage sales, to improve appearance, or to cut the costs of labor and materials. From 1875 to 1895 the ornamental system shifted away from thick, dark pieces of vigorously massed millwork to a more delicate treatment. The move corresponded with the last phase of what we might call the *stickwork cottage designs*. Instead of relying on layering or on the accumulation of multiples—a newel post with an octagonal base, a turned shaft in a couple of shapes, and a square top—the new version reduced the size of the newel and controlled the shape more tightly. In place of ridges and turnings, ornaments in shallow relief were cut into the faces of the newel, and the balusters had smaller diameters and rarely numbered more than two to a tread.

Despite these refinements, the ornamental system could not survive the progressive social movements that were redefining household environments. The ornamental was part of the general picturesque aesthetic that relied on irregularity and flamboyant profiles and which ultimately did not fit an age that was demanding recognition for women, especially of their housekeeping role. Gwendolyn Wright, in *Moralism and the Model Home* (1980), describes how the progressive design movement changed the house-keeper's status. She could now rise above the accumulation of multiple design effects and control the environment from *her* perspective. She might have to work with manufactured elements, but she was free to determine their assemblage and their relationships to each other and to herself.

The ornamental aesthetic had the capacity to overwhelm, partly because of its deep commitment to the celebration of industry. The clustering of motifs and the layering of surfaces were part of this celebration. It was a world of multiple surfaces, demonstrating faith in the power of edges, outlines, patterns, and parallel, intersecting, and curvilinear lines. Yet, despite all this busy-ness, the ornamental recognized privacy, the opportunity to withdraw, to become part of the context.

Ornamental
Aesthetic

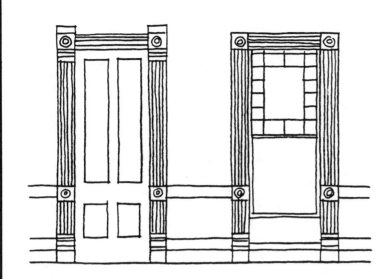

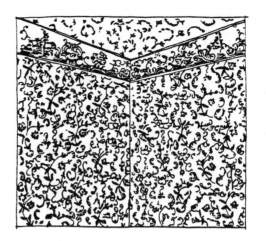

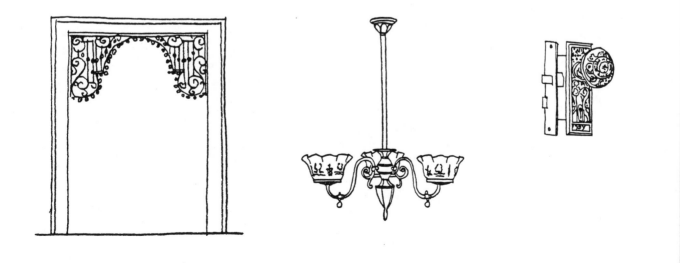

THE CLASSICAL, A TRANSITIONAL AESTHETIC

The aesthetic shelf life, if you will, of a series of solutions to interior design problems is not easily plotted. With so many elements in various stages of development, one may find a transitional condition overriding the effort to establish a new aesthetic. That is exactly what happened from about 1895 to 1910.

We think of this occurrence as a movement toward a classical aesthetic. At this point we are convinced that the aesthetic was legitimate, but we do not know how deeply embedded it was in the culture of its time. We lack sufficient evidence to locate the parameters of each series of design elements or to identify with certainty the effect of clustered elements. Before suggesting that this system was the equivalent of the others, we would need more conclusive information about the extent of its diffusion.

What we call the classical aesthetic exhibited strong links to the first generation of colonial designs after the Centennial celebration. Of the four different house types that utilized this approach, three of them were intentionally colonial designs. The fourth house was the hip-roofed, square type, which had a colonial-classical character because of its cube shape, stripped-down elevations, and colonial entry porch. The other houses were the formal colonial hip-roofed cottage, the gambrel-roofed cottage, and the hip-roofed bungalow.

As for the execution of the specific aspects of this aesthetic, a center hall plan (a colonial attribute) was used more frequently than a side hall plan, and the arrangements of rooms were no different from the prevailing form in all three houses. The significant differences occurred in the choices of individual elements and in the combinations of elements.

Millwork is once again the best indicator of how this aesthetic was structured. The fireplace mantel was rectangular in shape, and made with quarter-sawn oak or birch. It had a gloss finish, and the face was framed by columns extending from the hearth to the top of the overmantel. This mantel had some incised ornamentation and a few molding plants, but overall the number of ornaments had been greatly reduced. The overmantel often included a mirror.

The openings between rooms were spanned with grille columns, that is, with freestanding or low-pedestal colonnades that carried a deep architrave. Scroll work and spindle work grilles could be added to the opening. The placement of large columns is of historical interest, because in the next decade (1910s) interior columns became part of what we think of as colonnade furniture. This use of columns as an opening feature has not occurred since in a vernacular interior.

The stair plans were the same as those associated with these house types, but some of the elements of the stair were handled differently. For example, the newel post had a square base with a paneled shaft and a rather plain cap. At this time Sears sold its so-called anti-dust newel, which it identified as part of the artistic system as well as of this one. Balusters were square (a modern characteristic) or turned (colonial effect).

The interior finish also had two aesthetic options in that the baseboard had a three-part composition more or less like those in the ornamental system, but the pilaster casings around the doors and windows were either a reeded type or a plain, round-edge type. The plain casing was related to the "anti-dust" sensibility.

The classical aesthetic outdid all other systems in its use of cap trim over the head casing. Compositionally, a cap trim was a door cornice; most had a delicate molding—a bead or a row of small dentils—below the dust cap and the face of the casing. Wreaths and garlands sometimes were applied to the face. We have not found any cap trim in millwork catalogs before 1900, and after 1920 such trim is referred to as colonial cap trim.

The hardware system for this aesthetic was both colonial (oval escutcheons and knobs with beaded edges) and modern (plain, beveled-edge pattern). All of the designs were less ornamental than were their predecessors.

In summary, this aesthetic reflected the countervailing forces of tradition and change, which was implied in the language used to describe the system. For example, an article in a trade journal (1898) referred to a hip-roofed cottage as "somewhat of the colonial character, modernized in its treatment," with "inside finish of the simplest kind." In 1908 Sears sold a hip-roofed cottage with classical attributes, the Modern House, No. 102, which had a front porch of Tuscan columns, cottage windows, plain round-edge casings with circle-pattern blocks, and a moderately curved baseboard profile. This combination characterizes this eclectic moment in vernacular architecture.

Classical Aesthetic

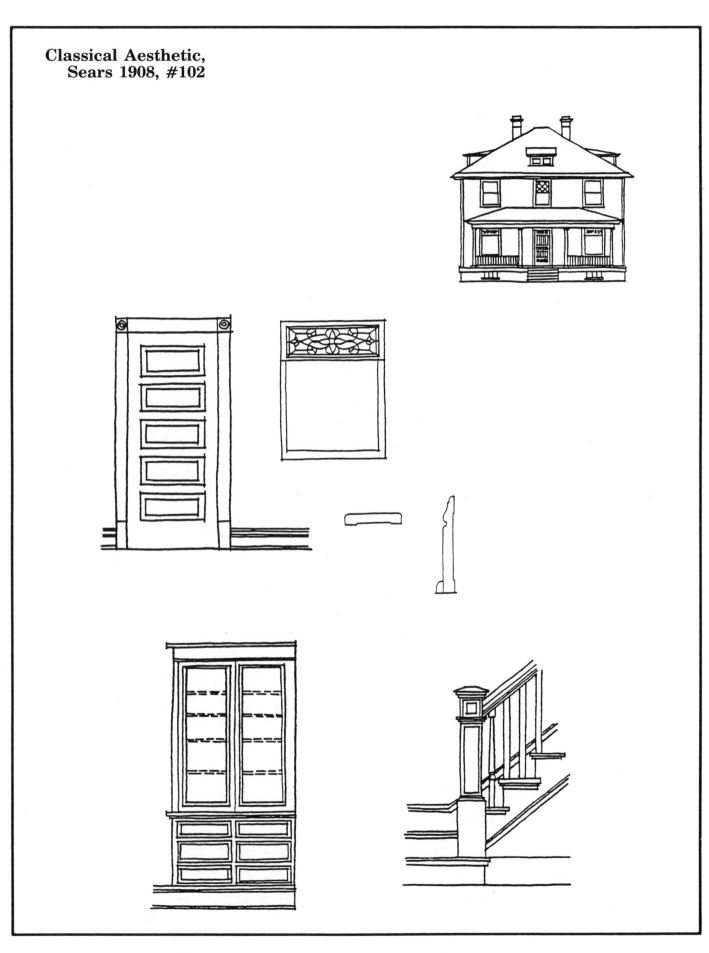

Classical Aesthetic,
Sears 1908, #102

THE ARTISTIC AESTHETIC

Dissatisfaction with previous design values and the search for an alternative were tied to overall changes in design philosophy for the period. Specifically, in their works and critical writings, William Morris and John Ruskin had a positive effect on design issues in America. Their rejection of industrially produced goods, their support for craft and the appropriate use of materials, and their belief in simplicity as an all-encompassing aesthetic found acceptance in America and played a key role in ending the sway of Victorian design. What is known as the Arts and Crafts Movement affected American culture, becoming a new arbiter of taste as well as the basis for a rational approach to design. The latter was especially helpful for various progressive movements that sought to redefine the home environment and the role of women in that environment.

The desire to create a modern theory of interior design can be traced also to the home reading courses and Extension Service bulletins published by land-grant universities. These tracts were disseminated throughout the United States as correspondence courses or self-study bulletins, the latter sometimes intended for use at group meetings. The publications reveal how modern design concepts and values were promoted—even deemed necessary—for quality rural and small-town life. When coupled with technological advancements, modern design, whether as taste or pure principle, was seen as a liberating force in the lives of rural women and their families. The authors' positions on their subject were progressive; they believed in the effects of the environment on life, and through design they saw relief from the drudgery of housework.

The Extension Service writers were pulling their clientele away from Victorian design values and toward modern values by instilling a belief in rational approaches to design problems. They taught respect for materials and function, for the power of line and plane in composition: they advocated relating design principles to taste, to right living, to hygiene and sanitation (the latter for disease control), and to a sense of beauty.

Beyond these general principles, there was also a belief in the power of the individual to construct a meaningful environment. The concept of the housekeeper as an artist—the home artist—was the key to broadcasting design values. The point was made that anyone could succeed in these decorating and designing activities, as long as she was willing to believe in herself and in the principles the writers set forth. The imposition of self in the design scheme was critical. There were no experts in rural areas to do it for you, anyway. The individual had the capacity to create the appropriate composition. The authority of the treatment, its credibility, was to be found within the eye and mind of the individual housekeeper. How one did this was theoretically simple. One created an environment that looked like and functioned like a picture, with rooms and furnishings brought into a harmonious effect. No matter the year—from 1902 to 1923—or the location, all of these home economists recommended creating "a simple unified effect" so that all parts of the picture produced a sustained impression. The overall design scheme was supposed to have a concept—say, repose, freedom, or cheer—which would be reinforced by every opportunity for design in the room.

Color was a key element in these theories, the writers recognizing color's psychological influence on human perception and behavior, its power to create a warm or cold emotional atmosphere. The application of color was reduced to a matter of natural tones. The primary toning of an interior included light-colored walls and dark wood. Professional decorators went further. They recommended a generalized brown tone for everything, with some rooms getting specific natural tones: russet for halls, green for living rooms, and brown for the dining area.

Color and nature were linked further in that natural materials, such as wood, were to *look* natural. Dark finishes that obscured the grain were to be avoided. Moreover, there was to be no artificial graining of wood since this was considered sham design. Being truthful about surfaces and the nature of materials, and using natural light and color, would produce a home picture that had spiritual as well as material worth.

The desire to create a unified effect, as of a picture, was linked to the bias for long vistas through interior spaces. That is, the interior of a house was to be connected visually and physically to the exterior so that both the perception of space and the movement through space would be experienced as continuous. This desire for inside-outside continuity had a major impact on space planning; it was especially helpful in breaking down Victorian compartmentalized spaces into the open planning we associate with modernism.

If an interior design was to be a unified picture, it had to be composed of a series of smaller pictures, a balanced arrangement of the structural parts of each room. For example, Helen Binkerd Young, writing in a Cornell reading course bulletin (Vol. II, No. 39, 1913), described a plan with these characteristics:

> On the rear wall of the living room is seen a central fireplace flanked by broad doorways of equal width, while the front wall opposite expands into a generous bay window centrally placed, with built-in bookcases to the right and left. These features so unite as to make of the living room a composition at once so dignified, so orderly and so effective that little furniture is needed to complete it.

Young, an architect, was a progressive in these matters. Her belief in

DINING ROOM, SKELETON WAINSCOT, BEAMED CEILING, SIDEBOARD

design principles helped women envision interior design in a larger context. Her design values, which were picked up by subsequent writers at other institutions, also helped tear readers away from a concern with material bits and pieces. The Victorian design system focused on the inherent value—the richness, if you like—of the object itself. Young taught that if the design had integrity, then the furnishings, regardless of their material and perhaps of their style, could be a secondary consideration. She reasoned that an interior design with a unified effect would cause a reconsideration of the material things that filled up a home. In the new scheme, those things that were not in harmony with the total picture could be discarded. Furniture, for example, that did not follow structural lines would seem inappropriate in a room so organized.

There was more to picture-making than references to vistas and analogies to artists. The home economists had a specific picture in mind—the landscape painting. The natural divisions of a room were likened to those of a landscape: the floor was like the earth: the walls, the foreground of the painting: the ceiling, the sky. In terms of light values, the scheme called for a darkened floor, walls of middle value, and a light-colored ceiling. Furthermore, horizon lines fitted into this idea as a way to establish proportions within a room. For instance, a plate rail or a picture molding could serve as a horizon line. An Iowa State University Extension bulletin (No. 17, December 1913) advised on its placement: "high enough to break the wall space into wall and frieze, or . . . low enough to divide the wall into wall and wainscoting. The best proportions are not more than one third from the top or one-third from the floor."

The modern, artistic, interior was therefore a picture based on principles—such as following structural lines—that could be composed by anyone who was willing to study. The principles were good for anything, from the entire farm to a piece of furniture or an arrangement of pictures on a wall. Over time, the principles became institutionalized; they were part of formal training in home economics and part of learning programs for the general public. They were strong enough to elicit this kind of writing in the 1920s: "The idea determines the form. The form controls the leading lines of the decoration. There is order and beauty when the rule is followed and lack of order and ugliness when the rule is violated" (Kansas State University Extension bulletin No. 43, June 1923).

The manufacturers of interior goods were not so spiritually involved with design principles, but they were interested in design effects, especially overall, harmonious effects. Industry could produce the appearance of integrated effects with millwork. The home economists' point of view about quality interiors became known as the *artistic view*. Manufacturers were reticent to make goods in a single style, since that would limit production and work against their belief in providing for individual tastes. But manufacturers could produce a range of goods with different elements that could be labeled as "artistic," and these could be assembled in a variety of ways.

In a 1915 trade catalog, an Iowa millwork company, Gordon-Van Tine, tried to appeal to those interested in artistic compositions by highlighting mantels, inglenooks, and stairs as the features of the house that allowed "the greatest play for the talents of the architect." Gordon-Van Tine assumed that properly placed elements, such as a mantel, had a major impact on overall effect. If a mantle could be combined with other wood pieces, cut from the same species of wood and finished the same way, then the impact of the effect could be increased significantly. The definition of interior

ENTRY HALL,
STAIR LANDING,
WAINSCOT

design as the control of a few effects, and the linking of those effects to a few architectural details, focused product design and merchandising on those issues. Engravings and photographs in advertisements and illustrated trade catalogs emphasized effects, and ancillary material in the pictures was intended to create the illusion of controlled effect. A Japanese flower arrangement or a piece of Southwest Indian pottery on a mantel signaled the viewer that this was indeed an artistic interior.

Sometimes the manufacturer suggested the special effect in the copy that accompanied the picture. A beamed ceiling might give a "massive" effect to a room, or a mantel might add a "rustic" quality. Portions of a space or a whole sequence of rooms might be "cheery" or "cozy." If affective appeals were not enough, there were appeals to the rational, design-principle side of things as well. Work was labeled "well proportioned" and "balanced" and the integration of parts was emphasized.

Millwork companies seemed unwilling to identify products with a style of design unless they were sure of sales. There were two styles—Mission and Craftsman, the names were used interchangeably—that were said to be capable of delivering artistic effects. These pieces were generally rectilinear in shape and were heavy visually and physically in that they revealed solid wood construction rather than the veneers of the Victorian styles. They exploited the character of the wood, emphasizing grain and simple joinery, and created novel effects. When combined with other elements in the artistic vocabulary such as rough plaster, burlap, art glass, and stenciling, the Craftsman and Mission work suggested an artistic environment. Part of the attraction to the artistic lay in the juxtaposition and proximity of materials: smooth, dull-gloss oak panel strips on the wall set against dyed burlap and rough plaster; brass against glass; the smooth glaze of ceramics against the grain of wood. This exploitation of natural materials gave a homespun quality to the interior and vested the room with the illusion of time. Time could be purchased for the vernacular interior with the installation of historical styles, but if one rejected that as inappropriate, or if something modern was preferred, one could turn to the strength of materials and references to craft as a substitute for academic historicism.

The key to integrating natural materials and design principles was the housekeeper, the woman in charge of the home. According to Helen Adler in *The New Interiors* (1916), this modern point of view about interior design required that women see themselves as artists. The implications of this role were sociological and political as well as stylistic. The home-artist concept implied a great deal of freedom and discipline—the willingness to eliminate the extraneous, to control the use of design details, to keep the unifying idea in perspective. The success of any interior's scheme was, therefore, a reflection of the housekeeper's personality and character.

As a final check on the artistic design system, let us turn to the country's premier purveyor of middle-class design values, the Sears, Roebuck Company. Sears produced pre-cut houses from 1908 through the 1930s. Throughout this period it used the term *artistic* to describe a number of individual products or ensembles. For Sears, artistic items had a higher pictorial value than other things; the artistic was unconventional. Glass, tile, or wood products that received special surface treatments were thought to be artful. Sears was also careful not to limit the idea of the artistic to a single line of goods. The company would often combine effects in illustrations of designs. A Craftsman door might be grouped with Queen Anne windows, with a colonial colonnade, and with a rustic fireplace (a feature in most of its designs).

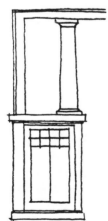

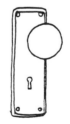

THE COLONIAL AESTHETIC

Every design aesthetic we examined in this period had the same intention, to be modern. Even the colonial, which had tradition and practice to fall back on, insisted on being contemporary.

Most studies of American cultural history agree that the 1876 Centennial Exposition in Philadelphia was a watershed for American design. The exhibition not only exposed Americans to the materials and forms of their own past, but it also introduced Americans to the new English cottage styles. The gap between the American vernacular and the imported, between the two craft traditions, was to be bridged by technology: colonial imagery produced through manufacturing. Distribution was important, because the frontier regions of the country did not have the sense of architectural history that people in the original colonial states enjoyed.

Over time the concept of "colonialism" became generalized into a few building types, for example, the saltbox house and the garrison house, which were successful popular culture forms, and the Georgian-inspired public building. Precisely what kind of colonial design American buildings were to display seemed at first a rhetorical question. Centennial fever had builders and manufacturers focusing on authentic detailing—mantels in the Massachusetts mode or wainscots in the manner of the Tidewater states. This archaeological approach had been part of the English movements to revive historical styles. Authenticity could produce a feeling of legitimacy, it would buy time.

Colonial materials, such as shingles and hand-wrought iron, and the patterns and textures they created were also of interest. Designers were well aware that texture produces effects whether the element is a rough-cut beam or an enameled classical molding. In the end, the Georgian style, in a much reduced state, won the day over the rustic. Colonial vernacular was going to look rational and enlightened rather than passively medieval and locally crafted.

In *Moralism and the Modern Home* historian Gwendolyn Wright attributes the emergence of the colonial to the Centennial and to the belief that colonial building types were economical, dignified, and simple (pp. 251–53). Common heritage and shared illusions, the turning to the English Arts and Crafts design aesthetic, the progressive spirit of the times which sought to reform housing conditions and housework environments, all this could be addressed through colonial design schemes. And indeed, as evidence for the strength of the system, colonial design has outlasted all others.

Colonial design was not a single-minded, all-pervasive system, but rather a series of effects to be interpreted broadly. The English reformers such as William Morris, who had many followers here, preached simplicity in all things. The colonial system succeeded by clustering simple effects. Moreover, progressives in this country declared ornamented cottage design inappropriate. Frank L. Lent, pattern-book writer and practitioner, put it this way:

> . . . whatever departure in minor details may be required in accommodation to our later mode of life or personal conveniences, the old Colonial grace, simplicity, and refinements are sure to make a favorable impression in contradistinction to foolish attempts at outward display, bedaubing with scroll-sawed brackets, freaks of the wood turner's fancy, fantastic color, lop-sided design, and cheap senseless ornaments. (*Sound Sense in Suburban Architecture,* 1895, p. 5)

In his own design work, Lent relied on the gambrel roof to organize the volumes of his commonsense houses. His interest in simplicity was translated as "utility and beauty" going hand in hand. While artistic design also promoted utility, the colonial was our most successful functional style. It delivered more modernism than the other systems, with straightforward, simple lines and forms, and at the same time it had associational value. History, John Ruskin told us, needed to be living history. With our enormous capacity to replicate anything and our hunger for a usable past, we made the colonial our national building style.

Overall, the colonial aesthetic existed in two types of design: the ornamental from 1890 to about 1920, and the modernized colonial between 1920 and 1940. In the first instance, colonial motifs, a Palladian window, for example, were added to cottage house forms. Cottage design was eclectic in this period, and colonial design was influenced by other styles, especially the Queen Anne, examples of which had been on display at the Philadelphia exhibition of 1876. The Queen Anne had vernacular roots, and Americans such as Henry Hudson Holly saw in it

> . . . a simple mode of honest English building, worked out in artistic and natural form, fitting with the sash windows and ordinary doorways which express real domestic needs. (*Modern Dwellings in Town and Country,* 1878, p. 11)

This passage suggests that Holly was attracted to the idea of effects, that windows and doorways had functional and symbolic meaning. Holly was a New York architect and pattern-book writer who liked the direct, simple, honest forms of the colonial because architects and workmen could work readily with the structure of the vernacular styles. It was something they knew. Holly's enthusiasm for the style was romantic, that is, he saw this kind of classicism as part of the picturesque cottage tradition—buildings with "irregularities." He liked the interaction of the roofs, dormers, and chimneys. Holly imagined the colonial adapted to modern purposes, but his method for creating the modern was to express the ornamental: "stained glass in the upper sash, walls and ceilings in harmonious colors, relieved by rugs of Oriental pattern . . . dado of Indian matting . . . sideboard and fireplace Jacobean."

The ornamental attitude toward colonial design gave way to the modernized system in the 1920s. The shift away from surface ornamentation was tied to the general reform of housing types in which the almost square, hip-roofed cottage replaced the Queen Anne. Colonial interior architecture became generalized into a few historical motifs that created a unified impression. Scaled down and simplified, with fewer elements for each effect, the colonial aesthetic boiled down to millwork, hardware, and some architectural furniture.

The illustration shows a typical modernized colonial interior, built between 1915 and 1935, whether in a straight gable or in a gambrel-roofed cottage, its ridgepole parallel to the street. Most had a central hall plan. They were two-story buildings with social and service spaces on the ground floor level and bedrooms and bathroom on the second. The stair was either a straight flight on axis with the entrance or a quarter-turned stair on axis. The floors were hardwood, at least on the ground floor level, with linoleum and tile in the kitchen and bath. The wall organization included a modest picture molding, with the rest of the area plastered or papered in a small-pattern motif. Walls were also paneled with paper and dining rooms might have an historic scene mural. Painted walls often were stippled. The standing finish was painted—ivory was the most popular color—and the risers on the stairs received the same color as the woodwork. The treads, rail, and newel were stained a dark color, usually mohogany. Baseboard design was restrained: most had a shoe molding at the bottom, but very few added a molding to the top.

CORNER CHINA
CABINET

Ceilings generally were left as finished plaster, but ceiling moldings and panels as well as center pieces were common. To a lesser degree, living rooms were beamed with the same oak as in the artistic system, but in the colonial the beams were painted to match the woodwork. Stenciling died out in the 1920s and had little significance in the colonial system. According to trade catalogs, the traditional entrance door was a six-panel stile-and-rail unit with raised panels, and interior doors were the five-cross-panel type. Inventories of colonial motifs reveal many alternative choices. French doors for access to the hall from a living room or dining room or for access to a sun parlor or porch became a standard element. Windows were predominantly double-hung sash types with divided lights. Window placement included singles that were wider on the façade, a leftover cottage motif, and doubles and triples especially in living and dining rooms. Sun rooms and sleeping porches often were glazed on all three sides.

Most large interior openings were cased with pilaster finish, but uncased, plastered openings and arches worked their way into the design vocabulary, just as colonnades had done in the ornamental version of the colonial. Grilles remained part of the older system. The colonial aesthetic had such a strong tie to the open fireplace that it became a requirement for colonial schemes. Most were end-wall types, with or without a chimney breast, and featured wood mantels with pilasters or columns and an entablature as a shelf, brick facing, and a brick hearth. The molding work on the mantel, whether applied or stuck, was often the most delicately designed work in the house. Architectural furniture for the colonial included bookcases (more often open rather than closed), a buffet, corner china closets, and during the 1920s a breakfast nook.

Hardware was either machined-finished in brass, bronze, or pewter, or hand-worked in iron. Most pieces had little ornamentation. There might be beading around the edge of the escutcheon plate or knob: a plate with an overall shape, such as an oval; or plates with different terminations: square, eared, round, half-round. Glass doorknobs were part of the modern and the colonial systems.

MAHTEL, BOOKCASE, FRENCH DOOR

Lighting installations for the colonial seemed to require candle lights as brackets or as parts of a large dining room luminaire. Most of these designs were made to look historic and to integrate with other colonial effects. For instance, the reflectors on bracket lights looked a great deal like the hardware on the doors—a decorated edge on the plate, a ball-shaped bulb not unlike the spheroid knob on the door. And yet lighting features were always modern.

To learn more about the application of colonial design systems, we turn to examples of the style's millwork in a trade catalog. The company was Carr, Ryder and Adams of Dubuque, Iowa (hereafter noted as CRA), which had broad distribution of its product; the catalog is not dated but seems to be circa 1927.

CRA listed elements of design systems for several styles. Elements that could be assembled for a colonial effect included doors, wainscots, stair treatments (including newel, rail, and baluster types), storage units, windows, and mantels. CRA offered thirteen trim sets and each was illustrated in a design vignette so that its application could be imagined. A set could consist of a baseboard and a quarter-round shoe molding, a casing with or without a backband, a base block, a picture molding, a choice of stops for the windows, and an integrated window stool and apron.

Of the thirteen sets, six can be identified as having a colonial context; that is, elements are shown with another CRA product identified by the maker as "colonial" or are familiar enough to have been recognized as colonial by the trade. The term *colonial* is not used in the copy accompanying the illustrations of trim sets. The message here seems to be that if the buyer wants a colonial effect, she should choose one of the trim sets suggested as appropriate to a six-panel door, or a pilaster-framed fireplace mantel, or a divided-light window set in 6/1, 6/6, or 8/8 configuration. Besides the millwork products generally associated with the colonial system, each vignette has other design clues, such as wall finish. The colonial rooms have smoother plaster work, stippled painting, and wallpaper with narrow stripes, the very finishes recommended for colonial treatments during this time.

Carr, Ryder and Adams 1926 Millwork Catalog Trim Sets

Trim	shoe mold	base	base mold	base block	pic-ture mold	head case	head case stop	head case mold	casing	back band	stop	stool	apron
910	7073	7435		923	7261	7335	7186	7261	7347		7242 7244	7312	7307
912	7073	7435			7261				7352	7151	7242 7244	7312	7307
913	7073	7388			7261	7337			7356		7242 7244	7312	7307
915	7073	7434			7261				7352	7147	7242 7244	7312	7307
918	7073	7434			7216				7367	7148	7242 7244	7312	7307
921	7073	7388	7043	925	7216				7370		7236 7238	7316	7308

In order to understand the make-up of trim sets, we have analyzed each set by its components. The chart reveals that there were many repeats in the sets; for example, the window stop, stool, and apron pieces could work in almost any context. There were virtually no choices in some series; for example, the picture molding was the same in every set.

If the shoe molding, the picture molding, and the window stool, apron, and stop remained constant, the real variables were the casing, which could be augmented by a backband molding, and the baseboard. Of these colonial sets, only one had a molding for the baseboard and only two had a base block. The modernized colonial was, therefore, a system of fewer elements than the ornamental colonial, and the elements that featured raised moldings had shallower profiles than in the ornamental. The reduction in the number of surfaces and in the depth of the cuts in the surfaces also eliminated historical references. This strategy reduced the number of dustcatching edges from the older millwork elements, which no doubt pleased design reformers, and it extended colonial trim's use into contemporary settings. Some of the casings and baseboards were so generalized that they became ubiquitous, fitting colonial, artistic, and generally modern systems.

CRA manufactured other items that could be used in a colonial setting. They had five different designs for dining room corner china cabinets, all of which included cabinet space in the base and a glass door in front of the shelving: most units had two storage drawers as well. In each case, the overall size of the piece was the same—7 feet 1 inch by 3 feet, with a recess 1 foot 3 inches deep—but the glazing pattern on the upper doors was varied as was the trim around the cabinet and the cabinet head. The headpiece options included a broken-pediment, a keystone, and a continuous casing. There were also bookcases identified as suitable for colonial environments. The cases were open or closed (glass doors) with circle-top, flat, or segmental heads.

The breakfast nook usually was associated with bungalow design, but CRA produced a colonial nook with panels painted on the seat backs and turned legs for the benches and the table. In stairwork there were five colonial newels—both starting and angle newels—of turned stock; four of the five had a square base and one ended in a spiral volute. The balusters were thin, with round or tapered shapes. CRA also illustrated two stair systems, both with a straight flight and the appropriate elements, within the context of a colonial hallway. If buyers couldn't assemble a system on their own, they could buy one intact.

The final CRA product that had bearing on the colonial system was leaded glass doors for cupboards. CRA identified the patterns as "appropriate for the Modern home" as well as for the colonial and the English. Furnished with either lead or zinc metal bars, the glazing patterns were mostly a gridiron of rectangles and diamonds.

To complete the review of the colonial interior system, we offer the results of one field survey of ten colonial cottages—some of the straight gable type and others of the Dutch gambrel type. These single-family cottages were analyzed by inventorying the key elements in the interior design, including the baseboard, window and door trim, interior and entrance door types, stair plan, newel design, fireplace design, built-in features, hardware, ground plan of both floors, and window pattern. The cottages were built in two different Iowa counties from 1907 to 1942, with six erected during the 1930s. Among the ten cases, very few design elements were repeated. There is general agreement about house plan, but no two plans were exactly alike. Most had three or four rooms on the ground level and four bedrooms

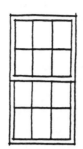

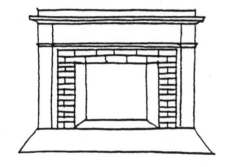

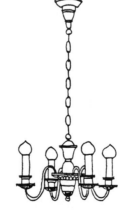

and a bath on the second floor. Two window patterns were repeated, but only one time each: 6/1 and 6/6. French doors, whether single or double, were included in six designs, but each door was in one of three glass patterns: twelve lights, fifteen lights (three times), and ten lights (two times). Seven of the ten stair plans had quarter-turned or hollow newel stairs. Three starting newels—a turned post with a volute—were the same, but all the others were singular. Eight of the houses had a living room fireplace, and of these, three units had comparable designs. Among interior door types, the single-panel door was repeated four times, the two-panel twice, and the six-panel twice. The only clustering of elements suggesting a unified approach to colonial design occurred among the houses built in the 1930s, but the correspondence was nowhere complete.

From the array of millwork products sold during the period 1870 through 1940, and from the information available from surveys of extant buildings, there seems never to have been a recognized formula for creating a colonial interior design. This conclusion holds up for the early, post-Centennial period as well as for the regenerated colonial of the 1920s. Based on what we now know of the Cape Cod house, which was first introduced as a colonial cottage, the situation remained the same throughout the 1940s. The colonial, like most interior architecture systems, was created from a series of effects within a range of intensities. Just as Henry Hudson Holly referred to the Queen Anne as the "free classic," the concept of the "free colonial" seems apt for this kind of design. The phrase suggests that the system from which it springs is not rigid, and that there is an overarching quality about the work that identifies it. You may not know exactly what that quality is, but you know it when you see it.

Colonial Aesthetics:
Elements

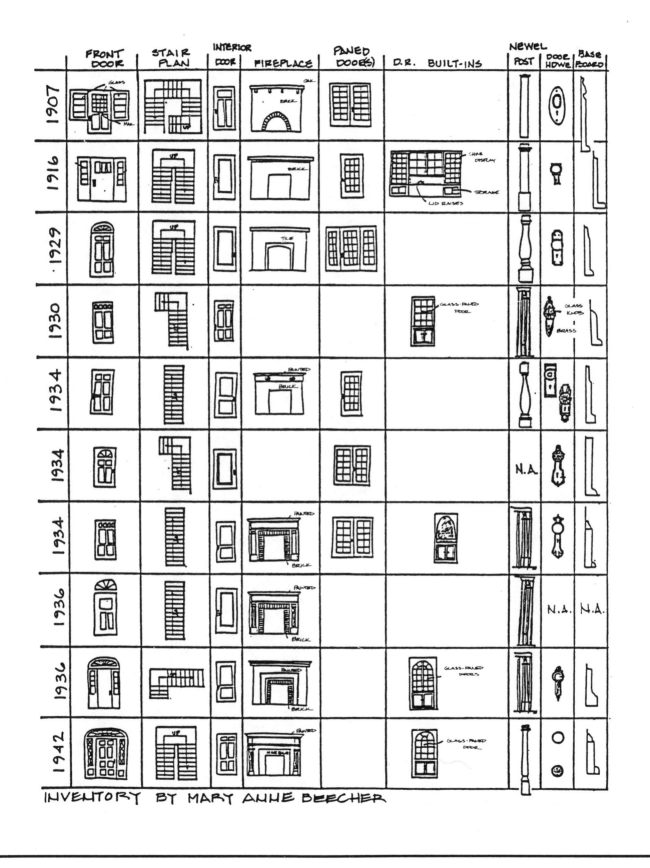

INVENTORY BY MARY ANNE BEECHER

BUILDING TYPES

INTRODUCTION

The following sections on building types consist of brief descriptions of buildings, including in each case the vernacular form and shape, the floor plan, and the salient features of the type. These are accompanied by schematic drawings of the general massing and plan arrangements and an isometric drawing that reveals the relationship between plan and form. Where appropriate, we include in each section a few pertinent phrases from the period to communicate something about the original intentions of the designers and manufacturers.

Each building type is designated either by its principal design element or by its historic name—the term used most frequently in the literature. In many cases the roof type (hip roof, gambrel roof) stands for a class of buildings.

The term *cottage* has been the most frequently used designation for vernacular houses. Almost any kind of single-family house with traditional cladding and fenestration has at one time been called a cottage. City houses, suburban and rural houses, and vacation houses have been called cottages. According to the *Oxford English Dictionary,* the term cottage "is found applied to dwelling places or holdings which under the feudal system were occupied by the cottars . . . and by the labourers of a farmstead." Historically, cottages were associated with poverty, with limited means both in buildings and in the circumstances of life. By the seventeenth century a cottage was a respectable dwelling with its own plot of land, but it remained a rural house type of limited means and tied to agriculture.

Current usage of the term relates to the effort to make the cottage a key element of the picturesque aesthetic—the *cottage orné,* an ornamented house type executed in natural materials and rustic effects. The change in definition and frame of reference signaled the rise of a middle class that could afford to convert a symbol of despair into an object of charm.

While the structure and ornamentation of an English cottage were made by hand, American cottages relied on millwork for effects. The American cottage also had a major role in reviving architectural styles, serving particularly as an appropriate model for country houses in the manner suggested by Andrew Jackson Downing and Alexander Jackson Davis. A suburban lot became the local equivalent of the English countryside, featuring gardens and verandas and visual and anecdotal references to historic architecture.

As for specific building types, we have classified six major categories of house forms consisting altogether of twenty-five subtypes. Commercial buildings and churches are divided into six classes each. In our original determination of building types, we examined the relationship between plan and form and assumed that each type would have an equally singular interior plan. We surmised that there could be a primary configuration and an alternative. In examining the issue of building type and plan thoroughly, however, we discovered that we had underestimated the entire relationship, so much so that variation, rather than exception, is the rule. Moreover, this conclusion encouraged us to reexamine whether ground plans of houses could readily be determined by exterior form. We decided that they cannot and will document why this is so.

Notes on Plan and Elevation Drawings

The drawings of ground plans in this section have a few notations that need explanation. For example, door openings are indicated by two notations—a quarter-circle swing for primary doors, and half that for closets. The reason for this is that a number of plans had doors in positions where the operation of one door could interfere with the other, certainly an example of poor planning. When we wanted the drawing to make a point, we used the two notations for doors to show the difference. Cased openings in all types are indicated by a pair of broken lines.

All of the plan and isometric drawings were done originally in one-eighth-inch scale and reduced for publication. Because the drawings in this section have been rendered in the same scale, they may be compared as to their relative size and volume. We have purposely not drawn basement and attic plans for those buildings that had them. We found both of these spaces to be of little importance for interior organization. For the most part, the attic and basement spaces remained unplanned and did not figure prominently in the rationale for form or interior aesthetic. There are a few common abbreviations to note: CL for closet, REC for reception hall or room, and PAN for pantry.

As indicated, the relationship between form and plan is not easily discerned; most housing types could vary in their choice plan. When looking at a house from the outside, however, it is possible to estimate aspects of the plan by looking for a few clues. The placement of a large window on a façade sometimes helps to locate the living room or parlor. Similarly, a small or otherwise unusual window by itself on a side elevation may indicate a stairway. Most vernacular house types have either a center hall plan, with an entrance door on the center axis of the building, a side hall plan, or entry into the living room. The placement of the entrance door also may indicate the general organization of the first floor.

When studying ground plans much can be learned about conceptual organization by the location of the stairs, the number of rooms on each floor, projections such as bay windows, and alignments of interior walls. Manipulation of these elements produced most interior arrangements.

Notes on Schematic Drawings

The building descriptions also include some schematic drawings of plans and interior volumes with roof plans. These drawings were intended to be analytical, to document the imprint of the plan on the site, and to reveal the volume. Ground plans do not show porch configurations unless the porch is covered by the main roof. Exceptions include the Bungalow Cottage and the Organic Cottages, where we analyze the relationship of porch to plan. In the Organic houses we also include some schematic drawings of circulation patterns.

The plan schematics focus on the organization of the main floor, with no drawings of upper floors. Sometimes we note the number of rooms on a second floor as part of the notes on general characteristics.

Variations in plan types are of two kinds: slight variations—a room added or subtracted—are labeled "variation," while clear alternative plans have a different designation, for example, "Bungalow Plan #3."

The interior walls are closed on the plans because we were trying to emphasize alignments between rooms. But all of the schematic drawings are proportional to each other, in order to facilitate comparisons.

GABLED COTTAGES

Gabled cottages are among the most prolific vernacular house types. They have been built in several formats, and sited in rural areas, small towns, and cities. The gable roof is traditional in vernacular building as an organizing element, whether parallel to or perpendicular to the street. By varying the roof pitch, the gable roof was easily adapted to all regions of the country. To accommodate different styling systems, slight modifications—clipping the apex of the gable, flaring the roof, and intersecting the gable with other roof forms, especially with another gable—were introduced.

WOODWARD'S NATIONAL ARCHITECT, DESIGN NO. 13 — 1869

LUCAS PAINT CO., "USUAL STYLE OF AMERICAN COUNTRY OR VILLAGE HOUSE" — 1887

W. K. WOOD HOUSE, MAXWELL, IOWA — 1877

Center Gable

The *center gable* is a very old house form and the American version of it probably derives from an English medieval vernacular form and from Tudor pattern books. This type of house was built long before 1870, but the precise time when it began to be built with industrial materials is not clear. One indication of its longevity is that in 1908 Sears offered it as Modern Home, No. 105, and by continuing to change a few exterior elements Sears continued to sell this house into the next decade.

The center gable house also derived from the romantic revival houses of the mid-nineteenth century, during which time houses had multiple gables as an expression of the picturesque. The center gable as a vernacular building had two types of volumetric organization: either one room deep or two rooms deep in one and a half or two stories. Both kinds were built during the 1870s and 1880s, and both types could include a vestibule on the façade or an ell in back. Older center gable houses had a large cornice and heavy projections, but these were reduced until the façade was flat and the roof had a modest overhang.

On plan, both models were wider than they were deep. The one-room-deep house was to have an ell rather than a vestibule. In our sample, more than half of these houses had a bay window, and, as is true for both kinds, the entrance was under the center gable. The two-room-deep house was slightly larger and usually had a vestibule, an ell, and a bay window. In both of these configurations, the ell was not aligned with either side wall. The typical floor plan was a center hall type with a stair in the hall rising from the entrance. Despite its predilection for symmetry, one cottage in this style was described as "domestic Gothic," alluding to the four-gable roof that might feature a "timber-trimmed gablet" (clipped gable).

SEARS, ROEBUCK AND CO.,
MODERN HOME NO. 105_1908

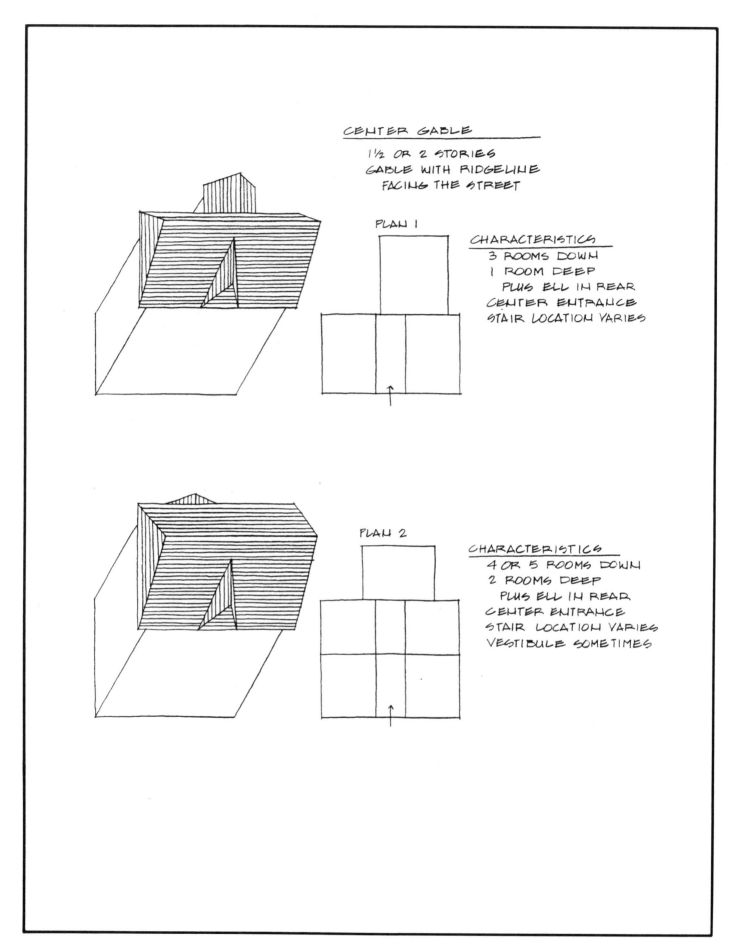

CENTER GABLE

1½ OR 2 STORIES
GABLE WITH RIDGELINE
FACING THE STREET

PLAN 1

CHARACTERISTICS
3 ROOMS DOWN
1 ROOM DEEP
PLUS ELL IN REAR
CENTER ENTRANCE
STAIR LOCATION VARIES

PLAN 2

CHARACTERISTICS
4 OR 5 ROOMS DOWN
2 ROOMS DEEP
PLUS ELL IN REAR
CENTER ENTRANCE
STAIR LOCATION VARIES
VESTIBULE SOMETIMES

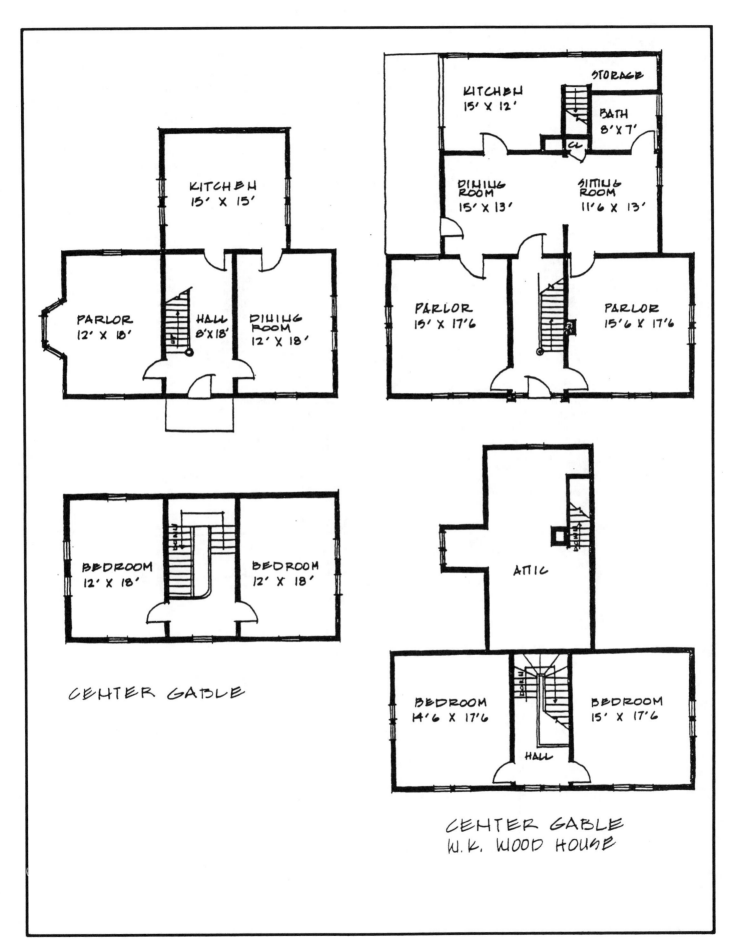

KITCHEN
15' X 15'

PARLOR
12' X 18'

HALL
8' X 18'

DINING
ROOM
12' X 18'

BEDROOM
12' X 18'

BEDROOM
12' X 18'

CENTER GABLE

KITCHEN
15' X 12'

STORAGE

BATH
8' X 7'

CL

DINING
ROOM
15' X 13'

SITTING
ROOM
11'6 X 13'

PARLOR
15' X 17'6

PARLOR
15'6 X 17'6

ATTIC

BEDROOM
14'6 X 17'6

BEDROOM
15' X 17'6

HALL

CENTER GABLE
W. K. WOOD HOUSE

Gabled Ell The *gabled ell* house was popular in rural areas, where it was identified as a "village residence." The distinctive feature of this two-story form was the massing of the large elements—a wing projected at a right angle to the main block. The ell had one of three configurations: the ell off center but still not aligned with the main block; the ell aligned with one side of the main block; and the ell centered on the main block. The interior organization of this house changed a few times from 1870 to 1920, which is about the extent of its duration. Overall it was a six- or eight-room house with a reception hall, either a straight or L-plan stair, a fireplace, a bay window, and a pantry.

THOMAS POPE HOUSE,
AMES, IOWA — 1877

CARPENTRY AND BUILDING,
BY T.I. LACEY OF
BINGHAMTON, NEW YORK —
1880

SYLVA, NORTH CAROLINA —
1903

This house has been referred to in the literature as an "upright and wing." In the early years of development, the wing was narrow but over time it widened, which paralleled the changing shape of the front room until the wing accommodated two rooms. The organizational plan included two rooms aligned with each other in the center of the building. There was usually a porch at one corner; some variations projected another one-story wing—a porch, shed, or other practical space—off the back of the main block.

The gabled ell received a number of different cottage treatments, several of which we illustrate. By the turn of the century the exterior stickwork and porch ornament had been stripped away, and the house had become classical in its repose on farmstead sites. "Its lines are American—straight, simple and massive." The interior organization was tied to the location of the porch, in that the porch served as the entrance. It was also common to find the stair in the middle of the volume at a right angle to the porch. This house was center-oriented in that the exterior walls were not aligned from room to room; instead, spatial units were clustered around the main block. The gabled ell was advertised as a "square layout . . . with a minimum construction and upkeep cost," and "easily adapted for group construction."

CARPENTRY AND BUILDING, "COTTAGE OF MODERATE COST," BY F.C. POLLMAR OF PETOSKEY, MICHIGAN — 1894

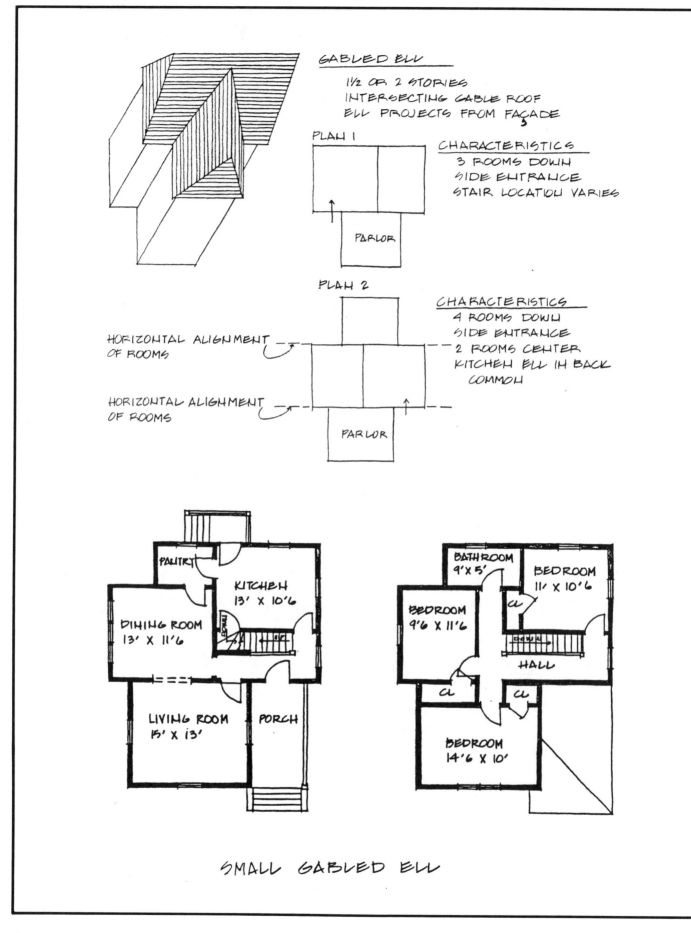

GABLED ELL

1½ OR 2 STORIES
INTERSECTING GABLE ROOF
ELL PROJECTS FROM FAÇADE

PLAN 1

PARLOR

CHARACTERISTICS
3 ROOMS DOWN
SIDE ENTRANCE
STAIR LOCATION VARIES

PLAN 2

HORIZONTAL ALIGNMENT OF ROOMS

HORIZONTAL ALIGNMENT OF ROOMS

PARLOR

CHARACTERISTICS
4 ROOMS DOWN
SIDE ENTRANCE
2 ROOMS CENTER
KITCHEN ELL IN BACK
COMMON

PANTRY

KITCHEN
13' X 10'6

DINING ROOM
13' X 11'6

LIVING ROOM
15' X 13'

PORCH

BATHROOM
9' X 5'

BEDROOM
11' X 10'6

BEDROOM
9'6 X 11'6

CL

HALL

CL

CL

BEDROOM
14'6 X 10'

SMALL GABLED ELL

278

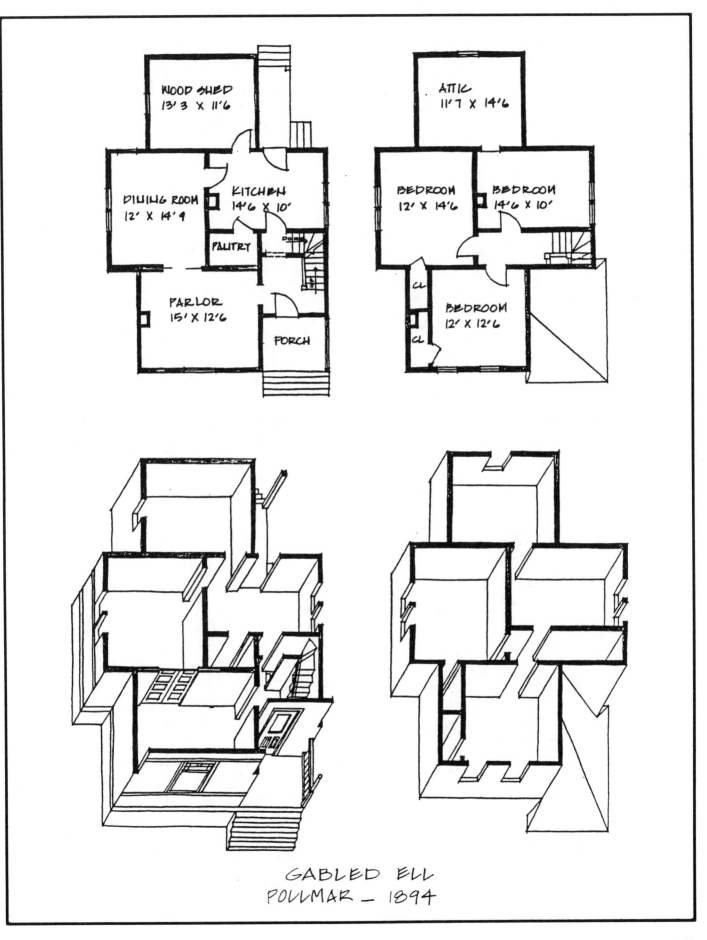

WOOD SHED
13'3 X 11'6

ATTIC
11'7 X 14'6

DINING ROOM
12' X 14'9

KITCHEN
14'6 X 10'

BEDROOM
12' X 14'6

BEDROOM
14'6 X 10'

PANTRY

Porch

PARLOR
15' X 12'6

CL

BEDROOM
12' X 12'6

CL

PORCH

GABLED ELL
POLLMAR — 1894

Plains Cottage The *plains cottage* was a single-family house type built in most states west of the Mississippi River, including the South. The cottage was a one-story building, with a projecting room off the front and two rooms side by side in the middle. The entry was located on the side as part of a modestly trimmed porch of turned posts, frieze, and brackets. The interior organization consisted of three to five rooms arranged so that the house was deeper than it was wide.

INTERSECTING GABLE ROOF, CHEYENNE, WYOMING

HIP AND GABLE ROOF, ASPEN, COLORADO

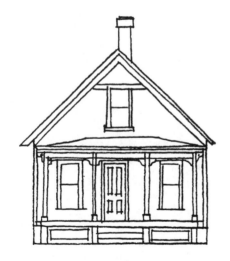

GABLE ROOF, CARPENTRY AND BUILDING, FOUR-ROOM COTTAGE — 1894

GABLE ROOF, THREE-ROOM COTTAGE, OURAY, COLORADO — 1908

Historically, this house has been labeled a country cottage, a western cottage, a cheap cottage, and a workingman's cottage. The range of descriptions reveals something about the purpose the house was to serve. We call it a plains cottage in response to its diffusion.

The plains cottage had three principal roof plans: a straight gable perpendicular to the street; two intersecting gables; and a hip-and-gable combination. Additional articulation included gable finish, art glass (especially in the large cottage window in the façade), and contrasting cladding materials such as shingles in the gables. These houses were built on narrow lots, typically on the "railroad" lots that were the major portion of the plats filed by railroads and developers in towns spawned by the presence of the rails.

The schematic drawings that accompany this entry illustrate the common arrangements of rooms, which, due to the size of the structure, required internal alignment. The interior aesthetic for this type was the ornamental system, which was reflected in its exterior details. Historically, most of the original plans for this house designated no bathroom. As a pragmatic design, the plains cottage was generally restrained. It was said of this house that, "having to combine usefulness and small outlay, there can be no latitude for architectural display," thus "the exterior . . . fairly expresses its domestic purpose."

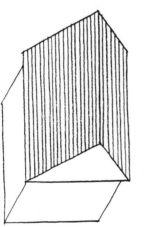

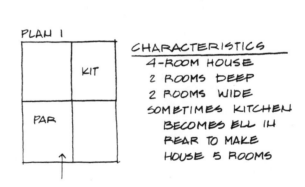

PLAINS COTTAGE

1 OR 1½ STORIES
GABLE END FACING STREET

PLAN 1

	KIT
PAR	

CHARACTERISTICS

4-ROOM HOUSE
2 ROOMS DEEP
2 ROOMS WIDE
SOMETIMES KITCHEN
BECOMES ELL IN
REAR TO MAKE
HOUSE 5 ROOMS

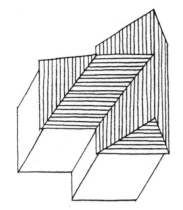

1 OR 1½ STORIES
INTERSECTING HIP AND GABLE
INTERSECTING GABLES

PLAN 2

CHARACTERISTICS
  4-ROOM HOUSE
  ENTRANCE FROM PORCH
    INTO PARLOR
  PARLOR LOCATED AT
    FRONT OR SIDE

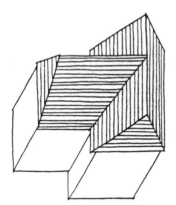

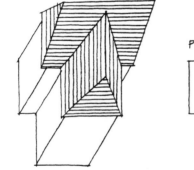

1 STORY
INTERSECTING GABLES

PLAN 3

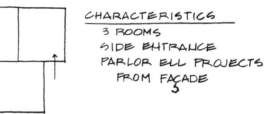

CHARACTERISTICS
  3 ROOMS
  SIDE ENTRANCE
  PARLOR ELL PROJECTS
  FROM FAÇADE

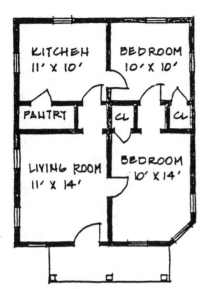

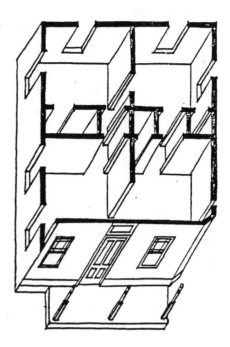

4-ROOM PLAINS COTTAGE

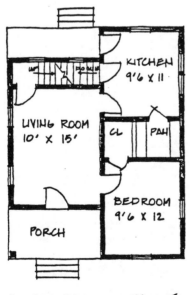

3-ROOM COTTAGE
OURAY, COLORADO

Shotgun and Industrial Houses

The so-called *shotgun house* was also a workingman's house, and thousands of these little houses were built next to or near industries of all kinds. The shotgun was easy to build, it could be erected in a day even with modestly skilled workers, and it could use local materials, which again saved on cost. These houses were built also in rural areas, especially in the South, and in one-industry or company towns. Narrower than a plains cottage, most shotguns were 12 to 15 feet wide and three to five rooms deep.

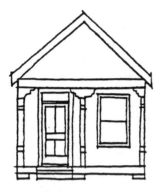

GABLE ROOF, MEMPHIS

HIP ROOF, LOUISVILLE

GABLE ROOF, BURBANK OIL FIELD, OKLAHOMA

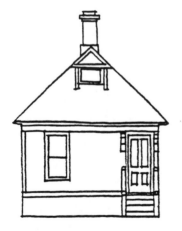

THE COMPLETE HOUSE BUILDER, DESIGN NO. 1, "CHEAP COTTAGE" 1890

MONTGOMERY WARD'S READY-MADE HOUSE, NO. 300 — 1910

Shotguns were wood-frame buildings with wood cladding, but brick was used also in cities. Although design concepts varied, the baseline model was a straight gable with a modest front porch. Other dimensions included an elaborate front porch, a cutaway side porch, gable finish of several kinds, fascia boards that girdled the building, and cottage-type porch detailing. The alternative roof for this house was the hip. Whatever the roof style, the interior organization was a jointed or segmented linear form of one room after another, with or without a connecting hall.

A housing type related to the shotgun was the *industrial house,* conceived to be built in clusters or in rows, like the shotguns, as part of an industrial development. More of them were built in this way than were built as single units. Most were literally "industrial houses" in that they were prefabricated.

Their standard width was 16 feet but their length varied; a typical three-room unit was 20 feet long. These were frame houses most likely clad with clapboards. The interior was finished in pine or fir. The industrial houses had a limited design vocabulary, and there was less individualization of units. Their architectural effect came from a uniform appearance, a common setback from the street, and common materials, something they shared with the shotgun house.

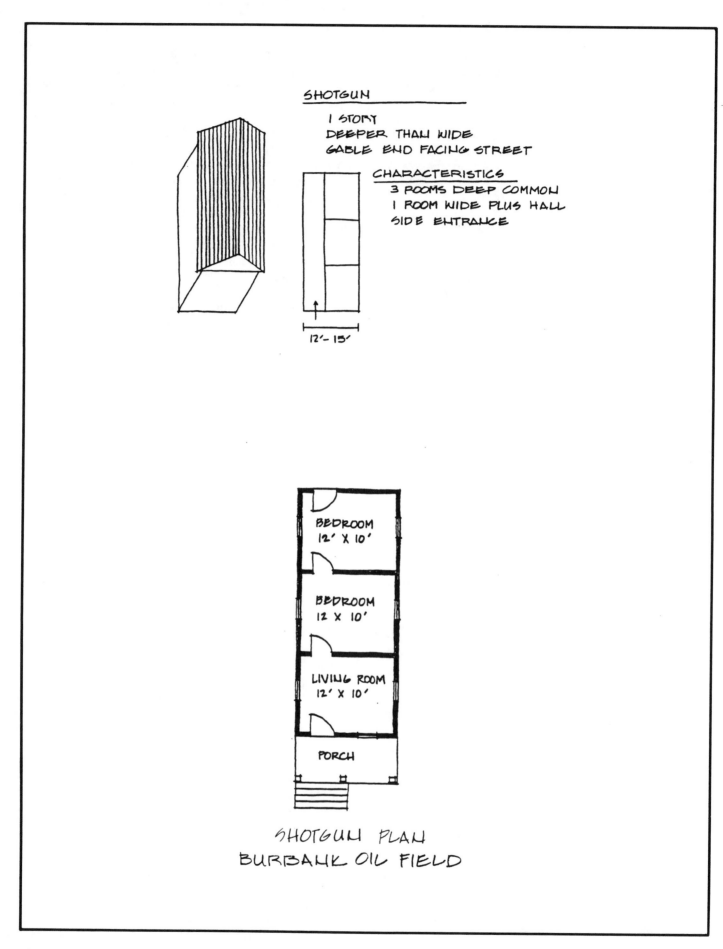

SHOTGUN

1 STORY
DEEPER THAN WIDE
GABLE END FACING STREET

CHARACTERISTICS
3 ROOMS DEEP COMMON
1 ROOM WIDE PLUS HALL
SIDE ENTRANCE

12'–15'

BEDROOM
12' X 10'

BEDROOM
12 X 10'

LIVING ROOM
12' X 10'

PORCH

SHOTGUN PLAN
BURBANK OIL FIELD

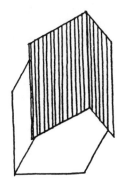

INDUSTRIAL

1 STORY
GABLE END FACING STREET

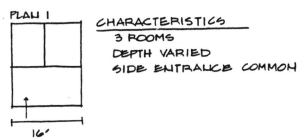

PLAN 1

CHARACTERISTICS

3 ROOMS
DEPTH VARIED
SIDE ENTRANCE COMMON

16'

PLAN 2

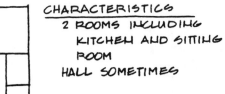

CHARACTERISTICS

2 ROOMS INCLUDING
   KITCHEN AND SITTING
   ROOM
HALL SOMETIMES

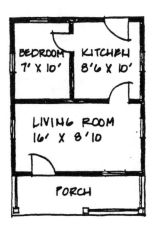

BEDROOM
7' X 10'

KITCHEN
8'6 X 10'

LIVING ROOM
16' X 8'10

PORCH

MONTGOMERY WARD'S
READY-MADE HOUSE #300

287

Open Gable The *open gable* was another modest house type, but its proportions were significant enough to include it in the cottage class of vernacular houses. Built in one-and-a-half and two-story models, the exterior form was a direct consequence of the interior organization. The roof ridge line was perpendicular to the street and carried short returns on the smaller houses. The roof edge projected about 2 feet over the side walls, making the wide eaves a distinctive characteristic of this design. A front porch spanned the façade.

TYPICAL FAÇADE,
2 STORIES

ALADDIN,
"THE SUBURBAN"
1920

TYPICAL FAÇADE,
1½ STORIES

The open gable had a side hall plan, with a living room across the front and two rooms behind it, or with the living room and a reception hall in front and a dining room and kitchen behind. The placement and plan of the stair was a significant variable in this house, with the quarter-circle and combination stair, with double access, as the principal arrangement. Fred Hodgson, pattern-book author and advisor to Sears, liked to turn the stairs in this type so that entry in the reception hall was from the side.

While the basic plan consisted of two rooms across and two rooms deep, the length was the greater dimension. The extra space could be absorbed by circulation, a pantry or breakfast nook, and a back porch. This was a plain, straightforward house, another of the type sometimes referred to in period literature as a "worker's house." It was marketed as a "conservative," simple design with straight lines.

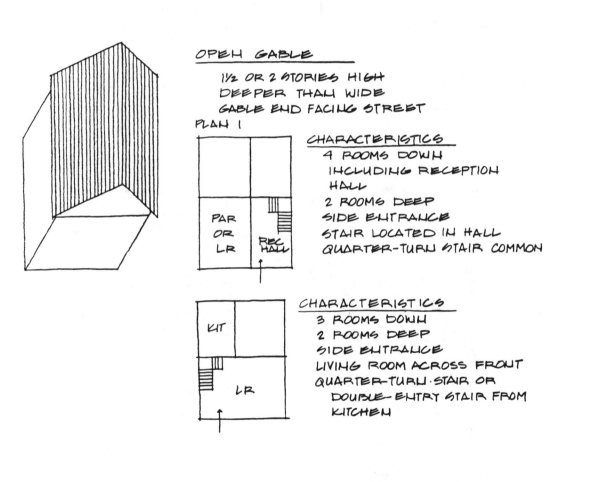

OPEN GABLE

1½ OR 2 STORIES HIGH
DEEPER THAN WIDE
GABLE END FACING STREET

PLAN 1

CHARACTERISTICS
4 ROOMS DOWN
INCLUDING RECEPTION
HALL
2 ROOMS DEEP
SIDE ENTRANCE
STAIR LOCATED IN HALL
QUARTER-TURN STAIR COMMON

PAR OR LR   REC HALL

CHARACTERISTICS
3 ROOMS DOWN
2 ROOMS DEEP
SIDE ENTRANCE
LIVING ROOM ACROSS FRONT
QUARTER-TURN STAIR OR
    DOUBLE-ENTRY STAIR FROM
    KITCHEN

KIT
LR

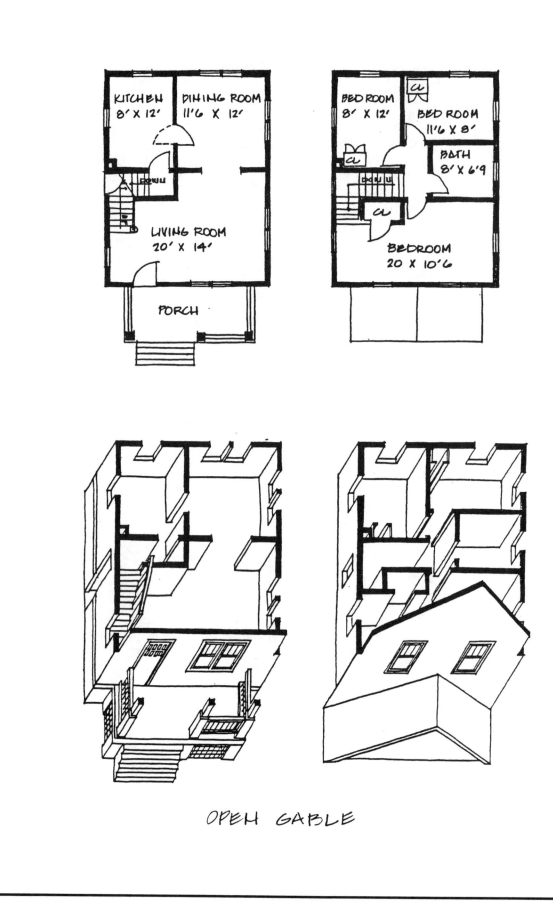

KITCHEN
8' X 12'

DINING ROOM
11'6 X 12'

LIVING ROOM
20' X 14'

PORCH

BED ROOM
8' X 12'

BED ROOM
11'6 X 8'

BATH
8' X 6'9

BEDROOM
20 X 10'6

CL

CL

CL

OPEN GABLE

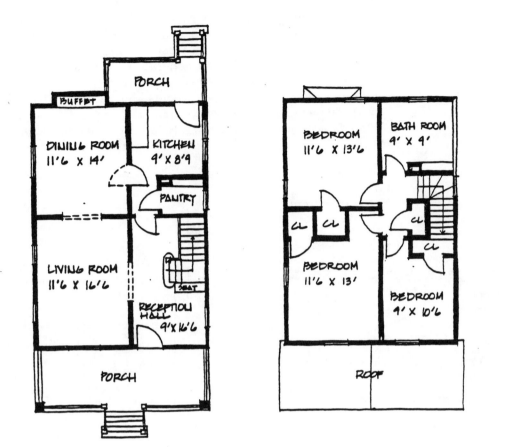

OPEN GABLE

Colonial Houses with *colonial* design characteristics were built in earnest after the 1876 Philadelphia Centennial exhibition. The first phase of this development focused on rediscovering the forms, details, and general qualities of colonial architecture. The translation of that information into vernacular building produced houses that were incorporated into the design language of the picturesque cottage. This first generation of houses was eclectic in that it was associated with the imported Queen Anne and the homegrown Shingle-style and hip-roofed cottages. During the 1880s and 1890s the key compositional elements were massive chimneys, bay windows, porticoes projected off the façades, unusual roof plans, Palladian windows, and moldings borrowed from Georgian sources, a general "adaptation of classic orders."

WASHINGTON, D.C. — 1936

RICHARD BECKMAN HOUSE, AMES, IOWA — 1936

BUILDING AGE AND NATIONAL BUILDER BLUEPRINT — 1925

While this first foray into America's past was a stimulus to vernacular design, the second revival of colonial architecture seemed to overwhelm house design. This model stripped away cottage detailing, an act that gave the historic form a lean and modern look. Linking historical forms and interior finish to the concept of modernity extended the colonial house deep into the architecture of the 1920s. The American preoccupation with progress somewhat inhibited the success of the colonial, but the illusion of history underpinned by modern living conditions was a powerful combination.

Generally, colonial house types fell into four subtypes of two-story or one-and-a-half-story frame buildings: a house clad in wood or brick veneer with three or five bays across the façade; the *overhang,* or *garrison,* house clad in shingles, clapboards, or combinations of materials; the wide-bodied *Cape Cod* that was called a colonial before it was a Cape Cod; and the *gambrel cottage,* or *Dutch colonial,* which will be discussed in a later section. The three gabled types were wider than they were deep, and all had a center hall plan. Many had a side porch or a sun porch on the ground floor or a sleeping porch on the second floor, and all had an end-wall chimney, although builders of Cape Cod houses sometimes included the more authentic central fireplace with multiple flues.

Interior organization of the colonial always relied on a symmetrical division of rooms along a central hall. Most stair plans were a straight flight up from the entrance. The early-twentieth-century aesthetic for the colonial was the artistic system, which was replaced by the modern colonial. The modern opened the plan and often added a knotty pine room to the ground floor or the basement, which was evolving into a finished space.

Interior finish for these houses was less ornamented than in the earlier colonials, but molded trim sets were still appropriate for doors and windows, cased openings, and baseboards. A chair rail and a picture molding also remained part of this system. Architectural furniture for the colonial cottage included corner china closets, open or closed bookcases, and a pilaster and architrave mantel. French doors to a porch, a sun room, or a hallway were a common passage effect.

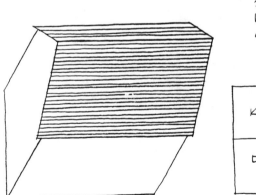

COLONIAL

2 STORIES
WIDER THAN DEEP
GABLE WITH RIDGE LINE
FACING THE STREET

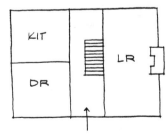

CHARACTERISTICS
2 ROOMS DEEP
2 ROOMS WIDE PLUS
CENTRAL HALL
CENTER ENTRANCE
STAIR LOCATED IN HALL
STRAIGHT-RUN STAIR
COMMON BUT PLANS
VARY
FIREPLACE ON OUTSIDE
LIVING ROOM WALL

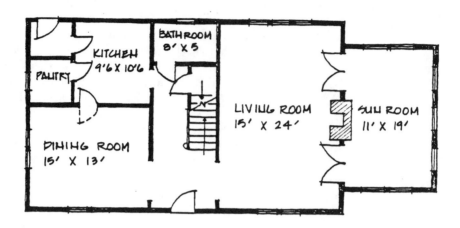

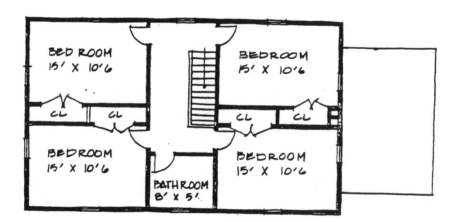

COLONIAL COTTAGE

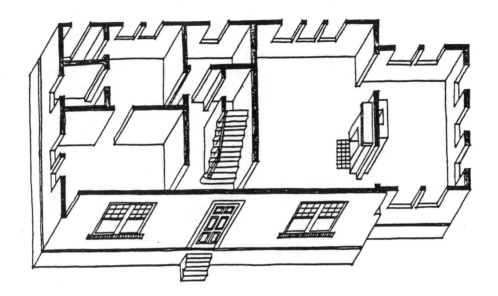

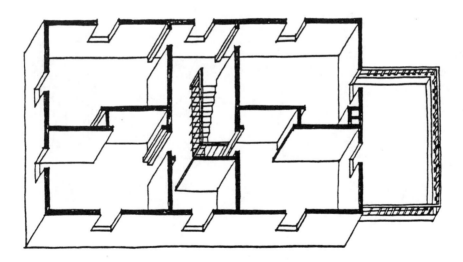

COLONIAL COTTAGE

Cape Cod The term *Cape Cod* has been in use in New England for almost two hundred years, but it was not used in trade literature until the 1930s. The original Cape Cod–colonial house form was not replicated faithfully throughout the land. The general form persisted, but the proportions and the elements of articulation have changed more than once. The wood-shingled exterior, left natural to weather gray, was replaced by clapboards, bricks, or asbestos shingles. The dimensions of this house varied, but it was wider than deep, with 32 feet across and 27 feet deep being an average size for a two-bedroom house. The Cape Cod was usually a story and a half in height and had dormers on one or both sides. Overall it was "simple and tidy in its lines."

The Cape Cod was an especially successful modern colonial, being designed with few embellishments outside or inside. Instead of using ornamentation as an historical reference, the Cape Cod relied on the severity of its lines and on a well-proportioned form, in which a broad roof and a wide gable brought the eaves close to ground. Closeness to the ground gave it an organic quality, and the concept of severe lines was carried into the interior as a straightedge casing or a uncased archway that divided the rooms. The time of the Cape Cod's greatest popularity coincided with the modern colonial aesthetic, and this was the interior system used for these houses.

TYPICAL FAÇADE

BUILDING AGE AND
NATIONAL BUILDER
BLUEPRINT — 1925

The interior organization was grouped around the central hall, with a long living room on one side and the dining room and kitchen on the other, and two bedrooms, a bath, and a connecting hallway upstairs. Most stair plans were straight, rising from the entrance. Despite the presence of popular elements such as breakfast nooks, sun rooms, and sun porches, the Cape Cod expressed "truly American traditions . . . more vividly than any other type."

CAPE COD

1 OR 1½ STORIES
SLIGHTLY WIDER THAN DEEP
GABLE WITH RIDGELINE
FACING THE STREET

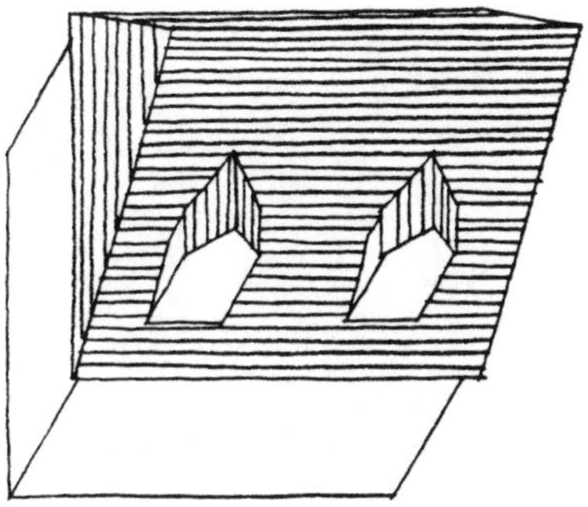

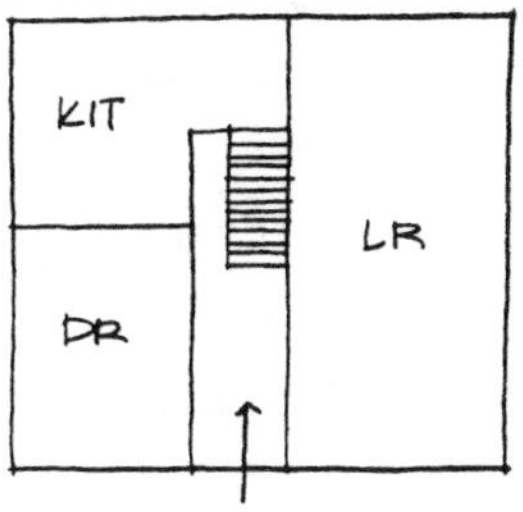

CHARACTERISTICS

3 ROOMS DOWN
2 ROOMS DEEP
CENTER ENTRANCE
STRAIGHT STAIR COMMON,
    PLACEMENT IN HALL
    VARIES
LIVING ROOM ACROSS
    ONE SIDE
2 BEDROOMS UP COMMON

VARIATION

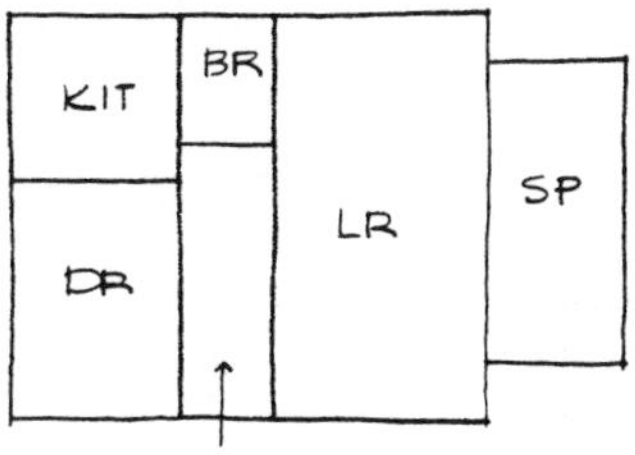

CHARACTERISTICS

BREAKFAST ROOM
SUN PORCH
ATTACHED GARAGE
    LATER

English Cottage The *English cottage* is one of the few imported, historically based house designs of the twentieth century. The primary source for this compact house was a vague notion of English vernacular characterized by irregular forms and surfaces in everything: steep roofs and contrasting roof lines, multiple cladding materials, fireplaces with tall, dramatically composed chimneys, asymmetrical massing and fenestration. The house was thought of as having "informal charm," a tone reinforced by details—gables of stucco and half timber, brick and stone effects, round-headed doors with strap hardware, round-headed archways between rooms, entrances that were not always visible from the street, diamond-paned casements, and "quaint dormers."

Interior planning, like that of the exterior, was varied because of the need to create a sense of casual arrangement, as if the spatial configurations were indigenous to the culture and therefore part of local custom. Generally, each house had three or four rooms down and up, with very few having a full second floor. Only portions of the main house, perhaps as wings, were raised to that height.

The English cottage reached the height of its popularity during the 1920s. Its success was based in part on a multitude of effects and special spaces, including a breakfast room or nook, a fireplace, a terrace or patio in an outside corner, and a reception hall or vestibule as a projecting gable off the front. All of this was intended to create "a dignified, restful house of surprising convenience and no extravagance."

BUILDING AGE AND
HATIONAL BUILDER
BLUEPRINT _1925

BUILDING AGE COVER DESIGN
MARCH 1913

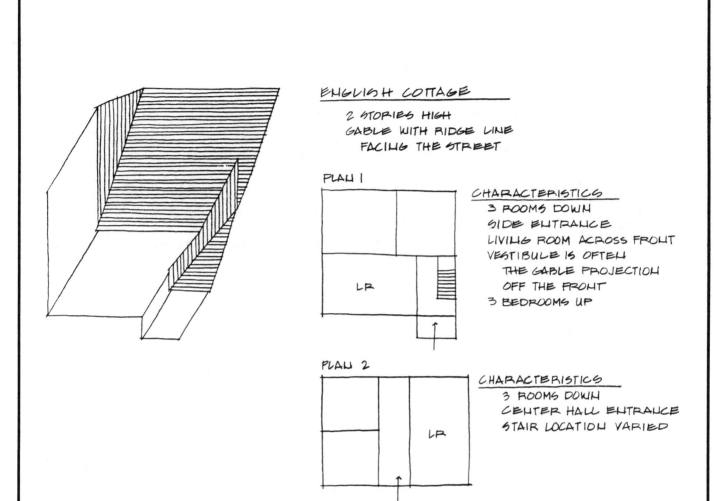

ENGLISH COTTAGE

   2 STORIES HIGH
   GABLE WITH RIDGE LINE
    FACING THE STREET

PLAN 1

CHARACTERISTICS
   3 ROOMS DOWN
   SIDE ENTRANCE
   LIVING ROOM ACROSS FRONT
   VESTIBULE IS OFTEN
    THE GABLE PROJECTION
    OFF THE FRONT
   3 BEDROOMS UP

PLAN 2

CHARACTERISTICS
   3 ROOMS DOWN
   CENTER HALL ENTRANCE
   STAIR LOCATION VARIED

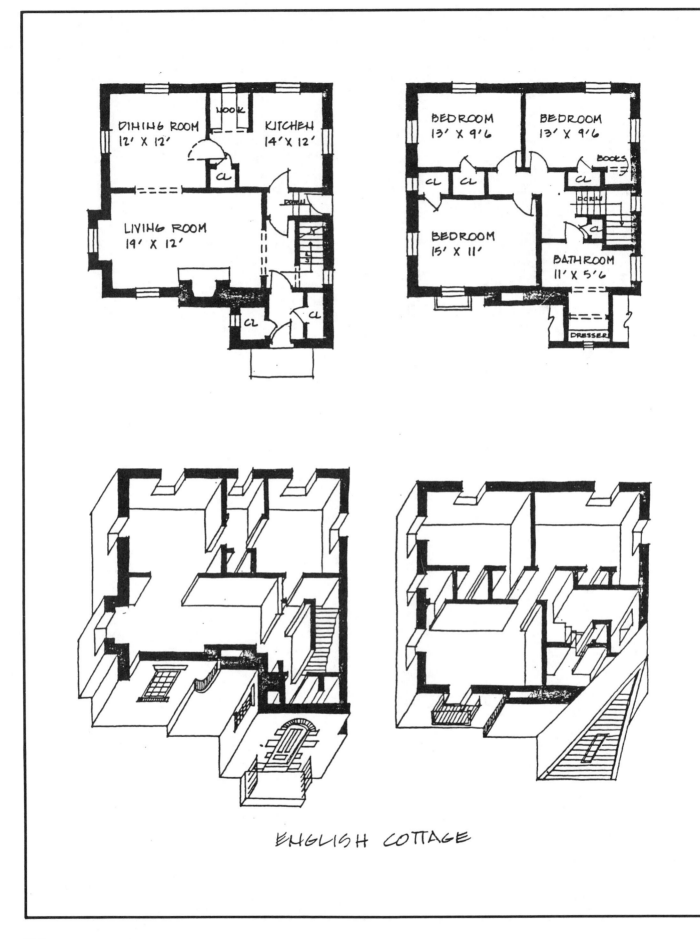

DINING ROOM
12' X 12'

NOOK

KITCHEN
14'X 12'

CL

LIVING ROOM
19' X 12'

DOWN

CL

CL

BEDROOM
13' X 9'6

BEDROOM
13' X 9'6

BOOKS

CL

CL

CL

DOWN

CL

BEDROOM
15' X 11'

BATHROOM
11' X 5'6

DRESSER

ENGLISH COTTAGE

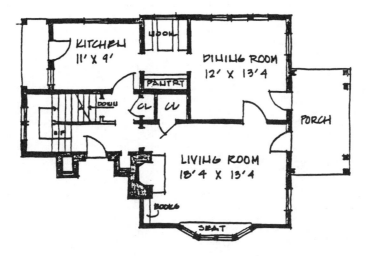

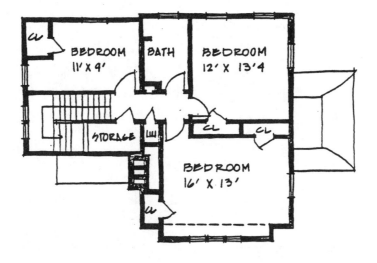

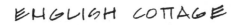

ENGLISH COTTAGE

HIPPED COTTAGES Among *hip-roofed cottages*, the baseline type for this class was referred to as a "square type," and plans offered within that form had several versions. The key elements in the floor plan of the square type were the placement of the reception space and the location of the stairs.

PLAN 1 VARIATION, LEE H. MC CLUNG HOUSE, SAPULPA, OKLAHOMA — 1909

PLAN 1 VARIATION, MRS. A.J. TROTT HOUSE, UNIVERSITY PARK, COLORADO — 1895

PLAN 3, SEARS, ROEBUCK AND CO., MODERN HOUSE NO. 102 — 1908

RECTILINEAR HIPPED COTTAGE, PLAN 1, F.S. COLLINS HOUSE, BERWYN, ILLINOIS — 1915

Square, Plan 1 The first model had a reception room as one of the four first-floor rooms. Average size for this house, which was wider than it was deep, was 25 feet wide by 31 feet deep. The square house had a full-width front porch. Several interior schemes utilized the reception room plan, which placed the quarter-turn stair to the side and included a small center hall on the upper level. A bay window, on a side elevation and part of the design of the dining room, was most often on the opposite side of the house from the stairs. Sold as a practical house without requiring the expense that comes from "making projections on a building," this type was referred to as a "modern square type" in which "square lines permit full utilization of every inch of floor space."

Focusing on the idea of square shapes, the Curtis Company advertised its square-type house as having an "absence of unnecessary ornamentation on the exterior" and having on the inside a stair with square balusters and newel as the "center of interest in a reception hall of square shape."

The variation of this type of cottage also had a reception hall, but the stair was placed behind the reception partition and was entered from the side. This house also had a bay window and the same distribution of rooms as the first model, with a slight increase in overall size, averaging 27 feet wide and 46 feet deep. The exterior had typical square-type elevations that could include a porch or pantry ell off the back side. The literature of the period cited this house for its "economy of space" which made it "suited for a narrow lot," its reception hall large enough "to be of some service," and its "excellent arrangement of stairs."

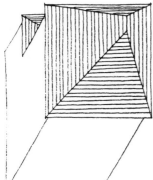

HIPPED COTTAGE

2 STORIES HIGH
SLIGHTLY DEEPER THAN WIDE
HIP ROOF

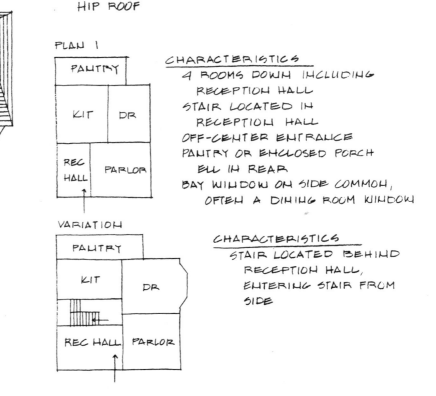

PLAN 1

PANTRY	
KIT	DR
REC HALL	PARLOR

CHARACTERISTICS
4 ROOMS DOWN INCLUDING
   RECEPTION HALL
STAIR LOCATED IN
   RECEPTION HALL
OFF-CENTER ENTRANCE
PANTRY OR ENCLOSED PORCH
   ELL IN REAR
BAY WINDOW ON SIDE COMMON,
   OFTEN A DINING ROOM WINDOW

VARIATION

PANTRY	
KIT	DR
REC HALL	PARLOR

CHARACTERISTICS
STAIR LOCATED BEHIND
   RECEPTION HALL,
   ENTERING STAIR FROM
   SIDE

Square, Plan 2 (Colonial)

A second type of hipped cottage had a colonial exterior treatment with a center hall plan and a center hall stair. The arrangement was comparable to the colonial house with a gable roof. There were three rooms and a reception hall on the ground floor and four bedrooms and a bath upstairs. Most plans extended the living room from front to back along one side.

As to its shape, the colonial was slightly wider than deep, averaging about 39 by 36 feet, which allowed for more square footage than the other cottages. Many of its exterior appointments were intended to imitate a Georgian colonial, and therefore included freestanding columns and colonnades between rooms or between rooms and halls. These houses were described as having general lines "taken from New England and Southern Colonial architecture," with dormers that were "severe, simple and quaint." As a building form, the house demonstrated "compactness without monotony" and conveyed a "truly American feeling."

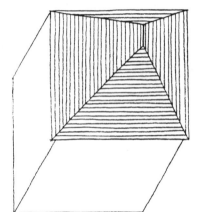

HIPPED COTTAGE

FORM BECOMES LARGER, WIDER

PLAN 2

KIT		DR
LR		PARLOR

CHARACTERISTICS
4 ROOMS AND HALL DOWN
2 ROOMS DEEP
CENTER ENTRANCE
STAIR LOCATED IN CENTER HALL, PLANS VARY
4 ROOMS PLUS BATH UP

VARIATION

LR		KIT
		DR

CHARACTERISTICS
3 ROOMS AND HALL DOWN
LIVING ROOM ACROSS SIDE

Square, Plan 3 The last of the square, hip-roofed cottages is the six-room type whose plan has the living room as the first room, spreading it across the entire front of the house.

This house was the smallest of its class. The form was sometimes cubical but more generally rectangular, with its depth only slightly greater than its width (27 feet by 32 feet). The overall shape was characterized by straight sides and a full-width porch. The lower level had three rooms and a quarter-turn stair behind which was the kitchen; on the second floor were bedrooms and a bath. This was a popular type because of its low cost, and it adapted well to a city or suburban lot. It was variously described as "a square roomy house" or a "square, center chimney type, a layout often used when strict economy is desired." If a client did not like the square look, there were alternatives with the same plan. In 1923, Curtis's *Better Built Homes,* Volume 16, offered the six-room square-type house under the trade name "Western." If buyers didn't like that, they could have the same plan with a colonial or English exterior.

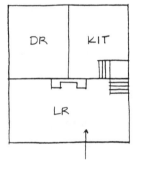

PLAU 3

CHARACTERISTICS
3 ROOMS DOWN
2 ROOMS DEEP
OFF-CENTER ENTRANCE
LIVING ROOM ACROSS FRONT
MOST NEARLY A SQUARE
QUARTER-TURN STAIR COMMON
FIREPLACE BETWEEN LIVING
  ROOM AND REAR ROOMS
  FREQUENT
3 BEDROOMS COMMON

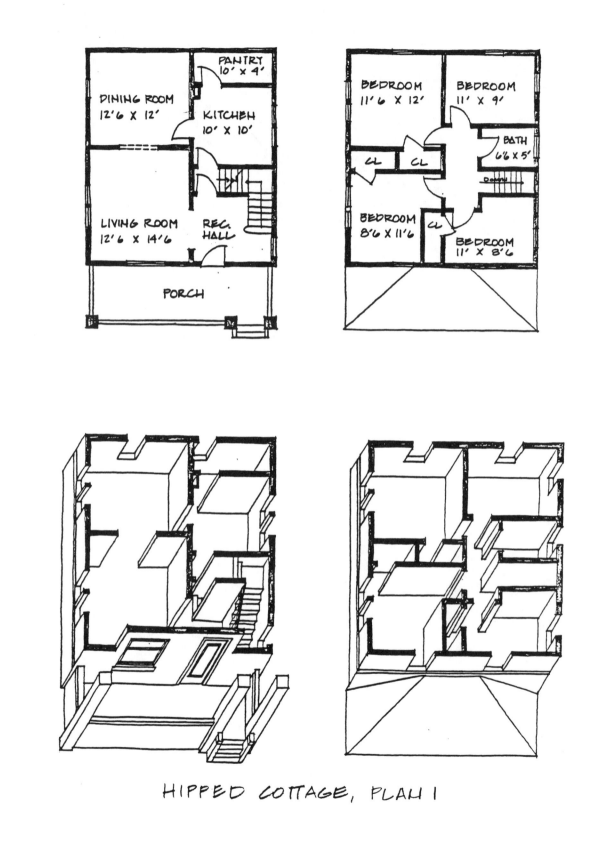

DINING ROOM
12'6 X 12'

PANTRY
10' X 4'

KITCHEN
10' X 10'

LIVING ROOM
12'6 X 14'6

REC.
HALL

PORCH

BEDROOM
11'6 X 12'

BEDROOM
11' X 9'

BATH
6'6 X 5'

CL   CL

BEDROOM
8'6 X 11'6

CL

BEDROOM
11' X 8'6

HIPPED COTTAGE, PLAN I

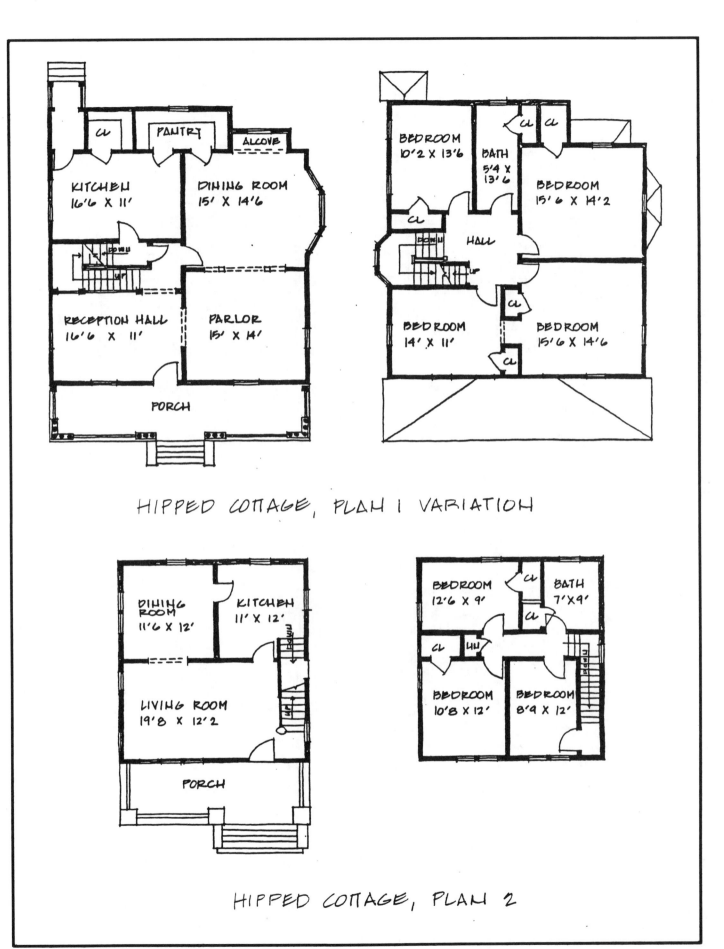

HIPPED COTTAGE, PLAN 1 VARIATION

Upper left floor plan (first floor):

CL
PANTRY
ALCOVE
KITCHEN 16'6 X 11'
DINING ROOM 15' X 14'6
DOWN
RECEPTION HALL 16'6 X 11'
PARLOR 15' X 14'
PORCH

Upper right floor plan (second floor):

CL CL
BEDROOM 10'2 X 13'6
BATH 5'4 X 13'6
BEDROOM 15'6 X 14'2
CL
DOWN
HALL
CL
BEDROOM 14' X 11'
CL
BEDROOM 15'6 X 14'6

HIPPED COTTAGE, PLAN 2

Lower left floor plan (first floor):

DINING ROOM 11'6 X 12'
KITCHEN 11' X 12'
DOWN
UP
LIVING ROOM 19'8 X 12'2
PORCH

Lower right floor plan (second floor):

BEDROOM 12'6 X 9'
CL
BATH 7' X 9'
CL
CL
UP
BEDROOM 10'8 X 12'
DOWN
BEDROOM 8'9 X 12'

307

COLONIAL HIPPED
COTTAGE, TYPICAL
FAÇADE WITH TWO-
STORY BAY

COLONIAL HIPPED
COTTAGE, TYPICAL
FAÇADE

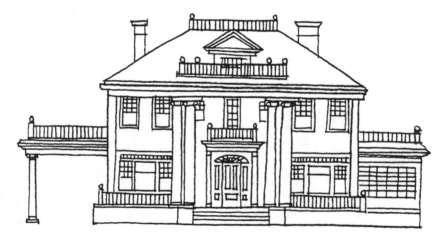

PLAN 3, SEARS, ROEBUCK AND CO.,
"THE MAGNOLIA," NO. 2089, PRECUT—
1918

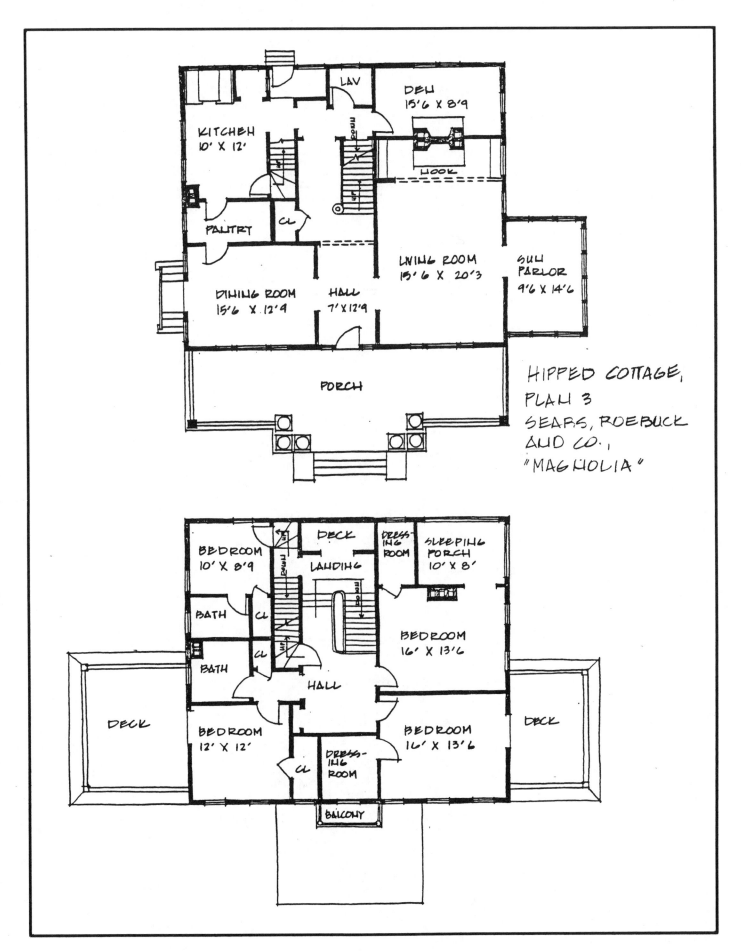

KITCHEN
10' X 12'

LAV

DEN
15'6 X 8'9

HOOK

PANTRY

CL

LIVING ROOM
15'6 X 20'3

SUN
PARLOR
9'6 X 14'6

DINING ROOM
15'6 X 12'9

HALL
7' X 12'9

PORCH

HIPPED COTTAGE,
PLAN 3
SEARS, ROEBUCK
AND CO.,
"MAGNOLIA"

BEDROOM
10' X 8'9

DECK

DRESS
ING
ROOM

SLEEPING
PORCH
10' X 8'

LANDING

BATH

CL

BATH

CL

HALL

BEDROOM
16' X 13'6

DECK

DECK

BEDROOM
12' X 12'

DRESS-
ING
ROOM

CL

BEDROOM
16' X 13'6

DECK

BALCONY

309

Villa The *villa house* was another type with a hipped roof and a central hall plan, although in this design the roof played a stronger role in the overall scheme than it did in others. The principal historical source for the villa was a generalized European-Mediterranean two-story form, with a main block wider than it is deep, a low broad roof, and an extension to one or both sides. In its exterior styling the villa house was either French, Italianate, or Spanish Colonial. These effects were produced by varying a few elements, such as roof shape, roofing material, the width of the eaves, the entrance design, and the handling of the cladding materials. The façades had three- or five-bay fronts covered with one or two materials, including brick veneer, stucco, clapboard, and shingles.

VILLA, PLAN 3 VARIATION, OAK PARK, ILLINOIS

VILLA, PLAN 3 VARIATION, OKLAHOMA CITY

There was an American-inspired alternative to the villa, derived from Prairie style houses and labeled "western" in the vernacular, but this was a minor development. Most western types were a version of the square-type house, producing a special cottage that we and others refer to as "the rectilinear." No matter what the form, this type did call attention to the idea that "straight, simple lines express true beauty." Other descriptions of the period referred to the "dignity and grandeur" of the house and stated that, although the "architectural lines are strong," the resulting form is "artistic."

VILLA, PLAN 3 VARIATION, <u>BUILDING</u> <u>AGE</u> SUPPLEMENTAL PLATE — 1915

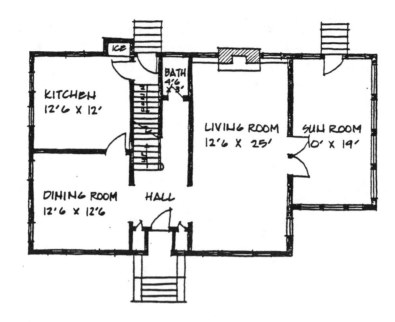

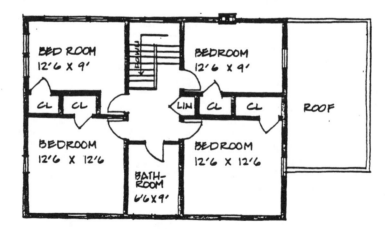

VILLA HIPPED COTTAGE

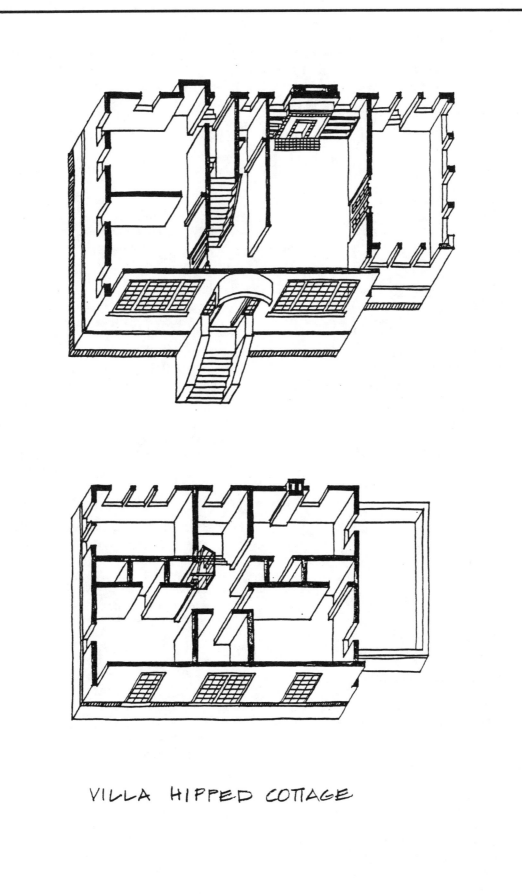

VILLA HIPPED COTTAGE

**ITALIANATE
HIPPED
AND
MANSARD
COTTAGES**

There is a special class of hip-roofed cottages whose design is based on the use of elements from an *Italianate* architectural style. In terms of composition, this type had a set of window, cornice, entry, and corner treatments that contributed to the styling effect. All of these elements were free adaptations of Renaissance motifs, reproduced in wood, tin, and iron. In the vernacular of the period, a cottage such as this was known also as a *bracketed cottage,* no doubt a reference to the heavy brackets that characterized the cornice.

ITALIANATE HIPPED,
PLAN 1, TYPICAL FAÇADE

ITALIANATE, HIP AND
GABLE ROOFS, PLAN 1
VARIATION, WOODWARD'S
NATIONAL ARCHITECT,
DESIGN NO. 16 — 1869

1½-STORY MANSARD,
PLAN 1, BICKNELL'S
VILLAGE BUILDER —
1872

2½-STORY MANSARD,
TYPICAL FAÇADE

The overall handling of exterior elements and interior organization was equally applicable to another cottage type, the *mansard cottage,* or *French cottage.* Both houses utilized the same kinds of plans—side hall and center hall.

The side hall plan was the more prevalent, and houses with this spatial configuration were typically one room and a hallway wide and three rooms deep, with a second level of bedrooms and bath. This arrangement fitted into several sizes, with Italianate types being one and a half to two and a half stories high, and mansard types being one and a half, two, or three stories high. Because of its roof shape, the mansard often included a third floor lighted by dormers.

Within the side hall plan, the stair plan was either a straight-run type or a quarter-turn type, with the latter often employing winder stairs to save space. The side hall plan also included a bay window projection off one side that lit a sitting room or dining room. This arrangement was especially true for houses built in the 1870s. Later examples included a bay window on the façade, sometimes tiered so that bay linked the floors.

The variant for the side hall plan had the same narrow, deep shape, but a new room was carved out of the center of the house just behind the stairs. The room usually was small and was used as a library or den; projecting the room slightly from the side elevation, or adding a bay window, turned it into a dining room.

The center hall plan had four rooms on the first floor, symmetrically arranged on each side, with a wide hall between them. Stair plans, again from the 1870s, often called for two stairs, the principal one accessible from the front door and the front rooms, and a second, hidden from view, connecting a small back hall to the upper floor.

The overall shape of these houses followed from the plan type, in that the side hall house had a narrower façade than the center hall type. In both cases, however, the rooms on the first floor were aligned with each other. There were also other kinds of plans that were used less frequently. These included a stem-and-crossbar type, on the order of a T-plan, in which a section of house one room wide intersected with a two-room-wide crossbar. A second alternative had an L-shape in which two sections, each one room wide, met at right angles, with the entrance, hall, and stair included in the intersection.

It has been our custom to include some references to building types from the trade literature of the period, but we were unable to find that kind of information for these cottages. Although accounts of these buildings were published, the houses were not characterized. Instead, there were lists of materials and engravings suggested siting. We can only surmise that for some reason—perhaps their construction dates—these cottages were not written about in the same way as the others.

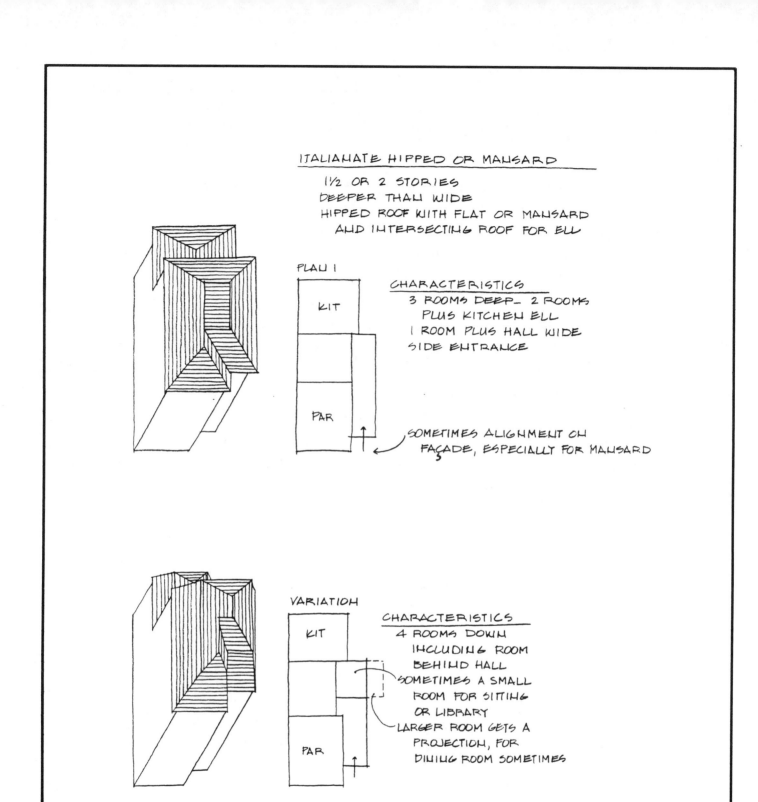

ITALIANATE HIPPED OR MANSARD

1½ OR 2 STORIES
DEEPER THAN WIDE
HIPPED ROOF WITH FLAT OR MANSARD
AND INTERSECTING ROOF FOR ELL

PLAN 1

KIT

PAR

CHARACTERISTICS
3 ROOMS DEEP— 2 ROOMS
PLUS KITCHEN ELL
1 ROOM PLUS HALL WIDE
SIDE ENTRANCE

SOMETIMES ALIGNMENT ON
FAÇADE, ESPECIALLY FOR MANSARD

VARIATION

KIT

PAR

CHARACTERISTICS
4 ROOMS DOWN
INCLUDING ROOM
BEHIND HALL
SOMETIMES A SMALL
ROOM FOR SITTING
OR LIBRARY
LARGER ROOM GETS A
PROJECTION, FOR
DINING ROOM SOMETIMES

316

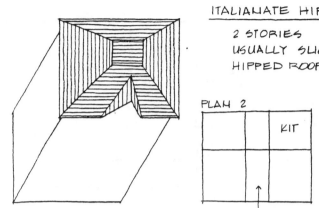

ITALIANATE HIPPED OR MANSARD

2 STORIES
USUALLY SLIGHTLY WIDER THAN DEEP
HIPPED ROOF WITH FLAT OR MANSARD

PLAN 2

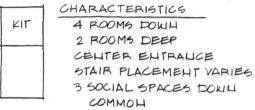

CHARACTERISTICS
   4 ROOMS DOWN
   2 ROOMS DEEP
   CENTER ENTRANCE
   STAIR PLACEMENT VARIES
   3 SOCIAL SPACES DOWN
      COMMON

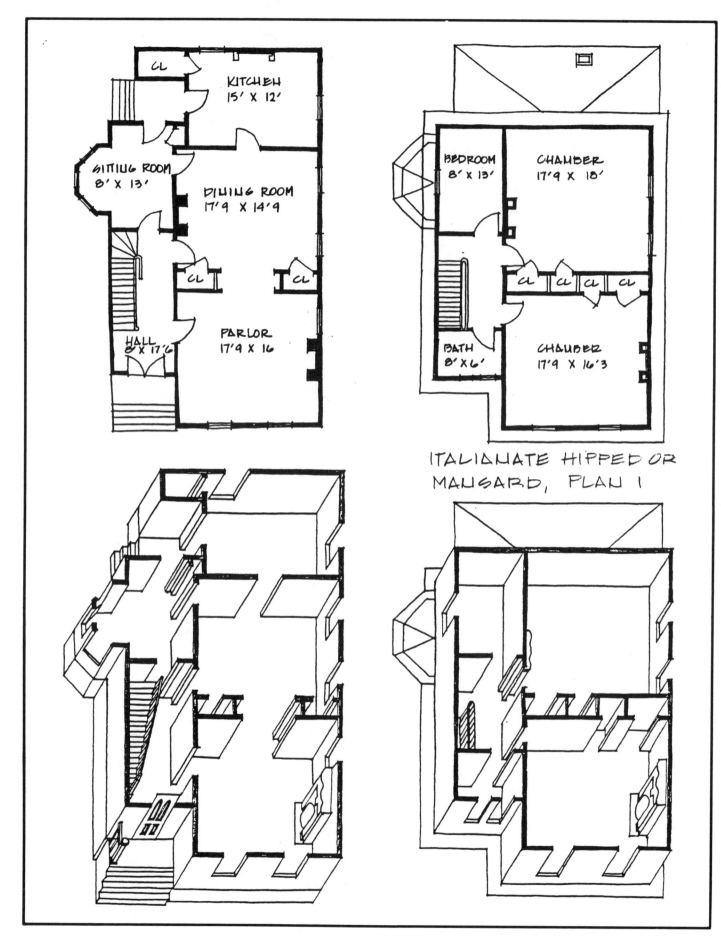

KITCHEN
15' X 12'

CL

SITTING ROOM
8' X 13'

DINING ROOM
17'9 X 14'9

CL

CL

HALL
8' X 17'6

PARLOR
17'9 X 16

BEDROOM
8' X 13'

CHAMBER
17'9 X 18'

CL CL CL CL

BATH
8' X 6'

CHAMBER
17'9 X 16'3

ITALIANATE HIPPED OR
MANSARD, PLAN 1

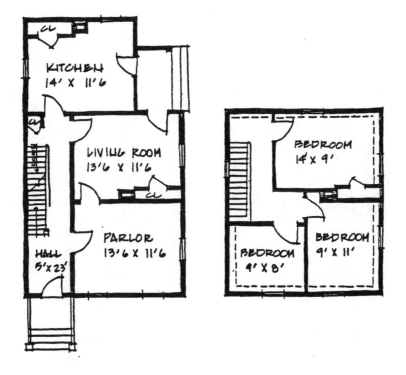

ITALIANATE HIPPED OR MANSARD
PLAN 1

GAMBREL COTTAGES

Gambrel cottages have always been associated with colonial design. Their source was, of course, the stone and clapboard houses of New York and New Jersey built by Dutch settlers. In the vernacular mode the house was referred to as "Dutch colonial." It had two forms based on its position vis-à-vis the street. In one form the roof—which had several distinct forms—was perpendicular to the street; in the other it was parallel.

2 STORIES, TYPICAL
FACADE

1½ STORIES, TYPICAL
FACADE

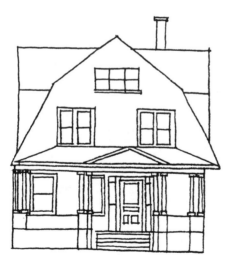

2½ STORIES, TYPICAL
FACADE

In the perpendicular mode the roof ran straight back or was intersected at a right angle by another gambrel. Other exterior characteristics included a projecting porch that spanned the house or a cutaway porch that created the equivalent of an outdoor room, that is, its dimensions were similar to those of the interior room next to it. The façade was organized into two or three bays.

The gambrel cottage with the roof parallel to the street had three or five bays and the same interior plan as the gable roof colonial cottage, including the division of space into the same social and functional spaces. The perpendicular model, which tended to have less square footage and less cubic footage, had a side hall plan. As in most colonial designs, fireplaces were prominent.

The major exterior variables for this type were the size and shape of the second-floor dormer, the manner in which the roof was brought down on the walls, and the different angles made by the roof planes. Conceptually, the gambrel cottage was thought of as having "sturdy, graceful lines," with "a good appearing yet economical roof, and . . . ample space for rooms in the upper story." As put by one writer of the period, "there is no style of architecture more suited to a suburban home."

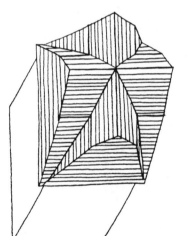

GAMBREL
_____

2 OR 2½ STORIES
DEEPER THAN WIDE
INTERSECTING GAMBRELS
    OR GAMBREL FACING STREET

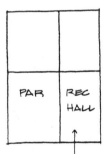

PAR | REC HALL

CHARACTERISTICS
_____

4 ROOMS DOWN
2 ROOMS DEEP
SIDE OR OFF-CENTER ENTRANCE
    INTO RECEPTION HALL
STAIR LOCATED IN RECEPTION
    HALL
STAIR PLANS VARY

PANTRY

KITCHEN
12' X 9'

DINING ROOM
12' X 13'6

DOWN

HALL
9' X 10'6

LIVING ROOM
15' X 14'

PORCH

BEDROOM
13' X 8'

CL

BEDROOM
11' X 14'

BATH
8' X 6'

DOWN

CL CL

CL

BEDROOM
11' X 13'

BEDROOM
13' X 16'

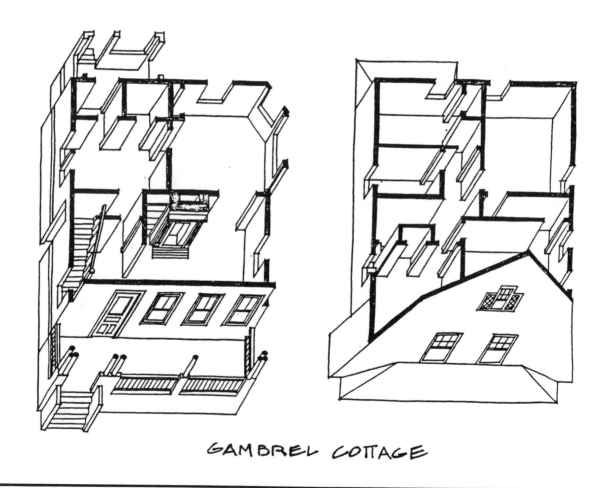

GAMBREL COTTAGE

WESTCHESTER COUNTY, NEW YORK

BUILDING AGE _ 1917

COLONIAL GAMBREL

  1½ OR 2 STORIES
  WIDER THAN DEEP
  GAMBREL WITH · RIDGELINE
    FACING THE STREET
    SHED DORMER COMMON

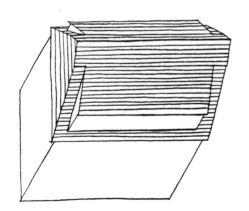

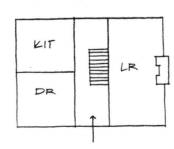

CHARACTERISTICS
  2 ROOMS DEEP
  2 ROOMS WIDE PLUS
    CENTRAL HALL
  CENTER ENTRANCE
  STAIR LOCATED IN HALL
  STAIR PLANS AND
    HALL PLACEMENT VARY
  FIREPLACE ON OUTSIDE
    LIVING ROOM WALL
  SUNPORCH COMMON

KIT

DR

LR

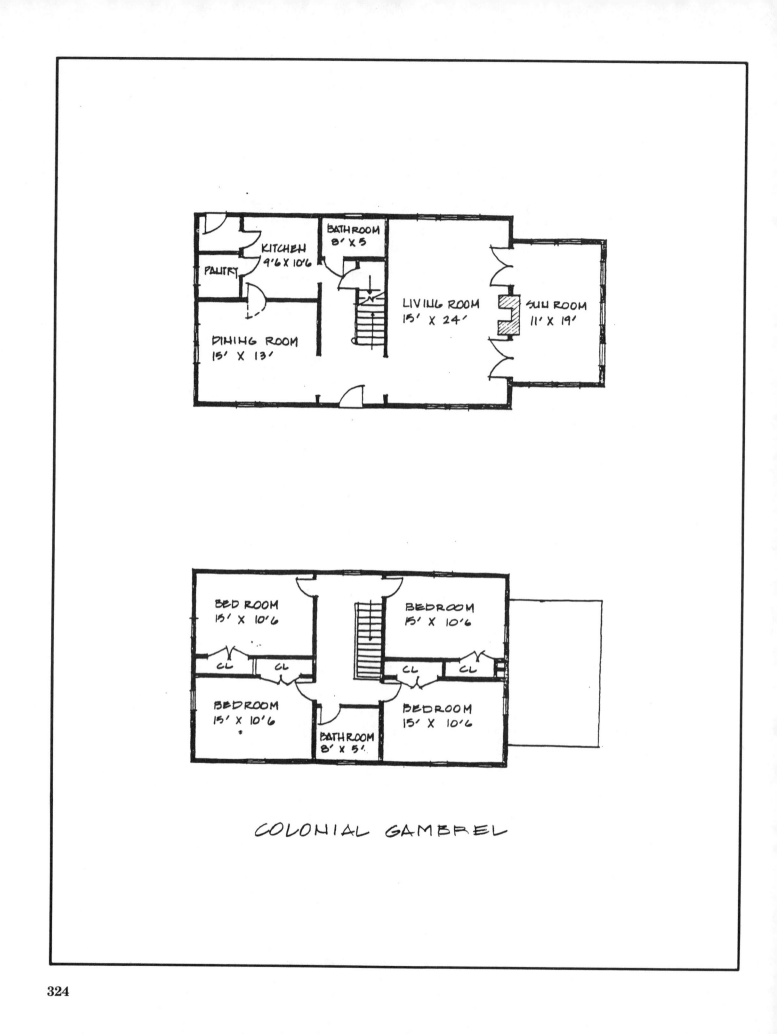

COLONIAL GAMBREL

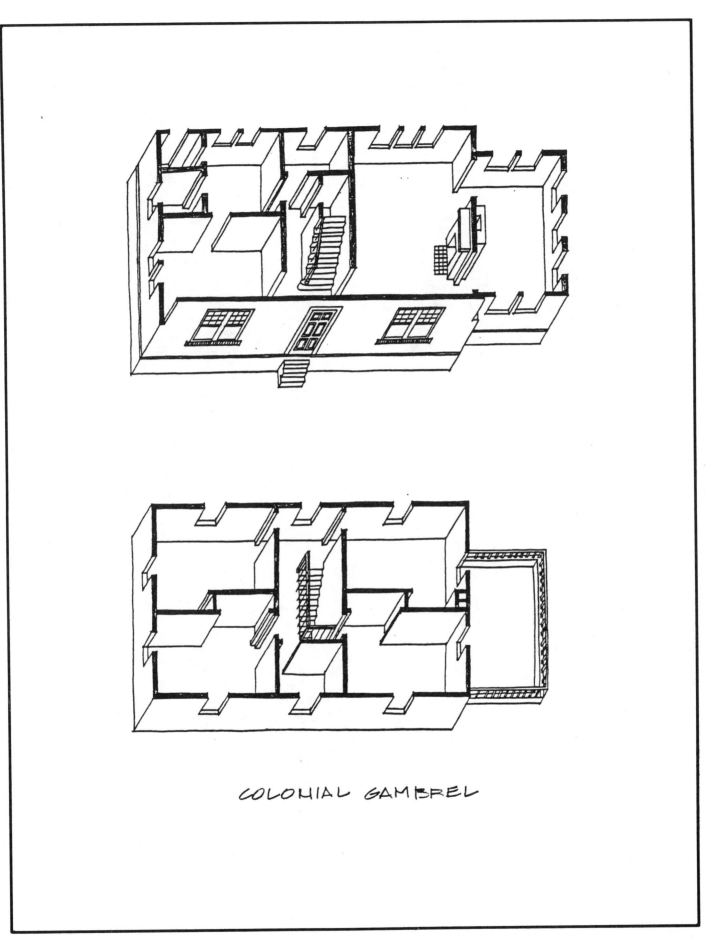

COLONIAL GAMBREL

ORGANIC COTTAGES

This category of house types is broad, because it concerns a number of houses with apparently differing stylistic interests. We have sorted houses that others identify as representative of styles—Shingle, Queen Anne, the

PLAN 5, CARPENTRY AND BUILDING, BY W. HOWARD WALKER, PROVIDENCE, RHODE ISLAND—1882

PLAN 1, CARPENTRY AND BUILDING, BY FRANK M. SNYDER, CHICAGO—1889

PLAN 2, CARPENTRY AND BUILDING, DESIGN SUBMISSION BY T.F. SCHNEIDER—1883

PLAN 1, CARPENTRY AND BUILDING, FIRST PRIZE DESIGN, BY JOHN P. KINGSTON, WORCESTER, MASSACHUSETTS—1903

so-called Stick style—under one rubric, consisting of two responses to cottage plans, with three versions of each solution. The attribution of an organic quality to these houses stems from the belief that the intention of their builders and designers was to satisfy the demand for a modern house by assembling an open-plan arrangement of rooms and passages within the confines of an accretive massing of volumes. By "accretive" we mean that there is in the organic cottage a reference to the kind of joining of seemingly disparate and historic sections of a house, as in many of the original colonial houses of New England. The combination of open circulation and an admixture

PLAN 1, JAMES G. HORN-
BECK HOUSE, PORT JERVIS,
NEW YORK — 1907

PLAN 2 FROM CEMENT
HOUSES AND PRIVATE
GARAGES — 1912

PLAN 1, CHATTANOOGA,
TENNESSEE — 1889

PLAN 1, BOSTON — 1889

of hipped and gabled roofs, with spaces emanating from the center, created a truly American house that could be distinguished from imported or otherwise Victorian models.

The new house was traditional: it was easily recognized as a member of the cottage order, and it utilized traditional materials for cladding and ornamentation. It was also modern, accommodating cisterns, bathrooms, kitchens, pantries, central heating, and gas and electric lighting. But its modernity was more subtle than that. The internal coherence of this class of houses did not come from the usual arrangement of rooms stacked across a building site. The internal coherence of the organic cottage was spatial, revealing continuities of space rather than alignments of partitions. The spatial basis for this type was expressed also in the number of projections from the core of each plan type.

We have identified five different schematic concepts for this general house type, and all of them stem not from a fixed physical element, like a fireplace or a stair, but from a space. The spatial center is part of the volumetric continuity that extends to other rooms, hallways, and in some instances to the outside.

Looking at schematic plans, the thrust of the core space can be read on the perimeter. Despite a few commonalities—a multisided projection off the front, a rectangular one off the back, and a straight or nearly straight side wall—the plan is unpredictable, and the shape, placement, and size of the porches reinforces the plan. The implication is that this expansive form could be continued.

As for the lumping of so many stylistic interests in a broad category, we think of these houses as part of a number of progressive and thoughtful solutions to the problem of building a truly modern house. While a number

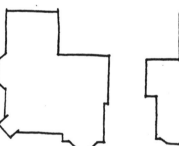
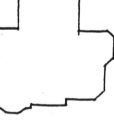
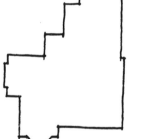
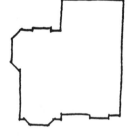

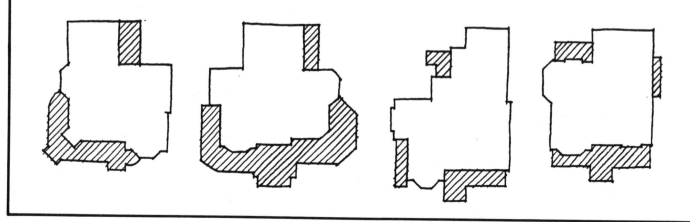

of house types have addressed the issue of incorporating modernity under their traditional skins or within their historical expectations—for instance, the way the colonial house adjusted so successfully to being modern in the 1920s—the organic cottage is fresh and original. It is an American product and a cultural resource that expresses its origins not through historical allusions but through space and form.

The exterior form of an organic cottage reflects the freedom with which it was assembled. Here organic spaces are accounted for within massing elements; geometric volumes cluster about the core, resulting in elevations different from each other but still interactive because of spatial interconnectedness.

An examination of the overall shapes of these houses, and of the relationship of parts to the whole, suggests that interruption is a value of higher order than the continuity of principal lines or materials. For example, there is the way a large element like a turret captures a corner, breaking the plane of two walls, or the way the cladding of one level abuts the cladding of another. Other characteristics include flaring walls; imaginative fenestration patterns combined with multiple roofs, with gables in different patterns; masses and voids in dynamic interplay. All this multivalent articulation does not exist unconnected. There are continuities that hold the elements within their bounds: string and belt courses, continuous sills and lintels, continuities of materials around elevations and between floors, repeated motifs.

In a larger sense, the interpenetration of lines and volumes suggests the spatial continuity that makes this house type unique. This is especially noticeable in the continuous circulation that is fundamental to these types. Access to all or almost all the ground floor rooms is possible from the entrance. We have illustrated some of these pathways around the core space.

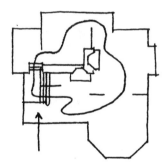

These patterns are really another layer of organic order overlaid in turn by the shapes of the principal rooms, which are in turn overlaid by the general shape of the house and porches, which are again overlaid by aspects of the site including its planting design. This imprinting of the organic cottage on its neighborhood or rural lot can be ascertained from schematic drawings of the plans.

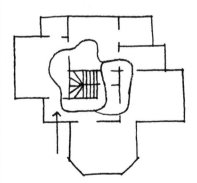

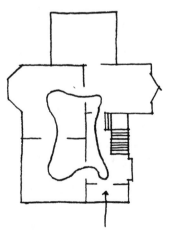

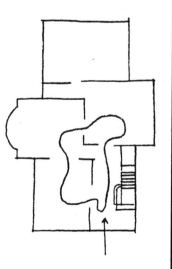

As for specific spatial configurations, we have identified five individual types of response to cottage planning: three side hall types and two center hall types. Taken together, these kinds of plans and their accompanying external forms were built from 1880 to 1910. In sorting cottages by plan typology, we find that almost every one of the plan types has a full complement of exterior style types. That is, there are Shingle, Queen Anne, and other-flavored treatments (what the builders call exterior finish) included in the plan types. The only exception is the organic cottage. Finally, because these cottages were introduced into older aesthetic and spatial systems, their first floor arrangements include parlors, sitting rooms, dining rooms, kitchens, and halls. Some of the halls are passageways and others are as large as a room and, indeed, function as one.

Side hall plans have been divided into three categories. The typical plan for side hall #1 begins with a projecting parlor, adjacent to or circumscribed by a porch, followed by a room-size reception hall and two adjoining rooms. These latter rooms are the physical center of the house, and they are both social spaces—a sitting room and a dining room. The sequence is completed by the kitchen and back porch. The back walls of the two central rooms are often in the same plane. In smaller houses of this type, the sitting room will be dropped from the plan, and the house will terminate with a pantry and a porch behind the kitchen.

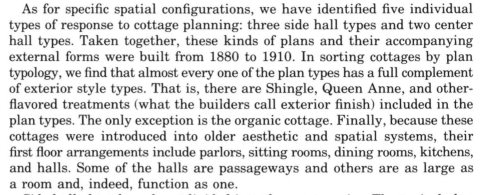

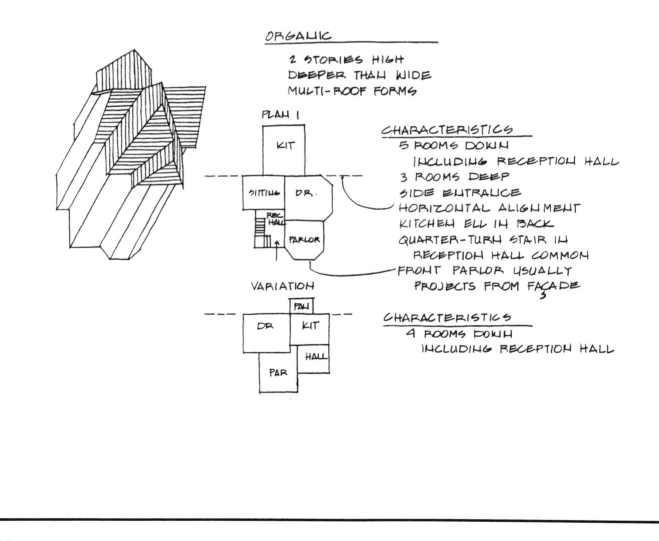

ORGANIC

2 STORIES HIGH
DEEPER THAN WIDE
MULTI-ROOF FORMS

PLAN 1

CHARACTERISTICS
5 ROOMS DOWN
INCLUDING RECEPTION HALL
3 ROOMS DEEP
SIDE ENTRANCE
HORIZONTAL ALIGNMENT
KITCHEN ELL IN BACK
QUARTER-TURN STAIR IN
RECEPTION HALL COMMON
FRONT PARLOR USUALLY
PROJECTS FROM FAÇADE

VARIATION

CHARACTERISTICS
4 ROOMS DOWN
INCLUDING RECEPTION HALL

KIT

SITTING | DR.

REC HALL

PARLOR

PAN

DR | KIT

HALL

PAR

330

Side hall plan # 2 has the following aspects. The parlor space has been pulled back toward the core of the house, and the hall, whose stair is a straight flight instead of a quarter-turn as in the first version, is narrower but longer. The center rooms—the sitting and dining rooms—have no lateral alignment, and the kitchen-pantry space is wider than the previous kitchen; in fact, their combined width is the same as that of the parlor and hall. The outside walls of the parlor and hall are continuous, and the sitting room usually has a bay window. In a smaller version of this type, the sitting room is left out of the plan and the parlor may include a bay window or a turret, with the overall dimensions of the plan being almost cubical.

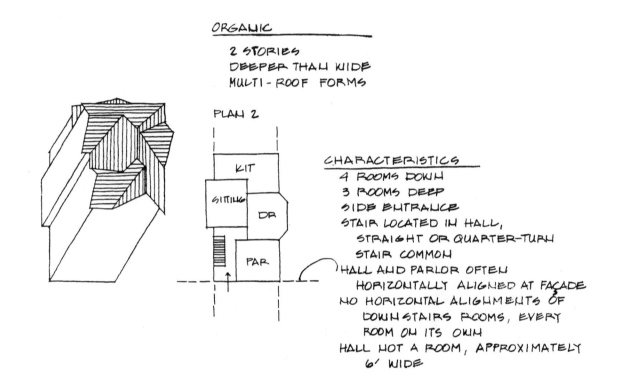

ORGANIC

2 STORIES
DEEPER THAN WIDE
MULTI-ROOF FORMS

PLAN 2

KIT
SITTING
DR
PAR

CHARACTERISTICS
4 ROOMS DOWN
3 ROOMS DEEP
SIDE ENTRANCE
STAIR LOCATED IN HALL,
    STRAIGHT OR QUARTER-TURN
    STAIR COMMON
HALL AND PARLOR OFTEN
    HORIZONTALLY ALIGNED AT FAÇADE
NO HORIZONTAL ALIGNMENTS OF
    DOWNSTAIRS ROOMS, EVERY
    ROOM ON ITS OWN
HALL NOT A ROOM, APPROXIMATELY
    6' WIDE

The third version of the side hall plan has a side entrance through a reception hall, a side stair located behind the hall and placed at a right angle to the flow of the house, and three social rooms on the first floor. The parlor once again projects off the core and the center rooms are aligned sequentially from front to back, with either a common partition or an exterior wall.

In the smaller house with this plan, the usual loss of one social room results in an increase in continuous walls, as the loss of volume makes larger interactions of massing elements less likely.

The center hall plan for the organic cottage enlarges the house to a square and cubic footage unmatched by any other type. The size of the hall, about 6 to 8 feet wide and three or four times that in length, expands the core, and the hall can become a full room. The hall space extends through about three-quarters of the house. As in many center hall plans, there is a suggestion of symmetry in the organization in that each half of the first floor has two rooms. However, each side of the house has been alternately pulled forward or pushed back along the axis of the hall. The usual configuration of three social spaces and functional space on the first floor is maintained.

The second floor of all two-story organic cottages repeats the general pattern of the first floor.

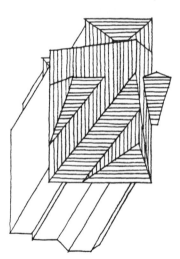

ORGANIC

2 STORIES
DEEPER THAN WIDE
MULTI-ROOF FORMS

PLAN 3

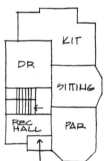

CHARACTERISTICS
  5 ROOMS DOWN
  SIDE ENTRANCE
  RECEPTION HALL ONE OF 5
    ROOMS DOWN
  STAIR LOCATED BEHIND
    RECEPTION HALL
  STAIR ENTRY FROM SIDE

In a house with less square footage, the hall area is significantly reduced, and although the hall may not have the physical presence it has in larger houses, the hall function is implied by the arrangement of the entrance on axis and by the various access routes through the interior. The hall function has been built into the plan where the hall itself could not be accommodated.

The alternative center hall plan has circulation patterns that intersect. We think of this plan as having a center hall with cross-axes. In order to establish this grouping, internal alignments are necessary, resulting in continuous walls inside and outside. Despite this accommodation, which also reflects smaller-sized plans, this cottage has multiple projections, including balconies and porches, and its spatial core is larger than that of some other plans. It creates, therefore, an organic imprint on its site.

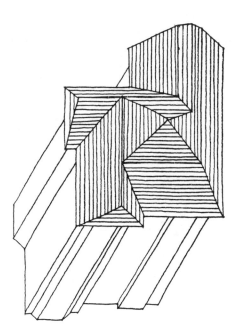

ORGANIC

2 OR 2½ STORIES
MULTI- ROOF FORMS
MOST ORGANIC FORMS

PLAN 4

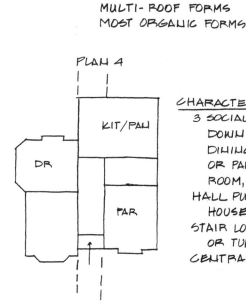

CHARACTERISTICS
3 SOCIAL SPACES
  DOWN — PARLOR,
  DINING ROOM, LIBRARY
  OR PARLOR, DINING
  ROOM, SITTING ROOM
HALL PUNCHES THROUGH
  HOUSE, CENTRAL AXIS
STAIR LOCATED IN HALL
  OR TURNED TO SIDE
CENTRAL ENTRANCE

As for the axes, many of these plans have several, and some identify hallways as "passage" spaces. It is also clear that a number of plans in this format include the staircase in the center hall, binding the spatial and physical core together. From our first sample of organic cottages, the diffusion of cross-axis floor plans does not seem as widespread as the other side hall and center hall plans. But, like the others, it too was built within several stylistic shells, in one- and two-story models. Very few of this type were built after 1900.

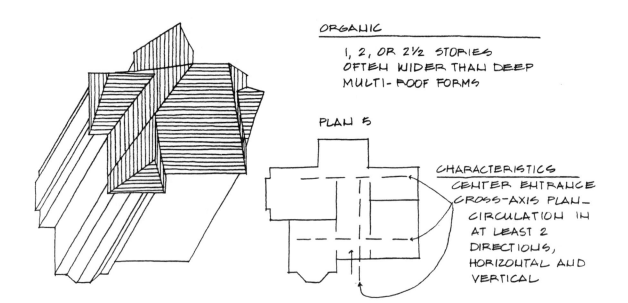

ORGANIC

1, 2, OR 2½ STORIES
OFTEN WIDER THAN DEEP
MULTI-ROOF FORMS

PLAN 5

CHARACTERISTICS
CENTER ENTRANCE
CROSS-AXIS PLAN—
CIRCULATION IN
AT LEAST 2
DIRECTIONS,
HORIZONTAL AND
VERTICAL

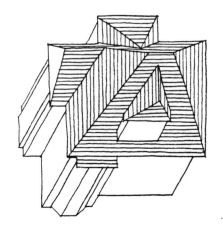

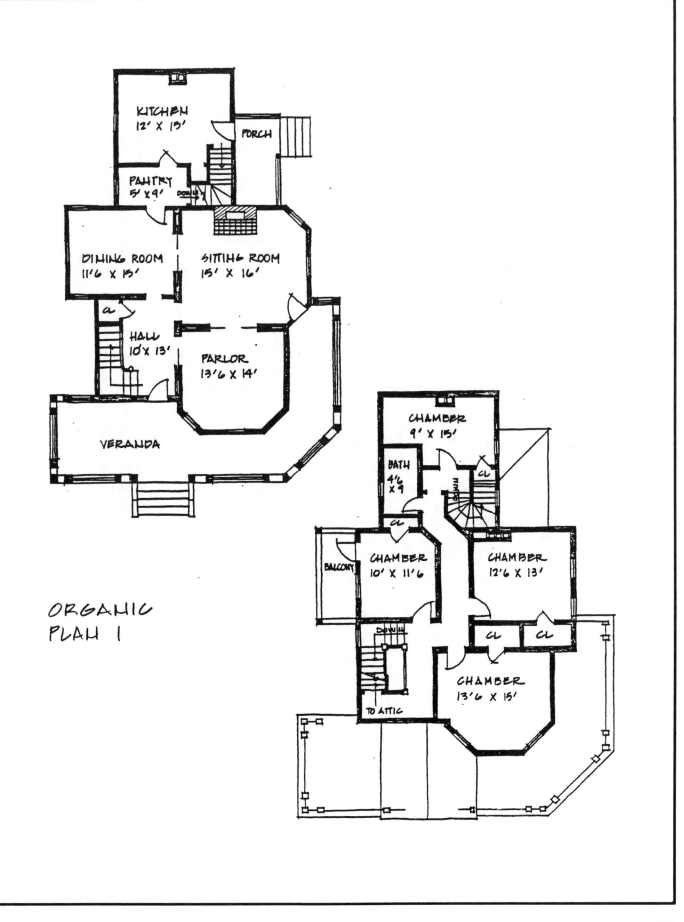

KITCHEN
12' X 15'

PORCH

PANTRY
5' X 9'

DOWN

DINING ROOM
11'6 X 15'

SITTING ROOM
15' X 16'

CL

HALL
10' X 13'

PARLOR
13'6 X 14'

VERANDA

CHAMBER
9' X 15'

BATH
4'6
X 9

CL

CL

BALCONY

CHAMBER
10' X 11'6

CHAMBER
12'6 X 13'

CL

CL

DOWN

TO ATTIC

CHAMBER
13'6 X 15'

ORGANIC
PLAN 1

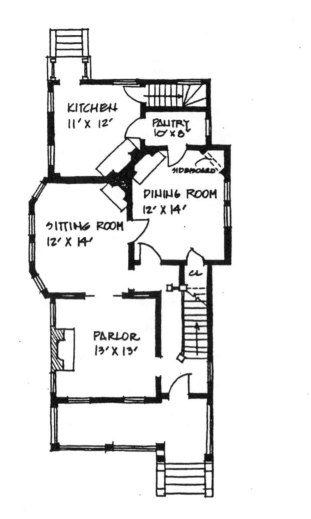

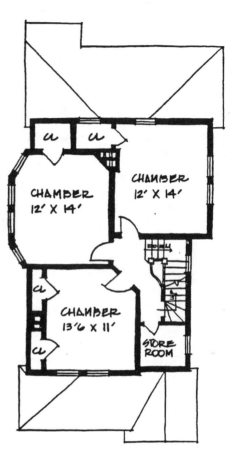

ORGANIC PLAN 2

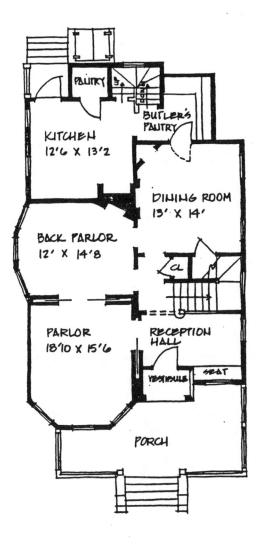

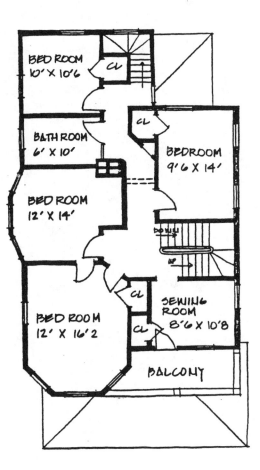

PANTRY

BUTLER'S
PANTRY

KITCHEN
12'6 X 13'2

DINING ROOM
13' X 14'

BACK PARLOR
12' X 14'8

CL

PARLOR
18'10 X 15'6

RECEPTION
HALL

VESTIBULE

SEAT

PORCH

BED ROOM
10' X 10'6

CL

CL

BATH ROOM
6' X 10'

BEDROOM
9'6 X 14'

BED ROOM
12' X 14'

DOWN

UP

BED ROOM
12' X 16'2

CL

CL

SEWING
ROOM
8'6 X 10'8

BALCONY

ORGANIC   PLAN 3

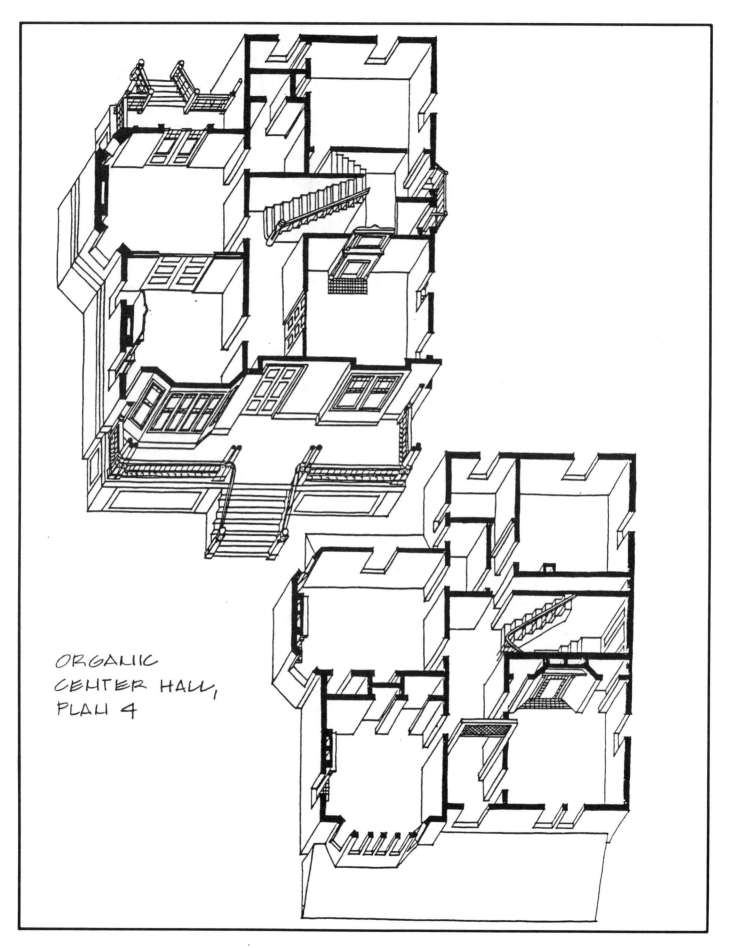

ORGANIC
CENTER HALL,
PLAN 4

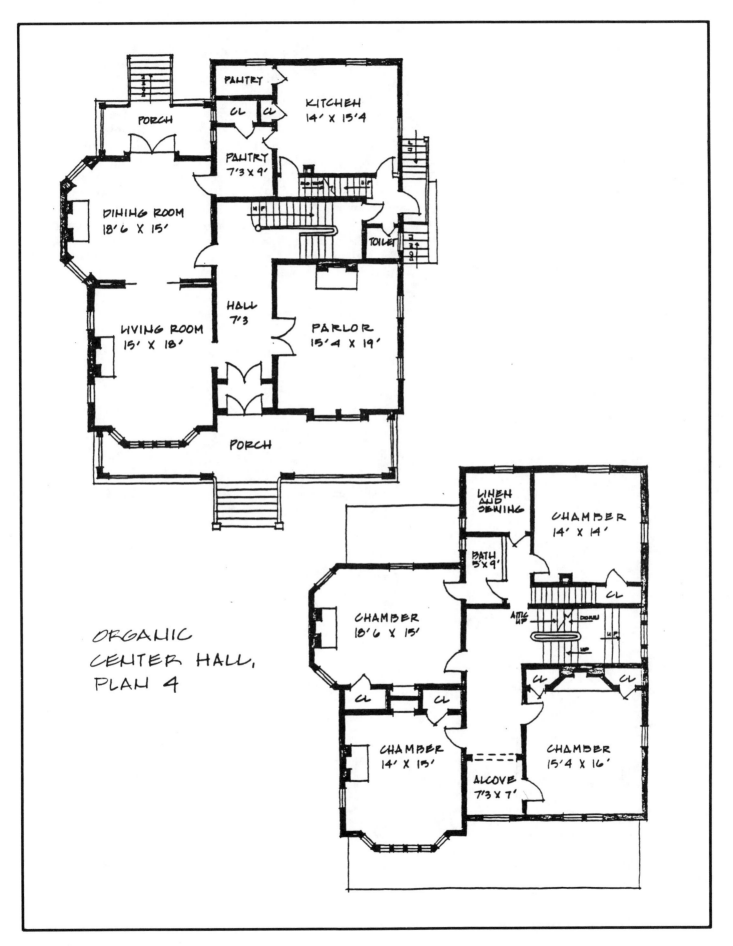

PANTRY

KITCHEN
14' X 15'4

CL CL

PORCH

PANTRY
7'3 X 9'

DINING ROOM
18'6 X 15'

TOILET

HALL
7'3

LIVING ROOM
15' X 18'

PARLOR
15'4 X 19'

PORCH

ORGANIC
CENTER HALL,
PLAN 4

LINEN
AND
SEWING

CHAMBER
14' X 14'

BATH
5' X 9'

CHAMBER
18'6 X 15'

CL

ATTIC
UP   DOWN

UP

UP

CL

CL   CL

CL   CL

CHAMBER
14' X 15'

CHAMBER
15'4 X 16'

ALCOVE
7'3 X 7'

One-story Organic Cottage

The one-story version of the cross-axis plan seems to be a regional house type. We have traced its appearance from California (as a so-called *California cottage*) across the Southwest to the Southeast, with a smattering of examples in the Midwest. In overall shape this cottage is a single story or a story and a half, with five or six rooms on the ground level and a center hall extending nearly the length of the house; this plan, when combined with the room shapes, creates a pronounced elongated form. Multiple roofs (typically a tall center hip with gables clustered around it) and curvilinear elements complete the exterior. Turrets, curved porches, and bay windows are examples of the latter.

This house was popular during the period 1890–1910. It was a logical solution to the compact three-room by two-room scheme, in which the logic is not easily read on the exterior. The rambling nature of this house also conceals the center hall, which, like almost everything else, disappears under the pyramidal roof that shelters the core.

PLAN 5, RALEIGH, NORTH
CAROLINA — CIRCA 1907

JOHN A. GUTHRIE HOUSE,
CANYON, TEXAS — BEFORE 1910

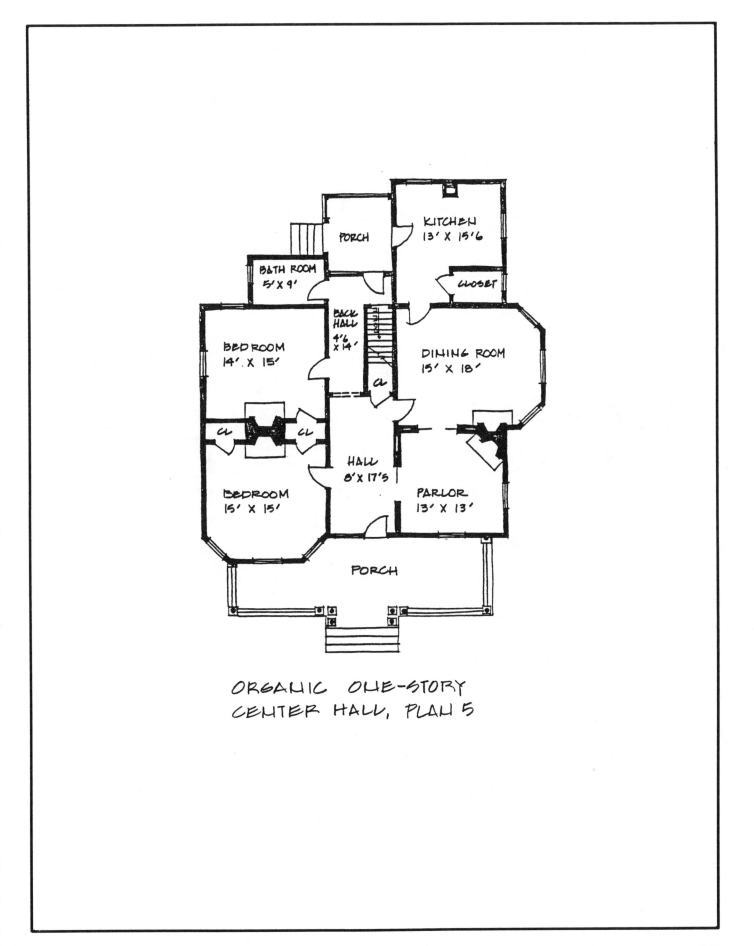

PORCH

KITCHEN
13' X 15'6

BATH ROOM
5' X 9'

CLOSET

BACK
HALL
4'6
X 14'

BEDROOM
14' X 15'

DINING ROOM
15' X 18'

CL

CL

CL

HALL
8' X 17'5

BEDROOM
15' X 15'

PARLOR
13' X 13'

PORCH

ORGANIC ONE-STORY
CENTER HALL, PLAN 5

BUNGALOWS The *bungalow* is one of the most successful vernacular houses ever built. It has been adapted for all regions and climates. It was built in clusters, in rows, and as single houses, finished in several aesthetics, and scaled up and down both as to size and cost. To the best of our knowledge the vernacular bungalow, which became known as a *California bungalow,* made its first appearance in the trade literature in 1904. A short article in the July 1904 issue of *Carpentry and Building* described the bungalow as "a low house, generally with a spacious interior . . . set snug and close to the ground, with overhanging eaves, and great surfaces of roof. They are only one story high, or at most one story and an attic, and are stained dark . . . porches are designed to be well-shaded. Rough stones are used for the chimneys and visible foundations."

TYPICAL FAÇADE

OKLAHOMA CITY

SEARS, ROEBUCK AND CO., "THE LORNE"—1921

JAMESTOWN, NEW YORK 1911

One of the first bungalow stock plan books was edited by Fred T. Hodgson, who as an editor and as a consultant to Sears, Roebuck and Co. figured prominently in the development of industrial vernacular architecture. In the preface of *Practical Bungalows and Cottages for Town and Country* (1906), Hodgson explained that bungalows "are the result of a popular tradition . . . a genuine expression of popular and wholesome habits of country living and . . . country building." Hodgson's comment is interesting in that he needed to justify a new form in terms of regional folk architecture, and he suggested that there was some moral imperative behind its presence. Perhaps this point of view was left over from the romantic revivals of the previous century. Whether Hodgson thought of it at this time or not, the bungalow would not turn out to be a country dwelling. It would be a subdivision house, reproduced by the hundreds in cities across the country. The bungalow would also be progressive and modern and consciously artistic in a manner unlike country houses and country living.

One year later, in 1907, a short unsigned article in the February issue of *Carpentry and Building* extolled the "breadth, strength, and simple beauty of the plainness" in the California bungalow, noting "there is a pleasing absence of 'millwork' and other ornamentation." The reference to millwork can be read as a reaction to picturesque cottage design, which the bungalow and the hip-roofed cottage would address. Moreover, the shift away from historic cottage designs was concerned not only with simplified exteriors but also with a new feeling for interior space and organization.

These early descriptions were remarkably accurate in terms of the purposes and aesthetics of this house type. The bungalow was to have a relaxed, informal, locally derived quality about it, which could not, however, be exported immediately to all regions of the country. The early versions of the bungalow relied on rustic effects derived from California living, and not all rusticity is the same. As the bungalow became more fully absorbed into the industrial production system, it lost some of its original qualities but it gained a stronger position among house types. This prominence was due, in part, to a significant expansion of the design language associated with the type, as we will discuss below.

Historically, the bungalow emerged during the first decade of this century, but it did not gain popularity until the second decade. From then through the 1930s, the number of bungalows built throughout the county increased dramatically. Basic, everyday bungalows were initially of two types, one with a gabled roof and the other with a hip roof. A number of plans were developed for each of these forms.

Gabled Bungalow The typical *gable-front bungalow* was a one-story, two-bedroom house. It had a front porch, a fireplace, and six rooms organized into parallel rows of rooms, with a living room, dining room, and kitchen on one side, and two bedrooms and a bath, connected by a short hall, on the opposite side. Adjoining rooms were connected by cased openings. The entry often was accommodated by a small vestibule or reception space that was actually part of the living room. The connection of the two front rooms created a passageway to the kitchen and the back rooms. The dining room often displayed a bay window, and many bungalows had a back porch that was a simple stoop or a cutaway porch tucked under the roof.

There is enough evidence to suggest that a simple variation on this plan added a third bedroom in line with the other bedrooms, which tended to extend the entire house.

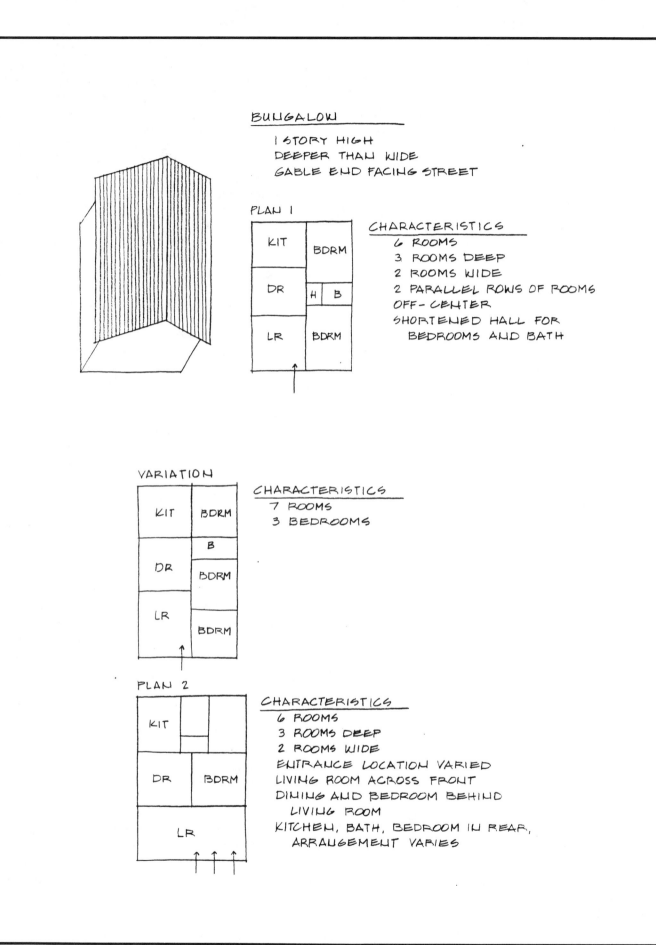

BUNGALOW

I STORY HIGH
DEEPER THAN WIDE
GABLE END FACING STREET

PLAN 1

KIT	BDRM
DR	H	B
LR	BDRM

CHARACTERISTICS

6 ROOMS
3 ROOMS DEEP
2 ROOMS WIDE
2 PARALLEL ROWS OF ROOMS
OFF-CENTER
SHORTENED HALL FOR
    BEDROOMS AND BATH

VARIATION

KIT	BDRM
DR	B
	BDRM
LR	BDRM

CHARACTERISTICS

7 ROOMS
3 BEDROOMS

PLAN 2

KIT	
DR	BDRM
LR	

CHARACTERISTICS

6 ROOMS
3 ROOMS DEEP
2 ROOMS WIDE
ENTRANCE LOCATION VARIED
LIVING ROOM ACROSS FRONT
DINING AND BEDROOM BEHIND
    LIVING ROOM
KITCHEN, BATH, BEDROOM IN REAR,
    ARRANGEMENT VARIES

The first alternative plan for the gabled bungalow placed the living room across the front of the house, making the entire living room a reception space. Half the living room was open to the dining room and the other was partitioned. The opening was cased or colonnaded. Having the entrance open directly into the living room called for some adjustments to restrict or delay visual or physical access to the inside. Bungalow builders used several devices: locating the entrance so that it opened in front of the living room back wall; setting the entryway on one side and dividing off a bit of the room for reception purposes; projecting a small vestibule onto the porch; and placing the entry in line with the dining room. In this last pattern, the sideboard built into the back wall of the dining room acted as the visual and physical terminus of the entry.

The placement of the living room across the whole width of the house aligned the interior partitions, so that from front to back rooms were bounded by successive planes of wall. The back wall of the dining room and that of the front bedroom were in the same plane, and the second bedroom, bath, and kitchen completed the back row and shared a continuous wall.

Specific interior elements included a fireplace as an end-wall unit—integrated storage, fireplace, and windows—located most often on the same side of the house as the dining room. Colonnades in bungalows usually included storage units too. A bay window could be included, as it was in the first plan, and its shape might be rectangular with multiple lights. Occasionally, the battered piers and columns of the front porch were repeated on a side porch, which was sheltered by a second gable. That motif, intersecting gables, was characteristic of all gabled bungalows.

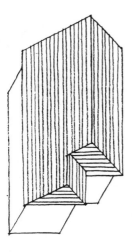

BUNGALOW

I STORY HIGH
DEEPER THAN WIDE
GABLE ENDS FACING STREET

PLAN 3

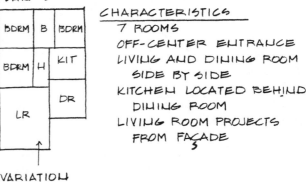

CHARACTERISTICS
7 ROOMS
OFF-CENTER ENTRANCE
LIVING AND DINING ROOM
SIDE BY SIDE
KITCHEN LOCATED BEHIND
DINING ROOM
LIVING ROOM PROJECTS
FROM FAÇADE

VARIATION

CHARACTERISTICS
LIVING AND DINING ROOM
HORIZONTALLY ALIGNED
ON FAÇADE
ENTRANCE LOCATION VARIES

ROOF TYPE VARIES

The third version of the gabled bungalow plan was a combination of the first two types, in that rooms were sequentially aligned behind each other, as in the first plan, but a center hall was introduced linking the living room with the back rooms. Both sides of this plan terminated in the same wall plane, but they started at different points. The living room projected, with the front portion serving as an entrance, and the dining room occupied a recessed position. The kitchen lay just behind the dining room, and the bedrooms were placed behind the living room and the kitchen, with the bath placed between the bedrooms and accessible from the hall.

There was also in this planning system an alternative of less consequence, in which the living room and dining room were placed beside each other, but the rooms were turned so that the overall shape of the house was wider than it was deep. The back walls of both rooms aligned, and a hallway, running parallel to the front rooms, linked the bedrooms, bath, and kitchen. The arrangement of the front rooms created the impression of a single room. The traditional arch and bookcase spanning the opening between the living room and dining room remained part of this plan, as did the built-in buffet and china closets. Some buffet closet pieces were projected off the dining room wall, in the manner of a bay window. The corner left open by the placement of the living room and dining room was filled with a porch or terrace which became part of the entrance system.

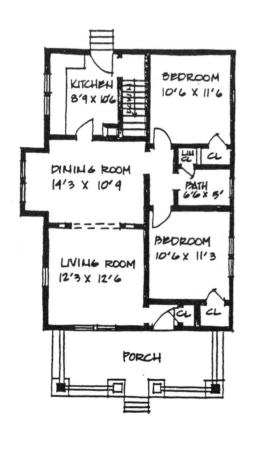

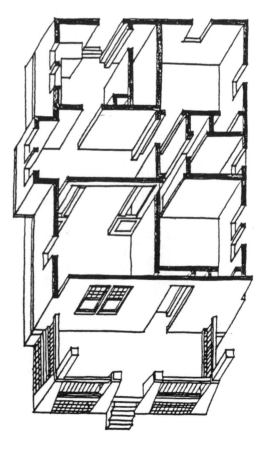

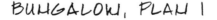

BUNGALOW, PLAN 1

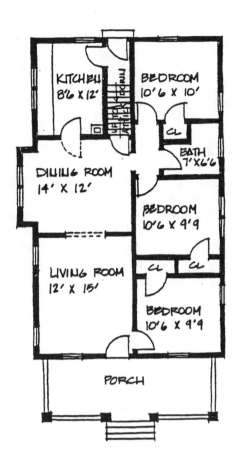

BUNGALOW, PLAN 1
VARIATION

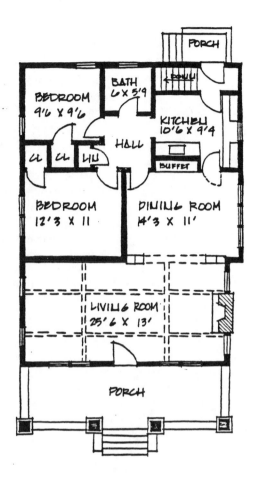

BUNGALOW, PLAN 2

Hipped Bungalow The *hip-roofed bungalow* dates from the same period as the gable-fronted bungalow. The exterior form of this type was dominated by the large hip roof, which was generally pyramidal and could be pierced by dormers that lit one or two rooms in the attic. The interior organization was of two types: a plan of sequentially ordered rooms, as in the first gable plan, with the living room, dining room, and kitchen on one side, and the two bedrooms and bath on the other; and a center hall plan with one half composed of the usual living, dining, and kitchen spaces front to back, and with the bedrooms on the opposite side and the bath sandwiched between the kitchen and the corner bedroom.

The composition of the hip-roofed bungalow had an air of formality not present in the rustic gabled types. Formality was reinforced by the porch and entrance designs. Most porches were covered by the principal hip roof, which integrated the façade and the porch, usually in a rhythmical pattern—four equally spaced columns. This front was orderly; even if the porch had been added on and supported its own roof, the effect was classical. There was also a feeling for centrality tied to the placement of the single dormer on the center line of the porch, which was sometimes reinforced by the placement of the entrance door on the same axis.

DESIGN BY FREDERICK
H. GOWING, BOSTON — 1922

TYPICAL FAÇADE

HIPPED BUNGALOW

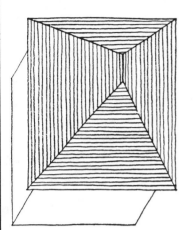

1 STORY, ATTIC COMMON
SLIGHTLY DEEPER THAN WIDE
HIPPED ROOF

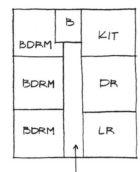

CHARACTERISTICS
7 ROOMS
3 ROOMS DEEP
CENTRAL ENTRANCE
CENTER HALL

BUNGALOW PLAN 1 IS MOST COMMON FOR
HIPPED BUNGALOW TYPE BUT THIS
CENTER HALL PLAN WAS A FREQUENT
VARIATION.

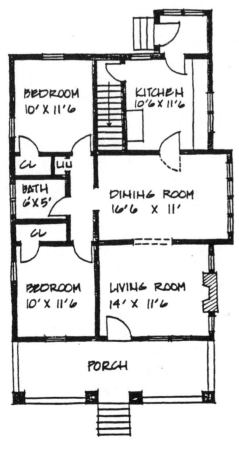

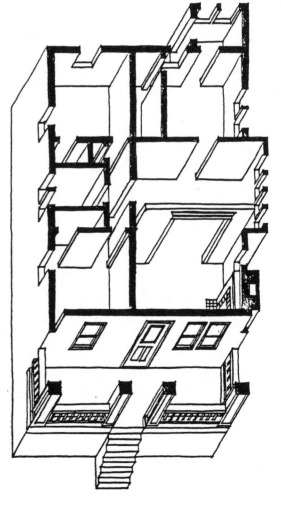

HIPPED BUNGALOW

Bungalow Cottage   There was an attempt to bridge the gap between the bungalow and the nineteenth-century cottage, and we call this hybrid a *bungalow cottage*. This cottage retained some of the characteristics of its predecessors, such as its overall shape and fenestration, but these were combined with the informality of the bungalow and its spatiality. The bungalow cottage was a story-and-a-half structure, with a broad gable roof parallel to the street and a large dormer facing in the same direction. The upper story was arranged with the rooms in the corners—two or three bedrooms and a bath—and a hall in the center at the head of the stairs.

TYPICAL FAÇADE

CURTIS, "ELLSWORTH," NO. 132 —
1923

The bungalow cottage was not built in earnest until the 1910s, and by 1930 its popularity was waning. Its plan types were of two varieties. The first type balanced the rooms in a left–right format: a large living room on the right responded to a dining room on the left, then a den or parlor on the right was answered by the kitchen on the left. The stairs for the second level were located behind the front rooms.

The second plan type extended the living space across the width of the house, having the entry open directly into the living room with the stairway off to the side. The living room divided the house approximately in half, and the dining room and kitchen subdivided the back portion.

As in all bungalow houses, fireplaces and built-in furniture were optional elements, and these were installed with regularity in bungalow cottages. Only the breakfast nook, for some unknown reason, did not seem to be a part of this development.

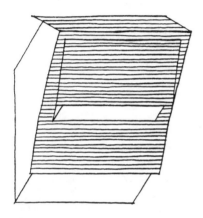

BUNGALOW COTTAGE

PLAN 1

	KIT
LR	DR
	PORCH

CHARACTERISTICS
- 4 ROOMS DOWN
- 2 ROOMS PLUS FRONT PORCH DEEP
- OFF-CENTER ENTRANCE
- STAIR OFTEN LOCATED BEHIND FRONT ROOMS
- 4TH ROOM DOWN — DEN, BEDROOM, PARLOR

PLAN 2

DR	KIT
LR	
PORCH	

CHARACTERISTICS
- 3 ROOMS DOWN
- LIVING ROOM ACROSS FRONT

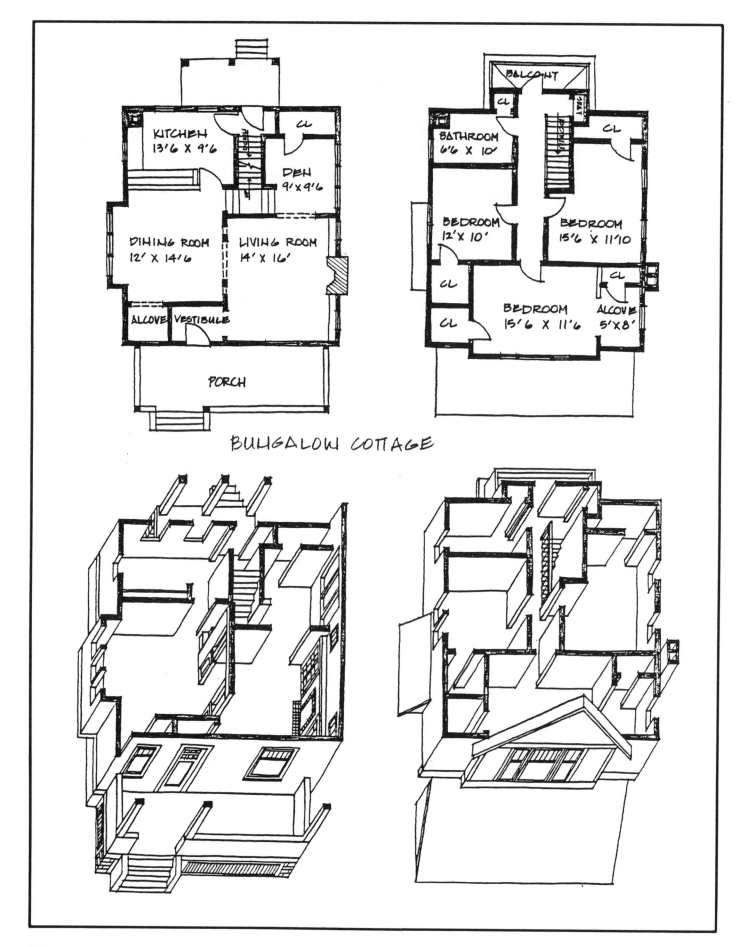

KITCHEN
13'6 X 9'6

CL

DEN
9' X 9'6

DINING ROOM
12' X 14'6

LIVING ROOM
14' X 16'

ALCOVE VESTIBULE

PORCH

BALCONY

CL

CL

BATHROOM
6'6 X 10'

BEDROOM
12' X 10'

BEDROOM
15'6 X 11'10

CL

CL

CL

BEDROOM
15'6 X 11'6

ALCOVE
5' X 8'

BUNGALOW COTTAGE

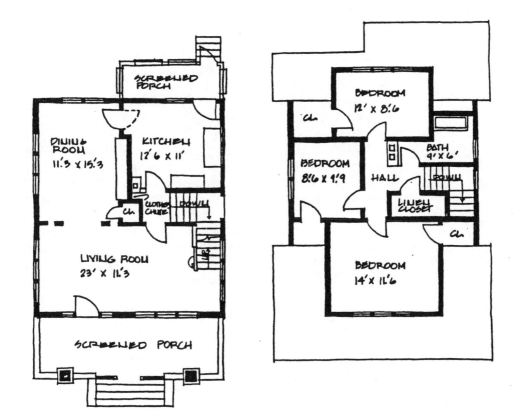

DINING
ROOM
11'3 X 15'3

KITCHEN
12'6 X 11'

SCREENED
PORCH

CLOTHES
CHUTE

DOWN

LIVING ROOM
23' X 16'3

SCREENED PORCH

BEDROOM
12' X 8'6

Ch.

BEDROOM
8'6 X 9'9

HALL

BATH
9' X 6'

DOWN

LINEN
CLOSET

Ch.

BEDROOM
14' X 16'6

BUNGALOW COTTAGE, PLAN 2

Airplane Bungalow

The so-called *airplane bungalow* was the largest bungalow house, having six to eight rooms on the ground level. Its broad plan was organized in two general patterns. The first type grouped the traditional social and functional spaces, adding a den, breakfast room, bedroom, back entry and porch on the first floor, and two bedrooms and a bath upstairs. The façade of this house was straight across the front, with adjacent rooms sharing the same outside wall. The back wall of the hall was also straight, thus the entire shape was very rectilinear, an attribute expressed by the squared nature of the plan.

The second plan type had a more traditional bungalow front in that one section of the house projected toward the street, creating a corner which was filled by a porch. The usual living room, dining room, and kitchen sequence covered one half of the plan, and the second half had a hall running through the entire house as well as an assortment of rooms such as a den, sleeping porch, sun parlor, and breakfast room. The stairs were located behind the principal rooms, just as they were in the bungalow cottage.

The airplane cottage was characterized by its low gable roof and multiple gables. The main gable covered the body of the house. Smaller gables that sheltered the porches and served as the roof for the second floor were positioned at a right angle to the main roof.

TYPICAL FAÇADE

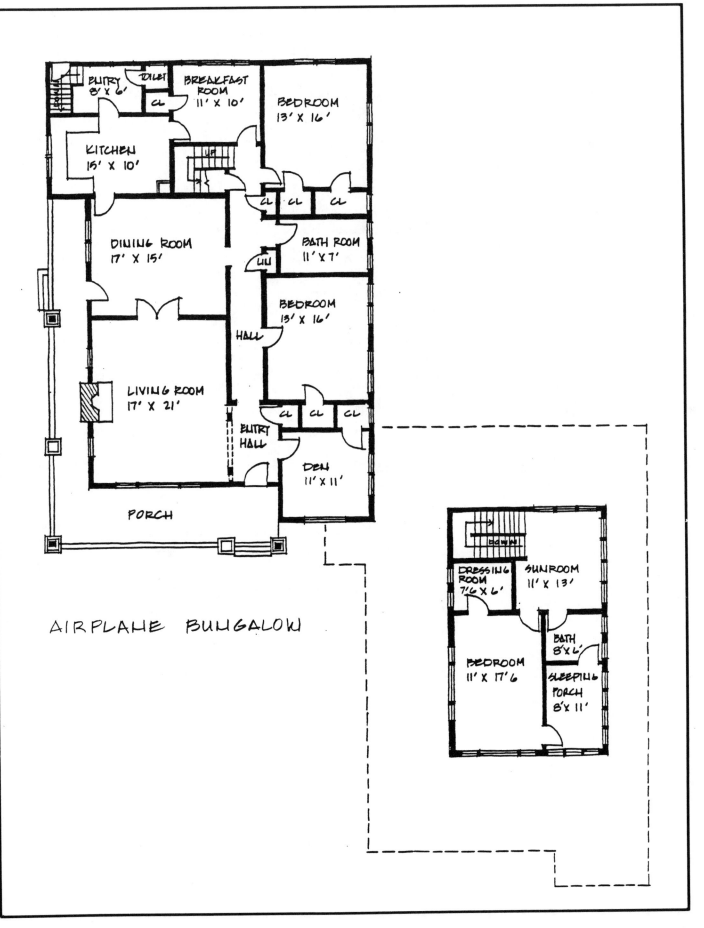

PURY
8' X 6'

TOILET

CL

BREAKFAST
ROOM
11' X 10'

BEDROOM
13' X 16'

KITCHEN
15' X 10'

UP

CL   CL   CL

DINING ROOM
17' X 15'

BATH ROOM
11' X 7'

BEDROOM
13' X 16'

HALL

LIVING ROOM
17' X 21'

CL   CL   CL

ENTRY
HALL

DEN
11' X 11'

PORCH

AIRPLANE BUNGALOW

DOWN

DRESSING
ROOM
7'6 X 6'

SUNROOM
11' X 13'

BATH
8' X 6'

BEDROOM
11' X 17'6

SLEEPING
PORCH
8' X 11'

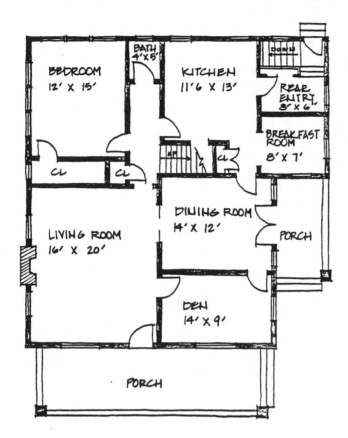

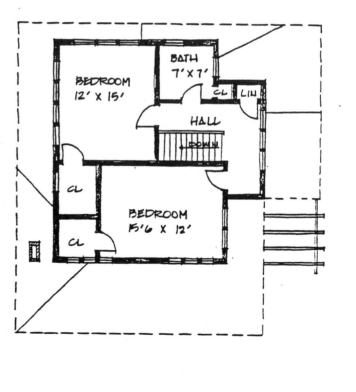

AIRPLANE BUNGALOW

356

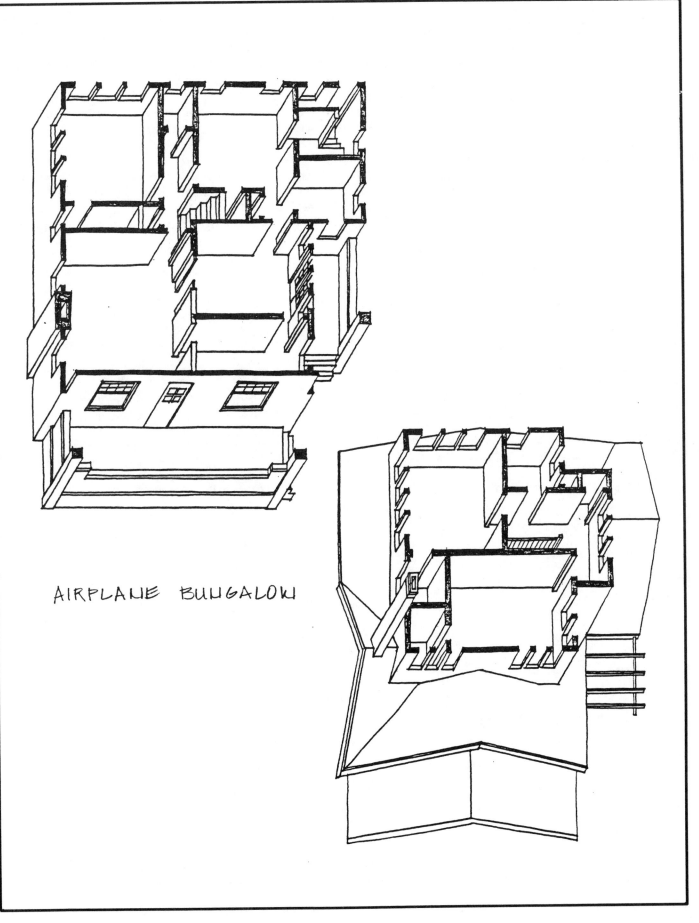

AIRPLANE BUNGALOW

Pedimented Bungalow

Bungalow design often boiled down to a few effects with a generalized convention that could be expressed in exterior and interior details and on plan. The *pedimented bungalow* was an example of this kind. The pediment above the entrance was a special effect which was integrated into a particular entrance system and into an interior floor plan to produce another bungalow prototype. The overall shape of this bungalow appears evenly divided between models that were either wider than they were deep, or vice versa. The entrance in both cases was on center, creating direct access to the living room.

The pedimented bungalow did not become a popular house type until the 1920s, when it might have gained some momentum from the success of colonial designs. It was the "colonial" aspect of this house that made it unique. The design was based on such things as detailing—the scaling

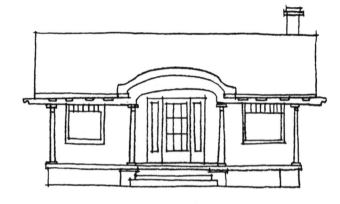

SOUTHERN PINES,
MODERN HOME NO. 1263_
1921

TYPICAL FACADE

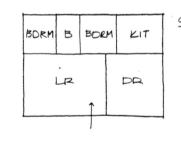

PEDIMENTED BUNGALOW

1 STORY HIGH
WIDER THAN DEEP
GABLE WITH RIDGELINE
FACING THE STREET

BDRM	B	BDRM	KIT
LR		DR	

CHARACTERISTICS
6 ROOMS
2 ROOMS DEEP
CENTER ENTRANCE
LIVING AND DINING
    ROOM SIDE BY
    SIDE
2 BEDROOMS
LIVING ROOM FIREPLACE

BUNGALOW PLAN 1 ALSO RECEIVES A SYMMETRICAL FRONT WITH PEDIMENTED CENTRAL ENTRANCE, CHANGING THE FORM TO SLIGHTLY DEEPER THAN WIDE.

down of historical elements, for instance—on symmetrical design, and on a sense of grace and simplicity accented with other colonial attributes such as shutters, white clapboards, and weathered shingles on the roof.

The internal organization was comparable to other bungalows, with social spaces across the front and service areas along the back. Within this configuration were a living room (with its required fireplace) connected to a dining room, and bedrooms, bath, kitchen, and breakfast nook. French doors leading to a terrace, side porch, or sleeping porch were options. But it was the entrance that characterized the pedimented bungalow. The pediment could be a dormer, a hood, or a small portico with Tuscan columns carrying a pediment. Another frequent façade feature was a pergola; it could be part of the entrance or part of a side porch or terrace and often carried latticework.

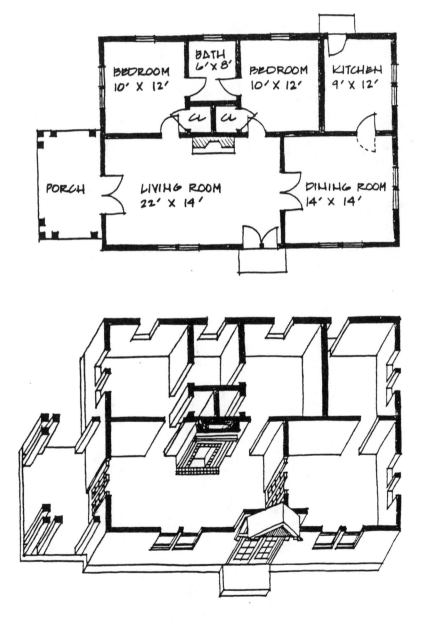

PEDIMENTED BUNGALOW

English and Spanish Bungalows

Because of its size and efficient plan, the bungalow was especially susceptible to imported styles. A basic plan could suffice for several surface treatments. For example, the April 1933 issue of *American Builder* carried an illustration of a bungalow in the Spanish style, derived from the "Mediterranean heritage," and advertised as suitable for Florida and the Southeast. The house pictured has an L-shape of unequal parts. The section pointed toward the street has a width of one room, while the second portion has a double row of rooms. This is an unusual shape, appropriate to the Spanish style; at least, its proportions and massing look as if they were derived from the Spanish. However, in the bottom right-hand corner there is an alternative design, labeled "Plan B"; this is a colonial design finished with brick veneer. There are, as well, changes in detailing to accommodate the alternative aesthetic.

H. F. MILLER HOUSE, LOS ANGELES — 1930

OKLAHOMA CITY

SEARS, ROEBUCK AND CO., "THE MANSFIELD," PRECUT — 1931

The most popular "cultural" treatments for bungalows were the Spanish and the English. For our purposes, these aesthetics are exterior variations of the same plan, so we have combined them into a single entry. There are different series of design elements for each type, which we will document.

The fundamental plan is angular, that is, the principal social space is at a right angle to the bank of bedrooms and bath, and the dining room and kitchen form the back section. There is at least one outside space. Inside, the living room has an end-wall fireplace, and arched openings with plaster finish separate the key rooms. The kitchen area includes a breakfast nook or alcove.

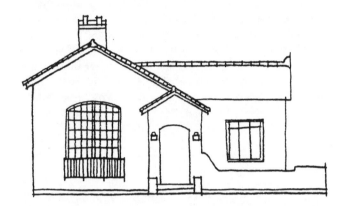

BUILDING AGE WORKING DRAWINGS, DESIGN 14110 — 1929

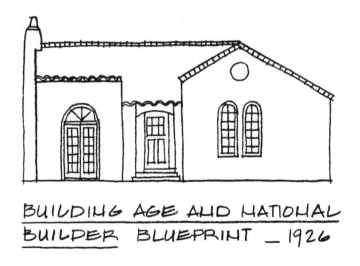

BUILDING AGE AND NATIONAL BUILDER BLUEPRINT — 1926

The application of *Spanish* motifs is usually identifiable because of its stucco exterior and tile roof. The roof lines are low with wide gables. The corner outside space may be a patio, and the entrance may be covered terrace space. Round-headed exterior arches and windows, some of wrought iron, and casement windows complete the inventory. Interior finish includes rough, tinted plaster and hewn rafters or a beamed ceiling.

The *English* bungalow relies on a projecting vestibule on the façade, covered with a steep gable to set the tone for the design. It is the broad, free sweep of the vestibule gable, carrying the roof almost to the ground, that establishes the dramatic profile characteristic of this style. Multiple roof forms (intersecting gables) on a low, rambling house clad with stucco or brick, perhaps a clipped gable or two, long casement windows with small panes, and a broad chimney with a pot for each flue—these are the design elements that underwrite this house.

Inside, the English bungalow may have a second floor in the main part of the house with space for a couple of bedrooms and a bath. If there are any rooms projecting from the main body of the house, these are typically the living room or a bedroom. Round-headed windows and doors and rough plastered walls are traditional details.

ENGLISH AND SPANISH BUNGALOWS

1 OR 1½ STORIES FOR ENGLISH
1 STORY HIGH FOR SPANISH
INTERSECTING GABLES, HIGH PITCH FOR
ENGLISH, LOW PITCH FOR SPANISH

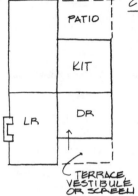

CHARACTERISTICS

6 ROOMS
OFF-CENTER ENTRANCE
LIVING ROOM OR BEDROOM
   PROJECTS OFF FAÇADE
TRIPLE WINDOWS IN LIVING
   ROOM COMMON
FIREPLACE ON OUTSIDE
   LIVING ROOM WALL COMMON
2 BEDROOMS
OUTDOOR LIVING SPACE PROVIDED,
   TERRACE IN FRONT, PATIO AT
   REAR

PATIO

KIT

LR   DR

TERRACE
VESTIBULE
OR SCREEN

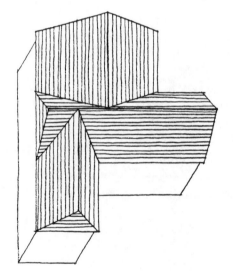

VARIATION

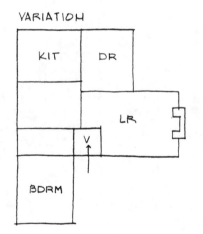

KIT   DR

LR

V

BDRM

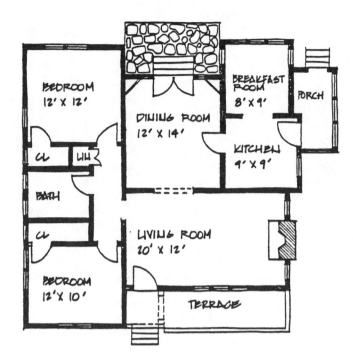

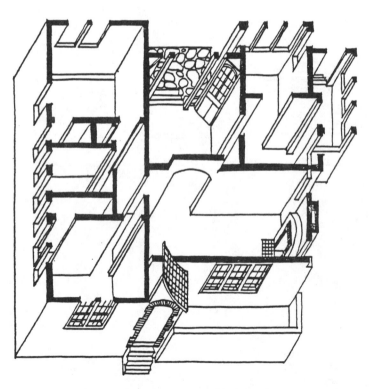

ENGLISH BUNGALOW

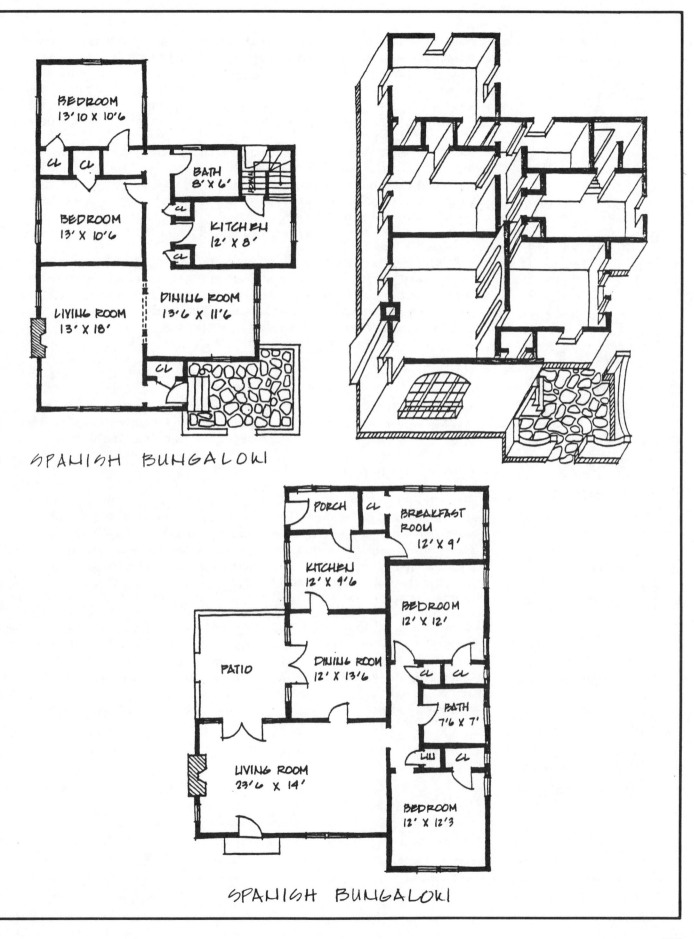

BEDROOM
13'10 X 10'6

CL   CL

BEDROOM
13' X 10'6

BATH
8' X 6'

KITCHEN
12' X 8'

CL

CL

LIVING ROOM
13' X 18'

DINING ROOM
13'6 X 11'6

CL

SPANISH BUNGALOW

PORCH   CL   BREAKFAST
ROOM
12' X 9'

KITCHEN
12' X 9'6

BEDROOM
12' X 12'

PATIO

DINING ROOM
12' X 13'6

CL   CL

BATH
7'6 X 7'

LIN   CL

LIVING ROOM
23'6 X 14'

BEDROOM
12' X 12'3

SPANISH BUNGALOW

ROWHOUSES

Rowhouses, or *contiguous houses,* as they were called in a few neighborhoods, were built by the hundreds in most of the "gritty cities" of the eastern United States. Not all rowhouses were the same; there were a number of different types with variations in the use of materials and costs. Design factors included the location of the house in relation to the front building line, the square footage, the degree of elaboration in plans, and the quality of the finish goods. The *flat-front rowhouse* was a less expensive type, sometimes built as philanthropic housing. The façade pattern was historical, but the industrial vernacular version had less charm. The flat-front house often was built on the building line; it was about 15 feet wide and two or three rooms deep. Many featured a pressed brick front topped by a bracketed cornice, others featured a parapet and a corbeled cornice. Mansard fronts were not uncommon with dormers and wood panels with incised ornament at the attic level.

The interior finish of this model was often pine, painted in some rooms and grained to look like oak or walnut in others. Mantels could be made of fiberboard to cut costs. The walls were papered and stock millwork was used for doors, windows, and wainscots in the kitchen and bath.

Bay-front rowhouses, with either a two-story bay or a single on the upper level, had more articulation than the flat-fronts. The façades carried references to cottage architecture with special parlor windows and front porches. As in the other types, the kitchen and bath often projected off the back of the house.

Inner-city housing in Philadelphia is dominated by the rowhouse. This represents one class of rowhouse in particular, and its inventory of elements provides some insight into the clustering of elements. One type of *Philadelphia rowhouse* was built just back from the front building line with a porch and a second story bay window, and it was part of a group of twenty-five houses.

The plan has a generous vestibule and reception hall that separates the parlor from the dining room. The house has a large parlor (cottage) window with a circle top of leaded glass. The vestibule finish has a raised panel wainscot and a ceramic tile floor, and a mantel with a gas-fired grate. Parlor finish consists of six-fold blinds and a "colonial" mantel with small columns and a marbleized slate fiberboard face. There is a sliding door between the dining room and hall, and a double-action door between the dining room and the kitchen. The stair has a quarter-turn plan and the balustrade is "semicolonial." The bathroom has an overhead ventilating skylight, tiled walls, an oak parquet floor, and a low closet with a copper tank. The interior door pattern has six cross-panels, with brass plates and wood knobs. There are gas fixtures, chandeliers, a pendant or two, and bracket lights. Electric attachments are fitted to the parlor, dining room, and toilet lights. There is hot-water heating with open plumbing work. It was customary to paper the walls throughout the house, using Lincrusta in both the halls and the dining room.

FLAT-FRONT, BALTIMORE AND PHILADELPHIA

BAY-FRONT OR PORCH-FRONT, TYPICAL FAÇADE

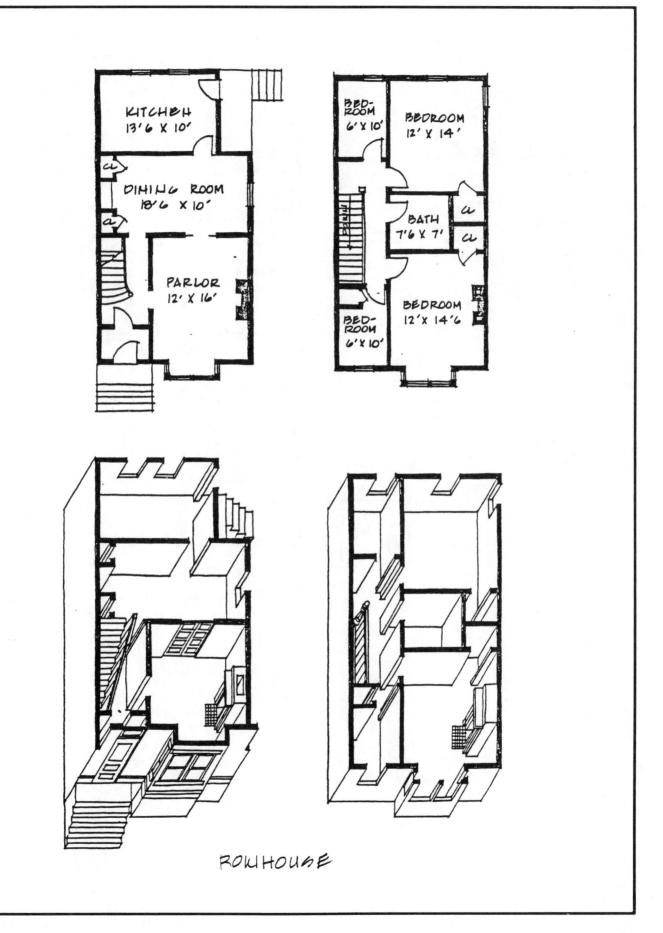

KITCHEN
13'6 X 10'

DINING ROOM
18'6 X 10'

PARLOR
12' X 16'

BED-ROOM
6' X 10'

BEDROOM
12' X 14'

BATH
7'6 X 7'

BED-ROOM
6' X 10'

BEDROOM
12' X 14'6

ROWHOUSE

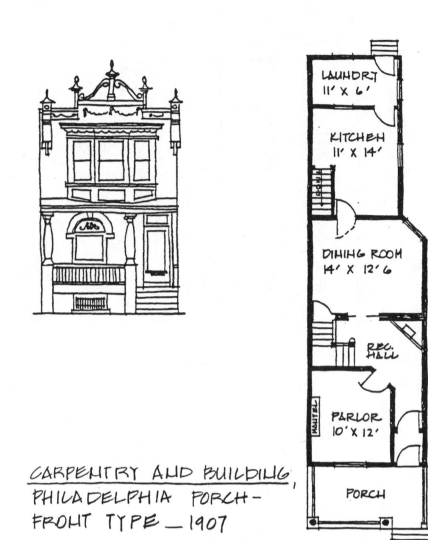

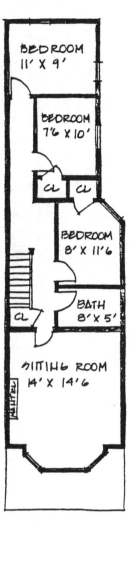

CARPENTRY AND BUILDING,
PHILADELPHIA PORCH—
FRONT TYPE — 1907

LAUNDRY
11' X 6'

KITCHEN
11' X 14'

DINING ROOM
14' X 12'6

REC.
HALL

PARLOR
10' X 12'

PORCH

BEDROOM
11' X 9'

BEDROOM
7'6 X 10'

BEDROOM
8' X 11'6

BATH
8' X 5'

DINING ROOM
14' X 14'6

COMMERCIAL BUILDINGS

The history of vernacular commercial building design is really the history of two phenomena. The first concerns the original installation of these buildings as part of some Main Street or courthouse square. In cities they might be located on a neighborhood corner or on streets that served as boundaries between districts. Of all the commercial buildings constructed in those places, stores were by far the most prolific type. And all the stores built before 1900, the prevailing types were the common brick-front store and the Italianate storefront made of cast iron or of iron and brick.

That we have had these storefronts for a long time brings us to the second phenomenon, which is that the history of commercial vernacular architecture is a history of remodeling. Commercial buildings have been susceptible to radical alterations of their façades and major alterations of their interior space. Storefronts have always been directly associated with myths about progress and change, especially about the need to change appearance in order to stay competitive.

Italianate and Brick-front Stores

The *Italianate* storefront often was constructed of cast-iron posts and beams with wood mullions and glass panels on the street level and some other cladding on the upper portion. The cornice line is significant in these buildings. In terms of design it is a heavy, elaborate element, composed of sheet metal on wood framing, and ornamented with numerous moldings and brackets. This same visual and physical heaviness is also present in the sills, the lintels, and the surrounds on the upper-floor windows.

The other principal storefront has a *brick façade* with a deep cornice of brick laid up in decorative patterns, in panels, or as corbeling. The first floor and the second are tied together by the facing brick—its color, bonding pattern, and mortar joints. Except for a transom light extending across the windows and entry door, the brick-front show windows are similar to those in the Italianate store, as are the bulkheads under the windows.

The interior organization is about the same for both stores. These buildings are long narrow shells enclosed by masonry load-bearing walls or by a wood frame with brick veneer or clapboards. The interior is created by

ITALIANATE

BRICK-FRONT

partitions and store furniture, the design and placement of which is somewhat determined by the nature of the business. We have chosen three typical plans, each with its individual display space and storage, service, waiting, and security requirements. Like everything in this kind of vernacular, store furniture and other fixtures were industrially produced from a slightly different system of parts, and most of these products were produced by millwork companies.

An article appearing in *American Builder and Building Age* (April 1935), entitled "Modernize Main Street," stated that according to Census Bureau data there were "more than 1,500,000 stores, shops, garages, offices and places of business of every kind." Of that total, more than one million were food, automotive, restaurant, apparel, and general supply businesses, and of that number the majority could have been accommodated in the kinds of stores discussed in this chapter.

A historical perspective on store design suggests that nineteenth-century storefronts were generally uniform in appearance. Stores often were built in twos and threes; when built as infilling structures they borrowed elements and materials from the buildings around them. The first decade of this century marked the beginning of a change in commercial façade design, a consequence of the store owners' desire to have their buildings express individuality. (This change had already occurred in housing design.) The logic for this change in attitude toward the function of the façade was related to the profit motive, which was linked to the idea of having "to catch and hold the attention of the casual observer." This enticement and engagement of the passerby was related to the idea that display space ought to have aesthetic appeal. The passerby would be induced to stop and enter by some display of "artistic beauty" or "striking effect." The building, by design, should please the customer.

Thus, storefront architecture became a problem to be solved with manufactured goods. The solutions expanded in several directions. The gross area allocated for display was increased: bulkhead, glass, and entry patterns were reconsidered: color became an essential element: and interior daylighting and artificial lighting became more significant in façade design. In reacting to all of this, passersby could now indulge in something known as windowshopping.

The success of plate glass as the principal display material was related ultimately to solving the problems of mullion, bulkhead, and tension for large plates. When plate glass could be set in metal, display windows could be larger, more unobstructed, and easier to maintain. With the development of metalwork in steel, copper, and bronze for use in moldings, corner bars, and division bars, with heavy-gauge metal in gutters and face members, designers could control the spring tension between the metal members and the window glass, making large windows possible. The metal could be finished in a number of ways to match other surface treatments. In this way storefronts increased their physical presence on the street through clear, dustproof glass and metal boxes.

Lighting was always a problem in a long, narrow store, and the introduction of transom lights helped illuminate these interiors. In time the transom panes were replaced by prism-glass panels of 4-inch squares glazed in sections. Electric lighting finally solved the problem of illumination. Electric lights, however, required new reflectors for store windows, and new indirect lighting for interiors. Lights were also required for cases and shelving, and so new bulbs, "daylight" or "blue bulbs," were developed to show true color indoors.

Artistic effects generally were tied to changing a few design elements, such as styling through detailing. For example, a new storefront of brick and terra-cotta ornament could transform an entire façade aesthetically. Other changes were linked to changing the bulkhead cladding from wood to something more exotic like marble, metal plates, or encaustic tiles, correlating materials with a new display and entrance pattern.

Stores also changed appearance to adjust to new types of business. For example, the display space for a jewelry store would not be suitable for a clothing store, nor would the raised floors of grocery store windows meet the display needs of a furniture store. Lastly, all these businesses needed special counters, tables, cases, cabinets, shelving, balconies, platforms, racks and fixtures, unobstructed floor space, ceiling and wall coverings, freight access, a ventilated toilet, a stock room, and sometimes a dumbwaiter or elevator.

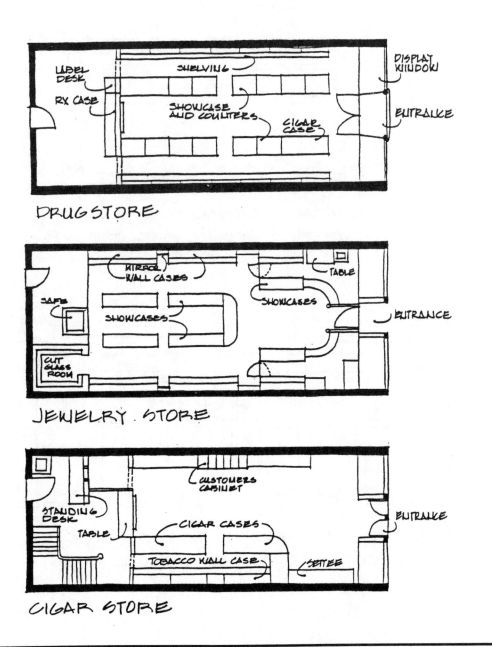

Broad-front Store The modern *broad-front* store building is a special class composed of patented storefront materials. This type had a unified front that was twice the width of a single store. The façade of this building was a large brick panel, symmetrically organized, with a continuous cornice, transom, and display windows. The broad-front could serve as one store or two. Terra-cotta or stone trimmings were used to cap a short parapet, and terra-cotta moldings and plaster panels filled the space between the transom and the cap. The entry was generally recessed, and truss-roof construction eliminated all supporting posts, leaving the interior free of obstruction.

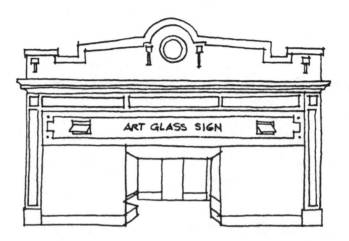

INTERNATIONAL STEEL AND IRON
CO.'S COMPLETE STORE FRONT__ 1922

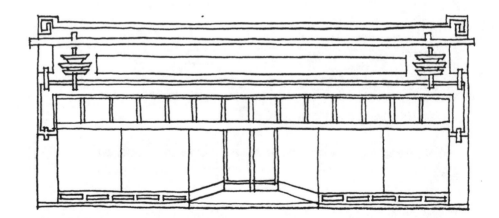

BASED ON A DRAWING BY THE RADFORD
ARCHITECTURAL CO., CHICAGO __ 1909

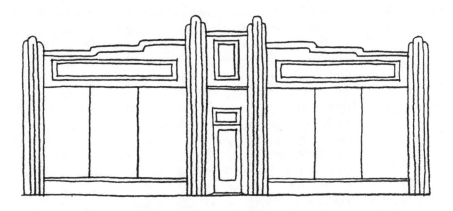

ART DECO BROAD-FRONT, CHEEVERS
FLOWER SHOP, OKLAHOMA CITY —
CIRCA 1916

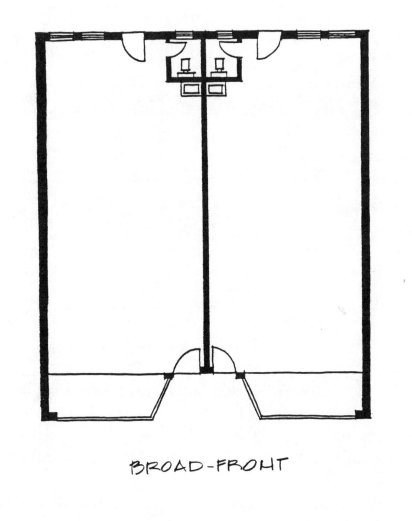

BROAD-FRONT

Artistic-front Store   One special category of store design is the *artistic front,* which was a group of stores and offices integrated by one design concept. Sometimes the group reflected a particular quality of craftsmanship that set it apart from its neighbors, or the buildings referred to art itself, that is, their motifs, surface treatments, and patterns were inspired by some style in the history of art. The phrase "artistic front" was of period usage.

Most artistic fronts had one large effect, say, a Spanish feeling that linked several stores. In some of these designs stores were allowed to keep their own identity, but in others all the units were subsumed under the grand gesture. Building materials used for exterior details included stucco, brick, stone, terra-cotta, tile, marble, tiling of several kinds, and wood. Interior finish was generally undetailed but it was not uncommon for an exterior treatment to be carried inside. Plastering, wood elements, color, and hardware, all might have a broad application.

Motivating this approach to store design was the belief that exterior treatments invite favorable notice and incite people to inspect the merchandise. The overall attractiveness of the artistic front was attained by clever proportioning and correct details. Much of this kind of commercial

ENGLISH ARTISTIC-FRONT, BASED ON THE TUDOR SHOPS BUILDING, EVANSTON, ILLINOIS — 1933

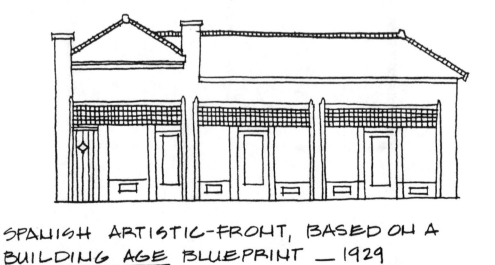

SPANISH ARTISTIC-FRONT, BASED ON A BUILDING AGE BLUEPRINT — 1929

development was done at a residential scale, so that the stores seemed to fit into the community and the shopping area looked and functioned something like a village. In other words, the stores were disguised.

Typical treatments included Spanish (stucco walls, tile roof), Tudor (stucco walls, slate roof, half timbering), Art Deco (glazed cladding, stylized ornament), Moderne (structural glass, metal trim), and broad front (multiple fronts linked by terra-cotta trim).

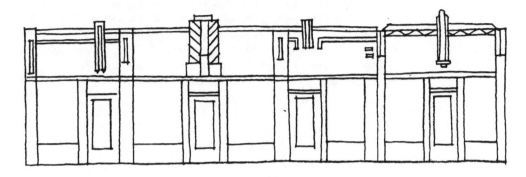

ART DECO ARTISTIC-FRONT, BASED ON AN OKLAHOMA CITY BLOCK — 1936

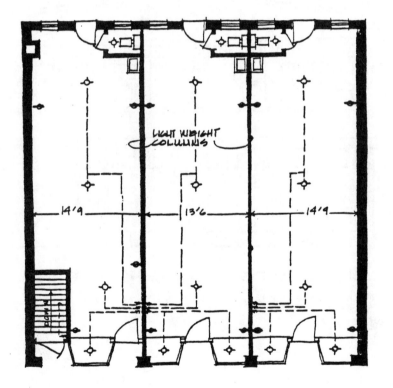

LIGHT WEIGHT COLUMNS

14'9   13'6   14'9

KEY TO WIRING SYSTEMS
◇ CEILING OUTLET
⊢● SINGLE CONVENIENCE OUTLET

ELECTRICAL PLAN, ARTISTIC-FRONT

Double Brick-front Stores

Some commercial structures were designed and built as *double stores*, and many of these were also residential buildings, with the second and third floors partitioned into two- or three-bedroom flats or apartments. These double-wide stores, also called *double-lot stores*, were related to the broad-front. They were of the same general width, 40 to 50 feet, and had the same overall composition, with strong piers on the corners and a large panel of brick and windows in between. Because of the size of the façade, the front had a three-part organization: show windows, commercial entry, and residential entry at the street level; upper-floor windows in rows, groups, bands, or as single units with cladding panels in between; and a cornice line that included the parapet, its coping, and other decorative elements. The most popular materials for this building were brick and terra-cotta.

DOUBLE-WIDE BRICK-FRONT, 2
STORES DOWN, 2 APARTMENTS
ABOVE

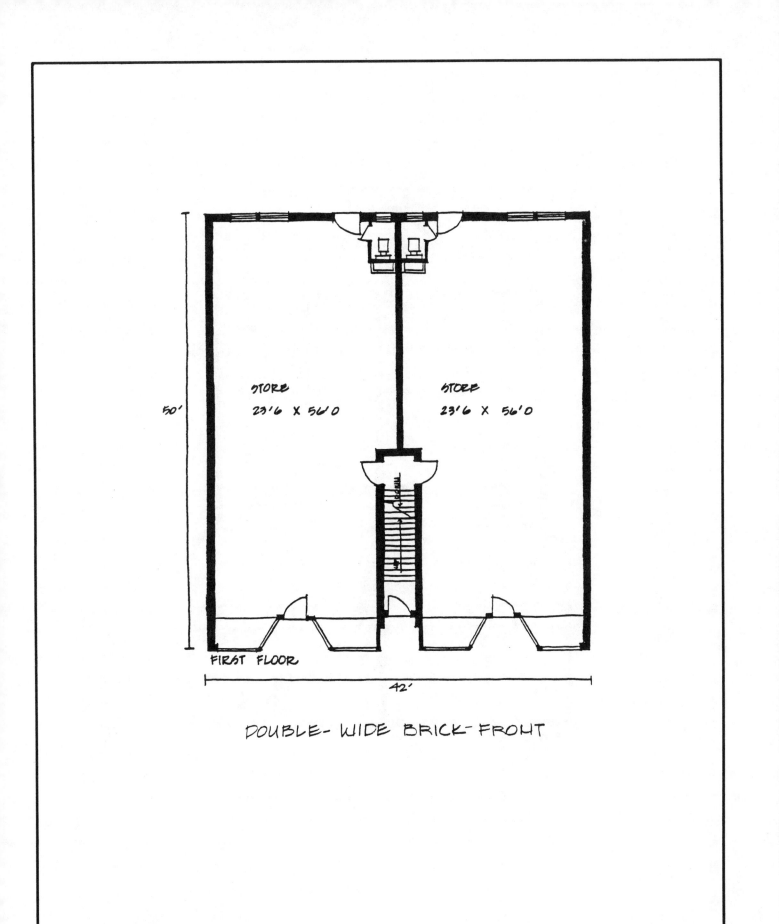

50'

STORE
23'6 X 56'0

STORE
23'6 X 56'0

FIRST FLOOR

42'

DOUBLE- WIDE BRICK-FRONT

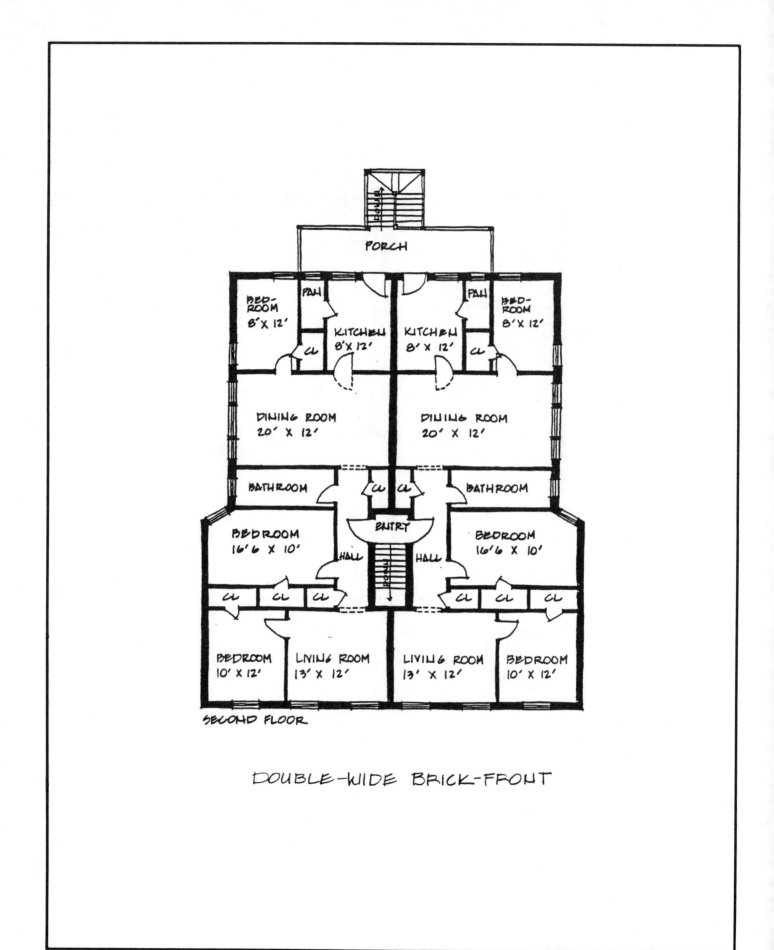

DOUBLE-WIDE BRICK-FRONT

378

Entrances Our study of commercial buildings showed that *store entrances* have been a special design problem. To understand that problem better, we sorted entrances by pattern for single, double, and multiple store structures; we reproduce them here in a schematic format. The patterns include alternative setbacks, display configurations, and access points: these features, taken together, influenced the store's presence on the street.

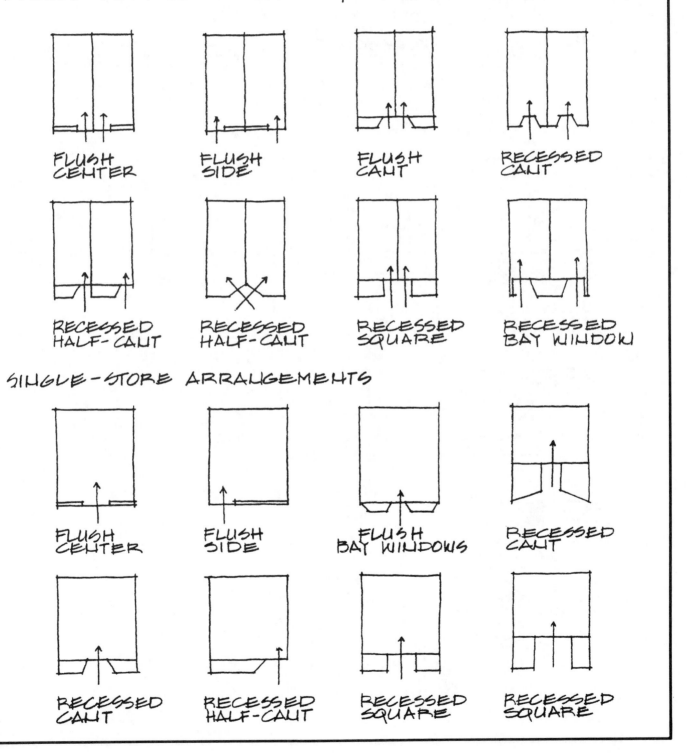

DOUBLE-STORE ARRANGEMENTS, ENTRANCE FOR EACH STORE

FLUSH CENTER

FLUSH SIDE

FLUSH CANT

RECESSED CANT

RECESSED HALF-CANT

RECESSED HALF-CANT

RECESSED SQUARE

RECESSED BAY WINDOW

SINGLE-STORE ARRANGEMENTS

FLUSH CENTER

FLUSH SIDE

FLUSH BAY WINDOWS

RECESSED CANT

RECESSED CANT

RECESSED HALF-CANT

RECESSED SQUARE

RECESSED SQUARE

SINGLE-STORE ARRANGEMENTS

RECESSED
SQUARE

RECESSED
T

RECESSED
STEPPED

RECESSED
STEPPED

MULTIPLE STORE ARRANGEMENTS

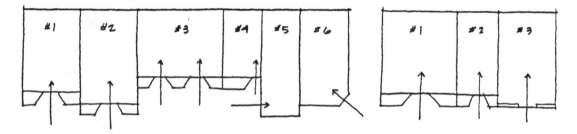

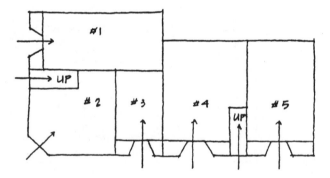

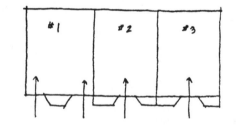

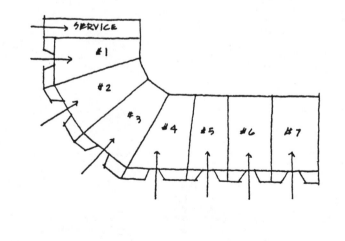

Store Layouts

To illustrate a typical store interior organization and furniture, we have assembled a plan and fixtures for a millinery store. The isometric drawing reveals half of the façade design and shows the spatial organization, starting with the splayed entry in the center between the show windows. The entry leads to the center aisle, which is fronted by counters and showcase furniture, behind which is the shelving against the wall. The back room in these stores was used for storage and toilet facilities, with larger storage and stockrooms in the basement. Special interior furniture for a specific store included in this case a console, a freestanding mirrored room divider finished in veneered wood; show cases consisting of a base, a glass or wood top (the latter for wrapping), and sliding doors in the back; and counters assembled from stiles, rails, and panels. Shelving was produced in units and it was common for the shelving to look like cabinetry and to be organized in bays by thin columns or pilasters with an architrave and cornice across the top.

MILLINERY STORE LAYOUT
AND ARCHITECTURAL
FURNITURE

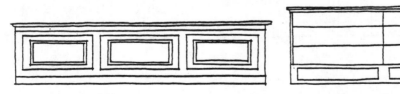

CONSOLE   DRY GOODS SHELVING

COUNTER   SHOWCASE

Drugstores   To extend the discussion of stores, we include a brief examination of another type, the *drugstore* as built from 1880 to 1940. Many vernacular commercial buildings established planning patterns in the nineteenth century that

PRESCRIPTION SCREEN AND SHELVING _ 1880

PRESCRIPTION CASE FRONT AND SHELVING __ 1910

remained intact for some time. This is true for the drugstore, which at first made up most prescriptions from raw materials, as it were, and also sold some patent medicines. As the pharmaceuticals industry grew, the drugstore began to rely more on dispensing patented products and medicines that did not have to be concocted in the store. This shift changed its storage requirements. The store also started to sell items related to general health care. Then drugstores added some food service—ice cream shops, candy counters, soda fountains, and the like. This last addition wrought a change in the store's interior design.

The furniture requirements for a commercial drugstore were as follows: a large case with shelves and drawers for tinctures used in the preparation of medicines; shelving for patent medicines; a prescription case that separated the public from the pharmacist's work space. This was the location, on axis with the entry, where prescriptions were filled. The inclusion of food service altered the character of the drugstore. The materials used for this service brought hard-finish, bright surfaces to what had been a somber, wood environment. The drugstore soda fountain had plastic countertops, metal and glass fixtures, and a whole new collection of millwork and furniture components—stools, benches, booths, back bars, mirrors, glass shelving, porcelain containers, and nickle-plated hardware. The ambience of the drugstore changed, becoming more social and less "scientific," a change from which it never recovered.

BEVELED
PLATE
MIRROR

PRESCRIPTION CASE: "NEAT, ARTISTIC, PRACTICAL, MODERN," 1910

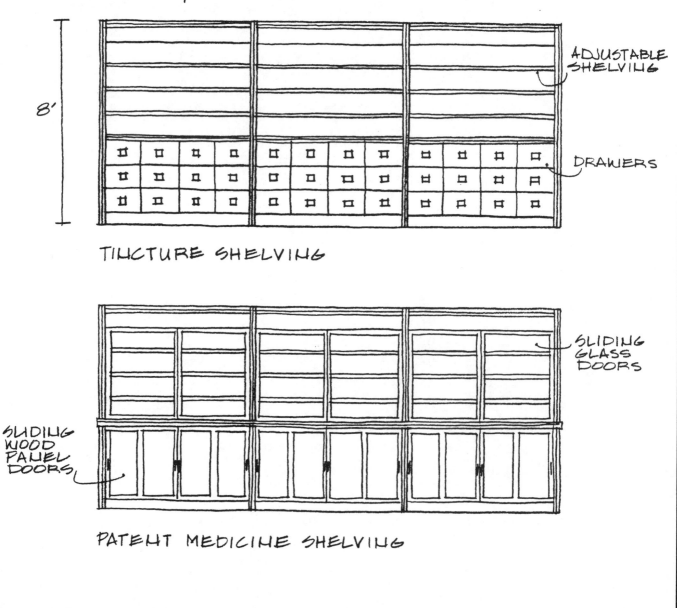

8'

ADJUSTABLE SHELVING

DRAWERS

TINCTURE SHELVING

SLIDING GLASS DOORS

SLIDING WOOD PANEL DOORS

PATENT MEDICINE SHELVING

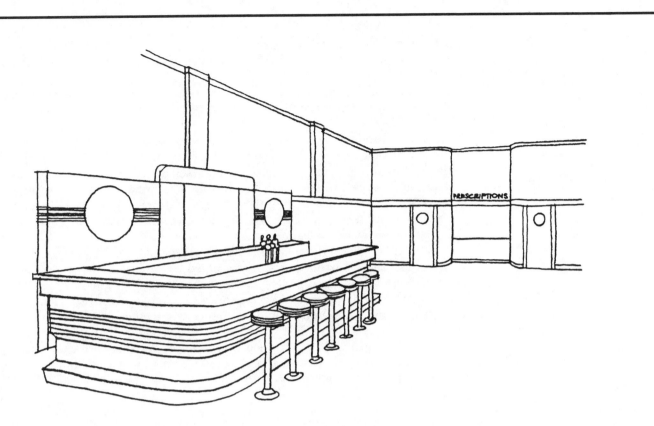

EMPHASIS MOVED FROM PRESCRIPTION CASE TO SODA
FOUNTAIN, COLONIAL PHARMACY, ORLANDO, FLORIDA — 1930

SODA BOOTHS AS ARCHITECTURAL FURNITURE — 1940

Banks Small-town or neighborhood *banks* started out their commercial life in buildings much like stores. First- and even second-generation banks in brick-front stores and in the more formal temple- or classical-front stores were located on the same streets as all the other businesses. Interior space design for a bank is rather simple. There is a public space separated from the work space by a partition, with special locations along the partition for different kinds of transactions. The work space also includes a space for tellers, an office space, a bank officer's desk, and a vault. This arrangement could fit into almost any space. In banks with more interior volume a mezzanine level was introduced for additional offices, and in even larger buildings a directors' room might be included in the plan. Bank designs and plans sometimes were included in pattern books, just as furniture was included in millwork trade catalogs.

Bank furniture was produced by millwork companies, and it was, therefore, susceptible to the aesthetic systems applied to other millwork products. Counters with ornamental panels, brackets, moldings, art glass, ornamental wickets for teller windows, railings, and other items made by assembling stiles, rails, panels, spindles, and balusters were made in the same way as goods for houses. Overall, bank interiors were somber, and their design effects and furniture had a unified appearance. As the vernacular bank became financially successful, there were changes in interior materials—substituting marble for wood—and a reworking of the façade.

BRICK FRONT

CLASSICAL FRONT

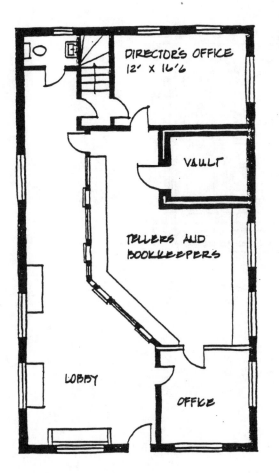

DIRECTOR'S OFFICE
12' X 16'6

VAULT

TELLERS AND
BOOKKEEPERS

LOBBY

OFFICE

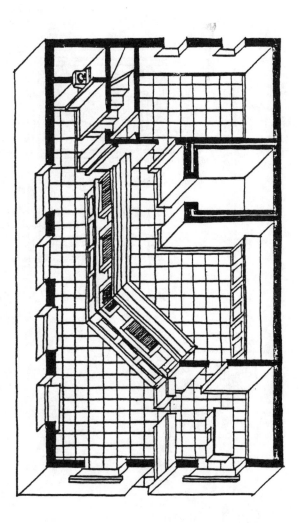

BANK

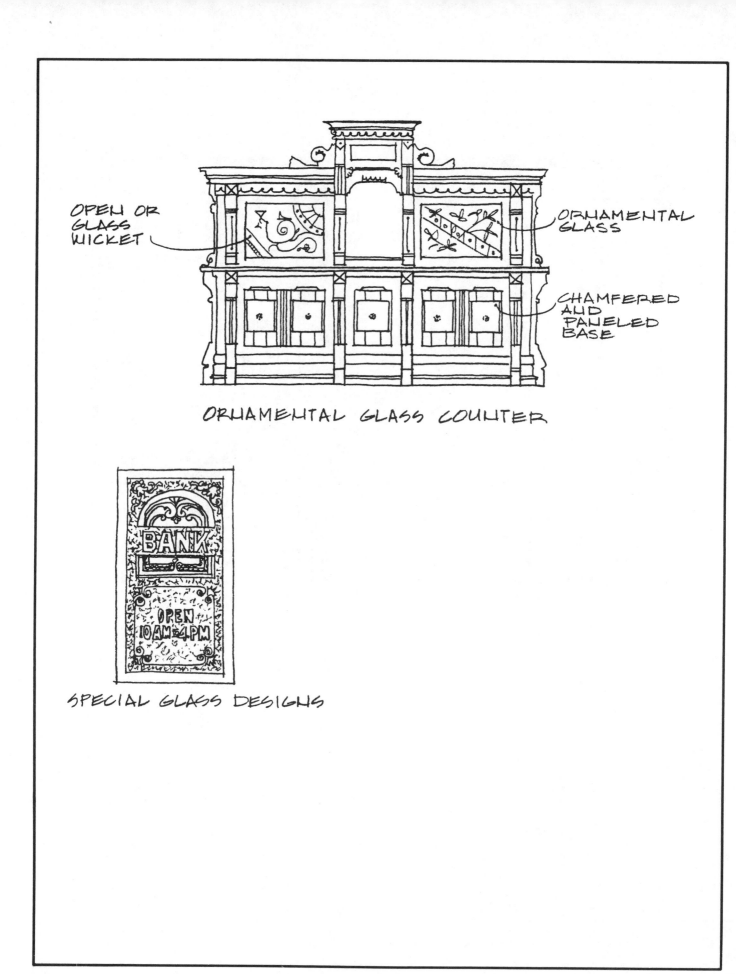

OPEN OR GLASS WICKET

ORNAMENTAL GLASS

CHAMFERED AND PANELED BASE

ORNAMENTAL GLASS COUNTER

BANK

OPEN 10AM-4PM

SPECIAL GLASS DESIGNS

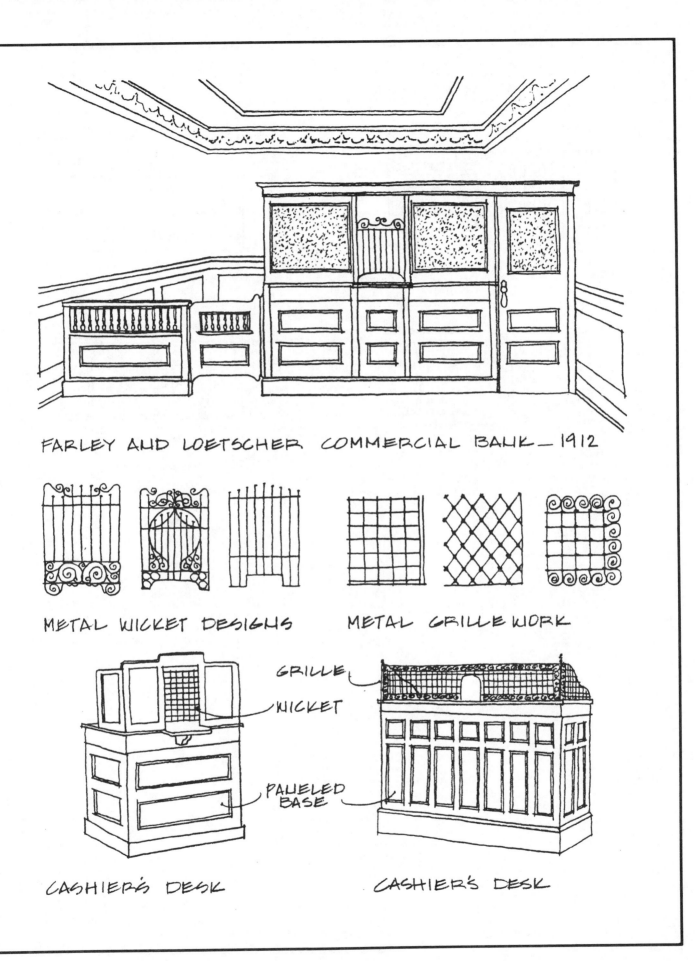

FARLEY AND LOETSCHER COMMERCIAL BANK – 1912

METAL WICKET DESIGNS   METAL GRILLE WORK

GRILLE
WICKET
PANELED BASE

CASHIER'S DESK   CASHIER'S DESK

OFFICE RAILING

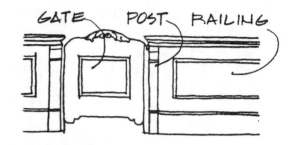
GATE POST RAILING

PANEL AND SPINDLE FRIEZE   PANELED

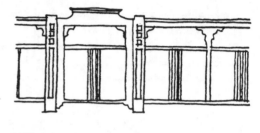

STICK   STICK

CHURCHES   The discussion of the design of vernacular churches focuses on the general form of the church building and the organization of its interior space. We have identified six different types of church structure, based on their essential design characteristics, and six different interior plans based on the proportion of length to width, the handling of aisles, and the arrangement of seats. Generally, the shape of a church does not necessarily dictate its interior plan. As in other aspects of vernacular architecture, there is a great deal of interaction between the exterior form and the interior organization. Some sanctuary plans cannot be read from the outside.

We do not discuss the development of the chancel and choir spaces in these churches because, while there are minor differences in the arrangements of these areas, the magnitude of the differences in vernacular churches was not great. We have also determined that a great number of the design concepts for churches originally were rather generic, perhaps done on the assumption that in finishing the church, adjustments would be carried out to suit specific needs. While consideration was given to all the religious denominations, the majority of the churches examined were Protestant.

The examples used to illustrate design concepts were taken from neighborhood, small-town, and rural sources. We tried to restrict our sample to churches drawn by architects but intended for replication, and churches designed and built by local people. A number of church organizations had architects design simple churches that could be erected in frontier, territorial, and developing community contexts. The idea of sowing the ubiquitous church as part of an evangelical mission was of interest to us. The institutionalization of spiritual life in a community through the building of a church is a fundamental part of the history of vernacular architecture. Our point here will be that the industrial system played much the same role in church construction that it played in residential, commercial, and other types of building activity. The industrial housing company Aladdin included a church design as part of its "company town," for example.

Most vernacular churches are of wood-frame construction with wood cladding, but brick, both as load-bearing wall construction and as brick veneer over frame, is common. There are also stone vernacular churches; some were built as imitations of traditional models and others were simply the work of local stonemasons. Of these materials stone is the most local, suggesting that many regions of the country at one time had people with the skill to build in stone but the skill was not passed on to succeeding generations.

Center Steeple and Steepled Ell

The *center-steeple church* was one of the most common types built. It is truly a national church type with plan options. The façade of this church relies on several center-oriented devices; the steps and porch, entry doors, window in the tower, belfry, and spire are all visually layered over each other. The attraction to the center is reinforced by the slope of the gable roof. The fenestration is symmetrical, and the rest of the wall is only modestly ornamented with corner boards and fascia.

Inside, the center-steeple has one of three seating plans: the center-aisle plan with rows of pews flush against the walls; a three-aisle format with a center aisle and an aisle on each side between the pews and the wall; and the so-called Akron plan with four aisles and segmented seating rows. The term *Akron plan* refers to the arrangement in which instructional rooms are adjacent to the auditorium, separated by a folding partition that can be opened for additional seating during services.

The *steepled-ell* church is best characterized by the intersection of its two broad wings, creating a large interior space. The broad gables created opportunities for interesting window groupings and stained glass, as well as for experiments with large-scale massing. The tower, for example, can be made to rise from the intersection in a number of ways, and in some designs the base of the tower is the entrance to the church.

The principal seating plan for the steepled ell includes a two-aisle configuration with the seats arranged in graduated segments, short rows in the front and long in the back. An alternative to this plan has a rectangular plan with the rows of seats at a right angle to the wall.

CENTER STEEPLE

STEEPLED ELL

Gable-end and Side-Steeple

The *gable-end* church is a widely diffused building, especially in rural areas; its simple gable roof and end wall have been suitable for many denominations. It was often sited in an open area where the understated, straightforward quality of the form created a strong profile, a sensible relief against a natural background. Larger versions of this church have two-story interiors and a broad west end which may be ornamented. Most of these frame churches were clad in clapboards, shingles, and boards with battens. They also had some gable finish in patterns borrowed from cottage design. This church was also built with brick and stone, and the dominant plan was a center aisle with a strong axis from the entry to the chancel.

Side-steeple churches have a west wall organization that relies on the interaction of the massing elements, the broad gable and the steeple, for effect. The steeple usually is composed in sections, building toward the spire, and the gable has a window grouping, sometimes of different shaped windows. The side-steeple church is likely to have either an oblong or a square plan. The oblong type has three different seating configurations: a three-aisle plan, a center-aisle plan, and a two-aisle plan. The churches with these plans are all nineteenth-century buildings. The square-plan examples are twentieth-century churches, built especially from 1905 to 1925. More often than not the pew arrangement in both the oblong and the square churches is segmented rather than rectangular.

GABLE END

SIDE STEEPLE

Twin-tower and Temple-front

Twin-tower churches rely on symmetrical massing for organization and aesthetic effect. The towers and the gable end usually have some detailing that links all three elements—watertables, string courses, and fascia boards. These churches were built as frame structures with clapboards and as masonry buildings made of brick.

The expressive qualities in this kind of church depend on the window treatment in the gable between the towers, on the entry, which is usually just below the window, and on the spire, which could be rendered in different shapes, profiles, and materials. As for seating plans, the format of rectilinear rows seems most common.

The *temple-front* church is the most classical of the vernacular types, because of the use of a temple-front portico or a façade organization based on pilasters at regular intervals. Compositions of this kind have linked this church also with colonial treatments, which allows the fenestration to be carried out with double-hung windows, sometimes with circle-top upper lights. The seating plan for this church favors three-aisle, segmented rows, but there is enough evidence that the straight-row plan has also been used.

TWIN TOWERS

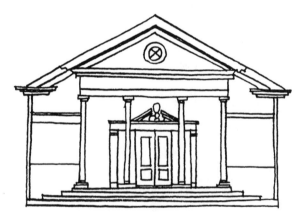

TEMPLE-FRONT

394

Church Design

With these rough sketches of the types of church buildings constructed from 1870 to 1940, we would like to turn to the rationale for vernacular church design. There is a body of literature that addresses this question. For example, in 1853, the Central Committee of the General Congregational Convention published *A Book of Plans for Churches and Parsonages* based on designs by leading architects: Upjohn, Downing, Renwick, Wheeler, Wells, Austin, Stone, Cleveland, Backus, and Reeve. The committee had requested designs that could be replicated in the new towns and villages of the West. The church reissued this book in 1892 without changing anything in the original, which makes it relevant for our discussion.

Almost every aspect of church design is covered in the essay that precedes the plates, and many of the Committee's concerns were related to issues in vernacular church architecture. Even the definition of what a church should be is of interest: "a place for the unified and intelligible worship of God by the whole assembled company" (p. 6). This statement is a not-so-veiled response to Roman Catholic church practice, which was liturgical and ritualistic, the priest being the primary celebrant. The Congregationalists, as their name suggests, intended to be democratic and social.

The Committee urged the church to adopt a simpler architecture, with rationality being more important than irrationality, and social values preferred over individual ones. Churches were not to be "temples of taste." The ideal church should have a commanding site and a spire (the recognized sign of religion). As for the interior, it should "correspond in style to the better class of dwellings possessed by those who occupy the church" (p. 11). The properly built church would also be properly equipped, with a businesslike environment and a workshop complete with tools. A church should not have to double up on the use of space. There was to be a minister's room and places for the congregation to socialize. The church was to be built of stone, and the church and its site should express a sense of time and place.

As for aesthetics, there should be no imitation of materials; things that looked like wood should be made of wood. There was an appeal to the organic—every church should utilize the resources of the site in construction. There was a pragmatic side to this design. Proper ventilation was important, and what we think of today as the human factor was to be taken into account in pew design. The preferred seating called for two aisles along the sides rather than a center-aisle format. Galleries were not to be hung by iron rods from the roof. Straight staircases were preferable, and the church should not have too many windows. Stained glass, in moderation, was acceptable but interior colors should be in harmony. A stark white interior was to be avoided.

Twentieth-century essays on the subject address most of the same issues. That church design should facilitate preaching was unanimously agreed upon. But there were disagreements on other things. Writing in 1906, Kidder says that for village churches the sanctuary should be square rather than polygonal, but Tralle (1921) states that the auditorium should be oblong, and never more than twice as long as it is wide. Brabham believes that the shape should be rectangular, in proportions of 3:4 or 4:6. Similarly, these writers have their own ideas about aisle width, pulpit placement, acoustics, and similar topics. Most writers recommend against center-aisle plans, since preachers believe that this plan divides the congregation. On the other hand, parishoners like the plan for weddings and funerals. These authorities are unanimous, however, in their rejection of the Akron plan. They all argue for separate worship and teaching rooms.

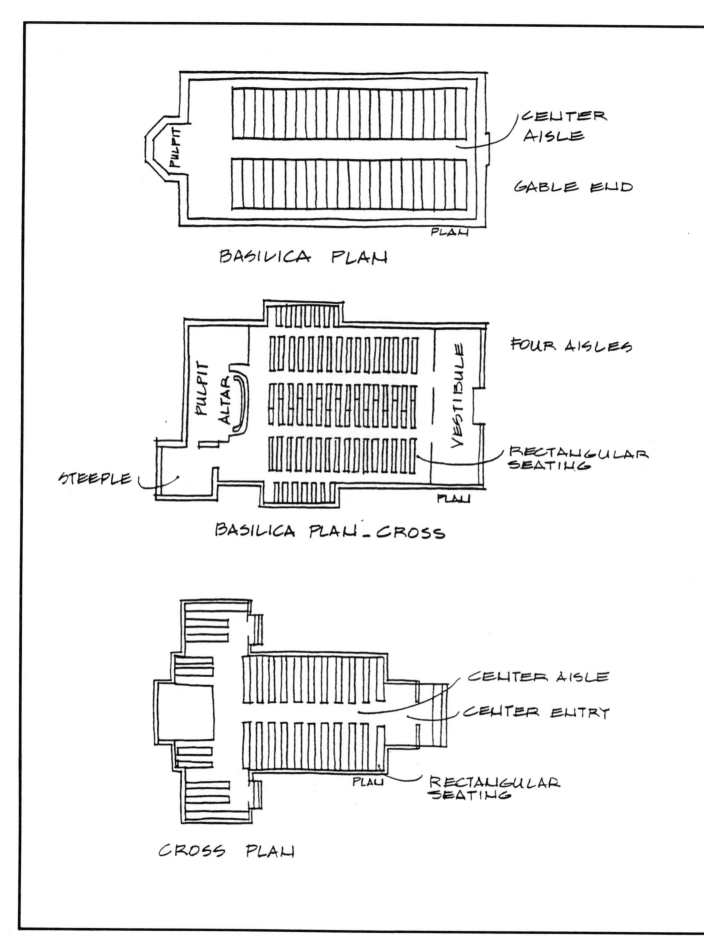

CENTER AISLE

GABLE END

PLAN

BASILICA PLAN

FOUR AISLES

RECTANGULAR SEATING

STEEPLE

PULPIT

ALTAR

VESTIBULE

PLAN

BASILICA PLAN - CROSS

CENTER AISLE

CENTER ENTRY

PLAN

RECTANGULAR SEATING

CROSS PLAN

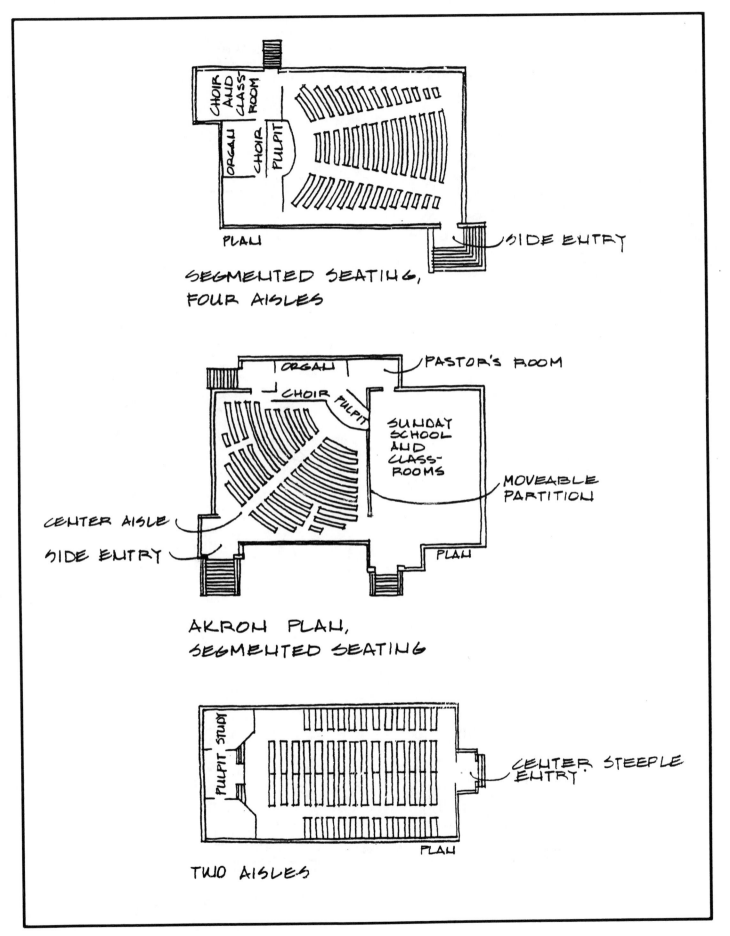

SEGMENTED SEATING,
FOUR AISLES

AKRON PLAN,
SEGMENTED SEATING

TWO AISLES

397

As already stated, the question of church plan was reduced to half a dozen popular formats, which could be installed in almost any kind of church. The basilica plan, regardless of the aisle arrangement, was the prevailing type. Vernacular churches did not use the cross plan extensively.

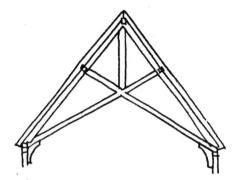

SCISSORS TRUSS
FOR FRAME CHURCHES ONLY

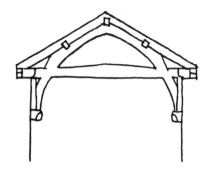

ARCH-BRACED TRUSS
WITH A TIE-BEAM

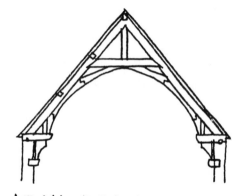

ARCH-BRACED TRUSS

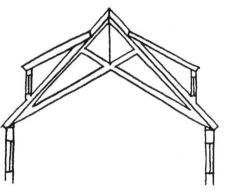

SCISSORS TRUSS
WITH A CLEARSTORY

RELATIONSHIP BETWEEN EXTERIOR AND INTERIOR

If these churches had cross arms or transepts—if the latter term can be used to describe vernacular churches—they were very shallow. The appropriation of seating plans—straight rows or curved or segmented rows—did not follow a precise logic. But the segmented rows were more popular in churches with wide (square floor plan) auditoriums. The concept of the wide room, perhaps derived from the Germanic *hallenkirche,* or the American meeting house, is a key element in vernacular buildings.

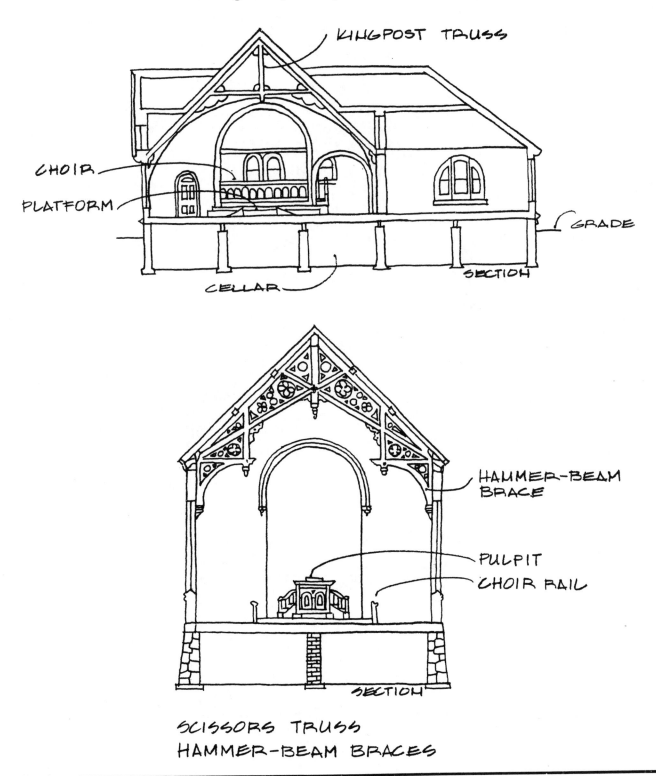

KINGPOST TRUSS

CHOIR

PLATFORM

GRADE

SECTION

CELLAR

HAMMER-BEAM BRACE

PULPIT

CHOIR RAIL

SECTION

SCISSORS TRUSS
HAMMER-BEAM BRACES

The principal church roof is the gable, and for a long time the shape of a gable, which sets a tone for the overall design, was a direct expression of the kind of roof truss used in construction. Scissors, arch-braced, and kingpost trusses were the most frequently used types. A scissors truss creates a sharply pitched roof, which is effective for Gothic treatments. The arch-braced truss has a wider gable, as does the kingpost. Trusses were more than supports for roofs. In many churches the trusses were left exposed

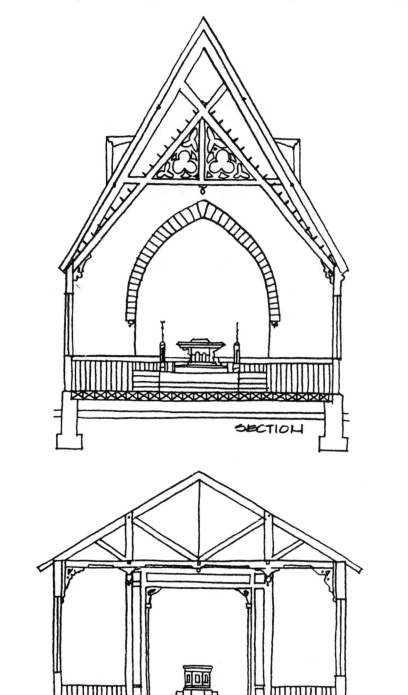

so that they were part of the ceiling and the overall scheme. Truss elements could be finished to add another dimension to a design concept.

We have included some section drawings to illustrate some kinds of interior organization—about the way the volume was subdivided, and about the relationship between the roof form and the interior. These drawings also provide an opportunity to illustrate the church's dependence on millwork products. Wood—as structure and as finish, as wall and as furniture—was the key material. Most church interior elements—stained glass windows (another kind of art glass), pews, rails, panels, interior doors, gallery columns, partition panels, windows, moldings, folding doors, and entrance doors—were manufactured by millwork companies.

Church furniture is millwork. The pulpit, one of the more significant objects within the sanctuary, was produced in two forms, console and lectern, and in styles that included Gothic, Mission, and colonial. Console design was ornamental, with panels and applied moldings built up from a base, and a top piece large enough to hold a Bible or other materials. Lecterns carried less ornament and were half the size of consoles.

Church pews were made of several parts. A section of seating sometimes had a special low partition, a pew front, a rail, and panel piece. Individual pews were put together from ends, a back, a seat, a center support, and sometimes a divider. Kneeling rails and racks for books—and at one time for hats—were part of pew design. Historically, pew ends set the tone for the interior design. The height of the end and its profile were the essentials. In the period we are studying here pew ends became shorter and more rectilinear. High, scrolled ends lost favor, as did heavy ornamentation. The size of a pew end is controlled by the angle of the pew back; a broadly inclined back needs a wide end. Pew ends were designed so that any of a number of panels could be inserted in them or one of several moldings could be applied. These elements addressed the question of aesthetics. In general, modern pew ends have less ornamentation and more abstraction of historical patterns.

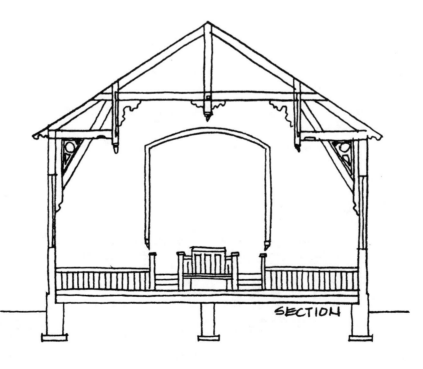

SECTION

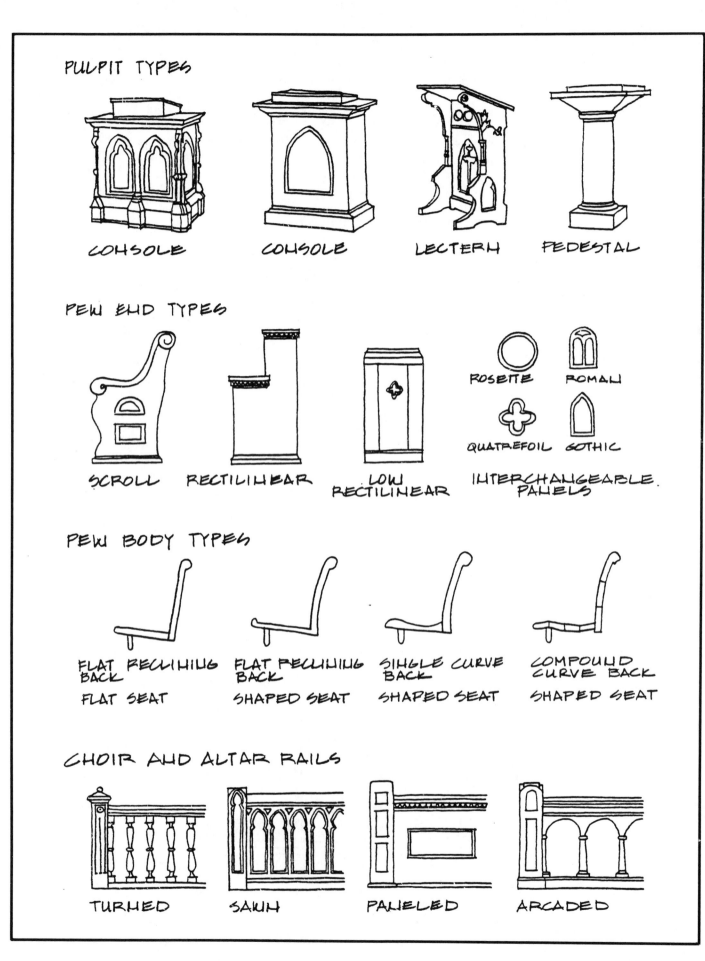

PULPIT TYPES

CONSOLE CONSOLE LECTERN PEDESTAL

PEW END TYPES

SCROLL RECTILINEAR LOW RECTILINEAR

ROSETTE ROMAN
QUATREFOIL GOTHIC
INTERCHANGEABLE PANELS

PEW BODY TYPES

FLAT RECLINING BACK
FLAT SEAT

FLAT RECLINING BACK
SHAPED SEAT

SINGLE CURVE BACK
SHAPED SEAT

COMPOUND CURVE BACK
SHAPED SEAT

CHOIR AND ALTAR RAILS

TURNED SAWN PANELED ARCADED

402

Bibliography

Parentheses ( ) following a title indicate that the cover title is different from the title page.

Extension Service, Government, and University Bulletins

Bailey, L. H. "Tasteful Farm Buildings." *Cornell Reading Course for Farmers*, Series VI, No. 26. Ithaca, N.Y.: College of Agriculture of Cornell University, Nov. 1905.

Bane, Geneva M., and H. P. Twitchell. *Just Kitchens*. Extension Bulletin, Vol. 20, No. 2. Columbus, Ohio: Agricultural Extension Service, Ohio State University, 1924–25.

———. *Just Kitchens*. Bulletin No. 66. Columbus, Ohio: Ohio State University Agriculture Extension Service, (Oct. 1927).

Barrows, Effie S. *Rural Kitchen Improvement*. Extension Service New Series, Circular No. 9. Logan, Utah: Extension Service, Utah Agricultural College, April 1928.

Conway, Mary Geneva. *Make the Farm Kitchen Convenient*. Publication 71. Knoxville, Tenn.: Division of Extension, College of Agriculture, University of Tennessee, Aug. 1918.

"Decoration in the Farm Home." *Cornell Reading—Course for Farmers' Wives*, Series I, No. 2. Ithaca, N.Y.: College of Agriculture of Cornell University, Dec. 1902.

Etherton, W. A. *Inexpensive Plumbing for Farm Kitchens*. Extension Bulletin No. 9. Manhattan, Kan.: Kansas State Agricultural College, Division of College Extension, April 1916.

Fenton, F. C., and H. E. Stover. *Farm Lighting*. Extension Bulletin 64. Manhattan, Kansas: Kansas State Agricultural College, Extension Service, June 1929.

———. *Wiring the Farmstead*. Extension Bulletin 63, revised. Manhattan, Kansas: Kansas State College of Agriculture and Applied Science, Extension Service, May 1938.

Frazier, F. F. *Sewage Disposal for Country Homes*. Extension Bulletin No. 6. Manhattan, Kansas: Kansas State Agricultural College, Division of College Extension, March 1916.

Gettemy, Winifred S. *Home Furnishing*. Extension Bulletin No. 17. Ames, Iowa: Iowa State College of Agriculture and the Mechanic Arts, Dec. 1913.

Goeppinger, Helen. "Walls and Wall Treatments." *Home Information*, Bulletin No. 8. Lafayette, Ind.: Better Homes in America, Purdue University, April 1936.

"Good Lighting in Houses." *Home Information*, Vol. 2, No. 30.

Lafayette, Ind.: Better Homes in America, Purdue University, June 1937.

Hoffman, Gertrude. *The Kitchen*. No. 75. Bozeman, Mont.: Montana Extension Service in Agriculture and Home Economics, Montana State College, Aug. 1925.

Holman, Araminta. *Art Applied in Home Furnishing and Decorating*. Extension Bulletin 43. Manhattan, Kan.: Extension Service, Kansas State Agricultural College, June 1923.

Keller, Lillian L. *The Country Home of Good Taste*. Publication 183. Knoxville, Tenn.: Agricultural Extension Service, University of Tennessee, Feb. 1934.

———. *The Living Room that is Livable*. Publication 134. Knoxville, Tenn.: Tennessee Extension Service, University of Tennessee, Dec. 1925.

———. *The Well Planned Kitchen*. Publication 202. Knoxville, Tenn.: College of Agriculture, University of Tennessee, Feb. 1937.

———, and M. M. Johns. *Farm Home Electrification*. Publication 198. Knoxville, Tenn.: Tennessee College of Agriculture, University of Tennessee, Feb. 1937.

Long, Marian. "Interior Decoration." *College Bulletin*, No. 78. Denton, Tex.: College of Industrial Arts, June 1, 1920.

Lynn, Gertrude. *The Step Saving Kitchen*. Home Economics Bulletin No. 47. Ames, Iowa: Iowa State College of Agriculture and Mechanic Arts, Extension Service, June 1924.

Martin, Clarence A. "The Plan of the Farmhouse." *Cornell Reading—Course for Farmers*, Series VI, No. 28. Ithaca, N.Y.: College of Agriculture of Cornell University, Jan. 1906.

"A Month of Education Study." *Cornell Reading—Course for Farmers' Wives*, Series VI, No. 27. Ithaca, N.Y.: New York State College of Agriculture at Cornell University, Jan. 1908.

Osmund, I. Thornton. *The Lighting of Farm Houses*. Bulletin No. 103. College Park, Penn.: Pennsylvania State College Agricultural Experiment Station, Sept. 1910.

Planning and Equipping the Kitchen. Home Economics Bulletin No. 8. Ames, Iowa: Iowa State College of Agriculture and Mechanic Arts, Extension Service, reprint Aug. 1923.

"Planning the Electrical Installation for Greatest Use." *Home Information*, Vol. 2, No. 29. Lafayette, Ind.: Better Homes in America, Purdue University, May 1937.

Pond, Julia, and Evelyn Turner. *Household Closets and Storage Spaces*. Extension Bulletin No. 142. East Lansing, Mich.: Extension Division, Michigan State College of Agriculture and Applied Science, Dec. 1934.

Reis, Gertrude. *Color in Home Decoration*. Extension Bulletin No. 169. East Lansing, Mich.: Extension Division, Michigan State College, Nov. 1936.

Richardson, Elsie. *Artistic Windows*. Home Economics Bulletin No. 73. Ames, Iowa: Iowa State College of Agriculture and Mechanic Arts, 2nd reprint, Aug. 1927.

———. *Color and Design in the Home*. Home Furnishing Booklets. Ames, Iowa: Iowa State College Extension Service, June 1928.

———. *Floor Coverings*. Home Economics Bulletin No. 87.

Ames, Iowa: Iowa State College of Agriculture and Mechanic Arts, Extension Service, Dec. 1925.

———. *Furnishing the Home*. Home Economics Bulletin No. 42. Ames, Iowa: Iowa State College of Agriculture and Mechanic Arts, Extension Service, April 1924.

Scott, Helen. *Home Decoration*. Extension Bulletin, Vol. IX, No. 10. Columbus, Ohio: Agricultural College, Ohio State University, June 1914.

Smith, L. J., Rudolph Weaver, and M. Minerva Lawrence. *Convenient Farm Homes*. Bulletin No. 91. Pullman, Wash.: Extension Service, State College of Washington, Sept. 1922.

Suggestions for Rural Housing Planning. Bulletin No. 102. Bozeman, Mont.: Extension Service, Montana State College, June 1929.

Ulmer, C. Paul. "Description and Cost Analysis of a House Built of Reinforced Concrete: House No. 3, Purdue Housing Research Project." *Home Information*, Vol. 1, No. 23 and 24. Lafayette, Ind.: Better Homes in America, Purdue University, Dec. 1936.

Walters, John Daniel. *The Water Supply of the Farmhouse*. Extension Bulletin No. 10. Manhattan, Kan.: Kansas State Agricultural College, Division of College Extension, April 1916.

Ward, Walter G. *Farm Buildings for Kansas*. Extension Bulletin No. 50. Manhattan, Kan.: Extension Service, Kansas State Agricultural College, Jan. 1925.

Wilder, Susan Z. *New Wall Finishes*. Circular 231. Brookings, S.D.: Extension Service, South Dakota State College of Agriculture and Mechanical Arts, Nov. 1925.

———. *Planning the Living Room*. Extension Circular 228. Brookings, S.D.: Extension Service, South Dakota State College of Agriculture and Mechanic Arts, Aug. 1925.

Wilson, Elmira T. *Modern Conveniences for the Farm Home*. Farmer's Bulletin No. 270. Washington, D.C.: U.S. Dept. of Agriculture, 1906.

Young, Helen Binkerd. "The Arrangement of Household Furnishings." *Cornell Reading—Courses*, Vol. IV, No. 85, Farmhouse Series No. 7. Ithaca, N.Y.: New York State College of Agriculture at Cornell University, April 1, 1915.

———. "The Farmhouse." *Cornell Reading—Courses Lesson for the Farm Home*, Vol. II, No. 39, Farmhouse Series No. 6. Ithaca, N.Y.: Cornell University, May 1, 1913.

———. "Household Decoration." *Cornell Reading—Courses Lesson for the Farm Home*, Vol. I, No. 5, Farm House Series No. 1. Ithaca, N.Y.: New York State College of Agriculture at Cornell University, Dec. 1, 1911.

———. "Household Furnishing." *Cornell Reading—Courses for the Farm Home*, Vol. I, No. 7, Farm House Series No. 2. Ithaca, N.Y.: New York State College of Agriculture at Cornell University, Jan. 1, 1912.

———. "Planning the Home Kitchen." *Cornell Reading—Courses for the Farm Home*, Farmhouse Series, Lesson 108. Ithaca, N.Y.: New York State College of Agriculture at Cornell University, July 1916.

General Works

Adler, Hazel H. *The New Interior*. New York: Century Co., 1916.

Architectural Interiors. Scranton, Pa.: International Textbook Co., 1931.

Bevier, Isabel. *The House: Its Plan, Decoration and Care*. Chicago: American School of Home Economics, 1907.

Brabham, Moklson William. *Planning Modern Church Buildings*. Nashville: Cokesbury Press, 1928.

Bruce, Alfred, and Harold Sandbank. *A History of Prefabrication*. Research Study 3. New York: John B. Pierce Foundation, 1944.

Brunner, Arnold W., and Thomas Tryon. *Interior Decoration*. New York: W. T. Comstock, 1887.

Caldwell, Frank C. *Modern Lighting*. New York: Macmillan Co., 1930.

Child, Georgie Boynton. *The Efficient Kitchen*. New York: McBride, Nast and Co., 1914.

———. *The Efficient Kitchen*. New York: Robert M. McBride, 1925.

Clute, Eugene. *The Treatment of Interiors*. New York: Pencil Points Press, 1926.

Coleman, Oliver. *Successful Houses*. Chicago: Herbert S. Stone and Co., 1899.

———. *Successful Houses*. New York: Fox Duffield and Co., 1906.

The Cost of Making A Settler's Home in the Famous Kern Delta. Bakersfield, Calif.: Kern County Land Co., n.d.

Crane, Caroline Bartlett. *Everyman's House*. Garden City, N.Y.: Doubleday, Page and Co., 1925.

Crane, Ross. *The Ross Crane Book of Home Furnishing and Decoration*. Chicago: Frederick J. Drake and Co., 1925.

Daniels, Fred Hamilton. *The Furnishing of a Modest Home*. Worcester, Mass.: Davis Press, 1908.

Eastlake, Charles L. *Hints on Household Taste*. Boston: James R. Osgood and Co., 1878. Reprint, New York: Dover Publications, 1986.

Eberlein, Harold Donaldson, Abbott McClure, and Edward Stratton Holloway. *The Practical Book of Interior Decoration*. Philadelphia: J. B. Lippincott Co., 1919.

———, and Donald G. Tarpley. *Remodeling and Adapting the Small House*. Philadelphia: J. B. Lippincott, 1933.

Ellis, Mary Heard, and Raymond Everett. *The Planning of Simple Homes*. Austin, Texas: University of Texas, 1916.

Ellis, Raymond A. *When You Build*. New York: Woman's Home Companion, 1920.

Ferro, Maximilian L., and Melissa L. Cook. *Electric Wiring and Lighting in Historic American Buildings*. New Bedford, Mass.: Preservation Partnership and AFC/A Nortek Co., 1984.

Frohne, Henry W., Alice F. Jackson, and Bettina Jackson. *Color Schemes for the Homes and Model Interiors*. Grand Rapids, Mich.: Dean-Hicks Co., 1919.

Gardner, E. C. *Home Interiors*. Boston: James R. Osgood and Co., 1878.

Gardner, F. B. *Everybody's Paint Book*. New York: M. T. Richardson, 1888.

Garner, John S. *The Model Company Town*. Amherst, Mass.: University of Massachusetts Press, 1984.

Gibson, Louis H. *Convenient Houses with Fifty Plans for the Housekeeper*. New York: Thomas Y. Crowell and Co., 1889.

Godinez, F. Laurent. *The Lighting Book*. New York: McBride, Nast and Co., 1913.

Goodnow, Ruby Ross. *The Honest House*. New York: Century Co., 1914.

Gray, Greta. *House and Home: A Manual and Text-Book of Practical House Planning*. Philadelphia: J. B. Lippincott Co., 1923.

Grow, Lawrence, ed. *Old House Plans*. New York: Universe Books, 1978.

Hellyer, S. Stevens. *The Plumber and Sanitary Houses*. 3rd ed. London: B. T. Batsford, 1884.

The Home. Supplement Given with Year's Subscription to *Woman's Weekly*. (n.p.): Magazine Circulation Co., 1922.

Home Building and Furnishing. New York: Doubleday, Page and Co., 1903.

The House Beautiful Furnishing Annual 1926. Boston: Atlantic Monthly Co., 1925.

Illsley, Charles E. *House Planning at Home; A Practical Manual for Self-Instruction for Members of Building Associations and Others*. St. Louis: C. B. Woodward Co., 1894.

Jennings, Arthur Seymour. *The Decoration and Renovation of the Home*. London: W. R. Howell and Co., 1923.

———. *Wallpapers and Wall Coverings*. New York: William T. Comstock, 1903.

Kellogg, Alice M. *Home Furnishing, Practical and Artistic*. New York: Frederick A. Stokes Co., 1905.

Luckiesh, M. *Lighting Fixtures and Lighting Effects*. New York: McGraw-Hill Book Co., 1925.

———. *Lighting the Home*. New York: Century Co., 1920.

McClelland, Nancy. *The Practical Book of Decorative Wall-Treatments*. Philadelphia: J. B. Lippincott Co., 1926.

Martin, Ray C. *Glossary of Paint, Varnish, Lacquer and Allied Terms*. St. Louis: American Paint Journal Co., 1937.

Mayhew, Edgar de N., and Minor Myers, Jr. *A Documentary History of American Interiors—From the Colonial Era to 1915*. New York: Charles Scribner's Sons, 1980.

Meloy, Arthur S. *Theatres and Motion Picture Houses*. New York: Architects' Supply and Pub. Co., 1916.

Myers, Denys Peter. *Gaslighting in America: A Guide for Historic Preservation*. Washington, D.C.: U.S. Department of the Interior, 1978.

Nylander, Richard C. *Wall Papers for Historic Buildings*. Washington, D.C.: Preservation Press, National Trust for Historic Preservation, 1983.

Parsons, Frank Alvah. *The Art of Home Furnishing and Dec-*

oration. Lancaster, Penn.: Armstrong Cork Co. Linoleum Dept., 1918.

———. *Interior Decoration*. New York: Doubleday, 1915.

Peterson, Charles E., ed. *Building Early America: Contributions toward the History of a Great Industry*. The Carpenters' Company of the City and County of Philadelphia. Radnor, Penn.: Chilton Book Co., 1976.

President's Conference on Home Building and Home Ownership. Committee on Farm and Village Housing. *Farm and Village Housing*. Washington, D.C.: n.p., 1932.

Rapoport, Amos. *House Form and Culture*. Englewood Cliffs, N.J.: Prentice-Hall, 1969.

Representative Plans for Farm Houses. Extract from a report submitted to the President's Conference on Home Building and Home Ownership by the Committee on Farm and Village Housing. N.p.: U.S. Dept. of Agriculture, Dec. 1931.

Robinson, L. Eugene. *Domestic Architecture*. New York: Macmillan Co., 1917.

Rolfe, Amy L. *Interior Decoration for the Small Home*. New York: Macmillan Co., 1917.

———. *Interior Decoration for the Small Home*. New York: Macmillan Co., 1924.

Sabin, Alvah Horton. *House Painting*. New York: John Wiley and Sons, 1918.

———. *The Industrial and Artistic Technology of Paint and Varnish*. New York: John Wiley and Sons, 1905.

Seal, Ethel Davis. *The House of Simplicity*. New York: Century Co., 1926.

Sell, Maud Ann, and Henry Blackman Sell. *Good Taste in Home Furnishing*. New York: John Lane Co., 1915.

Stansky, Peter, and Shewan, Rodney, eds. *The Aesthetic Movement and the Arts and Crafts Movement*. New York: Garland Publishing Co., 1978.

Sugden, Alan Victor, and Edmondson, John Ludlam. *A History of English Wallpaper, 1509–1915*. New York: Charles Scribner's Sons, 1925.

Sutherland, W. G. *Modern Wall Decoration*. Manchester, England: Decorative Art Journals Co., 1893.

Throop, Lucy Abbot. *Furnishing the Home of Good Taste*. New York: McBride, Nast and Co., 1912.

Tralle, Henry Edward. *Planning Church Buildings*. Philadelphia: Judson Press, 1921.

Varney, Almon C. *Our Homes and Their Adornments: Or How to Build, Finish, Furnish, and Adorn a Home*. Detroit: J. C. Chilton and Co., 1882.

Vieyra, Daniel I. *"Fill 'er Up"*. New York: Collier Macmillan Publishers, 1979.

Vollmer, William A., ed. *A Book of Distinctive Interiors*. New York: McBride, Nast and Co., 1912.

Waite, Diana S., ed. *Architectural Elements, The Technological Review*. The American Historical Catalog Collection. Princeton, N.J.: Pyne Press, 1972.

Wangner, Ellen D. *The American Home Book of Kitchens*. Garden City, N.Y.: Doubleday, Doran and Co., 1931.

Warner, Sam B., Jr. *Streetcar Suburbs: The Process of Growth in Boston*. Cambridge, Mass.: Harvard University Press and M.I.T. Press, 1962.

Wheeler, Candace. *Principles of Home Decoration*. New York: Doubleday, Page and Co., 1903.

White, Charles E. *The Bungalow Book*. New York: Macmillan Co., 1923.

White, Charles E., Jr. *Successful Houses and How to Build Them*. New York: Macmillan Co., 1914.

Winter, Robert. *The California Bungalow*. Los Angeles: Hennessey and Ingalls, Inc., 1980.

Wright, Richardson, ed. *House and Garden's Book of Color Schemes*. New York: Condé Nast Publications, (ca. 1929).

————. *House and Garden's Book of Houses*. New York: C. Nast and Co., 1920.

————. *House and Garden's Book of Interiors*. New York: C. Nast and Co., 1920.

————. *House and Garden's Complete Guide to Interior Decoration*. New York: Simon and Schuster, 1942.

————. *House and Garden's Second Book of Houses*. New York: Condé Nast Publications, 1925.

————. *Inside the House of Good Taste*. New York: Robert M. McBride and Co., 1922.

Your Wallpaper Tells Who You Are. New York: Wallpaper Guild of America, (ca. 1923).

Handbooks and Dictionaries

The Architects' and Builders' Reference Book. Chicago: Oscar M. Smith and Co., 1889.

Blackburn, Graham. *Illustrated Interior Carpentry*. Indianapolis, Ind.: Bobbs-Merrill Co., 1978.

Burbank, Nelson L. *Carpentry and Joinery Work*. New York: American Builder Publishing Corp., 1936.

Burke, Arthur E., J. Ralph Dalzell, and Gilbert Townsend. *Architectural and Building Trades Dictionary*. Chicago: American Technical Society, 1950.

Carpenter, J. H. *Hints on Building*. Hartford, Conn.: Case, Lockwood, and Brainard Co., 1883.

The Complete House Builder with Hints on Building. Chicago: Donohue, Henneberry and Co., 1890.

Corkhill, Thomas. *A Glossary of Wood*. London: Nema Press, 1948.

Ellis, George. *Modern Practical Carpentry*. 2nd ed. London: B. T. Batsford, 1915.

————. *Modern Practical Joinery*. London: B. T. Batsford, 1908.

Fleming, John, Hugh Honor, and Nikolaus Pevsner. *The Penguin Dictionary of Architecture*. Baltimore: Penguin Books, 1966.

Gwilt, Joseph. *Encyclopedia of Architecture*. Aberdeen: Aberdeen University Press, 1912.

Harris, Cyril M., ed. *Dictionary of Architecture and Construction*. New York: McGraw-Hill Book Co., 1975.

————. *Historic Architecture Sourcebook*. New York: McGraw-Hill Book Co., 1977.

Hodgson, Fred T. *The Carpenter's Cyclopedia*. For Sears, Roebuck and Co. Chicago: Frederick J. Drake, 1913.

———. *Common-Sense Stair Building and Handrailing*. (*Common Sense Hand-Railing, Modern Staircases*.) Chicago: Frederick J. Drake and Co., 1903.

Kidder, Frank E., and Harry Parker. *Kidder-Parker Architects' and Builders' Handbook*. 18th ed. New York: John Wiley and Sons, 1942.

Lloyd, William B. *Millwork: Principles and Practices*. Chicago: Cahners Publishing Co. and The National Woodwork Manufacturers Assoc., 1966.

Quin, Charles, W. *The Complete House Builder with Hints on Building*. Chicago: M. A. Donohue, 1904.

Radford, William A. *Practical Carpentry*. Vol. II. For Sears, Roebuck and Co. Chicago: Radford Architectural Co., 1907.

———. *The Steel Square and Its Uses*. Vols. I and II. For Sears, Roebuck and Co. Chicago: Radford Architectural Co., 1913.

Saylor, Henry H. *Dictionary of Architecture*. New York: John Wiley and Sons, 1952.

Scott, John S. *The Penguin Dictionary of Building*. New York: Penguin Books, 1964.

Sturgis, Russell. *A Dictionary of Architecture and Building*. New York: Macmillan Co., 1902.

Sylvester, W. A. *The Modern House-Carpenter's Companion and Builder's Guide*. Subscription ed., 7th Thousand. Boston: W. A. Sylvester, 1883.

Whiton, Sherrill. *Elements of Interior Design and Decoration*. Philadelphia: J. B. Lippincott Co., 1951.

Monographs and Articles

Alderson, Caroline. "Re-Creating a 19th Century Paint Palette." *APT Bulletin* 16, No. 1 (1984): 47–56.

Alto, J. E. "A Plea for Painted Walls." *American Homes*, Sept. 1900, pp. 562–63.

Armagnac, A. S. "Heating Steps Forward." *Building Age* 51 (April 1929): 136–37.

"Artistic Fronts for Small Business Buildings." *Building Age* 39 (Dec. 1917): 675–77

Baker, Henry G. "Hardware for Good Buildings." *Building Age* 51 (April 1929): 154–55.

Bigsby, J. M. "American Kitchens Glorified Too." *Building Age* 51 (April 1929): 142–43.

———. "Built-In Features and Furniture That Make Modernizing Desired." *Building Age* 51 (Jan. 1929): 68–69.

Bishop, C. H. "Plumbing—Sanitation Plus." *Building Age* 51 (April 1929): 138–39.

Blackman, Leo, and Deborah Dietsch. "A New Look at Linoleum." *Old House Journal*, Jan. 1982, pp. 9–12.

Bond, Alexander. "Floors Keep Step with Progress." *Building Age* 51 (April 1929): 116–17.

Bradbury, Bruce. "Anaglypta and Other Embossed Wallcoverings—Their History and Use Today." *Old House Journal*, Nov. 1982, pp. 231–34.

———. "A Layman's Guide to Historic Wallpaper Reproduction." *APT Bulletin* 16, No. 1 (1984): 57–58.

———. "Lincrusta–Walton—Can the Democratic Wallcoverings Be Revived?" *Old House Journal*, Oct. 1982, pp. 203–7.

Brownfield, Marion. "The Cozy Kitchen Nook." *Keith's Magazine*, March 1924, pp. 114–15.

———. "The Latest Ideas for the Kitchen." *Keith's Magazine*, Nov. 1924, pp. 221–23.

"Builders' Reference and Checking List: Large Buildings." *American Builder*, June 1925, pp. 195–203.

"Builders' Reference and Checking List: A Specification Guide for All Classes of Buildings." *American Builder*, June 1925, pp. 189–94.

"Building Bungalows." *Carpentry and Building* 26 (July 1904): 222.

Butterfield, Emily H. "A Family Kitchen." *Keith's Magazine*, Nov. 1923, pp. 208–9.

Byers, Charles Alma. "Concerning Modern Bedrooms." *Keith's Magazine*, Jan. 1923, pp. 11–15.

———. "Fireplaces That Add Beauty to the Home." *Building Age* 41 (June 1919): 186–87.

———. "Planning the Fireside Corner." *Keith's Magazine*, Dec. 1915, pp. 375–78.

———. "Practical Sleeping Porches." *Keith's Magazine*, July 1923, pp. 10–13.

Campbell, C. J. "Electrify All Buildings: Wiring the Home for Comfort." *American Builder*, April 1924, pp. 171, 172, 174, 176.

Clausen, Arthur C. "Construction Details of the Home—Built-In Sideboards." *Keith's Magazine*, Dec. 1911, pp. 382–85.

"Construction Details of the Home—The Bathroom." *Keith's Magazine*, Feb. 1912, pp. 93–95.

"Construction Details of the Home—Built-In Pantries." *Keith's Magazine*, Jan. 1912, pp. 20–23.

"Construction Details of the Home—Entrances, Front and Interior Doors, Advantages of Sidelights." *Keith's Magazine*, Sept. 1911, pp. 160–63.

"Construction Details of the Home—Windows, Their Location and Design." *Keith's Magazine*, Nov. 1911, pp. 230–33.

Coppes, D. W. "Lighting Your Home." *Beautiful Homes Magazine*, Sept. 1930, pp. 6–9.

"Creating Better Store Architecture." *Building Age and the Builder's Journal*, Oct. 1922, p. 30.

"Designs for Wood Ceilings." *Carpentry and Building* 1 (Feb. 1879): 21–22.

"Designs of Sash and Solid Partitions." *Building Age* 34 (June 1912): 307–8.

"Dining Room Mantel and Mirror." *Carpentry and Building* 2 (Nov. 1880): 201–3.

"Door Hardware Should be Selected for Its Permanence as Well as for Its Beauty." *Keith's Beautiful Homes Magazine*, May 1929, pp. 204–6.

Dunlea, Nancy D. "The New Home Hardware." *Keith's Magazine* 53 (May 1925): 230–31.

Ednie, John. "The Decoration of a City House." *House Beautiful*, Dec. 1903, pp. 34–42.

"Electrify All Buildings: The Electrical Home Efficient." *American Builder*, May 1924, pp. 184, 186, 190, 192.

"The Equipment of the Ideal Home." (The Muncie Star) *Better American Homes Almanac and Year-Book for 1923*. Chicago: American Homes Bureau, 1922, pp. 3–14.

"Fireplace Treatments." *Keith's Magazine*, Jan.–Dec. 1908, n.p.

"Foster-Munger Hard Wood Mantels." *Carpentry and Building* 22 (Jan. 1900): xii.

Fox, C. J. "Ornamental Tile Work." *Carpentry and Building* 29 (Oct. 1907): 331–32.

Frangiamore, Catherine Lynn. *Wallpapers in Historic Preservation*. Washington, D.C.: National Park Service, Technical Preservation Services, 1977.

"Fully Rented Before Completion." *American Builder*, Nov. 1933, p. 44.

"Furnishing and Decorating the Home." *Modern Homes*, June–July 1914, p. 9.

Garvin, James L. "Mail-Order House Plans and American Victorian Architecture." *Winterthur Portfolio* 16 (1981): 309–34.

Gerth, Ruth L. "The Dining Room." *Keith's Magazine*, Oct. 1923, pp. 155–59.

Hale, O. H. "Outlets Outlaw Housework." *Building Age* 51 (April 1929): 140–41.

"Halls and Entrances." *Home Decoration*, April 17, 1886, p. 89.

Harris, Ralph G. "Hot Water Systems in the Home." *American Builder*, June 1922, pp. 119–21.

Hart, Arthur A. "M. A. Disbrow & Company: Catalogue Architecture." *The Palimpsest* 20, No. 4 (July–Aug. 1975): 98–119.

Harvey, L. H. "Effective Design with Wallboard." *Building Age* 41 (Aug. 1919): 266–67.

———. "How Wallboard Was Used in Remodeling an Old Home." *Building Age* 40 (Dec. 1918): 552–54.

Harvey, Thomas. "Mail-Order Architecture in the Twenties." *Landscape* 25, No. 3 (1981): 1–9.

Harwood, Buie. "Stencilling: Interior Architectural Ornamentation." *Journal of Interior Design Education and Research* 12 (Spring 1986): 31–40.

Higbie, H. H. "Good Lighting Adds to Comfort and Charm in the Home." *Beautiful Homes Magazine*, Dec. 1929, pp. 167–69, 187.

Hill, Amelia Leavitt. "The Sunroom." *Keith's Magazine*, May 1924, pp. 248–51.

Hill, W. R. "Door Hardware for the Modern Home." *Building Age* 41 (Aug. 1919): 253–54.

Hillen, R. C. "Designing a Store in a Residential District to Have Same Characteristics and General Appearance of a Home." *The Home Designer*, Sept. 1921, p. 69.

"Hints on Home Adornment, Number Four." *Godey's Lady's Book and Magazine* 96, No. 574 (1878): 350–51.

Hubka, Thomas C. "In the Vernacular: Classifying American Folk and Popular Architecture." *The Forum*, 7, No. 2 (Dec. 1985), n.p. Insert in *Newsletter, The Society of Architectural Historians*, 30, No. 1 (Feb. 1986).

"Interior Decoration: Suggestions for the Hall, Dining Room, Bedrooms, Etc." *Shoppell's Homes, Decorations, Gardens*, Jan. 1907, pp. 14–18.

"Japanese Lattice-Work." *Carpentry and Building* 8 (July 1886): 123–25.

Johnson, Louise H. "Our Bedroom." *Keith's Magazine*, April 1919, pp. 245–48.

Kauffman, Elizabeth Macy. "Wooden Walls Again." *Your Home*, Nov. 1929, pp. 45–47, 70.

Kingsley, K. S. "What Makes a House Colonial?" *Building Age* 51 (Aug. 1929): 66–67.

"The Kinnear Improved Steel Ceiling." *Carpentry and Building* 21 (Jan. 1899): xiv.

Kraft, Gertrude. "Looking at the Ceiling." *Beautiful Homes Magazine*, Jan. 1931, pp. 23–26.

Kupsinel, Morgan M. "Interior Architectural Millwork Components in the Plains States (1900–1930)." Thesis, University of Nebraska, 1980.

Lancaster, Clay. "The American Bungalow." *The Art Bulletin* 40 (Sept. 1958): 239–53.

Lawall, G. R. "Bringing Light to the Kitchen." *Keith's Magazine*, March 1923, pp. 134, 136.

———. "Lighting the Dining Room." *Keith's Magazine*, June 1923, pp. 284, 286.

———. "Luminaires for the Living Room," *Keith's Magazine*, Oct. 1923, pp. 182–84.

"Lincrusta-Walton." *Carpentry and Building* 5 (Feb. 1883): 30.

Luckey, Gertrude Appleton. "Breakfast Alcoves." *Keith's Magazine*, April 1917, pp. 242–45.

"Mantels, Tiles and Grates." *The National Builder*, Oct. 1887, pp. 50–51.

Marlatt, Abby L. "Consider the Housewife First!" *American Builder and Building Age*, March 1933, pp. 16–17, 50, 52.

Martin, John Howard. "The Overmantel and Fireplace." *Keith's Magazine*, Feb. 1920, pp. 68–70.

"Modern Builders Hardware." *American Carpenter and Builder*, April 1911, p. 41.

"Modernized Store Buildings Get the Trade." *American Builder*, June 1925, pp. 233–35.

"The Modern Kitchen—Most Important Room in the House." *American Builder and Building Age*, March 1933, p. 15.

"The Modern Living Room." *Modern Homes*, Feb. 1915, pp. 5, 21.

"Mosaics." *American Homes*, Oct. 1900, pp. 621–25.

"Mosaic Vestibule Tiling." *Carpentry and Building* 8 (Nov. 1886): 210.

National Park Service. *The Preservation of Historic Pigmented*

Structural Glass (Vitrolite and Carrara Glass). Preservation Brief 12. Washington, D.C.: Dept. of Interior, Feb. 1984.

Newberry, Mary. "A Model Bath-Room." *House Beautiful*, July 1904, pp. 21–22.

"New Factory-Finished Flooring at Low Price." *American Builder*, Dec. 1932, p. 37.

"1930 Trend of Style." *American Builder*, Feb. 1930, pp. 85–92.

"1936 Building Outlook BEST in Years." *American Builder and Building Age* 58, No. 1 (Jan. 1936): 28–31, 74.

Northend, Mary H. "The Dining Room As It Should Be." *Keith's Magazine*, Feb. 1911, pp. 76–82.

———. "The Impression of the Hall." *Keith's Magazine*, Oct. 1911, pp. 220–25.

Oren, E. M. "The Wide Range of Textured Wall Finishes." *American Builder*, June 1927, pp. 114–15.

Otter, Paul D. "Built-In Furniture That Adds Convenience to the Home." *The Building Age* 40 (April 1918): 184.

———. "Embossing on Wood." *Carpentry and Building* 21 (June 1899): 151.

"Painting Floors." *Carpentry and Building* 8 (July 1886): 128.

Parsons, D. J. C. "Tiling the House." *Keith's Beautiful Homes Magazine*, Sept. 1929, pp. 80–82, 95.

Parsons, Frederick. "Modern House Decoration—Part I: Decorative Wall Coverings." *The Western Painter*, April 1896, pp. 165–79.

Pickett, A. D. "Tile Floors and Tile Walls." *Building Age* 51 (April 1929): 112–13.

Pillsbury, Richard. "Patterns in the Folk and Vernacular House Forms of the Pennsylvania Culture Region." *Pioneer America* 9, No. 1 (July 1977): 12–31.

"Planning the Modern Kitchen." *American Builder and Building Age*, March 1933, pp. 18–20.

Powell, A. W., and H. A. Smith. "Better Illumination for Bedroom and Bath." *American Builder*, Sept. 1922, pp. 100–2.

———. "Improved Illumination for the Dining Room." *American Builder*, Aug. 1922, pp. 98–100.

———. "Trend of Electric Fixture Design in Modern Home." *American Builder*, June 1922, pp. 102–4, 150.

———. "Trend of Electric Fixture Design in Modern Home." *American Builder*, July 1922, pp. 104–7.

"Queen Anne Sideboard and Mantel." *Carpentry and Building* 1 (Jan. 1879): 19.

Randall, Kate. "The Modern Kitchen." *Keith's Magazine*, Oct. 1912, pp. 250–52.

Reedy, William B. "The Rooms in the House: The Bedroom." *American Builder*, April 1922, pp. 86–87.

"Restyling Main Street for the New Deal in Beverages." *American Builder and Building Age*, April 1933, pp. 32–33.

Romanoff, Victoria, and Sarah W. Adams. *New York State Storefronts*. Trumansburg, N.Y.: Tompkins Co., n.d.

Sakier, George. "Permanent Floor Coverings—A Review." *House and Garden*, Feb. 1935, pp. 37–39, 69.

Sautter House Five, Wallpapers of a German-American Farmstead. Omaha, Neb.: Papillion Area Historical Society and Douglas County Historical Society, 1983.

Scofield, Merle. "Achieving an Harmonious Interior." *The Home Designer*, Nov. 1921, pp. 147, 157.

Sexton, R. W. "A Successfully Planned Business Center." *American Builder*, Jan. 1935, pp. 36–37.

"Sheet-Metal Ceiling." *Carpentry and Building* 8 (Oct. 1886): 188–89.

"Sheet Metal in Interior Decoration." *Carpentry and Building* 22 (March 1900): 69, 70; (April 1900): 117–19; (July 1900): 201–2.

"The Sleeping Porch is Now Considered Indispensable." *Modern Homes*, Dec. 1914, p. 7.

"Some California Bungalows." *The Architectural Record* 18 (Sept. 1905): 217–23.

"Some Characteristics of the California Bungalow." *Carpentry and Building* 29 (Feb. 1907): 53.

Sovereign, O. E. "The Readi-Cut Structure Demands Attention of the Home Owner." *Modern Homes*, March 1915, pp. 14–15.

Sterling, Florence J. "What Comprises a '100% Modern Kitchen'?" *American Builder and Building Age*, Jan. 1931, pp. 94–95.

Stewart, Ross E. "Millwork and Interior Finish, The Elements that Produce Satisfactory Work." *The American Architect* 127 (June 1925): 519–20.

Stillwell, E. W. "What is a Genuine Bungalow?" *Keith's Magazine*, April 1916, pp. 273–91.

Stowell, Kenneth K. "Today's Home, Looking Backward—and Ahead." *Building Age* 51 (April 1929): 89–91.

"Style Review—New and Tested Products." *American Builder and Building Age*, April 1933, pp. 14–19, 56, 58.

"Suggested Treatment of Wall Spaces in Suburban Homes." *Building Age* 34 (Aug. 1912): 413.

Swiatosz, Susan. "A Technical History of Late Nineteenth Century Windows in the United States." *APT Bulletin* 17, No. 1 (1985): 31–37.

Taylor, John. "Interior Decoration." *Keith's Magazine*, Feb. 1908, pp. 74–75.

Teasdale, O. R. "Wood for Fine Interiors." *Building Age* 51 (April 1929): 114–15.

"The Tendency in Home Architecture." *Carpentry and Building* 22 (June 1900): 165.

"Twenty-five Years." *American Builder*, April 1930, pp. 87–88.

"Wall Decorations—Paper Hangings." *Carpentry and Building* 1 (April 1879): 61–62.

"Wall Papers." *Carpentry and Building* 2 (Dec. 1880): 221–24.

"Walls and Ceilings." *Home Decoration*, June 12, 1886, p. 138.

Warren, James. "Standardized Millwork Cuts Costs." *Building Age* 51 (April 1929): 106–7.

"Why Build Stores that Look Like These; When for the Same Money You Can Have Artistic Designs Like These?" *Building Age and National Builder*, June 1926, p. 108.

Williams, E. A. "Bathrooms, Don't Neglect a Single Detail." *Building Age* 51 (Oct. 1929): 58–59, 96.

Worth, John. "Flexible Finishes, Today's Style." *Building Age* 51 (April 1929): 118–19.

Selected Pattern Books/Stock Plans

Cottage Designs with Constructive Details. Carpentry and Building Series, No. 1. New York: David Williams Co., 1897.

Davis, Francis Pierpoint, et al. *Ideal Homes in Garden Communities: A Book of Stock Plans*. 4th ed. New York: Robert M. McBride and Co., 1919.

Hodgson, Fred T. *Modern Carpentry: A Practical Manual*. Vols. I and II. Chicago: Sears, Roebuck and Co., 1917.

Home Plan Book Co. *The Book of Small Homes: 33 Designs*. St. Paul, Minn.: Home Plan Book Co., n.d.

Hopkins, David S. *Houses and Cottages, Book No. 6, A Collection of House and Cottage Designs, Containing 56 Designs Costing from $150 to $1,500*. 4th ed. Grand Rapids, Mich.: D. S. Hopkins, 1897.

Keith, Max Le Roy. *Beautiful Homes, 200 Plans*. Minneapolis, Minn.: Keith Corporation, 1925.

Modern Bungalows. Oklahoma City: Aurelius-Swanson Co., n.d.

Radford, William A. *Modern House-Plans for Everybody*. New York: Orange Judd Co., 1902.

———. *The Radford American Homes: 100 House Plans*. Riverside, Ill.: Radford Architectural Co., 1903.

———. *Radford's Portfolio of Plans*. Chicago: Radford Architectural Co., 1915.

———. *Radford's Stores and Flat Buildings*. Chicago: Radford Architectural Co., 1909.

Saylor, Henry H. *Inexpensive Homes of Individuality*. Vol. 2. New York: McBride, Nast, and Co., 1915.

Smith, Henry Atterbury, ed. *The Book of a Thousand Homes*. New York: Home Owners Institute, 1927.

Woodward, George E., and Edward G. Thompson. *Woodward's National Architect; Containing 100 Original Designs, Plans and Details, to Working Scale, for the Practical Construction of Dwelling Houses for the Country, Suburb and Village*. New York: George E. Woodward, 1869.

Selected Trade Catalogs

Catalog Companies, Stores, and General Supply Houses

Chicago Wrecking House Co. *Catalog No. 160 A, 1909–1910*. Chicago: Chicago Wrecking House Co., 1909.

Harris Brothers Co. *Harris Brothers Co*. Chicago: Harris Brothers Co., 1926.

Home Builders Catalog Co. *Home Builders Catalog*. New York: Home Builders Catalog Co., 1925.

Sears, Roebuck and Co. *1897 Sears Roebuck Catalogue*. General Catalog. Chicago, 1897; reprint, New York: Chelsea House Publishers, 1968.

——. *The Sears, Roebuck Catalogue*. General Catalog. Chicago, 1902; reprint, New York: Crown Publishers, 1969.

——. *Sears, Roebuck and Co. Catalogue, No. 140*. General Catalog. Chicago: Sears, Roebuck and Co., Spring 1920.

"Sweet's" Indexed Catalogue of Building Construction. New York: Architectural Record Co., 1906.

Ceramic Tile

Associated Tile Manufacturers. *Ceramic Mosaic*. Publication No. K-500. Beaver Falls, Penn.: Associated Tile Manufacturers, 1922.

Floors

Armstrong Cork Co., and Agnes Foster Wright. *Floors, Furniture and Color*. Lancaster, Penn.: Armstrong Cork Co., Linoleum Division, 1924.

Armstrong Cork Products. *Pattern Book, 1936, Armstrong's Linoleum. (Armstrong's Linoleum Quaker Rugs Floor Covering, 1936.)* Lancaster, Penn.: Armstrong Cork Products Co., Floor Division, 1936.

Congoleum. *Congoleum Nairn 1942*. N.p.: Congoleum, 1942.

George W. Blabon Co. *Blabon Art Linoleums, Styles for 1921*. Philadelphia: George W. Blabon Co., 1921.

Glass

Macbeth-Evans Glass Co. *Fifty Years of Glass Making, 1869–1919*. Pittsburgh: Macbeth-Evans Glass Co., 1920.

Pittsburgh Plate Glass Co. *Glass, Paints, Varnishes and Brushes—Their History, Manufacture, and Use*. Pittsburgh: Pittsburgh Plate Glass Co., 1923.

——. *Vitrolite Fixtures. Furniture for Restaurants and Drug Stores*. Chicago: Vitrolite Co., 1927.

Hardware

Gardner Hardware Co. *Gardner Hardware Co., Wholesale and Retail, Builders' Hardware and Contractor's Supplies*. Minneapolis, Minn.: Gardner Hardware Co., (ca. 1910).

P. and F. Corbin. *Catalog*. New Britain, Conn.: P. and F. Corbin, 1871.

Reading Hardware Co. *Reading Hardware Company's Illustrated Catalog of Locks and Hardware*. Reading, Penn.: Reading Hardware Co., 1897.

Russell and Erwin Mfg. Co. *Illustrated Catalogue of American Hardware of the Russell and Erwin Manufacturing Company*. New Britain, Conn., 1865; reprint, (n.p.): Assoc. for Preservation Technology, 1980.

Yale and Towne Mfg. Co. *"Yale Products."* Catalog No. 26. Stamford, Conn.: Yale and Towne Mfg. Co., 1929.

——, and Henry R. Towne. *Locks and Builders Hardware*. New York: John Wiley and Sons, 1904.

Heating and Technologies

Allen Mfg. Co. *Sales Plan, Allen's Parlor Furnace.* Nashville, Tenn.: Allen Mfg. Co., n.d.

Burlingame and Darbys Co. *New Perfection Oil Cook Stoves.* North Adams, Mass.: Burlingame and Darbys Co., 1916.

Michigan Radiator and Iron Mfg. Co. *Michigan Radiator and Iron Mfg. Co.* Detroit: Michigan Radiator and Iron Mfg. Co., n.d.

Perfection Stove Co. *Superflex Oil Burning Heaters.* Cleveland, Ohio: Perfection Stove Co., n.d.

Sears, Roebuck and Co. *Book of Stoves.* Chicago: Sears, Roebuck and Co., 1906.

———. *Modern Heating Systems.* Chicago: Sears, Roebuck and Co., 1912.

———. *Modern Plumbing and Heating Systems.* Chicago: Sears, Roebuck and Co., 1924.

———. *Sears Plumbing, Heating, Water Supply.* Chicago: Sears, Roebuck and Co., 1935.

———. *Sears Plumbing, Heating, Water Supply.* Chicago: Sears, Roebuck and Co., 1938.

Lighting

DeKosenko Mfg. Co. *Catalogue No. I. The DeKosenko Manufacturing Co. Electric, Gas, and Combination Fixtures.* (*DeKosenko Manufacturing Co., Catalogue No. I, Electric, Gas and Combination Fixtures.*) Philadelphia: DeKosenko Mfg. Co., n.d.

General Electric Co. *Home Lighting Fundamentals.* Cleveland: General Electric Co., Nela Park Engineering Dept., May 1931.

Moran and Hastings Mfg. Co. *Moran and Hastings Mfg. Co., Catalogue No. 23, Gas Fixtures.* Chicago: Moran and Hastings Mfg. Co., n.d.

Sears, Roebuck and Co. *Electric, Gas and Combination Lighting Fixtures.* Chicago: Sears, Roebuck and Co., 1918.

———. *Lightmaster Lighting Fixture Style Book.* Chicago: Sears, Roebuck and Co., 1938.

Metalwork

Canton Art Metal Co. *Catalog "F": Canton Line Stamped Steel Ceilings.* (*Canton Line Steel Ceilings.*) Canton, Ohio: Canton Art Metal Co., n.d.

Detroit Steel Products Co. *Fenestra Fencraft Casements.* Detroit: Detroit Steel Products Co., 1930.

Garry Iron and Steel Roofing Co. *Catalogue of Garry Iron and Steel Roofing Company.* Cleveland: Garry Iron and Steel Roofing Co., 1892.

St. Paul Roofing, Cornice and Ornament Co. *Section "O"—Steel Ceilings, Paneled and Continuous.* St. Paul, Minn.: St. Paul Roofing, Cornice and Ornament Co., 1904.

Waite, Diana S., ed. *Architectural Elements, The Technological Review.* The American Historical Catalog Collection. Princeton, N.J.: Pyne Press, 1972.

Millwork

Angel Novelty Co. *Angel's New Line of Standardized Woodwork for the Home*. Fitchburg, Mass.: Angel Novelty Co., 1942.

Bardwell-Robinson. *Catalogue of Bardwell-Robinson Co., Wholesale Manufacturers—Windows, Doors, Blinds*. Minneapolis, Minn.: Bardwell-Robinson Co., 1904.

Builders Wood-Working Co. *Built-In Furniture*. Minneapolis, Minn.: Builders Wood-Working Co., 1922.

Carr and Adams. *Illustrated Catalog, 1911–12 Carr and Adams Co*. Des Moines, Iowa: Carr and Adams Co., 1912.

Carr, Ryder and Adams Co. *"Bilt-Well" Millwork, Catalog No. 40*. Minneapolis, Minn.: Carr, Ryder and Adams Co., n.d.

Chicago Millwork Supply Co. *Millwork and Building Material of Guaranteed Quality, Catalog No. 355*. Chicago: Chicago Millwork Supply Co., 1924.

Curtis Brothers. *Book of Designs, 1899*. Clinton, Iowa: Curtis Brothers and Co., 1899.

———. *Curtis Catalog, General Millwork*. Clinton, Iowa: Curtis Brothers and Co., 1914.

Farley and Loetscher Mfg. Co. *Farley and Loetscher Mfg. Co., General Catalog No. 9*. 2nd ed. (*Design Book No. 9, Farley and Loetscher Mfg. Co., Makers of Everything in Millwork*.) Dubuque, Iowa: Farley and Loetscher Mfg. Co., 1912.

Gernet Brothers. *Gernet Bros. Lumber Co*. Louisville, Ken.: Gernet Bros. Lumber Co., 1898.

Gordon-Van Tine Co. *Gordon-Van Tine Co*. Davenport, Iowa: Gordon-Van Tine Co., (ca. 1920).

———. *Grand Millwork, Catalog for Home Builders*. Davenport, Iowa: Gordon-Van Tine Co., Spring 1911.

Huttig Brothers Mfg. Co. *Catalogue of Huttig Bros. Mfg. Co. Wholesale Manufacturers of Doors, Glazed Sash, Blinds . . . and Everything in the Line of Millwork in any Wood, Foreign or Domestic*. Muscatine, Iowa: Huttig Brothers Mfg. Co., 1900.

Joseph Hafner Mfg. Co. *The Jos. Hafner Mfg. Co. Combined Book of Sash, Doors, Blinds*. St. Louis: Joseph Hafner Mfg. Co., 1891.

Late Victorian Architectural Details. Combined Book of Sash, Doors, Blinds, Mouldings, Chicago, 1898; reprint, Watkins Glen, N.Y.: American Life Foundation and Study Institute, 1978.

Louisiana Steam Sash, Blind and Door Factory. *Roberts and Co. Illustrated Catalogue of Mouldings, Architectural and Ornamental Woodwork, Door, and Window Frames, Sash, Doors and Blinds*. New Orleans: Louisiana Steam Sash, Blind and Door Factory, 1891.

M. A. Disbrow and Co. *Book of Designs*. Lyons, Iowa: M. A. Disbrow and Co., 1891.

Morgan Co. *The Door Beautiful*. 7th ed. Oshkosh, Wisc.: Morgan Co., 1916.

Morse and Co. *Catalogue for Carpenters and Builders*. Bangor, Maine: Morse and Co., n.d.

Roach and Musser Sash and Door Co. *Stock-List Catalogue*.

Muscatine, Iowa: Roach and Musser Sash and Door Co., 1908.

Sears, Roebuck and Co. *Builder's Supplies*. Chicago: Sears, Roebuck and Co., 1900.

———. *Building Material and Millwork*. Chicago: Sears, Roebuck and Co., (ca. 1918).

———. *Building Material and Millwork*. Chicago: Sears, Roebuck and Co., 1925.

———. *Honor Bilt Building Materials*. Chicago: Sears, Roebuck and Co., 1931.

———. *Sears Building Materials*. Philadelphia: Sears, Roebuck and Co., 1936.

Smith and Wyman. *Price List, Smith and Wyman, Sash, Doors, Blinds*. Minneapolis, Minn.: Smith and Wyman, January 21, 1884.

Southern Hardwood Producers. *Southern Hardwood Interiors*. Southern Hardwood Information Series, No. 3. Memphis, Tenn.: Southern Hardwood Producers, 1937.

Wholesale Sash, Door and Blind Manufacturer's Assoc. of the Northwest and the General Sash and Door Assoc. *Universal Millwork Design Book No. 20*. Dubuque, Iowa: Universal Catalogue Bureau, 1920.

———. *The Victorian Design Book*. Universal Design Book, Oct. 15, 1903; reprint, Ottawa, Ontario: Lee Valley Tools, 1984.

Miscellaneous Materials

American Face Brick Assoc. *A Manual of Face Brick Construction*. Chicago: American Face Brick Assoc., 1920.

Cutting and DeLaney. *Price List of the Cutting and DeLaney Decorative Lattice Work. (Decorative Lattice; Our Doors and Windows; How to Decorate.)* Buffalo, N.Y.: Cutting and DeLaney, (ca. 1889).

Decorators Supply Co. *Illustrated Catalogue of Composition Capitals and Brackets*. Chicago: Decorators Supply Co., June 1909.

Faithorn Co. *Interiors*. Compliments of the Rexall Store. West Union, Iowa. Chicago: Faithorn Co., n.d.

Hart, Bliven and Mead Manufacturing Co. *1876 Centennial Appendix to the Hart, Bliven and Mead Manufacturing Co.'s Catalogue of 1873*. New York: Hart, Bliven and Mead Manufacturing Co., 1876.

Kimball Brothers Co. *Kimball Elevators*. Council Bluffs, Iowa: Kimball Brothers Co., (ca. 1921).

National Lumber Manufacturers Assoc. *Modern Home Interiors*. Washington, D.C.: National Lumber Manufacturers Assoc., 1929.

Tyler Co. *Elevator Cars*. Chicago: W. S. Tyler Co., 1932.

Paint

Carter White Lead Co. *The Paint Beautiful*. Chicago: Carter White Lead Co., n.d.

Montgomery Ward and Co. *Coverall Paint, 1918*. Chicago: Montgomery Ward and Co., 1918.

National Lead Co. *Nuggets of Wisdom from an Old House Painter*. New York: National Lead Co., 1899.

Sherwin-Williams Co. *The Home Painting Manual*. Cleveland: Sherwin-Williams Co., 1922.

Toch Brothers. *The "R.I.W." Book*. Long Island City, N.Y.: Toch Brothers, 1908.

Pattern Books by Companies, Precut Buildings, Portable Buildings

Adams-Herr Co. *Rural Architecture*. Minneapolis, Minn.: Adams-Herr Co., 1884.

Aladdin Co. *Aladdin Homes, Built in a Day, Catalog 31, 1919*. Bay City, Mich., 1918; reprint, Watkins Glen, N.Y.: American Life Foundation, 1985.

———. *Aladdin Houses, "Built in a Day," Catalog No. 19, Spring 1910*. Bay City, Mich.: North American Construction Co., 1910.

———. *Aladdin Readi-Cut Homes*. Catalog No. 49. Bay City, Mich.: Aladdin Co., 1937.

———. *Aladdin Readi-Cut Houses*. Catalog No. 43. Bay City, Mich.: Aladdin Co., 1929.

Blodgett and Osgood. *Ready-Made Houses*. St. Paul, Minn.: Blodgett and Osgood, (ca. 1890).

Brown-Blodgett Co. *The Book of 100 Homes, Book C*. (Hayes-Lucas Lumber Co.) St. Paul, Minn.: Brown-Blodgett Co., 1936.

Chicago House Wrecking Co. *A Book of Plans*. No. 54. Chicago: Chicago House Wrecking Co., 1909.

Curtis Companies. *Better Built Homes, Volume 16*. 2nd ed. Clinton, Iowa: Curtis Companies, 1923.

E. F. Hodgson Co. *Hodgson Houses*. Boston: E. F. Hodgson Co., 1935.

Gordon-Van Tine. *Gordon-Van Tine Co., Architectural Details, 1915*. Davenport, Iowa, 1915; reprint, Watkins Glen, N.Y.: American Life Foundation, 1985.

———. *Gordon-Van Tine's Grand Book of Plans for Everybody*. Davenport, Iowa: Gordon-Van Tine Co., n.d.

Harris Brothers Co. *A Plan Book of Harris Homes, Edition No. 73*. Chicago: Harris Brothers Co., 1917.

Hinkle and Co. *Hinkle and Co.'s New Book on Building*. Cincinnati, Ohio: Hinkle and Co., 1869.

Portland Cement Assoc. *Portland Cement Stucco*. Chicago: Portland Cement Assoc., (ca. 1925).

Sears, Roebuck and Co. *Book of Modern Homes*. Chicago: Sears, Roebuck and Co., (ca. 1911).

———. *Book of Modern Homes and Building Plans*. 1st ed. Chicago: Sears, Roebuck and Co., (ca. 1908).

———. *Homes of Today*. Chicago: Sears, Roebuck and Co., 1931.

———. *Honor Bilt Modern Homes*. Chicago: Sears, Roebuck and Co., (ca. 1921).

———. *Honor Bilt Modern Homes: Leading Eastern and Western Designs of Bungalows, Houses, Cottages, Flat-Buildings, Farm-Houses and Farm-Buildings*. Chicago: Sears, Roebuck and Co., (ca. 1917).

Southern Pine Assoc. *Homes for Workmen: A Presentation of Leading Examples of Industrial Community Development.* New Orleans: Southern Pine Association, 1919.

West Coast Lumbermen's Assoc. *Distinctive Homes of Red Cedar Shingles.* Seattle: West Coast Lumbermen's Assoc., (ca. 1910).

Weyerhaeuser Forest Products. *A Dozen Modern Small Houses.* St. Paul, Minn.: Weyerhaeuser Forest Products, 1926.

Plumbing

Cochran-Sargent Co. *Cochran-Sargent Company General Catalogue "C."* St. Paul, Minn.: Cochran-Sargent Co., 1921.

Crane Co. *Crane Plumbing Catalog B.* Minneapolis, Minn.: Crane Company, 1915.

George H. Cole Supply Co. *Catalogue C—Geo. H. Cole Supply Co. Plumbing and Heating Supplies.* Troy, N.Y.: George H. Cole Supply Co., 1917.

H. Mueller Manufacturing Co. *Mueller Water, Plumbing and Gas Brass Goods. Catalog E.* Decatur, Ill.: H. Mueller Mfg. Co., 1918.

Iron City Sanitary Manufacturing Co. *Iron City Enameled Plumbing Fixtures.* Pittsburgh: Iron City Sanitary Mfg. Co., 1924.

J. M. Kohler Sons Co. *Catalog, J. M. Kohler Sons Co.* Catalogue edition 7105. Sheboygan, Wisc.: J. M. Kohler Sons Co., n.d.

N. O. Nelson Manufacturing Co. *"Nonco" Plumbing Fixtures.* 5th ed. St. Louis: N. O. Nelson Mfg. Co., 1928.

Roberts-Hamilton Co. *Rohaco Dealers Catalog and Simplified Price Book, Manufacturers of Plumbing, Heating and Electrical Supplies.* Minneapolis, Minn.: Roberts-Hamilton Co., April 1921.

Rundle-Spence Manufacturing Co. *Catalogue H—Rundle-Spence Mfg. Co., Producers of Supplies for Plumbers and Steam Fitters.* Milwaukee, Wisc.: Rundle-Spence Mfg. Co., 1915.

Standard Sanitary Manufacturing Co. *Color and Style in Bathroom Furnishing and Decoration.* Pittsburgh: Standard Sanitary Mfg. Co., 1929.

Weil-McLain Co. *Weil Plumbing Fixtures, Catalogue C.* Chicago: Weil-McLain Co., 1920.

Storefronts, Fountains, and Fixtures

American Kerament Corp. *Kerament Store Front Details.* A.I.A. File No. 239. New York: Amer Kerament Corp., n.d.

M. Winter Lumber Co. *Winter's Catalogue No. 87, Commercial Furniture.* Sheboygan, Wisc.: M. Winter Lumber Co., 1910.

Mueller Fountain and Fixture Co. *Mueller Fountain and Fixture Co., Masters in the Manufacture of Drug Store Equipment, Soda Fountains, and Interior Store Fittings.* Decatur, Ill.: Mueller Fountain and Fixture Co., n.d.

Pittsburgh Plate Glass Co. *Easyset Store Fronts.* Pittsburgh: Pittsburgh Plate Glass Co., 1930.

Wall Surfaces

M. H. Birge and Sons. *The Birge Special Designs Paper Hangings and Birge Velours for Season of 1889 and '90. (Illustrations, Special Designs of the Birge Paper Hangings and Velours*

‾for the Season 1889 and 90.) Buffalo, N.Y.: M. H. Birge and Sons, 1889.

———. *A Book of Illustrations of New Patterns of Paper Hangings for the Season of 1916.* Buffalo, N.Y.: M. H. Birge and Sons Co., 1916.

Montgomery Ward. *Wallpaper at Wholesale Prices—Newest Styles for 1910.* Chicago: Montgomery Ward and Co., 1910.

———. *Ward's Fine Non-Fading Wallpaper—Wallpaper Style Book for 1934.* Chicago: Montgomery Ward and Co., 1934.

Niagara Blue Ribbon. *Gregory and Gregory.* Westfield, N.Y.: Niagara Blue Ribbon, (ca. 1925).

Richard E. Thibaut. *Thibaut's Art Wallpapers.* New York: Richard E. Thibaut, 1900.

Robert Graves and Co. *The Robert-Graves-Co., Manufacturers of Fine Wall Papers and Decorations, Season of 1889.* New York: Robert Graves Co., 1888.

Sears, Roebuck and Co. *A Book of Wall Paper Samples from Sears Roebuck & Co.* Chicago: Sears, Roebuck and Co., (ca. 1906).

———. *High Grade Wallpapers.* Chicago: Sears, Roebuck and Co., (ca. 1902).

———. *High Grade Wall Papers, Season 1915.* Chicago: Sears, Roebuck and Co., 1915.

———. *Master-Art Wall Papers—Wall Paper Samples, Season 1928.* Philadelphia: Sears, Roebuck and Co., 1928.

———. *Wallpaper, Certified Fadeproof, New Styles for 1932.* Chicago: Sears, Roebuck and Co., 1932.

———. *Washable, Fadeproof Wallpaper.* Chicago: Sears, Roebuck and Co., 1935.

W. O. Dresser. *Artistic Wallpapers.* Tonopah, Nev.: W. O. Dresser, 1922.

Serials

Aladdin's Magazine; (Aladdin's Weekly). Bay City, Mich.; before 1917–21?

American Builder; (American Carpenter and Builder). Chicago; 1905–69.

American Gas-Light Journal and Chemical Repertory. New York; before 1871–?

American Homes and Gardens. New York; 1905–15.

The Architect, Builder and Decorator; (Northwestern Builder, Decorator and Furnisher; Northwestern Builder and Decorator; Builder and Decorator). Minneapolis, Minn.; 1882–95.

Beautiful Homes. St. Louis; 1908–10.

Beautiful Homes Magazine; (Homebuilder; Keith's Home-Builder; Keith's Magazine on Home Building; Keith's Beautiful Homes Magazine). Minneapolis, Minn.; 1899–1931.

Building Age; (Carpentry and Building). New York; 1879–1930.

Building Systems Design; (Heating and Ventilating Magazine; Heating and Ventilating; Air Conditioning, Heating and Ventilating). New York; 1904–79.

The Cement Age. New York; 1904–12.

Concrete; (*Concrete-Cement Age*). Detroit; 1904–12.

The Craftsman. Eastwood, N.Y.; 1901–16.

Creative Designs in Home Furnishings; (*Creative Design*). New York; 1934–39.

Curtis Service. Clinton, Iowa; 1913–15?

Edison Electric Light Company Bulletin. New York; 1882–84.

Edison Monthly. New York; 1908–28.

E.E.I. Bulletin; (*Edison Electric Institute Bulletin*). Philadelphia; 1933–74.

General Electric Company; (*Edison Lamp Works*). Harrison, N.J.; 1911–18?

Home Decoration. New York; 1886–89.

Home Improvements. Chicago; 1936–39?

House Beautiful. Chicago; 1896–current.

House and Garden. Greenwich, Conn.; 1901–current.

Ladies Home Journal; (*Ladies Home Journal and Practical Housekeeper*). Philadelphia; 1883–current.

The Millwork Magazine. Louisville, Ken.; 1909–10.

Modern Home Builder. Racine, Wisc.; 1902–?

Modern Paint and Coatings. New York; 1911–74.

Rock Products. Louisville, Ken.; 1902–current.

ROHACO Price Bulletin. Minneapolis, Minn.; 1919–?

Your Home; (*Own Your Own Home*). Dunellen, N.J.; 1925–31.

Index